JN238289

ネイティブの感覚で前置詞が使える

Ross Noriko
ロス典子
著

改訂合本

べレ出版

はじめに

なぜ本書では「前置詞」にフォーカスしたのか

▶前置詞{副詞}とは

下の①②の絵を見ながら以下の質問に答えてください。

(Question) Where is the cat?

日本語で「どこ？」と聞かれた場合、「かど」と答えることができます。
　英語で Where? と聞かれたら on the corner, in the corner, at the corner などのように必ず場所を示すことばの on, in, at などを、ものを示すことばである the corner の前に置きます。
　the corner だけでは「もの」だけを表現していて、「場所」は表していません。これら on, in, at などの場所を示すことばを前置詞と呼びます。英語では前置詞を使ってこそはじめて「どこ？」に対する答えの「どこどこです」を伝えることができるのです。

　前置詞は場所のほかにも時間、季節、期間、期限、動き、移動するプロセス、方向、視線や意識を向ける場、状態や状況、感情の状態、原因、手段などを表わします。

また

On Monday I came to school with my friend.

のように、基本文「主語＋動詞＋(目的語)」の前や後に、前置詞を使うと文をつなげていくことができます。そして、より詳しい状況やこまやかな表現ができるので、豊かな文かどうかは前置詞が鍵をにぎっているといえます。

　さらに take off, put on のように、前置詞 {副詞} は基本の動作を表す take, put, get, have, be, make, go, come などの動詞と一緒に用いることで熟語としても使います。動詞＋前置詞 {副詞} の熟語は日常会話で頻繁に使われていますので、日常会話を上達させたければまず前置詞 {副詞} を学習することをお勧めします。

　ところで come in のように in が動詞の一部として使われ、in の後ろに、どこに入るのか場所を示す名詞句がない場合の in は、up, out, away などと同じように副詞と呼ばれます。この本でとりあげる前置詞の中で副詞として使われないのは at, from, towards などのごく一部です。
　go out of the house のように副詞 out も前置詞 of をつけ加え、後ろに名詞句 the house を使うとどこからなのか場所を示すことができ、out of が前置詞のような役割をします。
　さらにほとんどの前置詞を前置詞として使おうとも副詞として使おうとも、基本のイメージは同じです。本書にたずさわったネイティブスピーカーたちは前置詞の in と副詞の in をあえて区別しませんでした。基本となるイメージが同じだからでしょう。そのためこの本では on, in, over, around などの前置詞が副詞として使われる場合も、up, down, out, away のような副詞もとりあげています。

　はじめによく使われる前置詞 {副詞} にはどのようなことばがあるかを知ってください。
　私はアメリカ人のおばあさんから、小学校で習ったという前置詞の歌を聞きました。それらの前置詞が元となり、この本ではよく使われるほぼ全ての前置詞と一部の副詞を含めて 62 のことばをとりあげました。本書の目次を見ると今まで

前置詞{副詞}だと知ってはいたけれども、どのように使ったらよいのかわからなかったことばだったり、これも前置詞{副詞}だったの？とあらためて気づくことばもあるかもしれません。

それにしてもおもな前置詞{副詞}の数が 62 もあるということ、数が多過ぎます。そのときどきに応じてどの前置詞{副詞}を使えばよいのか本当に頭の痛い問題です。

一体、62 ある前置詞{副詞}の中から自分の言いたいことを言うための前置詞をどのようにして選んだらよいのでしょうか。

そのためにはクライテリア＝選択基準を知ることが必要です。

▶クライテリアとは？

それではもう一度、上の絵を見て on, in, at のいずれかを選び、各絵を表わす文章を作ってみてください。

① There is a cat (　　　) the corner.
② There is a cat (　　　) the corner.
③ There is a dog (　　　) the corner.

さてあなたが on, in, at のいずれかを選んで文章を作るときにどのように考え、どのような基準をもって on, in, at の中から「これだ」と思うことばを選びましたか。

中に入っているから in だろうとか、on は「上」というイメージがあるとか、いろいろと頭に浮かんだかもしれません。そして最終的に一つの前置詞を選び、

絵の状況を表す英文をつくったことでしょう。

　私たちは言いたいことを表現するとき、知っている多くのことばからそのとき表現したいことばをひとつ選んでいます。このときクライテリアが必要です。
　クライテリア（**criteria**）とは基準のこと。どれを選ぶか判断するための、決定するための基準のことをいいます。自分のことばで表現するためには誰もがいつもクライテリア（＝選択基準）を使っています。
　英語のクライテリアとは「英語で表現するときに、自分が表現したいことばを選ぶ基準のこと」をいいます。日本語にも日本語のクライテリアがあります。

　日本語では数を表現することばは多くの日本語学習者を悩ませるほどたくさんあります。
　1本2本と数えるもの、1枚2枚と数えるもの、1個2個と数えるものなどがあります。それぞれ1本、1枚、1個と数えるものをイメージしてみてください。xxxが1本、xxxが1枚、xxxが1個というとxxxが何かわからなくてもなんとなく形を想像することができるでしょう。その形はどんなイメージですか？
　1本2本と数えるエンピツや棒、木などは「線のイメージ」として、1枚2枚と数える紙や皿、木の葉などは「面のイメージ」として、1個2個と数えるりんごや箱、ボールなどは「立体のイメージ」としてとらえていませんか？逆に線のイメージととらえたボトルを1本2本と数え、面のイメージでとらえたピクニックシートを1枚2枚、立体のイメージでとらえたマンゴーを1個2個と数えていませんか？

　「線」「面」「立体」が日本語の数えることばを選ぶときのクライテリアです。
　このクライテリアは私たちが幼いときにイメージとして洞察してしまったもので、すでにしっかりと身についているのであらためてことばで説明することが非常に難しいのです。それにもかかわらず、ことばを知れば知るほど、自分自身のクライテリアは確実に進化していきます。英語の前置詞のクライテリアも同じ。

ことばを知れば知るほど自分自身の英語の前置詞のクライテリアが磨かれていきます。

▶クライテリアが身につくと言いたいことばを選べる

　ネイティブスピーカーの子どもたちは単語数が少ないにもかかわらず、例えば get という動詞に前置詞｛副詞｝をプラスして get at, get in, get on, get off, get along, get around のように使って、さまざまな表現をすることができます。
　しかし多くの英語学習者はすぐに get on の意味は？ get along の意味は？と、それぞれの前置詞の定義を知りたくなります。また暗記に頼ってしまうと、状況が変わると言いたいことをどう表現したらいいのかわからなくなる場合もあります。
　ネイティブスピーカーの子どもたちはどのようにして前置詞｛副詞｝の使い方の区別ができるようになったのでしょうか。
　私たち日本人が日本語の数の数え方を習得してきたプロセスについても考えてみましょう。日本語の数の数え方で使う1本、1枚、1個、1台、1頭、1匹、1棟…などの違いを私たちはどのようにして区別することができるようになったのでしょうか。
　英語のネイティブスピーカーの子どもたちが前置詞｛副詞｝のクライテリアを習得するプロセスと、日本人が日本語の数の数え方のクライテリアを習得するプロセスはほぼ同じでしょう。
　私たちは子どもの頃から周りの人たちが話すことばを聴き、目にする場面や状況を観察し、ことばを結びつけては表現し、普遍化し、時には間違いを修正されながら、細長くて「線」のようなイメージのものは1本、薄い「面」のイメージのものは1枚、そして「立体」のイメージのものを1個と言うように洞察し、それぞれの違いをだんだんと区別できるようになりました。説明はできなくても日本語のネイティブスピーカーには「点」「線」「面」「立体」のイメージが数を数えることばを選ぶときのクライテリアとなっています。

英語のネイティブスピーカーの子どもたちも同じようなプロセスを経て、前置詞｛副詞｝のクライテリアを身につけてきました。私は子どものように状況や場面から前置詞｛副詞｝のクライテリアを洞察したいと考え、イラストレーターたちに前置詞｛副詞｝のイメージの絵を描いてもらいました。10枚位から始まり、結果的に8000枚以上の絵を描いてもらいました。それらの絵を描いてもらってはネイティブスピーカーに聞き、自分の間違いを発見し、さらに繰り返しイメージを洞察してはネイティブに聞いてみるということを続けました。そして描いてもらった絵を共通のイメージをもつ前置詞ごとに分類し、それぞれのグループにはどのような核となるイメージがあるのかを探っていきました。そして何度も試行錯誤しグループ分けをした結果、0次元「点」、1次元「線」、2次元「面」、3次元(3D)「立体」のイメージが英語の前置詞句のクライテリアであることを発見しました。

　クライテリアが身につくと自分の中に基準ができ、暗記に頼らないで自分が言いたいことを自分で選ぶことができるようになります。なぜなら**自分の中にクライテリア(＝基準)があるので、自分が言いたいことを伝えるためのことばを選択することができるからです。**

　前置詞｛副詞｝を使いこなすことができるようになることは前置詞｛副詞｝のクライテリアが身についているということです。同時に相手が話していることを的確にキャッチすることができるようになるので、こまやかな表現力、豊かな表現力をもってコミュニケートすることができるようになります。間違えたときにもなぜ間違いなのかを理解しやすくなります。

　映画のセリフや英文の本、絵本、ニュース、そして歌詞などを意識して見たり聴いたりしてみてください。日常会話においていかに多くの前置詞｛副詞｝が使われているかを再発見することでしょう。そしてその場面や状況で使われた前置詞｛副詞｝が印象に残り、自分でも使いたくなることでしょう。

▶前置詞句の核となるイメージは
０次元「点」、1次元「線」、2次元「面」、3次元(3D)「立体」。
そして前置詞は命令している

　さらに私はこの絵を何回も何回も眺めているうちにごく最近、英語では前置詞がとても力をもっていて、「名詞句を０次元(点)、1次元(線)、2次元(面)、3D(立体)として見なさい」と命令していることに気づきました。
　例えば in the corner のような前置詞句は前置詞(in)＋名詞句(the corner)で成立しています。名詞句は限定詞(the)＋名詞(corner)で成立しています。日本語では「もの」自体を線や面や立体のイメージとして、例えば棒は線、紙は面、りんごは立体としてとらえています。言い方を変えると日本語では、数を数える「もの」自体を線としてとらえるときには1本2本と数え、面としてとらえるときには1枚2枚と数え、立体としてとらえるときには1個2個と数えています。
ところが英語では名詞句の前にある前置詞、例えば on が「もの」(名詞句) the corner を1次元線として見なさい、と命令します。前置詞が on か in か at かによって、「かど」が点にも線にも面にもなるのです。「もの」の形が変わるのです。
　つまり前置詞は場所や時間を「**０次元、1次元、2次元、3Dととらえなさい**」と指示しているのです。
　そこで本書では新たな視点を加えて提示します。

　前置詞はあとに来る名詞句をどのようなイメージで見るかを聞き手に命令している。
　「**０次元(点)として見なさい**」
　「**1次元(線)として見なさい**」
　「**2次元(面)として見なさい**」
　「**3D(立体)として見なさい**」と命令しているのです。

「前置詞が場や時のイメージを変える」ということをぜひ意識して、本書の膨大な量の絵を見ていってください。今までの前置詞に対するとらえ方、視点が大きく広がります。そして表現の幅がぐんと広がっていきます。

では皆さんに見ていただいた絵と「線」「面」「点」のイメージで表現した図を見比べてみましょう。そして「線として見る」「面として見る」「点として見る」ということを意識しながら、あらためて絵を見てください。

※「はじめに」で使用した絵は本編に載っています。英文例は本編 p.262-201, 203 と p.613-31 をご参照ください。

本書の使い方一例 •••••••••••••••••••••••••••••••••••••••

○どこから始めても構いません。本編では「線」(1次元)、「面」(2次元)、「点」(0次元)、「立体」(3D)の順にそれぞれのイメージの絵を4章に分けて提示していますが、どこから始めても構いません。絵をざっと眺めながらページをどんどんめくっていってください。

　繰り返し絵を見ていくことで、絵と絵の共通点や違いが見えてきて、他の前置詞{副詞}のイメージとの共通点や違いにも気づいてくることでしょう。

　日常生活で目にする状況や状態を表していますので、繰り返し本書を使うことでネイティブスピーカーたちが前置詞句のクライテリアを身につけていったプロセスに似た体験をしていくことができます。共通点や違いを発見しながら核となるイメージを洞察する練習をしていくことにより、次第に場所や時間を「線」(1次元)、「面」(2次元)、「点」(0次元)、「立体」(3D)としてとらえるコツを自分自身でつかんでいくことができるようになります。

○英語初心者の方はまず各章の「基本イメージ」のところを見ていくと前置詞{副詞}の全体のイメージがつかみやすくなることでしょう。イメージがなんとなくつかめるようになったら「連想するイメージ」「イメージを比較する」へと進んでみましょう。

○大切なのは読者の皆さん自身がご自分なりの感覚で前置詞{副詞}のイメージをつかんでいくことです。英文例を参考にすると、何を主語にするとわかりやすいか、どこに視点を当てたらよいのかのヒントになります。

　イメージをつかむことに慣れてきたら、それぞれの絵の状況を英文で表現するとしたらどのようになるのか英文を作ってみましょう。回答例として一例を脚注に載せています。

　ご自分で作った英文が間違っていることがあるかもしれませんが、間違うことはとても大切です。間違うことで多くの発見があります。皆さんの想像力を広げて「線」「面」「点」「立体」のイメージの特徴を自分で探してみてください。観察し、気づき、発見し、洞察する。この繰り返しがポイントです。

○時々、映画のセリフや歌詞、英語の本やニュースなどの実際の英語に触れてみましょう。英語をとらえる感覚がアップしていることに気がつくことがあります。シンプルな英語からでもこまやかなイメージが湧いてきて、情景や状態などの描写が以前よりも豊かに感じられることを実感することでしょう。

○巻末(p.680〜685)にはおもな前置詞{副詞}のイメージをイラストで示しています。前置詞{副詞}それぞれの核となるイメージを俯瞰して見ることができます。

○目次(p.13〜34)や索引(p.693〜699)などにも繰り返し目を通すことで、絵を見たときの洞察力を深めるためのヒントとなります。

▶ **注意点**

※前置詞によっては他のグループの前置詞と比較しながら見ていくほうがイメージがつかみやすいという場合があります。その場合は違うグループ(章)に入れていますことをあらかじめご了承ください。

※各ページの上の部分につけている見出しは参考として使ってください。グループ分けをした絵から共通のイメージをことばにしてみました。あくまでもイメージする際のヒントとして載せています。

※脚注には英文例を載せていますがこれだけが回答ではありません。それぞれの絵が表わす英語はその話者の数だけあるといっても過言ではありません。ここではネイティブスピーカーがこの絵を見たときに表現する可能性が高い英文を一例として載せています。

　それでは本編が始まります。
　イメージを描くということに何のルールもありません。正しい・間違いもありません。読者の皆さんがご自身でイメージをふくらませ前置詞{副詞}の世界を楽しんでいただけますように。
　そして皆さんが英語で自分の表現したいことを自分のことばで表現することができる、こまやかで豊かな表現力をもってコミュニケートできるためのサポートとなる1冊となれば大変嬉しいです。

改訂合本
ネイティブの感覚で前置詞が使える
CONTENTS

はじめに……3

本書の使い方……11

1章 | 1次元（線）として見なさい

on ――――――――――― 線と見る

Ⅰ 基本のイメージ
① 線上にいる / ある on……36
② 線上で動いている on……44

Ⅱ 連想するイメージ
① のっている……46
② 重さがのっている……52
③ タッチしている……56
④ ついている……60
⑤ 点いている……64
⑥ 線上で動いている……66
⑦ 動き続ける……70

Ⅲ イメージを比べる
① 乗る on と in……72
② ついている on と入りこんでいる in……78
③ タッチしている on……79
④ タッチしている on と in……80

- ⑤ 下についている on と under……82
- ⑥ 下がっている on と from……84
- ⑦ 着ける put on と脱ぐ take off……86
- ⑧ 方向・方角の on, to, in……88

onto ──────────── 線と見る

Ⅰ基本のイメージ
- ① 線上に着く onto……92

off ──────────── 線と見る

Ⅰ基本のイメージ
- ① 線上から離れる off……94

Ⅱ連想するイメージ
- ① 降りる……98
- ② それる……100
- ③ 切り離す……102
- ④ 離れる……104

Ⅲイメージを比べる
- ① 蒸発する off と out……106
- ② 点いている on と消えている off……108
- ③ だんだんと消えていく out……109

over ──────────── 線と見る

Ⅰ基本のイメージ
- ① 線を越える over……110
- ② 線をカバーしている over……114

II 連想するイメージ

① 越える……118
② ひっくり返す……122
③ くり返す……124
④ 終わった……126
⑤ 視線が越えていく……128
⑥ 向こうに目的がある over/across と比べる……132
⑦ カバーしている……134

III イメージを比べる

① ジャンプする over と off……138
② 落下している down/over と比べる……140
③ ひっくり返る over, down, off……142
④ ころぶ over, down, off……143
⑤ knock over と knock down……144
⑥ knock down/over と比べる……146
⑦ 「上に」の over, on, above……148

under ——————————— 線と見る

I 基本のイメージ

① 線をくぐる under……154
② 線がカバーしている under……156
③ 下にいる/ある under……158

II 連想するイメージ

① 下にいる/ある……160
② カバーされている……164
③ 状況下にいる/ある……168
④ かくれている……170

| Ⅲ イメージを比べる | ① コントロールの **under, over, out of**……176 |

| コラム① | **under** と **below** の違いって何?……179 |

along ——————————————— 線と見る

| Ⅰ 基本のイメージ | ① 線に沿って動いている **along**……180 |

| Ⅱ 連想するイメージ | ① 連れていく **take ~ along to** と **take ~ to**……182
② **follow along** と **follow after**……184
③ 寄り添う **get along**……185 |

| Ⅲ イメージを比べる | ① 沿って動いている **along/alongside**……186
② そばにいる/ある **along, alongside, beside**……188 |

for ——————————————— 3Dと見る

| Ⅰ 基本のイメージ | ① 意識だけが向かっている **for**……190 |

| Ⅱ 連想するイメージ | ① 意識が向かう……192
② 目的のため……196
③ サポートしている……198 |

| Ⅲ イメージを比べる | ① 意識が向かう **for** と到着する **to**……200
② **do for** と **do to**……203 |

against ──────────────── 3Dと見る

❶基本のイメージ
① はね返っている against / into と比べる……204
② 逆らっている against……206
③ 反している against……208
④ 対称にいる / ある opposite……209

like ──────────────── 3Dと見る

❶基本のイメージ
① 似ている like……210
② 〜のような like……211

2章 | 2次元（面）として見なさい

in ──────────────── 面と見る

❶基本のイメージ
① 境界内にいる / ある in……214
② 境界内で動いている in……218

❷連想するイメージ
① 中にいる／ある……220
② 入りこんでいる in とついている on……221
③ 囲まれている (in the 〜) (in a 〜) (in 〜)……224

④ 状況の中にいる (in a ～) (in ～) (in ～ s)……230
⑤ 状況の中にいる (in ～) と場所の (in the ～)……234
⑥ 状況の中にいる (in ～)……236
⑦ (in ～) と (in/at/on the ～) を比べる……237
⑧ 境界を意識する……238
⑨ 境界内に入る……248
⑩ 属している (in the ～) (in a ～) (in ～)……252
⑪ 属している (in a ～) (in ～) (in ～ s)……258

Ⅲ イメージを比べる
① 境界内に入っている in と線上にのっている on……260
② in/on/at the corner……262
③ at/on/in the edge of ～……264
④ at/on/in the end of ～……265
⑤ 心の中で想像している in his mind……266
⑥ 心から離れない on his mind……267

within ──────────── 面と見る

Ⅰ 基本のイメージ
① 境界をはみ出さない within……268

Ⅱ イメージを比べる
① within と in……270
② in, inside, within……272

into — 面と見る

Ⅰ 基本のイメージ
① 境界内に入っていく into……276

Ⅱ 連想するイメージ
① 中に入っていく into……278
② 中にいる／ある in……279
③ 突入する……280
④ ばらばらになる……281
⑤ 変身する……282

Ⅲ イメージを比べる
① 変身する into……284
② 変わっていった to……285

out of — 面と見る

Ⅰ 基本のイメージ
① 境界内から外に出る out of……286
② 境界内から出ている out……288

Ⅱ 連想するイメージ
① 中から外に出る……290
② 出している……292
③ なくなってしまう……294
④ 出ている……296
⑤ 「(5人)のうちの(2人)」の out of と in……301

Ⅲ イメージを比べる
① 離れる out of と off……302
② 離れる out of, off, away (from)……304

of ——————————————— 面と見る

Ⅰ 基本のイメージ
① 「a of B」でaはBの一部である of……310
② 「a of B」のBが強調される……312
③ 「A of b」でAの中のbを選び出す of……313

Ⅱ 連想するイメージ
① 一部分……314
② 一部分をとり出す……316
③ とり出す……318

Ⅲ イメージを比べる
① 一部の of, 選ぶ of, 所有の「～ 's」……320
② B's a と Ba……322
③ 所有する / 正式な / 子どもっぽい父親……323
④ 「～の」はいつも of ではない……324

through ——————————————— 面と見る

Ⅰ 基本のイメージ
① 境界内を通り抜けている through……326

Ⅱ 連想するイメージ
① 通り抜けている……330
② 通り抜けたものを強調する……332
③ 始めから終わりまで……334

Ⅲ イメージを比べる
① 始めから終わりまでの through……336
② カバーする over……337
③ インフォメーションの through, by と on/in……338

［コラム②］間違った絵から大発見あり……341

throughout ——————————————— 面と見る

❶基本のイメージ
① 境界内にいきわたっている throughout……342
② through, across, in と比べる……343

across ——————————————————— 面と見る

❶基本のイメージ
① 境界内を横切っている across……344

❷連想するイメージ
① 横切っている……348
② スペースをはさんで向き合っている……350

❸イメージを比べる
① across/on/over/through the border……353

around ——————————————————— 面と見る

❶基本のイメージ
① 境界内の周囲を回る around……354
② まわりにいる / ある around……355
③ 境界内のあちこちをめぐる around……356
④ 境界のあたりにいる / ある around……357

❷連想するイメージ
① 自ら回る(**1**)……358
② 他を回す……359
③ 自ら回る(**2**)……360
④ 「そのあたりのどこかに」……362

Ⅲ イメージを比べる	① around, over, along を比べる……363
	② 見て回る look around……364
	③ 調べ回る look over……365

about ———————————————— 面と見る

Ⅰ 基本のイメージ	① 境界内をあちこち回る about……366
	② around と比べる……367
	③ 境界内のあちこちにいる／ある about……368
	④ around と比べる……369

Ⅱ 連想するイメージ	① およその about と around……370

Ⅲ イメージを比べる	①「およそ〜について」の about(1)……372
	② on, over と比べる……373
	③「およそ〜について」の about(2)……374
	④ of と比べる……375

between / among ———————————— 面と見る

Ⅰ 基本のイメージ	① 2つの間にいる／ある between……376
	② 3つ以上の間にいる／ある among……377

Ⅱ 連想するイメージ	① 2つの間にいる／ある……378
	② 仲間うちで……380
	③ 仲間うちで分ける……382
	④ 異なった力を合わせる……384

Ⅲ イメージを比べる	① 異なった力を合わせる **among**……386
	② 一緒に〜する **together**……387
	③ 間にある **among** と中にある **in**……388

with ――――――――――――――――― 面と見る

Ⅰ 基本のイメージ	① 境界内で一緒になり共に動いている **with**……390
	② 手と共に動いている **with**……392

Ⅱ 連想するイメージ	① 共に動いている……394
	② 共にある……398
	③ 共にいる／あるものを強調する……400

Ⅲ イメージを比べる	① 共に動いている **with** と逆らう **against**……404
	② 共に動いている **with／by** と比べる……406
	③ 手段の **with, by, in**……408

without ――――――――――――――― 面と見る

Ⅰ 基本のイメージ	①「〜なしで」の **without**……410

except (for) ――――――――――――― 線と見る

Ⅰ 基本のイメージ	①「のぞいて」の **except (for)**……411

besides ——————————————— 3Dと見る

Ⅰ基本のイメージ　①「異なるものをさらに加えて」のbesides……412

3章 0次元(点)として見なさい

at ———————————————————————— 点と見る

Ⅰ基本のイメージ
① この時この点にいる/ある at……416
② 点のあたりにいる/ある at……418

Ⅱ連想するイメージ
① この時この点に……420
② 視線が点にある……426
③ 心が点にある……430
④ ここに目的がある/byと比べる……434
⑤ ここに目的がある……436
⑥ そこにいる/ある……440
⑦ そのあたりにいる/ある……442
⑧ そのあたりを強調する……448
⑨ atを使わない!……449

Ⅲイメージを比べる
① この時この点にいる arrive at……450
② 着いている場所を強調する arrive in……451
③ この時この点にいる work at……452

④ サポートする **work for** と属する **work in** ……453

⑤ 目的がある **at** と状況の中にいる **in** ……454

⑥ 目的がある **at/by** と比べる……456

⑦ 目的がある **at/in, on** と比べる……458

⑧ 攻撃的な **at/to** と比べる……460

⑨ **at** と **on**（**1**）……462

⑩ **at/on/the top of** ……464

⑪ **at** と **on**（**2**）……465

⑫ **at/on/in the bottom of** ……466

⑬ **at/on the side of** ……468

⑭ **at, in, by** ……469

to ── 点と見る

Ⅰ 基本のイメージ
① 点に着いている **to** ……470
② 点へ向かっている **to** ……472

Ⅱ 連想するイメージ
① 〜に着いている……474
② 〜に合わせる……476
③ 最終点に着く……478
④ 〜へ向かっている……480
⑤ 点から点への **from 〜 to 〜** ……483

from ——————————————————— 点と見る

Ⅰ 基本のイメージ
① 点から離れていく from……484
② 点から出ている from……486

Ⅱ 連想するイメージ
① 〜から出ている……488
② 選べる点から離れていく /out of と比べる……490
③ 選び出している /off と比べる……492
④ 選び出している……494
⑤ 選び出せない from, off, out of……495
⑥ 引き離している……496
⑦ のがれている……498

Ⅲ イメージを比べる
① 起点が原料の from とつくり出す out of……500
② be made of/from/out of……502
③ 疲れる be tired from……504
④ あきる be tired of……505
⑤ 原因となる of, from, by……506
⑥「〜から」の of と from……508

close to ——————————————— 点と見る

Ⅰ 基本のイメージ
① 点に近づく close to……510
② 近くにいる /ある close to と near……511
③「近い」close to, near と「遠い」far away (from)……512

away from ———————————— 点と見る

I 基本のイメージ
① 点から離れていく **away from** ……514

II 連想するイメージ
① 離れていく……516
② 時が過ぎ去っていく……518
③ 遠ざける……520
④ **away** は使わない!……521
⑤ 遠ざけてしまう……522
⑥ みんなあげてしまう……523

III イメージを比べる
① 切ってしまう **cut away** と **cut off**……524
② 遠ざけている **keep away from**……526
③ 分かれている **apart (from)**……527

by ———————————————— 点と見る

I 基本のイメージ
① 点を経由していく **by**……528
② 点を通過していく **by**……530
③ そばにいる／ある **by**……532

II 連想するイメージ
① 選べる手段を経由している……534
② 数量を経由している……536
③ 経由しているものを強調している……540

III イメージを比べる
①「そばに」を比べる……542
② **stand by** を比べる……544

up

❶ 基本のイメージ
① 自ら上がっている up……546
② 他を上げている up……548

❷ 連想するイメージ
① のぼっている……550
② 到達点までのぼる up to……551
③ 自ら大きくしている……552
④ 他を強くしている……553
⑤ 「近づく」を強調している up to……554
⑥ 合わせる up to……555
⑦ 自ら起き上がっている……556
⑧ 他を起こしている……558
⑨ 「何が起きているの?」の up to……559
⑩ 上げている……560
⑪ up は使わない!……563
⑫ し上げている……564
⑬ 終わりに達している……568

down

❶ 基本のイメージ
① 自ら下げている / 降りている down……572
② 他を降ろしている down……574

❷ 連想するイメージ
① 自らを下げている……576
② 落下している……578
③ 弱くしている……580

Ⅲ イメージを比べる
① 上る **up** と下る **down** ……582
② 前方の **up** と **down** ……584
③ **up and down** ……585

4章 3次元（立体）として見なさい

beside ─────────── 3Dと見る

Ⅰ 基本のイメージ
① 立体の横にいる／ある **beside** ……588
② 点のとなりにいる／ある **next to** ……589
③ 横の **beside** と、となりの **next to** ……590
④ 「脇へ」の **aside** ……591
⑤ 立体の中— **inside** 外— **outside** ……592

behind ─────────── 3Dと見る

Ⅰ 基本のイメージ
① 立体の向こう側にいる／ある **behind** ……594
② 影響している **behind** と場所だけの **in back of** ……595
③ 背後にいる **behind** ……596
④ あとを追う **after** ……597

in back of ──────────────── 面と見る

Ⅰ基本のイメージ
① 後ろにいる / ある **in back of**……598
② 後ろの方にいる / ある **in the back of**……599

before ──────────────── 3Dと見る

Ⅰ基本のイメージ
①「時間的に前に」の **before**……600
②「位置的に前に」の **in front of**……601
③ 目の前の **before**……602
④ **before** と **in front of** を比べる……603

in front of ──────────────── 面と見る

Ⅰ基本のイメージ
① 前にいる / ある **in front of**……604
② 前の方にいる / ある **in the front of**……605

toward(s) ──────────────── 3Dと見る

Ⅰ基本のイメージ
① 立体に向かっている **toward(s)**……606
② 立体に向いている **toward(s)**……608

Ⅱイメージを比べる
① **toward(s)** と **to**……610
② **toward(s), to, at**……612

forward(s)

I 基本のイメージ	① 前に向かう forward(s) ……614
	② 先に行く ahead of ……615

II イメージを比べる	① forward(s) と ahead ……616

backward(s)

I 基本のイメージ	① 後ろに下がる backwards ……618
	② 逆向きの backward(s) ……619

II イメージを比べる	① もとにかえる back ……620

beyond ——————————— 3Dと見る

I 基本のイメージ	① はるか遠くを越えている beyond ……622
	② はるか遠くを過ぎている beyond ……624

II 連想するイメージ	① はるか遠くを越えている /over と比べる ……626

III イメージを比べる	① over, past, beyond ……628

above ——————————— 3Dと見る

I 基本のイメージ	① 立体より高いところにいる / ある above ……630
	② より高い above ……632

below ──────────── 3Dと見る

Ⅰ基本のイメージ
① 立体より低いところにいる / ある below……634
② より低い below……636

Ⅱイメージを比べる
① below と under……638

underneath ──────────── 3Dと見る

Ⅰ基本のイメージ
① 下にかくれている underneath……642
② かくれている underneath……644
③ 下の方にいる / ある underneath……645

Ⅱイメージを比べる
① かくれている underneath/under, below と比べる……646

beneath ──────────── 3Dと見る

Ⅰ基本のイメージ
① はるかに深い beneath……648
② 重さのかかる beneath……649

Ⅱ連想するイメージ
① 影響をおよぼしている……650
② まったく気づかない……651

Ⅲイメージを比べる
① 影響をおよぼす beneath/under と比べる……652

時間

① **Time**を点として見る**at**……654
② 日にちの**on**……660
③ 意識している「時」の**for**……661
④ 一点の**at**，線上の**on**，境界内の**in**……662
⑤ **at the / on / in time**……664
⑥ 「〜から〜まで」の**from〜to〜**……665
⑦ 〜から今も続いている**since**……666
⑧ 〜から(〜まで)の**from**……667
⑨ 時間の長さを表わす**for**……668
⑩ 距離を表わす**for**……669
⑪ 「(2日)後には」の**in**……670
⑫ 「(2日)間」の**for**……671
⑬ 「〜の間に」の**during**……672
⑭ 「〜の間ずっと」の**throughout**……673
⑮ **in, during, throughout, for**……674
⑯ **before**と**after**……676
⑰ **in, before, after**……677
⑱ 通過する時間を表わす**by**……678
⑲ (6時)までずっとの**until / till,** (6時)前までの**before,** (6時)までにの**by**……679

Timeを表わすおもな前置詞……680
Spaceを表わすおもな前置詞……682
　　①場を1次元(線)と見るように指示している……682
　　②場を2次元(面)と見るように指示している……683

③場を0次元（点）と見るように指示している……684
④場を3D（立体）と見るように指示している……685

キャラクター紹介……686

あとがき……689

索引……693

Chapter 1
1次元（線）として見なさい

on
onto
off
over
under
along
for

on：線と見る

①線上にいる / ある on

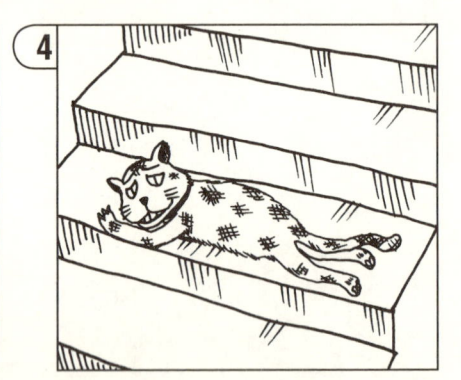

on the power line

1. There is a bird on the power line.
2. Bakunsai is walking on the tightrope.
3. There is some food on (top of) the table.
4. Dora is on the stairs.
5. Teria is on a stool.
6. Tim is on the roof.

【Ⅰ】基本のイメージ　37

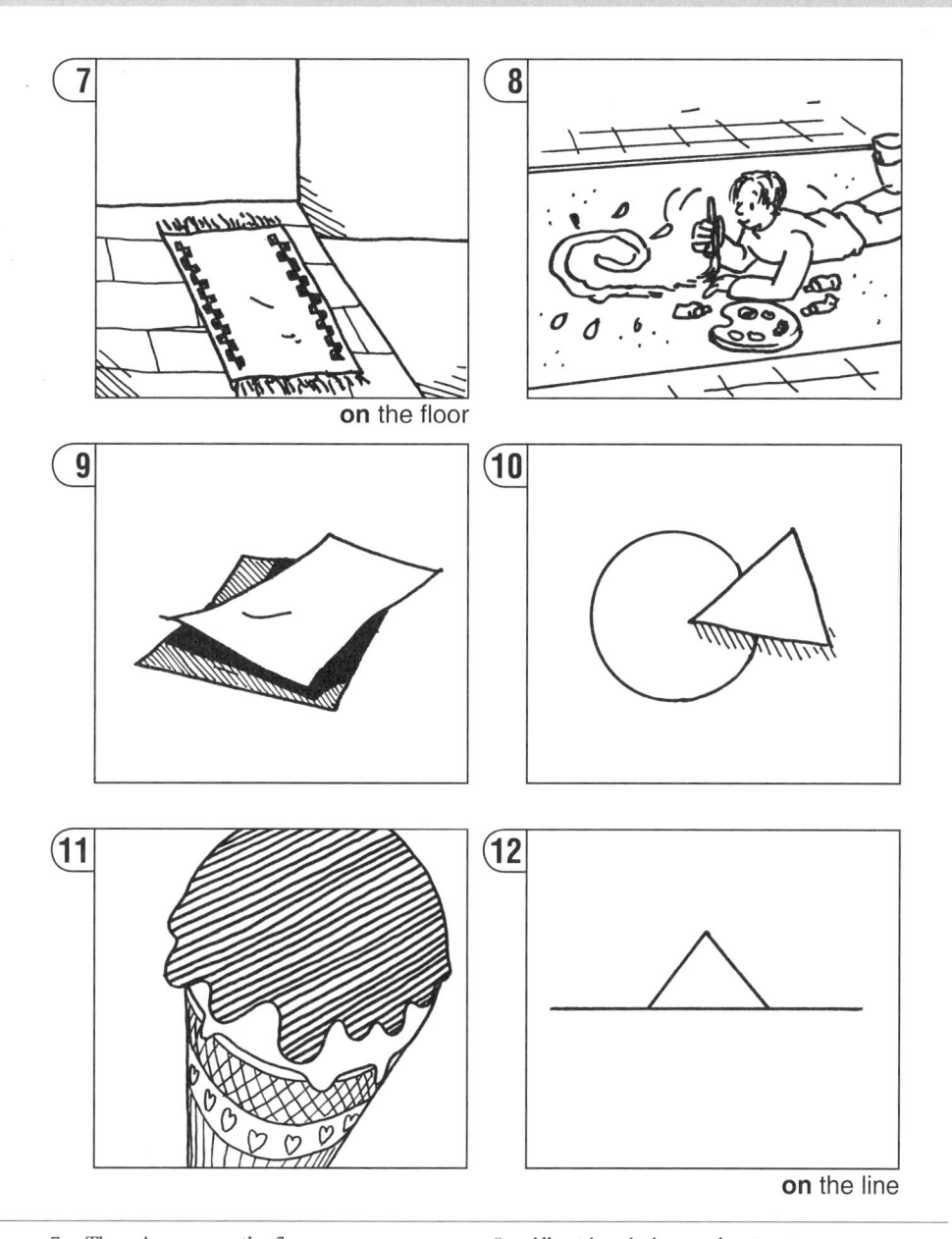

on the floor

on the line

7　There is a rug on the floor.
8　Albert is painting on the street.
9　There is a piece of white paper on top of the black piece/one.
10　The triangle is on the circle.
11　There is some chocolate on (top of) the ice cream.
12　The triangle is on the line.

on：線と見る

①線上にいる／あるon

on the wall

13　There is a picture (hanging) on the wall.
14　The sign is on the building.
15　The shower head is on the wall.
16　There are some decorations on the tree.
17　Ruby has a bee sting on her face.
　　The bee stung Ruby on her face.
18　There is a ring on her finger.

【 I 】基本のイメージ

on the pole

from

on the line

19　The flag is on the pole.
21　The sign is on the side of the building.
23　The astronaut is on the outside of the space ship.
20　The flag is hanging from the pole.
22　Somebody drew graffiti on the side of the car.
24　The triangle is on the line.

①線上にいる／ある on

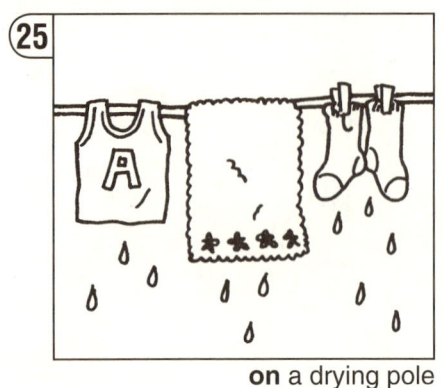

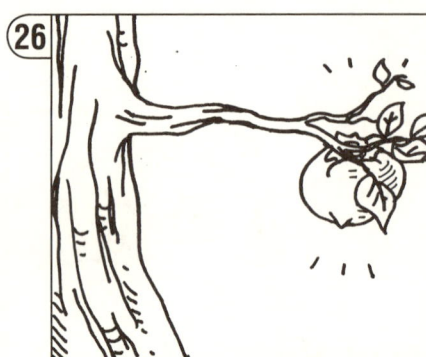

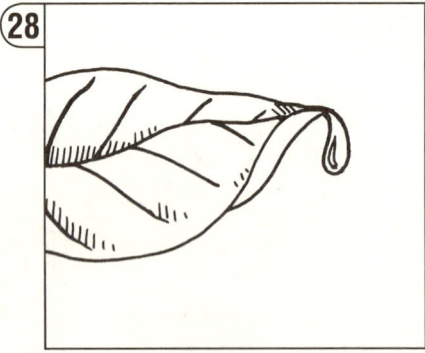

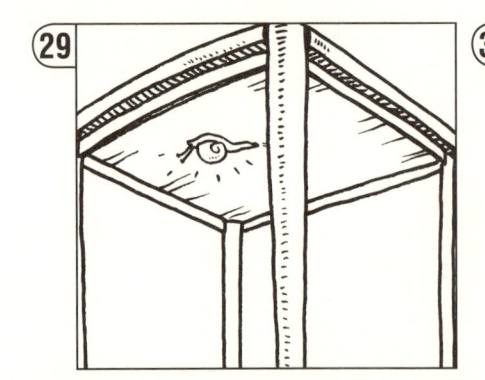

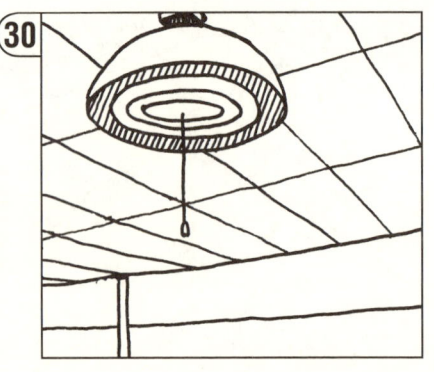

on a drying pole

25 There are some clothes (hanging) on a drying pole/a clothes line.
26 There is a persimmon (hanging) on/from the branch.
27 There is a ladybug on/under the leaf.
28 There is a drop of water on the leaf.
29 The snail is on/under the table. [on the bottom of]
30 There is a light hanging on/from the ceiling.

【Ⅰ】基本のイメージ 41

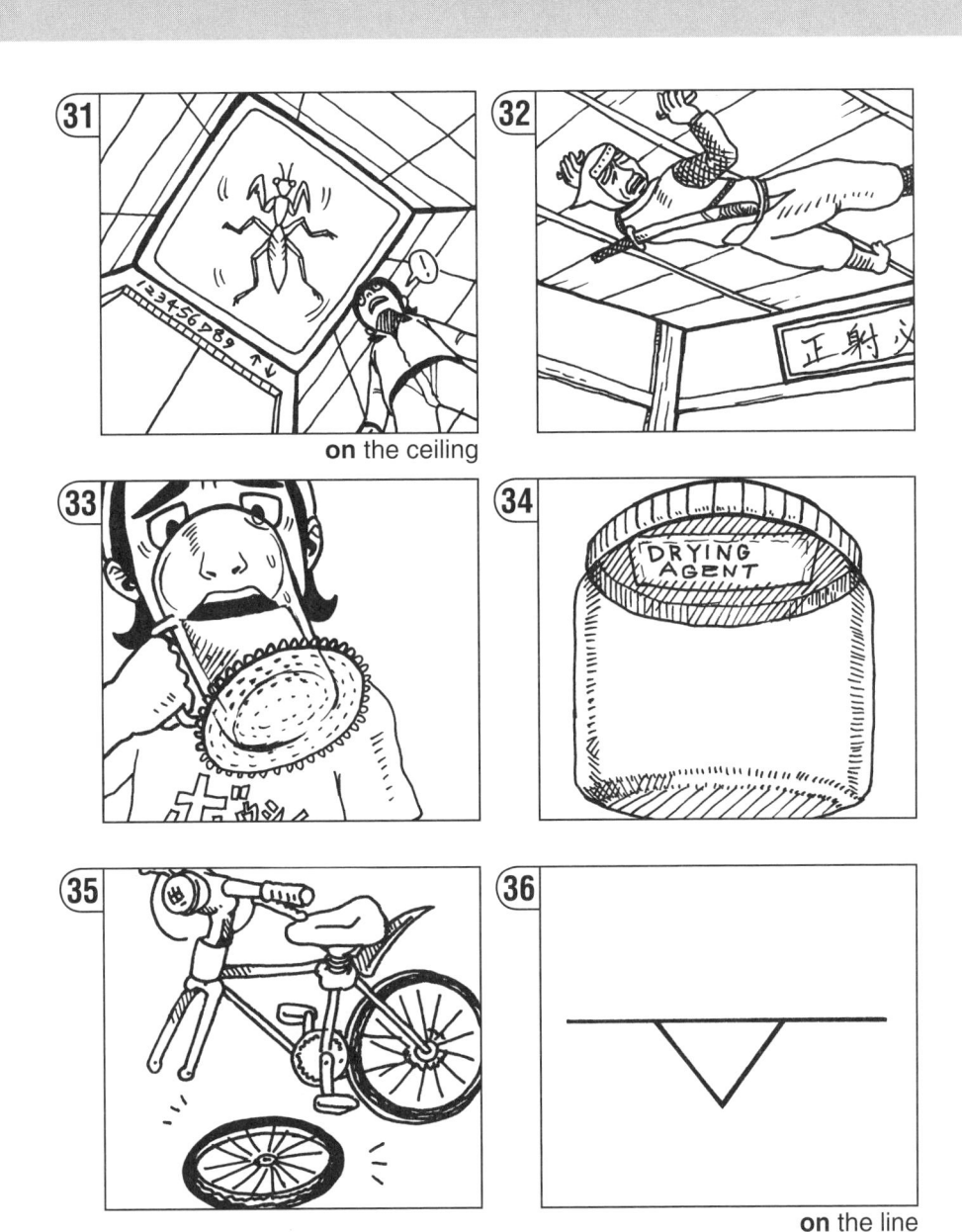

on the ceiling

on the line

31 There is a mantis on the ceiling.
32 The ninja is on the ceiling.
33 The doily is on the bottom of the glass. The doily is stuck to the glass.
34 There is a drying agent on the bottom of the lid. [under]
35 The front tire is not on the bike.
36 The triangle is on the line.

① 線上にいる / ある on

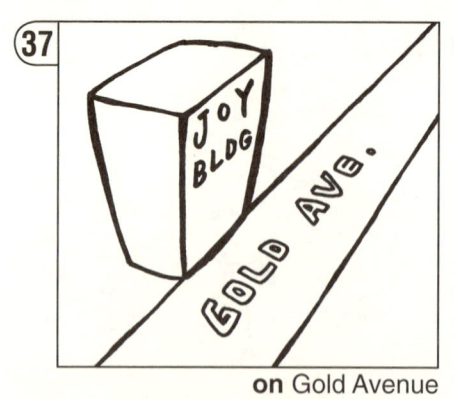

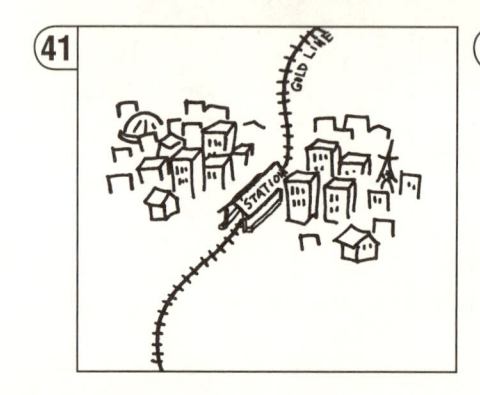

on : 線と見る

on Gold Avenue

37 The Joy Building is on/along Gold Avenue.
38 The Gold Building is on Gold Street.
39 The house is on the lake.
40 The house is on the river.
   [next to, beside, by]
41 The town is on the Gold Line.
42 The town is on (either side of) the river.

【Ⅰ】基本のイメージ 43

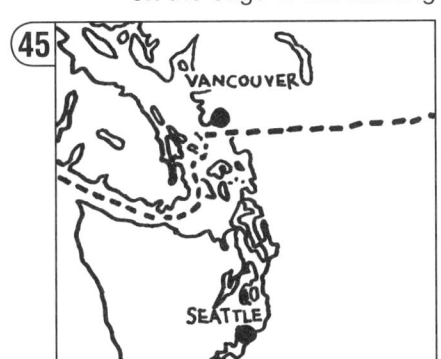

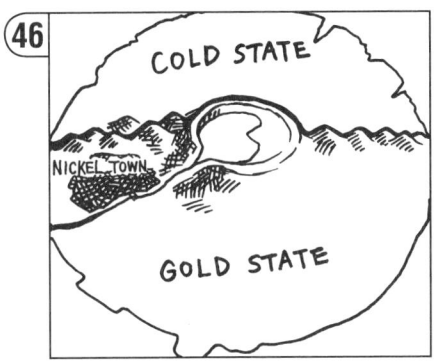

on the edge of the building

on the border between

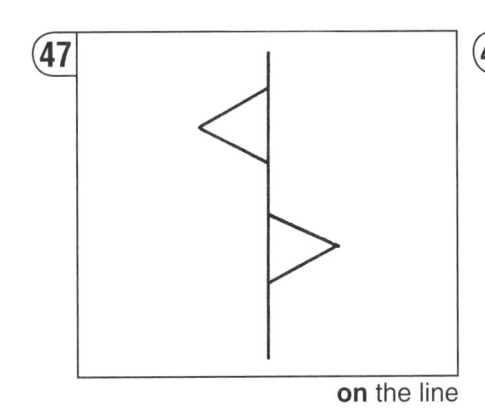

on the line

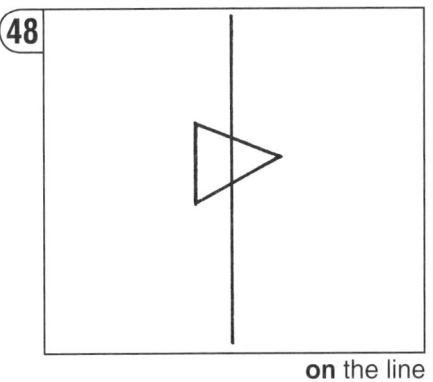

on the line

43 Teria is on the edge of the building.
44 Teria is on the edge of the cliff.
45 Vancouver is on the border between the US and Canada.
46 Nickel town is on the border between Gold State and Cold State.
   The mountains are on/along the border.
47 The triangles are on (either side of) the line.
48 The triangle is on the line.

②線上で動いている on

walk **on** the log

on her way

49 A monkey is walking on the log.
50 Olivia is on her way to her Grandmother's house.
51 The truck is on the way to Gold Harbor.

【Ⅰ】基本のイメージ 45

walk **on** and **on**

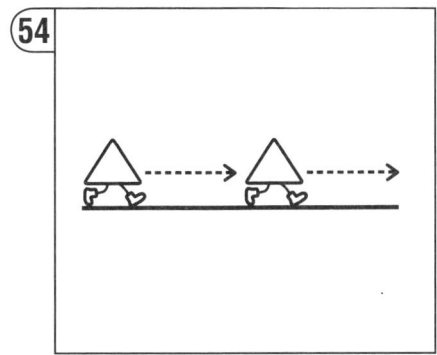

walk **on** the line

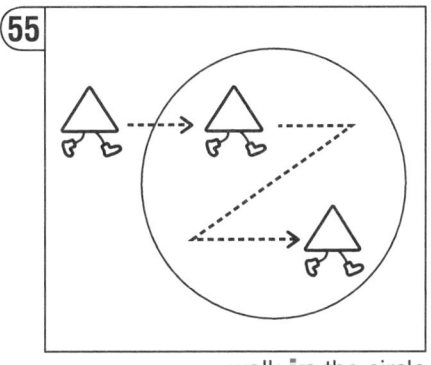

walk **in** the circle

52 Indy is walking on and on into the distance.
53 Indy told the sea munchkins to move on.
54 Mr. T is walking on the line.
55. Mr. T is walking in the circle.

on：線と見る

①のっている

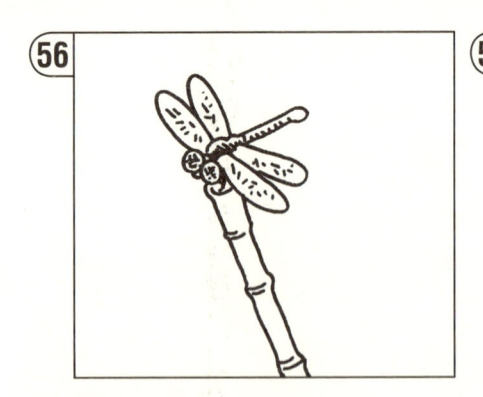

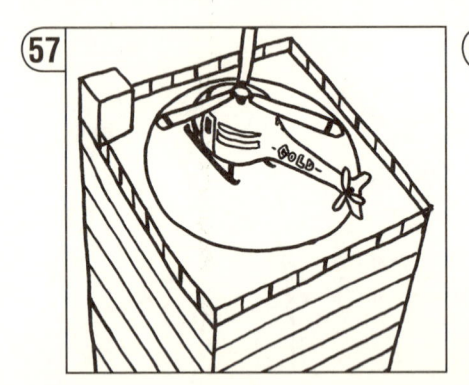

on the fire

56 There is a dragonfly on (top of) the bamboo pole.
57 There is a helicopter on top of the building.
58 Baby is on top of the school building.
59 Thumbelina is on a flower.
60 The shish kebabs are being grilled on the fire.
61 The blanket is on the grass.

【Ⅱ】連想するイメージ

62 Teria is on the/an asteroid.
63 The UFO is landing on Earth.
64 There are some soldiers on the hill.
65 Bowsheeman is on the island.
66 The boat is on the lake. [in]
67 There is some whipped cream on top of the coffee. [in]

on：線と見る

① のっている

68 The ninja has a hat on his head.
70 Baby is standing on Mama's feet.
72 Butch is on the horse's back.
　 Butch is on horseback.
69 The headphones are on Teria's head/ears.
　 Teria has (the) headphones on.
71 The little turtle is on (top of) the bigger one.
73 They are riding (on) camels.

【Ⅱ】連想するイメージ 49

74 Nautilus is riding (on) a motorcycle.
75 Candy is on the back of the bike.
76 Tim is traveling on a ship. [by ship]
77 Tim is traveling on a train. [by train]

| 50 | ···on：線と見る

① のっている

78　b. Someone is putting the lid on the pot.
79　a, b. Olivia is putting the rabbit on a/the chair.
80　She/He is putting some butter on the bread.

【Ⅱ】連想するイメージ

put it on to boil

81 a, b. He is stepping on the bottle.
   c. He cut his foot on the bottle.
   　 He has cuts on his foot.
82 He/She is stepping on some flowers.
83 His/Her feet are on the flowers.
84 Mama put the water on to boil.

②重さがのっている

on：線と見る

85 Butch is carrying some logs on his shoulder.
86 Olivia is on Tim's back.
87 Mama is carrying Baby on her back.
88 Bowsheeman is standing on his hands. Bowsheeman is doing a handstand.
89 Baby is crawling on his hands and knees.
90 Candy is jumping on one foot.

【Ⅱ】連想するイメージ 53

91　on / against
92　on / against
93　on / against
94　on / against
95　on
96　on / against

91　Bowsheeman is leaning against/on the wall.
92　Albert is leaning on/against the door.
93　Tim is leaning the ladder on/against the wall.
94　The bat is leaning against/on the desk.
95　The old man is leaning on a cane.
96　The paper is leaning on/against the ball.

②重さがのっている

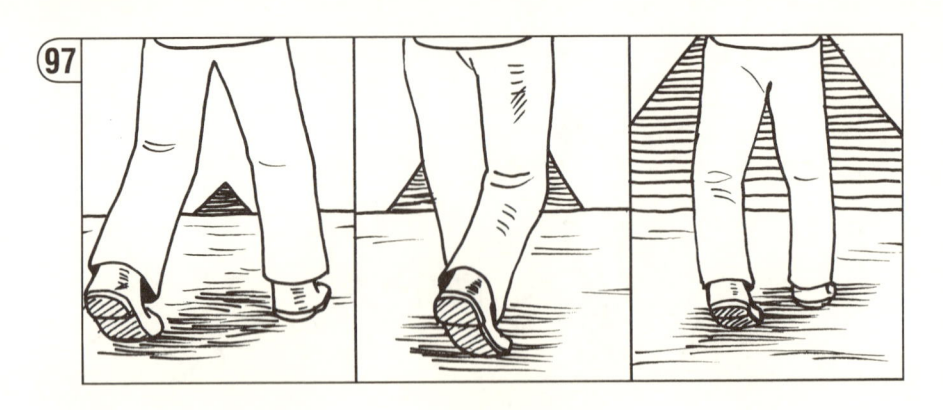

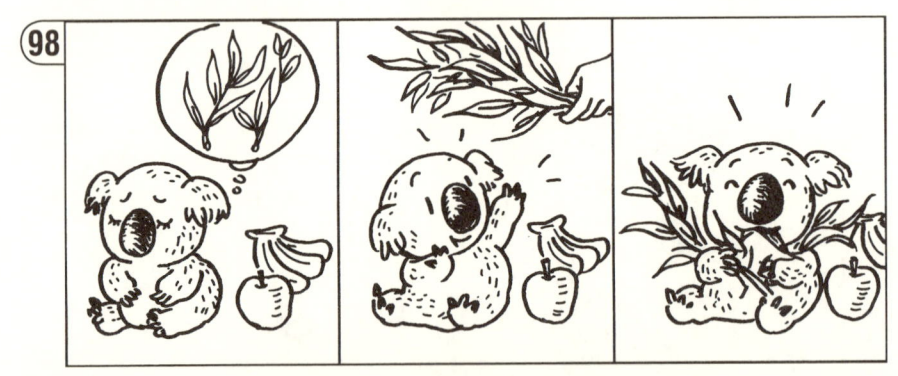

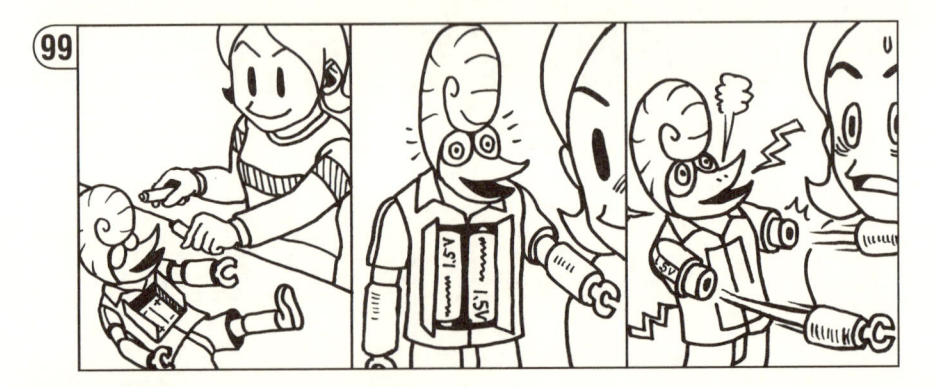

97 He is going to the pyramid on foot.
98 The koala lives on eucalyptus leaves.
99 The Nautilus toy runs on batteries.

100 Albert depends on his mother.
101 Albert depends on his father for money.
102 The test is unsupervised.
　　b. The students are on their honor.
　　c. But Candy is cheating on the test.

③タッチしている

103 b, c. Teria is typing on the computer.
104 Teria is playing jazz on the piano.
　　Teria is playing the piano.
105 The people are striking 108 times on the bell.
　　The people are striking the bell 108 times.

【Ⅱ】連想するイメージ　57

106 (The) rain is falling on the leaf.

107 The woman is pouring water on the girl's hands.

108 Water is pouring on the rock.
110 The sun is shining on the man.

109 Mama is blowing on Baby's cheek.
111 The sun is shining on the earth.

on：線と見る

③タッチしている

on / at the line

112 A/The light is shining on the wall.

113 The arrows are coming together on/at the line.

114 The spotlight is focused on the wrestler.

115 Bowsheeman is focusing on Katarina.

116 Indy is spying on the UFO.

【Ⅱ】連想するイメージ 59

about

117 Dr. Bizarro is giving a speech on/about the robot.
118 This is a book on/about rabbits.
119 This is a book on/about flowers.
120 This is a book about Ms. Flower.
　　This book is about Ms. Flower.

on：線と見る

④ ついている

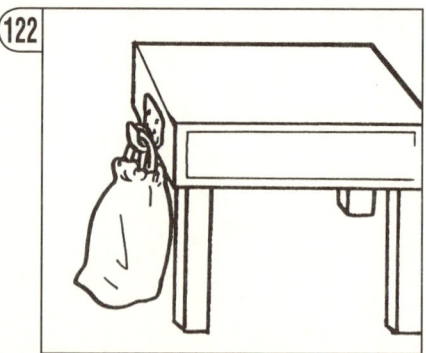

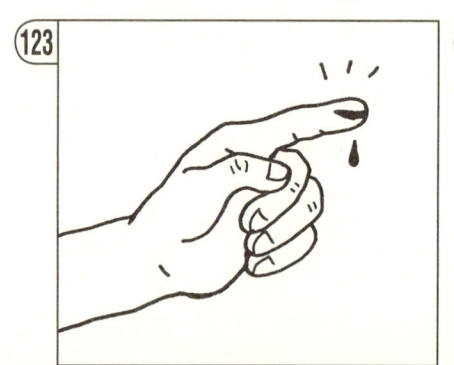

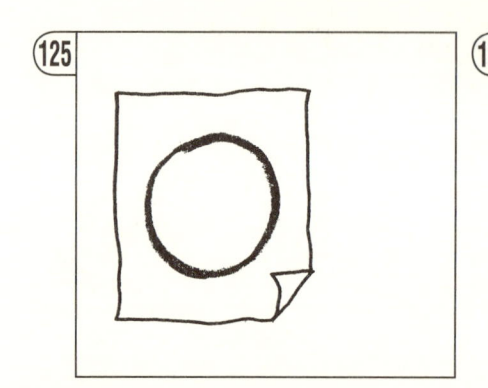

121 The lizard is on the wall.
123 He/She has a cut on his/her finger.
125 The circle is on the paper.
　　There is a circle on the paper.
122 The bag is hanging on/off/from the desk.
124 There is mud/are footprints on the rug.
126 There is a picture on page 11.

127 b. Olivia is putting on her nightgown.   c. She is wearing her nightgown.
128 Mama is a bad influence on Tim.
    Mama has a bad influence on Tim's behavior.
129 Alcohol has a bad effect on Mr. Gold's driving.

④ ついている

on fire

on duty

on business

130 The house is on fire.
　　The house is in flames.
131 The sea munchkin is on duty.
132 The sea munchkin is on vacation.
　　He is off duty.
133 Papa came to Hawaii on business.

【Ⅱ】連想するイメージ 63

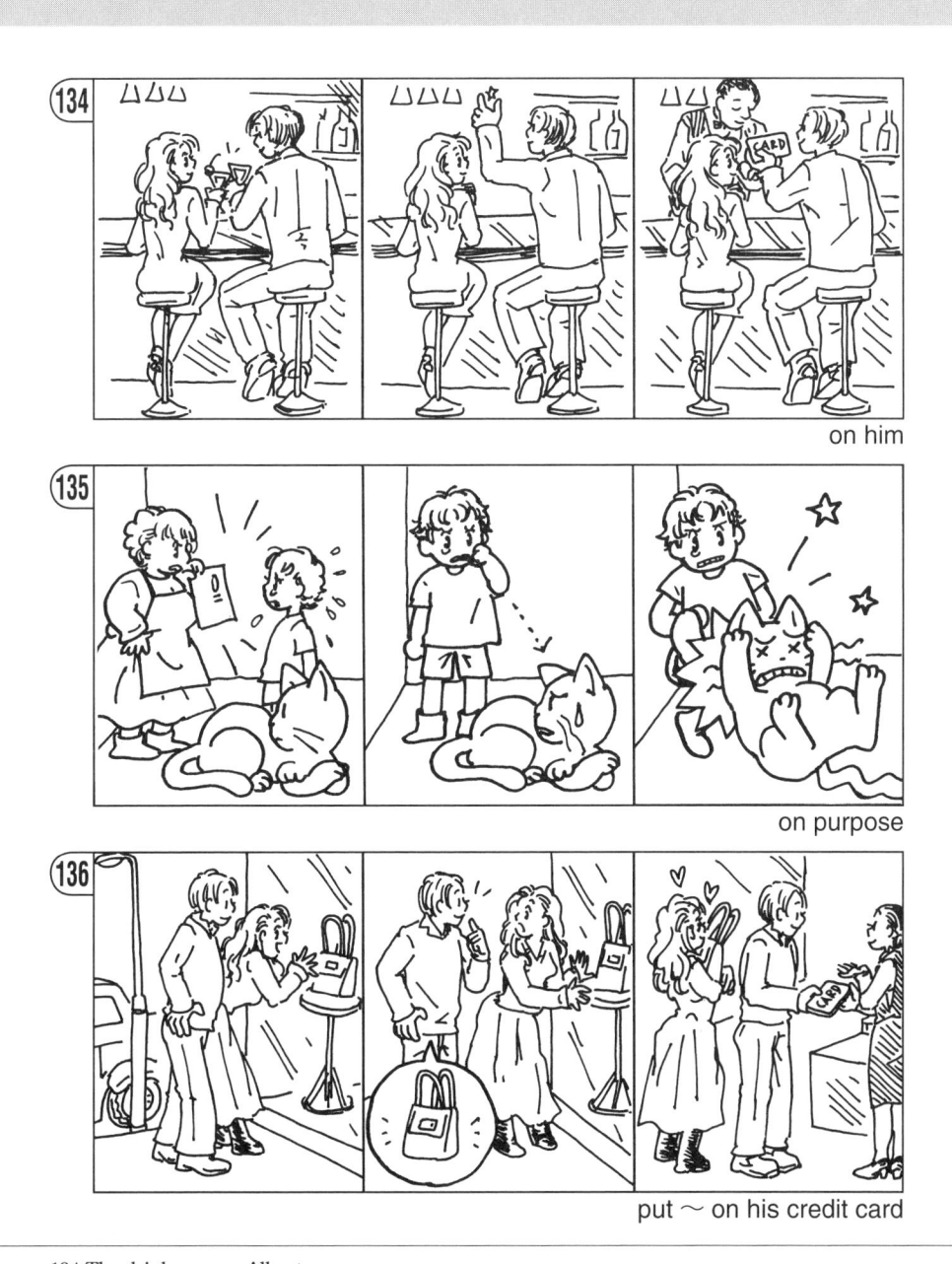

on him

on purpose

put 〜 on his credit card

134 The drinks are on Albert.
135 Tim kicked the cat on purpose.
136 Albert is putting the present on his credit card.

64 … on：線と見る

⑤ 点いている

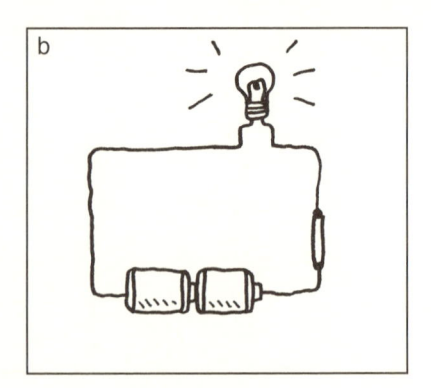

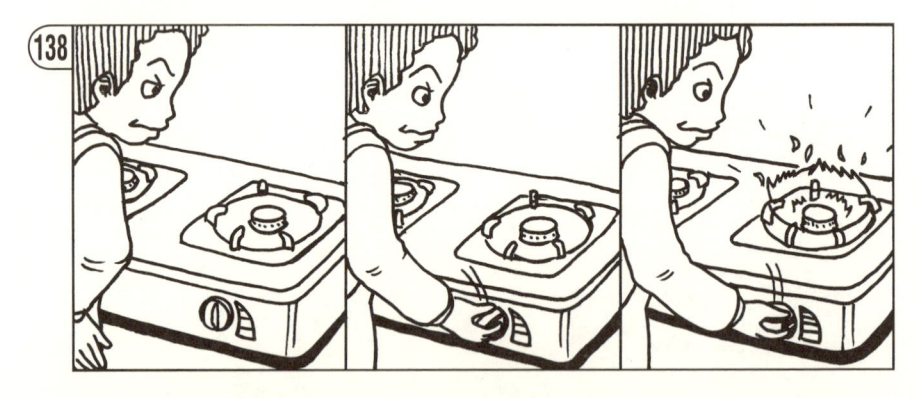

137 a. The light is off.   b. The light is on.
138 Okan is turning on the gas.
139 b. Okan is turning on the TV.   c. Okan has turned on the TV.

140 "Teriyaki Ninja 3" is on this week.
   Next week, "Vampire Tom" will be on.
141 School is on in spite of the typhoon.
142 The party is still on (in spite of the rain).

⑥ 線上で動いている

on a trip

on sale

143 b, c. Katarina has gone on a trip to Nautilus Island.
144 Indy is (going) on a journey.
145 The dress is on sale.

146 a, b. Teria is going on/to a picnic.　c. Teria is on a/the picnic.
147 a. Papa is going to a picnic.　b, c. Papa is at/on a/the picnic.
148 a. Teria's family is going on a picnic.　c. Teria's family is on a/the picnic.

⑥線上で動いている

work on

149 Papa is working on his taxes.
150 a, b. Albert is working on a book.
151 Dr. Bizarro is working on his project.

on a committee

on his advice

152 Mama is on a committee.
153 Teria took up swimming on her doctor's advice.
154 Oton used the chemical on Dr. Bizarro's advice.

⑦ 動き続ける

155 Mr. Gold keeps on winning.
156 Bowsheeman keeps on losing.
157 Mama is talking on and on.

【Ⅱ】連想するイメージ 71

158 Papa is working on and on until late at night.
159 Butch kept yelling, "Come on" at Albert.
160 "Come on," Tim screamed/yelled at Puppy.

⋯ on：線と見る

①乗る on と in

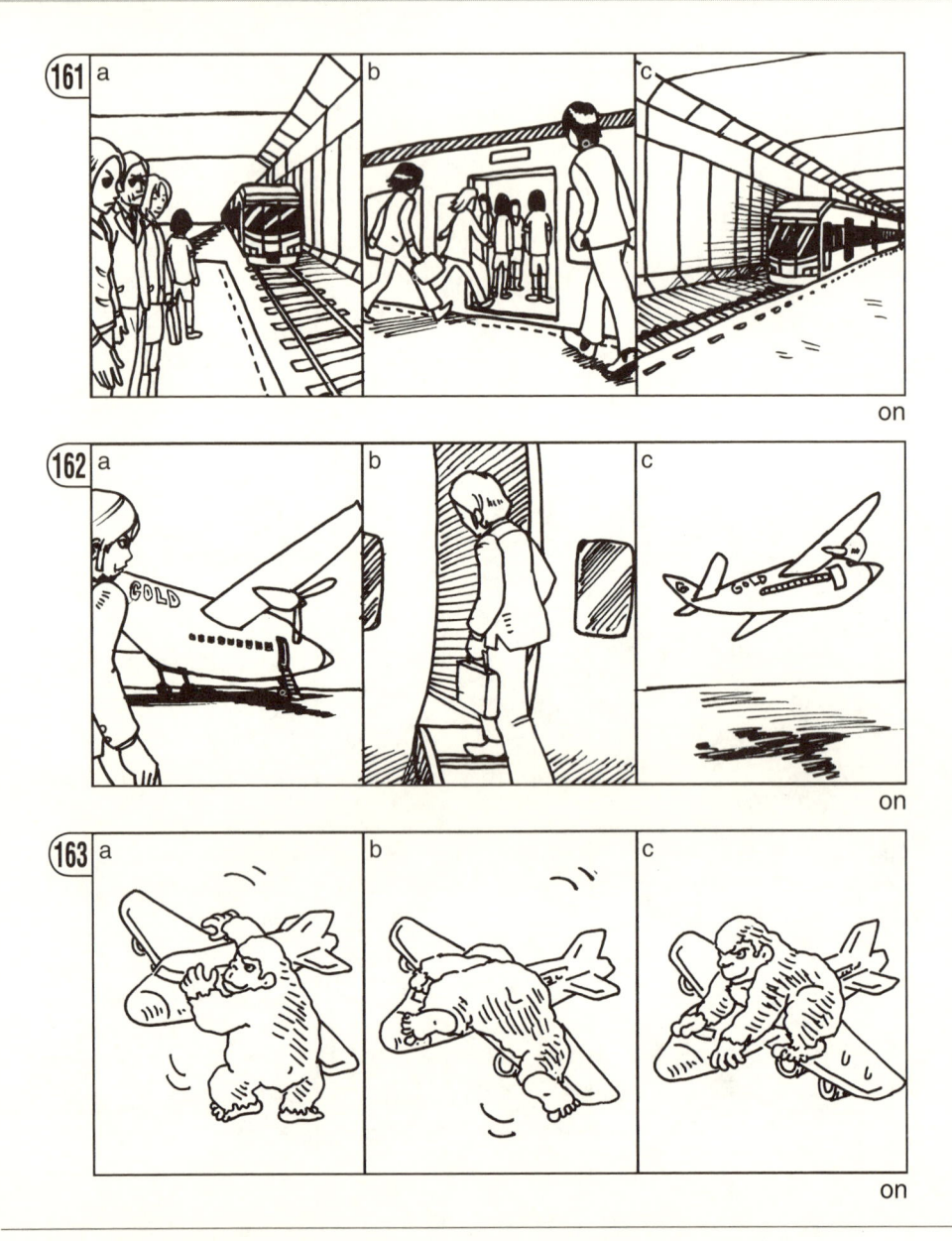

161 b. The passengers are getting on the train.　c. The passengers are on (board) the train.
162 b. Mr. Gold is getting on the plane.　c. Mr. Gold is on (board) the plane.
163 b. The gorilla is getting on/onto the plane.

【Ⅲ】イメージを比べる

in

in

in

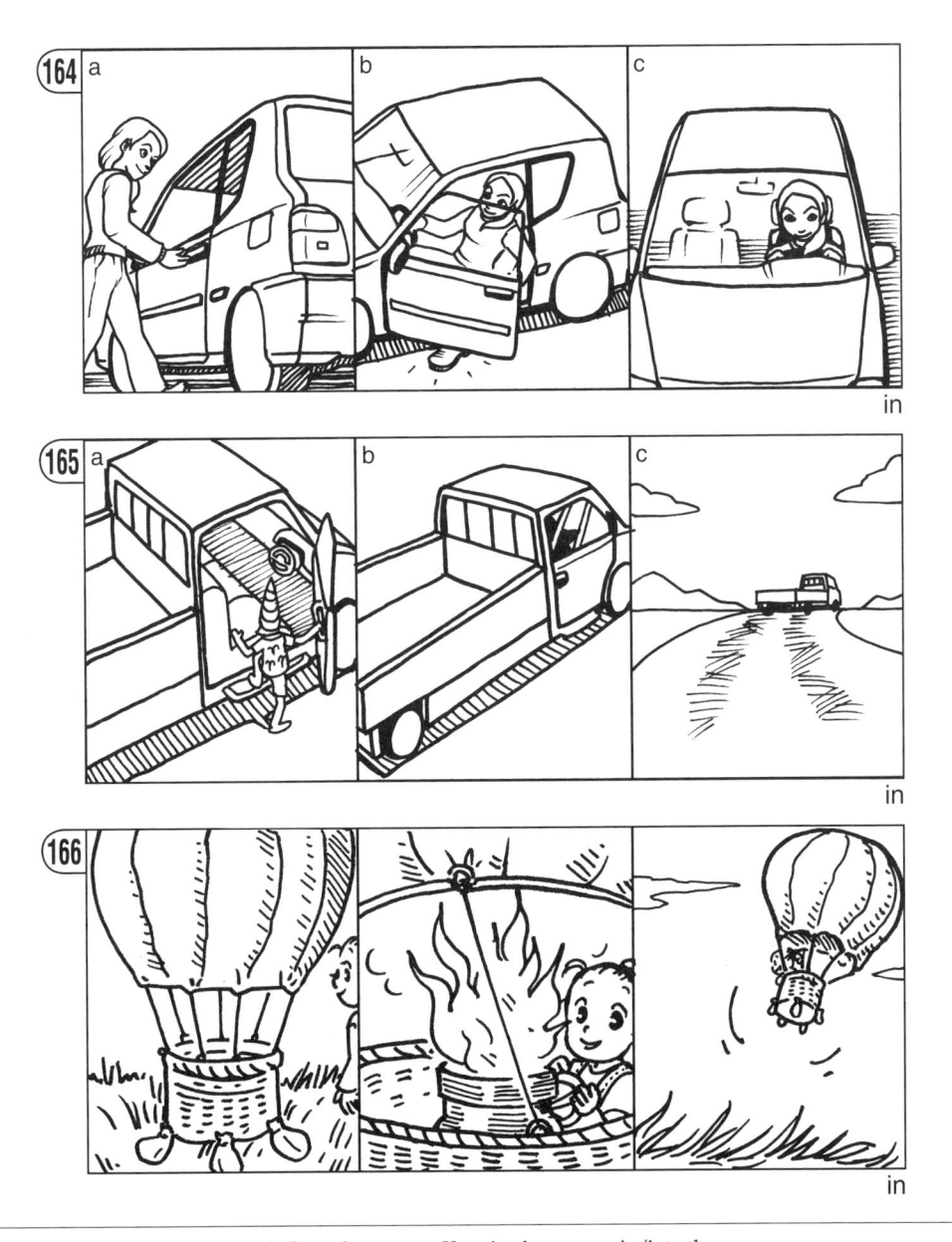

164 b. Katarina is getting in/into the car.   c. Katarina has gotten in/into the car.
165 a. The sea munchkin is getting in/into the truck.
    b, c. The sea munchkin has gotten in/into the truck.
166 Teria got into/in the balloon.

74 … on：線と見る

①乗る on と in

on / in

on

on / in

---

167 The sea munchkins got on/in the truck.
168 b. The sea munchkin is getting on the truck.　c. The sea munchkin is on the truck.
169 a. Bowsheeman is putting the goods on/in the truck.　b, c. The goods are on/in the truck.

【Ⅲ】イメージを比べる   75

on / in

on

in

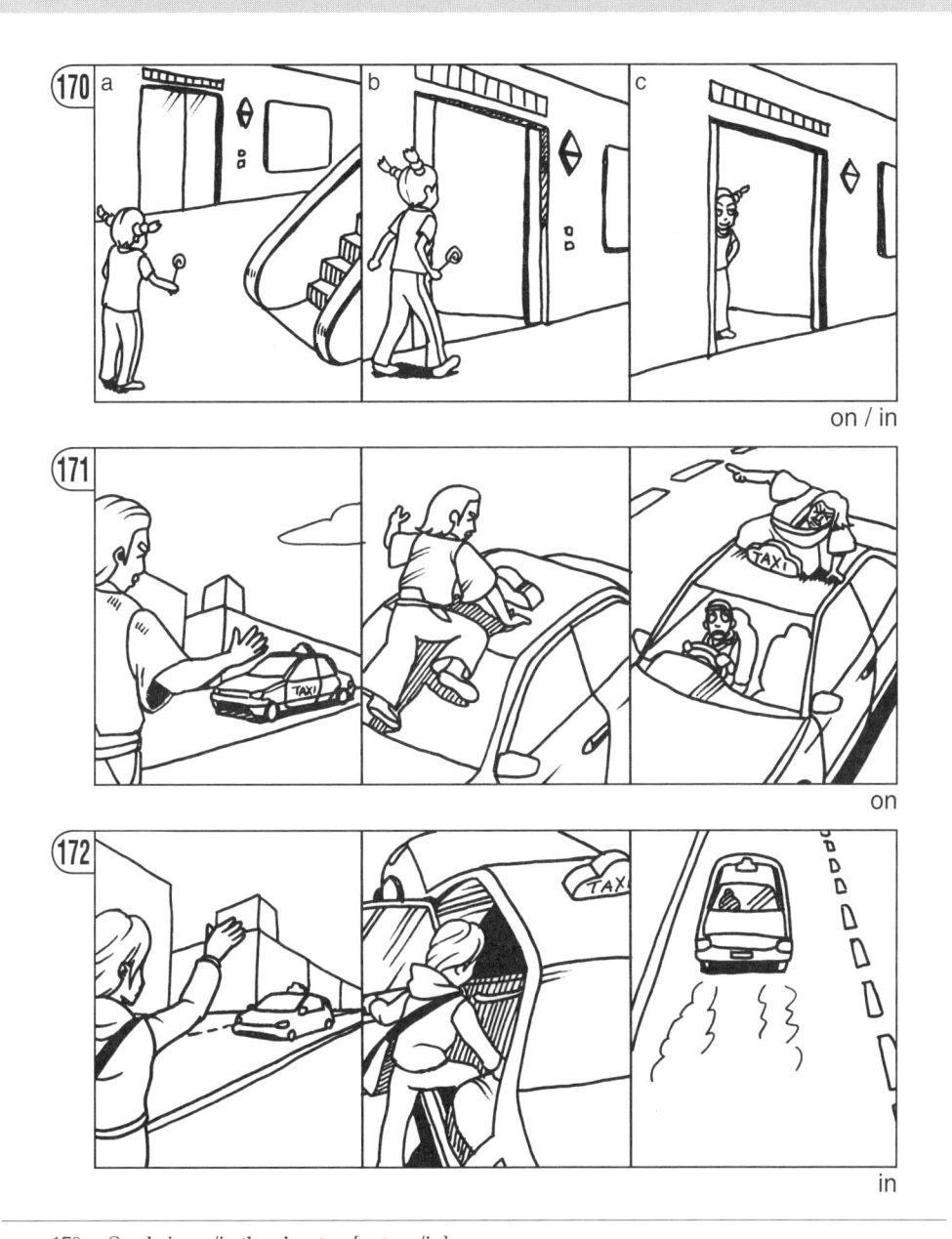

170 c. Candy is on/in the elevator. [got on/in]
171 Bakunsai got on the taxi.
172 Katarina got in the taxi.

① 乗る on と in

on / in

on

on

in

in

173 b. Katarina is getting on/in the bus.　　c. Katarina is on (board) the bus.
174 Bowsheeman is on the bus.　　　　　　176 The sea munchkin is on the truck.
175 Bowsheeman is in the bus.　　　　　　　177 The sea munchkin is in the truck.

【Ⅲ】イメージを比べる

178 b. The passengers are getting on/in the ship.　c. The passengers are on (board) the ship.
179 Ruby is on the boat.
180 The sea munchkin is in the boat.
181 Katarina is on the train.
182 Indy is drinking in the train bar.

②ついている on と入りこんでいる in

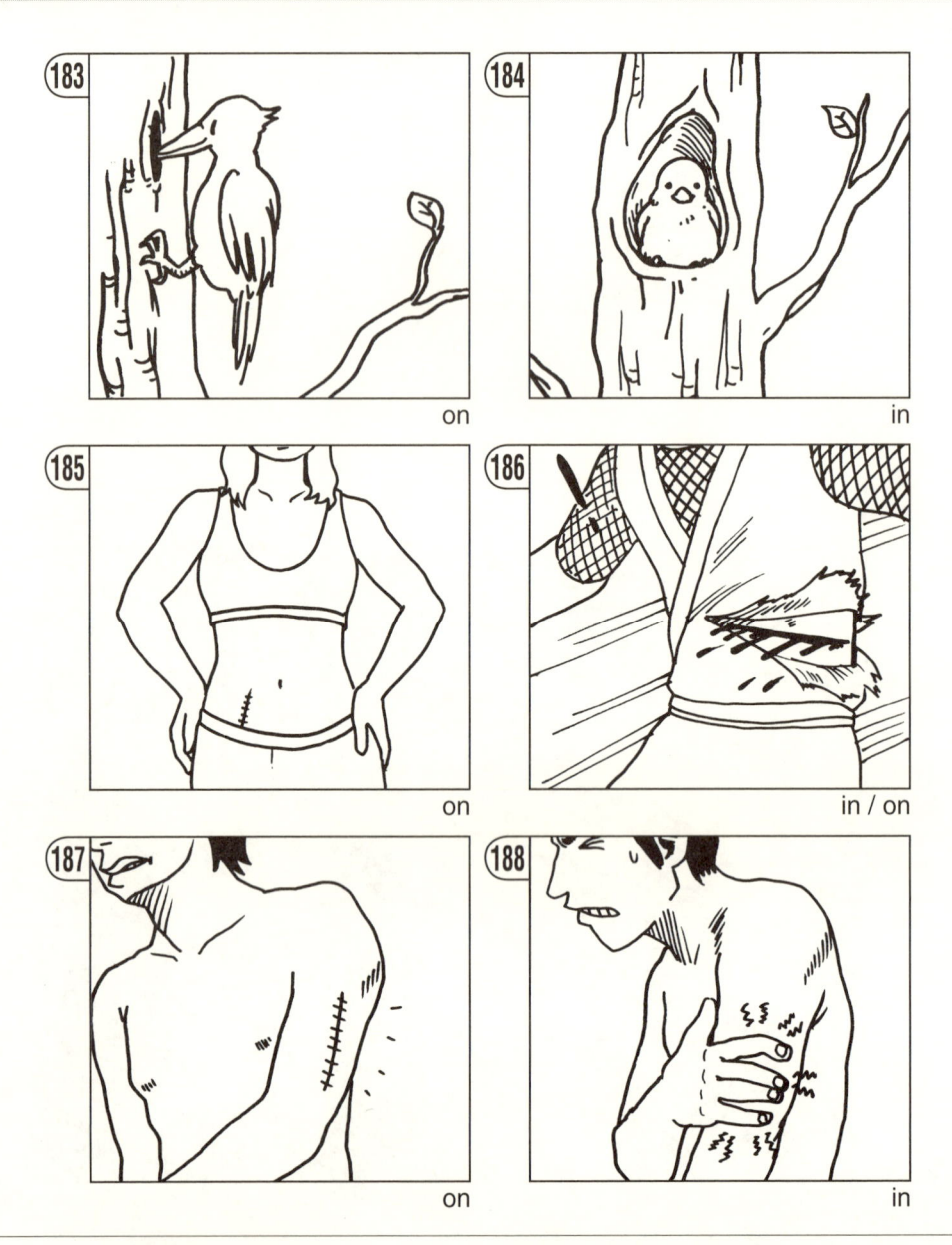

(183) on
(184) in
(185) on
(186) in / on
(187) on
(188) in

183 There is a bird on the tree.
185 She has a scar on her stomach.
187 He has a scar on his arm.
184 There is a bird in the tree.
186 The ninja has a cut in/on his stomach.
188 He has a pain in his arm.

③タッチしている on

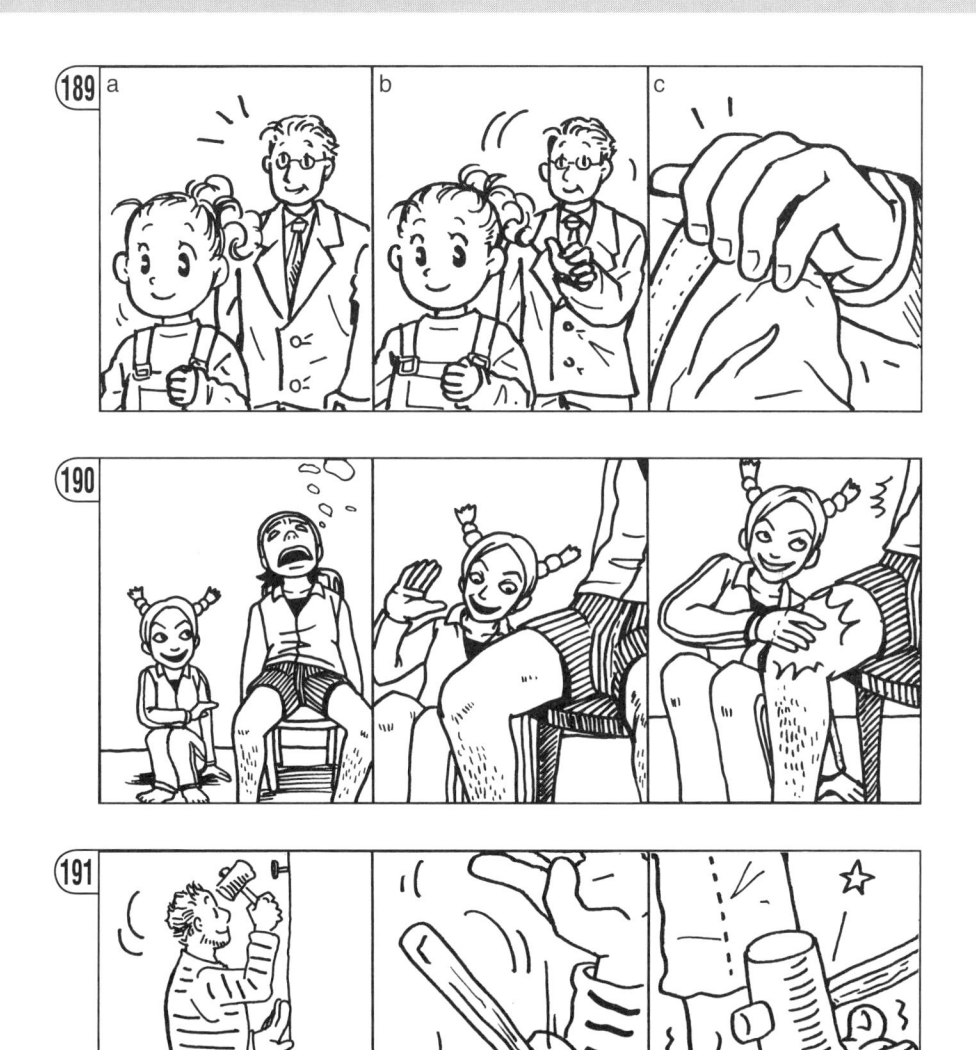

189 c. Papa is touching Teria on the shoulder.
190 Candy slapped Bowsheeman on the knee.
191 Butch dropped the hammer on his foot.

④タッチしている on と in

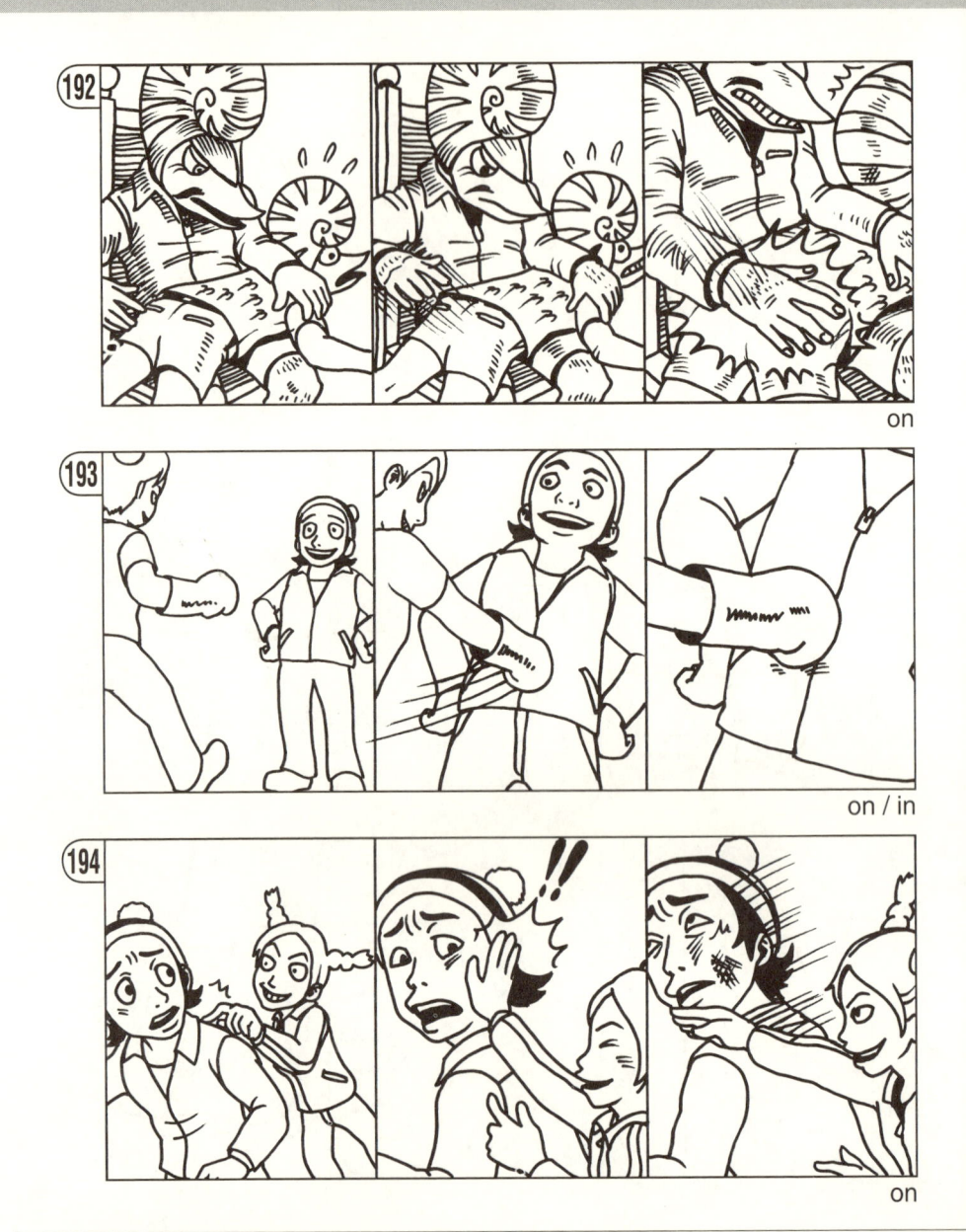

on

on / in

on

192 Father spanked Nautilus on his bottom.
193 Candy is hitting Bowsheeman in/on the stomach.
194 Candy is slapping Bowsheeman on the face.

195 Bakunsai is jabbing the ninja in the eyes.
196 Bakunsai struck the ninja in (the pit of) the stomach.
197 Candy is hitting Bowsheeman in the face.

⑤ 下についている on と under

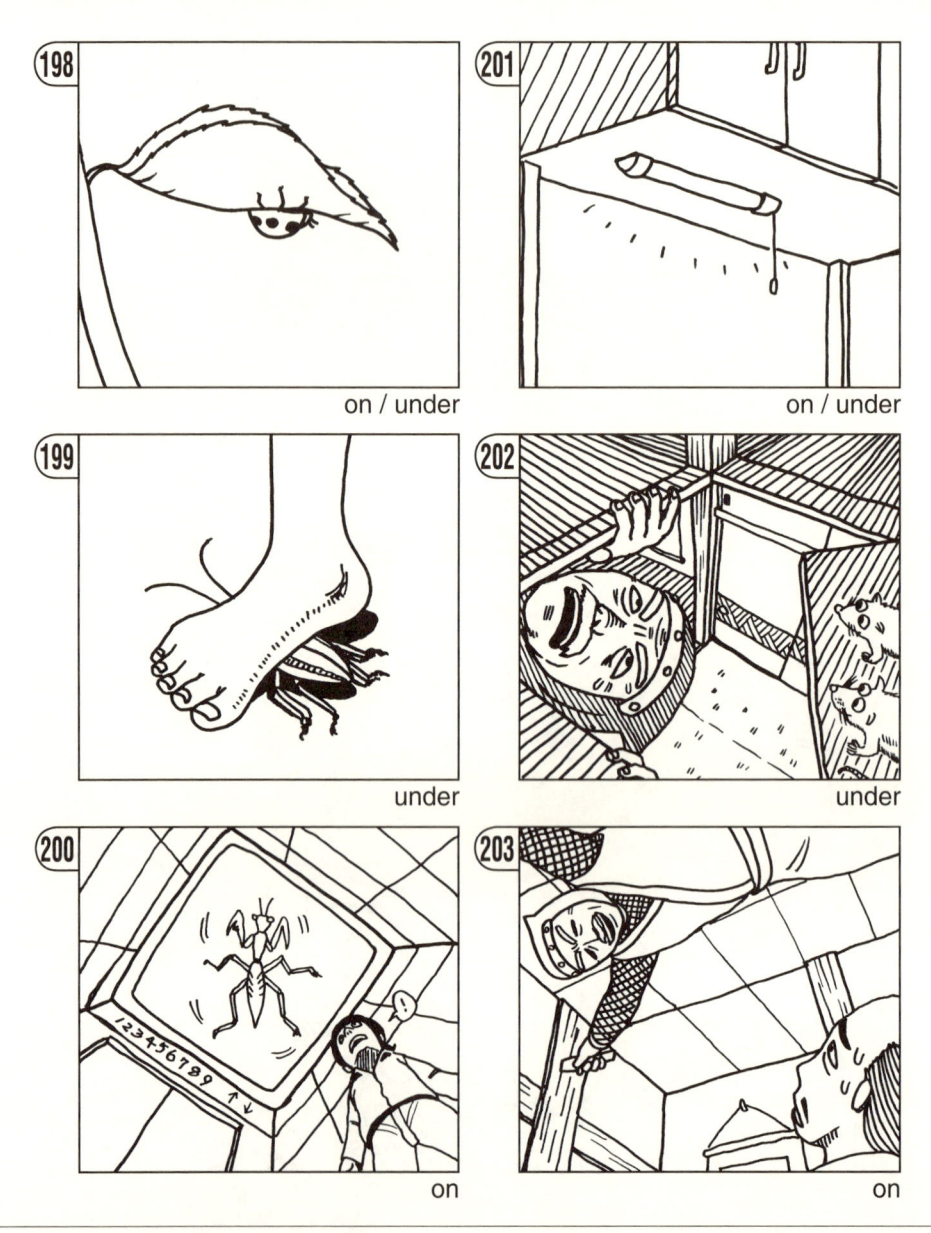

on / under (198)
on / under (201)
under (199)
under (202)
on (200)
on (203)

198 There is a ladybug on/under the leaf.
199 There is a cockroach under his foot.
200 There is a mantis on the ceiling.

201 The lamp is on (the bottom of)/ under the cupboard.
202 The ninja is under the ceiling/attic.
203 The ninja is on the ceiling.

【Ⅲ】イメージを比べる 83

204 on / under

205 under

206 on

207 on / under

208 under

209 on

204 The bug is on (the bottom of)/ under the table.
205 The cat is under the table.
206 The doily is on the bottom of the glass.
207 There is a drying agent on the bottom of/under the lid.
208 There is a letter under the bottle.
209 There is a drying agent on the bottom of the lid.

⑥ 下がっている on と from

(210) on / from
(213) on / from
(211) from
(214) from
(212) on
(215) on

210 The koinobori are hanging from/on the pole.
211 The ring is hanging from the pencil by a string.
212 The ring is hanging on a string.
213 The dress is hanging on/from a drying pole.
214 The socks are hanging from a laundry rack.
　　The socks are hanging from /on the clothes pins.
215 Some clothes are (hanging) on a drying pole.

【Ⅲ】イメージを比べる　85

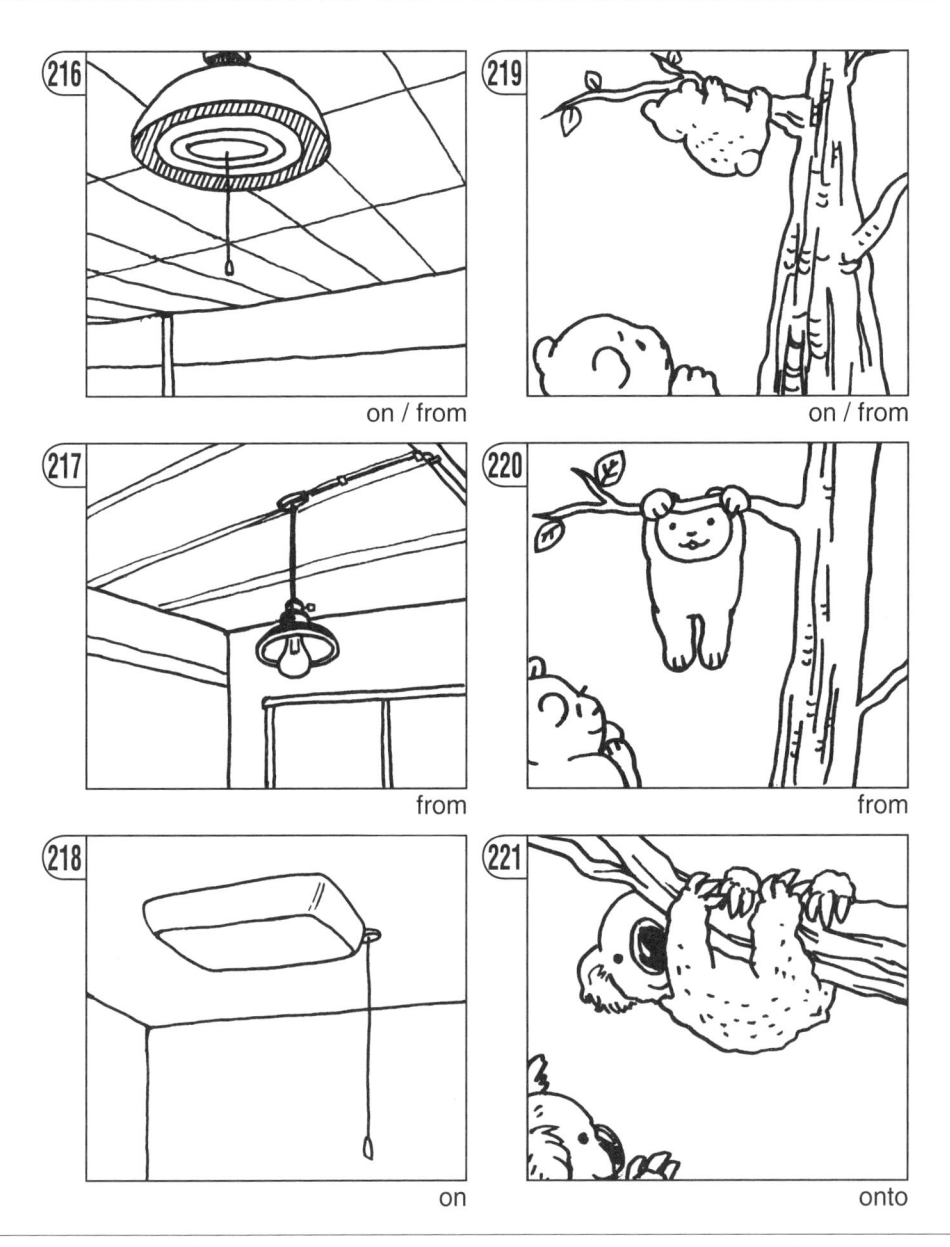

216　on / from
217　from
218　on
219　on / from
220　from
221　onto

216 There is a light hanging on/from the ceiling.
217 There is a light hanging from the ceiling.
218 There is a light on the ceiling.
219 The bear is hanging on/onto/from the branch.
220 The bear is hanging from the branch.
221 The koala is hanging onto the branch.

⑦ 着ける put on と脱ぐ take off

put on

222 b. Bowsheeman is putting on his cap.　c. He is wearing his cap.
223 Sylvia is putting on her lipstick.
224 Candy is putting on her glasses.

【Ⅲ】イメージを比べる　87

take off

225 a. Grandma is wearing a hat.　b. She took her hat off.
226 a. Olivia is wearing her pajamas.　b. She took her pajama bottoms off.
227 a. She is wearing her boots.　b. She took her boots off.

88 ··· on：線と見る

⑧方向・方角の on, to, in

228 on / to

229 on / to

230 on / to

231 on / to

232 on

228 The fox is on/to Teria's left.
229 The theater is on/to the left of the road.
230 The Gold Building is on the right side of the river. [on/to the right of the river]
231 Ruby's house is on the right.
Ruby's house is to the right (side) of the road.
232 a. Bowsheeman lives on the poor side of town.
b. Mr. Gold lives on the rich side of town.

【Ⅲ】イメージを比べる 89

233 on / to

234 to

235 on

236 on / to

237 to

238 on

233 Bowsheeman's apartment building is on/to the north side of the river.
234 Northern Island is to the north of Cold State.
235 Mt. Gold is on the north (side) of Gold State.
236 The apple is on/to Teria's right.
　　The orange is on/to Teria's left.
237 The chopsticks are to the left of the bowl.
238 The orange is on Teria's left.

⑧方向・方角の on, to, in

(239) on
(240) to
(241) on / to
(242) on / to
(243) on / to
(244) on / to

239 The lighthouse is on the south edge of Bowshee Island.
240 Nautilus Island is to the south of Bowshee Island.
241 The Sea of Gold is on/to the south side of Bowshee Island.
242 The Sea of Gold is on/to the east of Bowshee Island.
243 The Gold Building is on/to the south of the Gold River.
244 Bowsheeman's apartment building is on/to the north (side) of the Gold River.

【Ⅲ】イメージを比べる　91

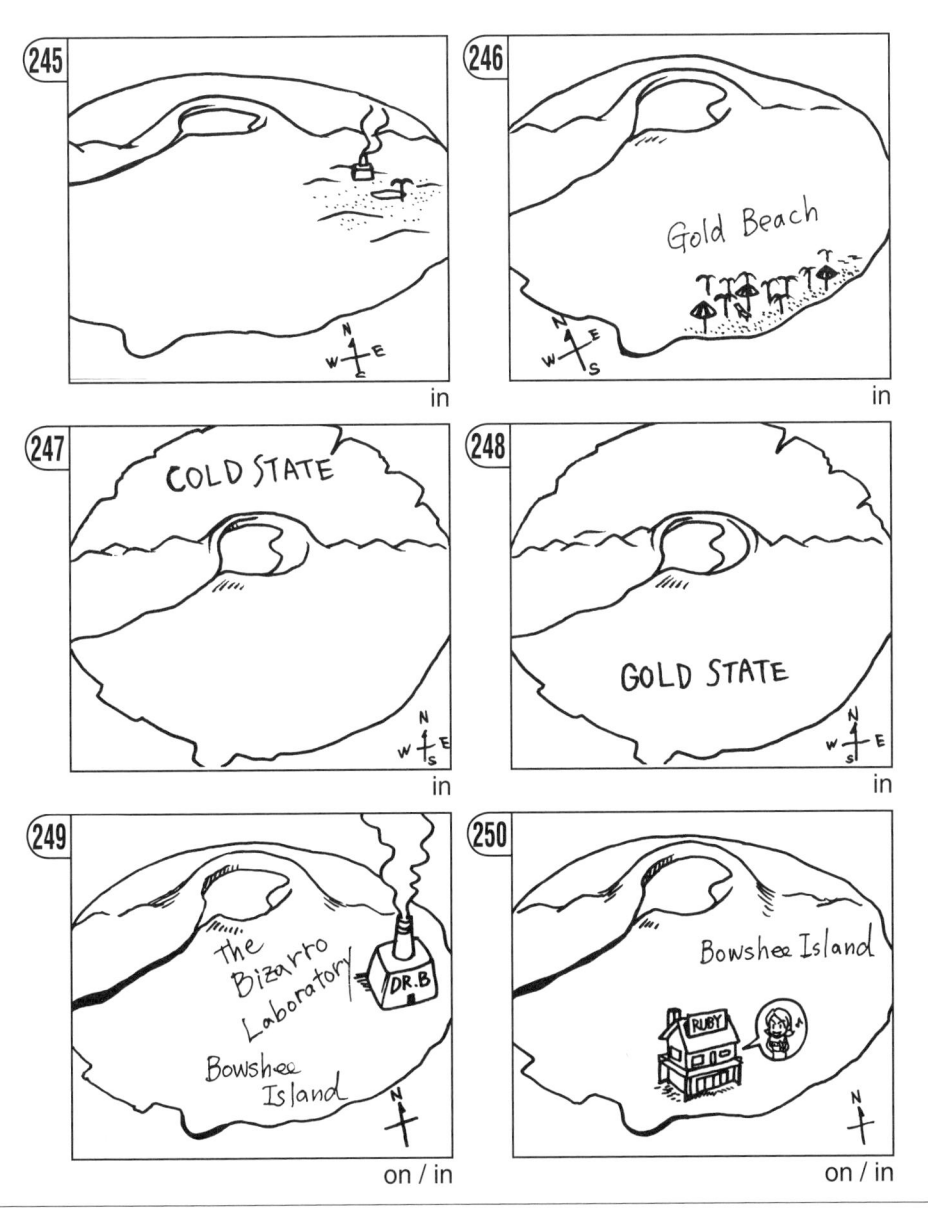

245　The desert is in the East.
247　Cold State is in the north/northern part of the island.
249　The Bizarro Laboratory is in the East.
　　 The Bizarro Laboratory is on the east side of Bowshee Island.
246　Gold Beach is in the South.
248　Gold State is in the south of the island.
　　 Gold State is in the southern part of the island.
250　Ruby's house is in the South.
　　 Ruby's house is on the south edge of Bowshee Island.

① 線上に着く onto

onto the table

1 Kitten jumped onto the table.
2 Pooch jumped onto the sofa.
3 The actress walked onto the stage.

onto the ground

on / **onto**

4　b. The apple is falling onto the ground.　　c. Some of the apples are on the ground.
5　a, b. Butch is pulling the boat on/onto the land/the shore.　　c. The boat is on land/the shore.
6　a, b. The bird is descending onto the lake.　　c. The bird has landed on the lake.

⋯ off：線と見る

① 線上から離れる off

on

off the tightrope

on

off

1 a. Bakunsai is on a tightrope.　b. Bakunsai fell off the tightrope.
2 a. There is a bug on the leaf.　b. The bug fell off the leaf.
3 a. Teria is cleaning the table off.　b. The dishes have been taken off the table.
　　She is cleaning off the table.

【Ⅰ】基本のイメージ 95

on

off the ceiling

onto

from

4　a. The ninja is on the ceiling.　　b. The ninja fell off the ceiling.
5　a. The koala is hanging onto the branch.　　b. The koala fell off the branch.
6　a. Icicles are hanging from the eaves.　　b. One of them fell off.

①線上から離れる off

come off

come off

tear ～ off

7　a. There is a knob on the door.　b. The doorknob came off in his hand.
　　He pulled the doorknob off.
8　b. The mannequin's arm came off.　Leaf knocked the mannequin's arm off.
9　b. The cat tore the wallpaper off.

【Ⅰ】基本のイメージ

sail **off**

take **off**

take **off**

10 b. The ship is sailing off into the ocean.   The ship is sailing away.
11 b. Butch took off (like a flash) from the starting line.
12 b. The plane took off from the runway.

off：線と見る

①降りる

on

off

in   out of

13 a. Olivia is on the rug.   b. Mama shooed Olivia off the rug.
　　　　　　　　　　　　　　Mama told Olivia to get off the rug.
14 b. Eluca is getting off the train.
15 Katarina got out of the car.

16 a. The farmer is on his property.   b. The farmer ran off his property.
　　　　　　　　　　　　　　　　　　　The farmer left his property.
17 a. Olivia and Tim are on the grass.   b. The gardener is telling them to keep off the grass.
18 a. The cat is in the grass.   b. The cat is coming out of the grass.

②それる

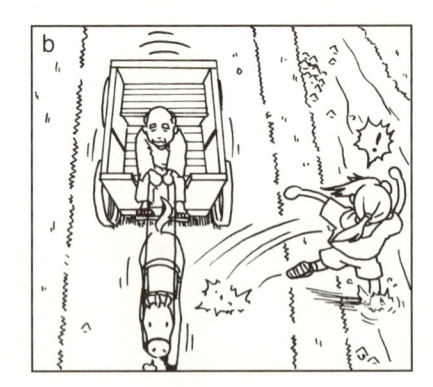

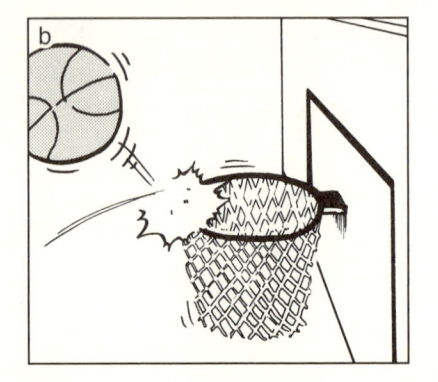

19 b. The boy jumped off/out of the road.
　　 The boy jumped aside.
　　 The boy jumped out of the horse's way.
20 Tim turned off the road to school, but Teria went on.
21 b. The ball bounced off the hoop.

22 c. The dog is running off.
23 c. Pooch ran off the sidewalk.
24 The cat was on the way to his food, but he jumped after the mouse instead.

③切り離す

25 Baby tore off a piece of toilet paper.
26 b. Papa cut off a piece of paper.
27 c. Tim cut out a piece of paper.

28 b. Bakunsai cut off the fish's head.
29 b. The cat is walking off/away with the fish. c. The cat is running away from Bakunsai.
30 b, c. Sylvia slept off her drunkenness.

④ 離れる

31 b. Teria is keeping off fatty foods.
32 b. Butch is off cigarettes.
33 b. Sylvia is off alcohol.

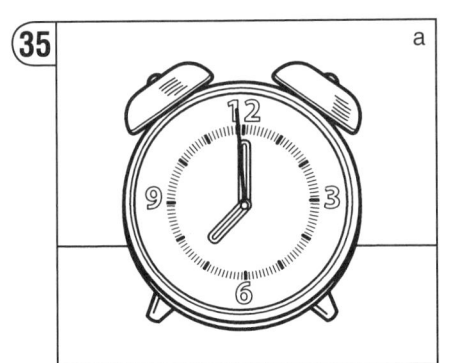

34 a. Tim stepped on a turtle. b. Tim took his foot off the turtle.
35 b. The alarm clock went off.
36 The socks are giving off an odor.   37. The garbage is giving off an odor.

off：線と見る

①蒸発する off と out

off

off

dry her hair

38　b, c. Eluca dried off the car.
39　c. The umbrella dried off.
40　Sylvia dried her hair.

【Ⅲ】イメージを比べる 107

out

out

off the line

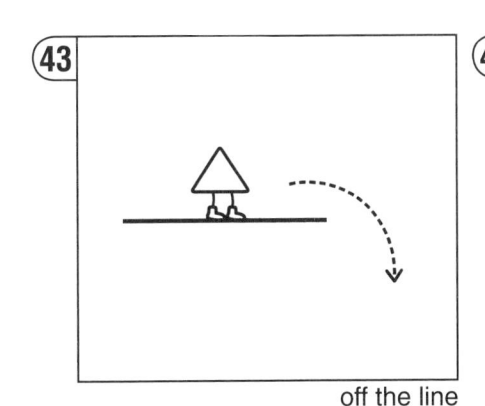

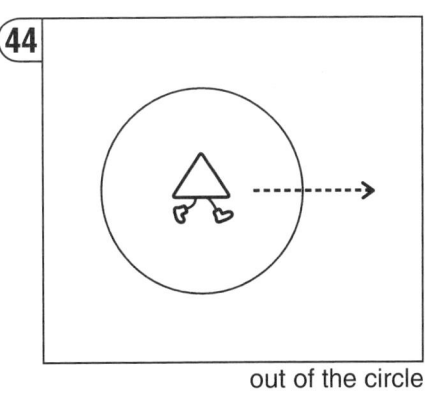

out of the circle

41　c. The sun dried out the mattress.
42　c. Butch's shirt has dried out.
43　If Mr. T walks any further, he will fall off the line.
44　Mr. T is getting out of the circle.

②点いている on と消えている off

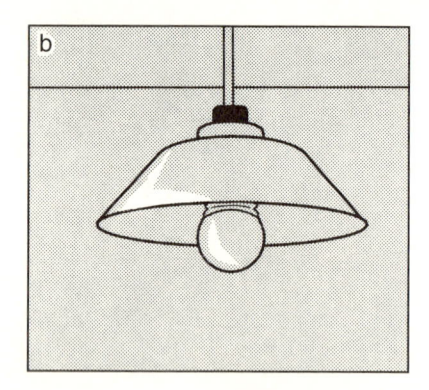

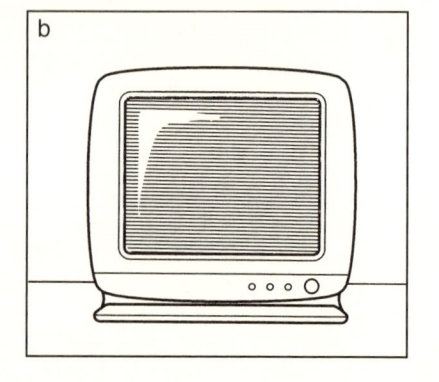

45　a. The light is on.　b. The light is (turned) off.
46　a. The gas (heater) is on.　b. Mama turned the gas (heater) off.
47　a. The TV is on.　b. The TV is (turned) off.

③だんだんと消えていく out

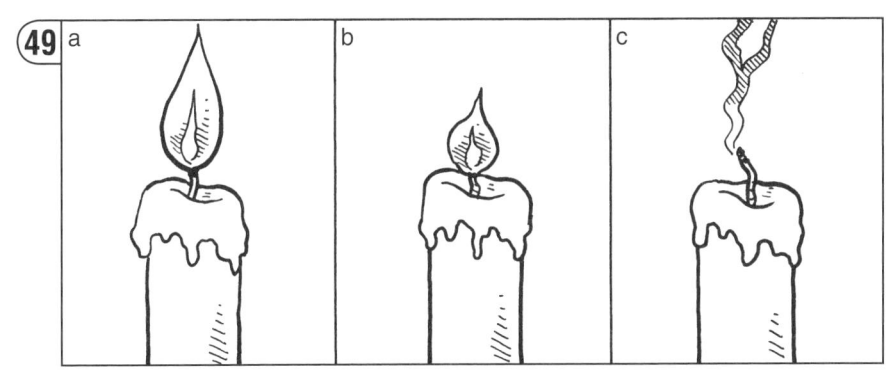

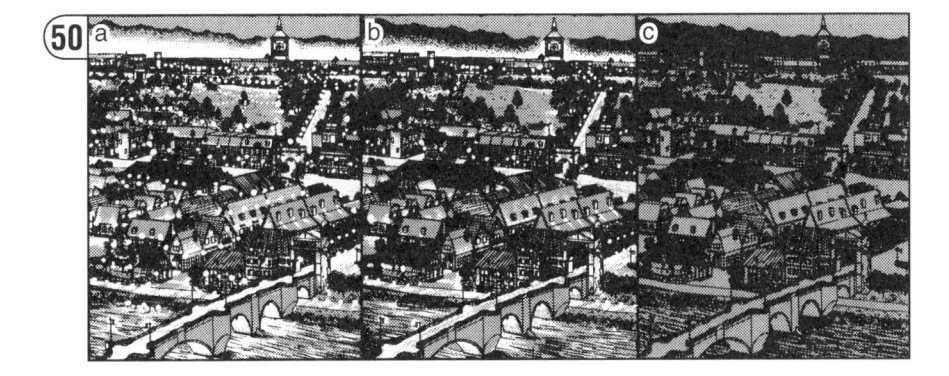

48 c. The fire is out.
49 c. The flame is out.　The candle went out.
50 c. The city's lights are out.

① 線を越える over

over the fence

1 The horse jumped over the fence.
2 c. The ninja is just over the fence.
   The ninja is on the other side of the fence.
3 b. The ball went over the fence.   c. Teria is looking over the fence.

over the fence

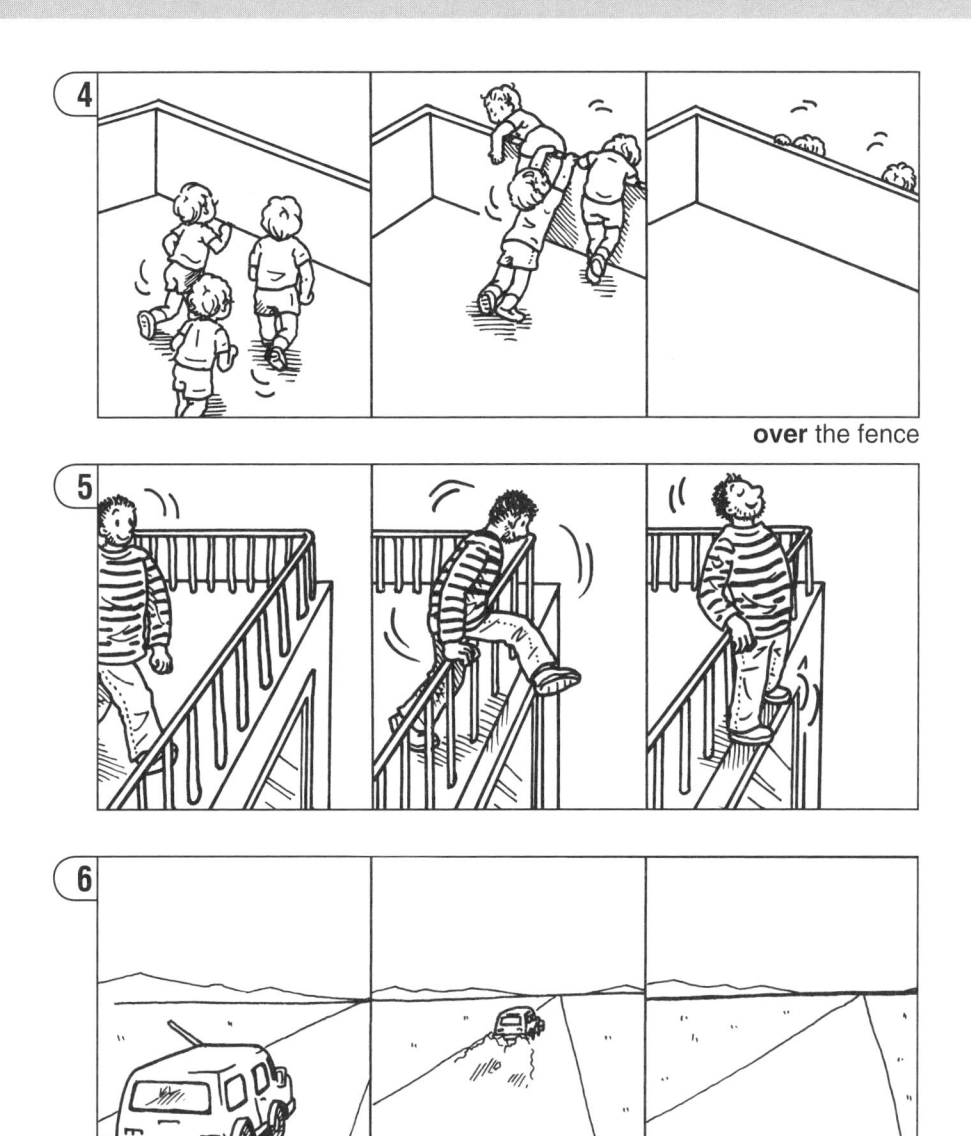

4　The children climbed over the fence.
5　Butch stepped over the fence/the railing.
　　Butch stepped onto the edge of the building.
6　The car drove over/beyond the horizon.

①線を越える over

over the frog

7　The car ran over the frog.
8　The plane flew over the lighthouse.
9　The bird is flying over/above the houses.

over the puddle

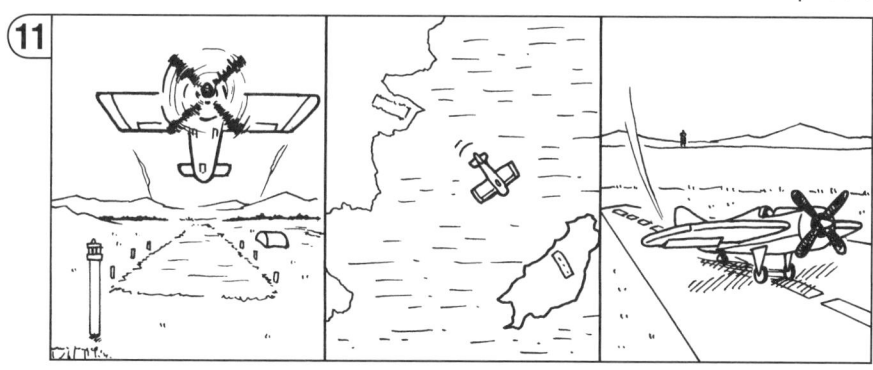

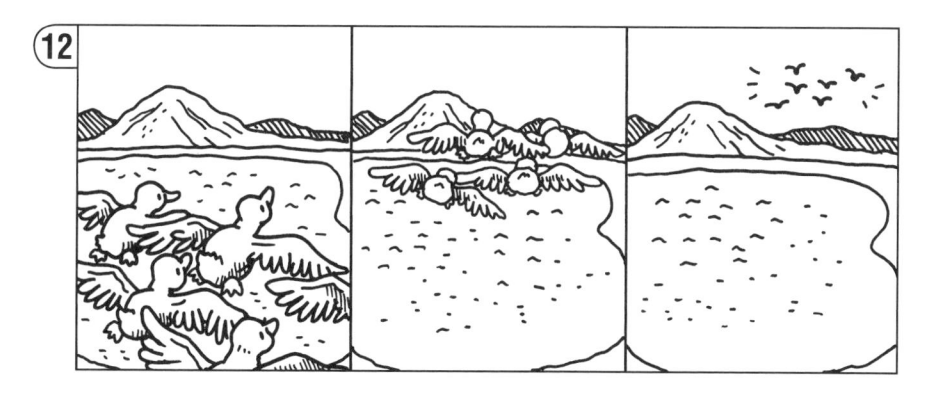

10 Bakunsai jumped over/across the puddle.
11 The plane flew over the sea.
12 The birds flew over the lake.

114　over：線と見る

②線をカバーしている over

over him

13　Mama is putting a blanket over/on Baby.
14　c. Someone is holding his/her hand over/on the bottle.
15　Someone put a cover over the food (on the plate).

【Ⅰ】基本のイメージ 115

16 **over** the fish

18 **over** / on

19 on

16 There is plastic wrap over the fish.
17 There is mosquito netting over Baby.
18 There is a sheet of paper over/on the pencil.
19 There is a pencil on the paper.
20 There is a cloth over/on the basket.
21 There is a glass cover over/on the light bulb.

②線をカバーしている over

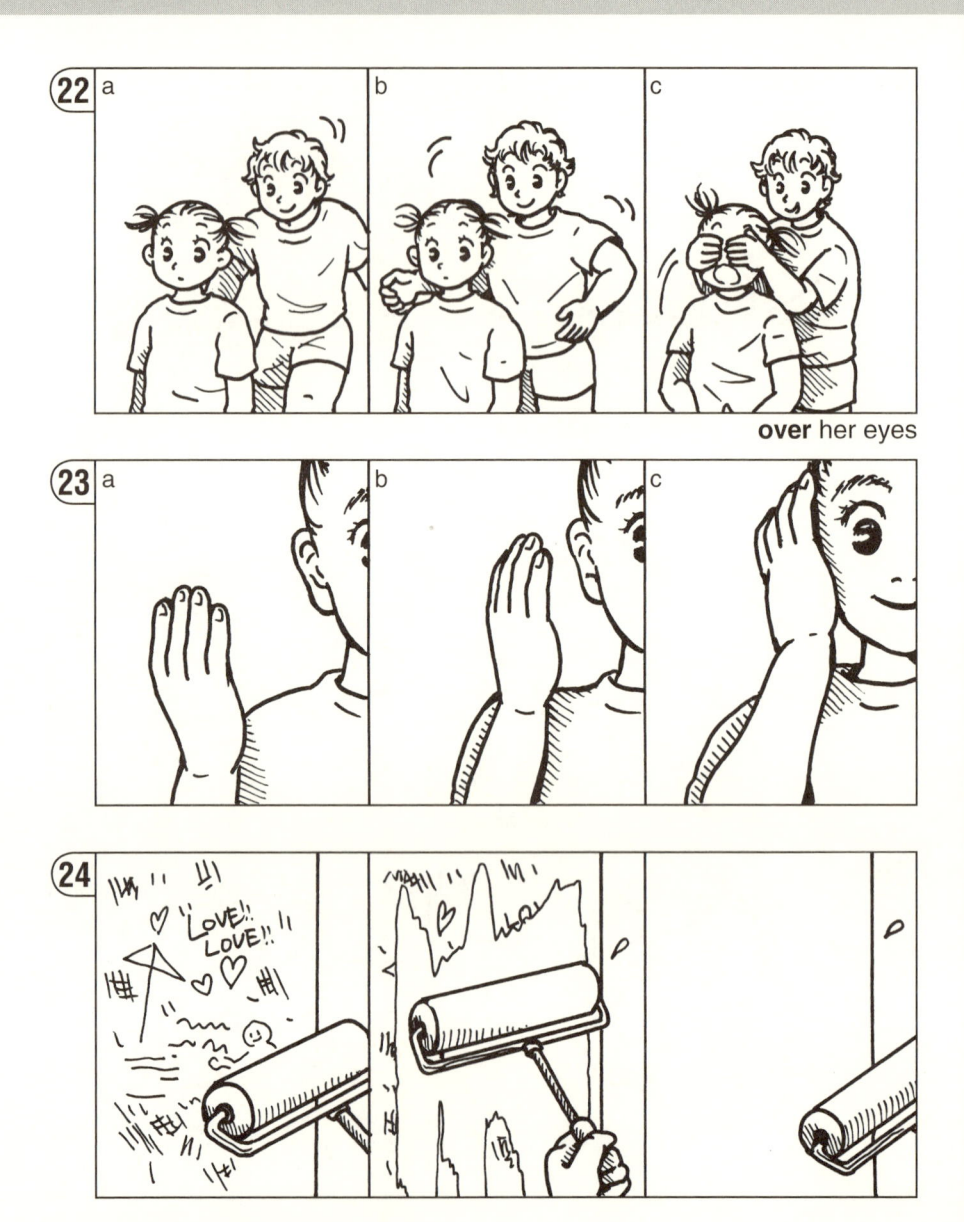

over her eyes

22　c. Tim put his hands over Olivia's eyes.
23　c. Teria has her hand over her ear.
24　Someone painted over the writing on the wall.

【Ⅰ】基本のイメージ 117

over the mouse

against

25 Olivia put a basket over the mouse/the hole.
26 Tim is covering over the hole.
27 Teria swatted a fly against the ceiling.

① 越える

28 Someone stepped over Pooch.
29 The helicopter flew over the hill.
30 Teria and her friends are hiking over the hill.

【Ⅱ】連想するイメージ 119

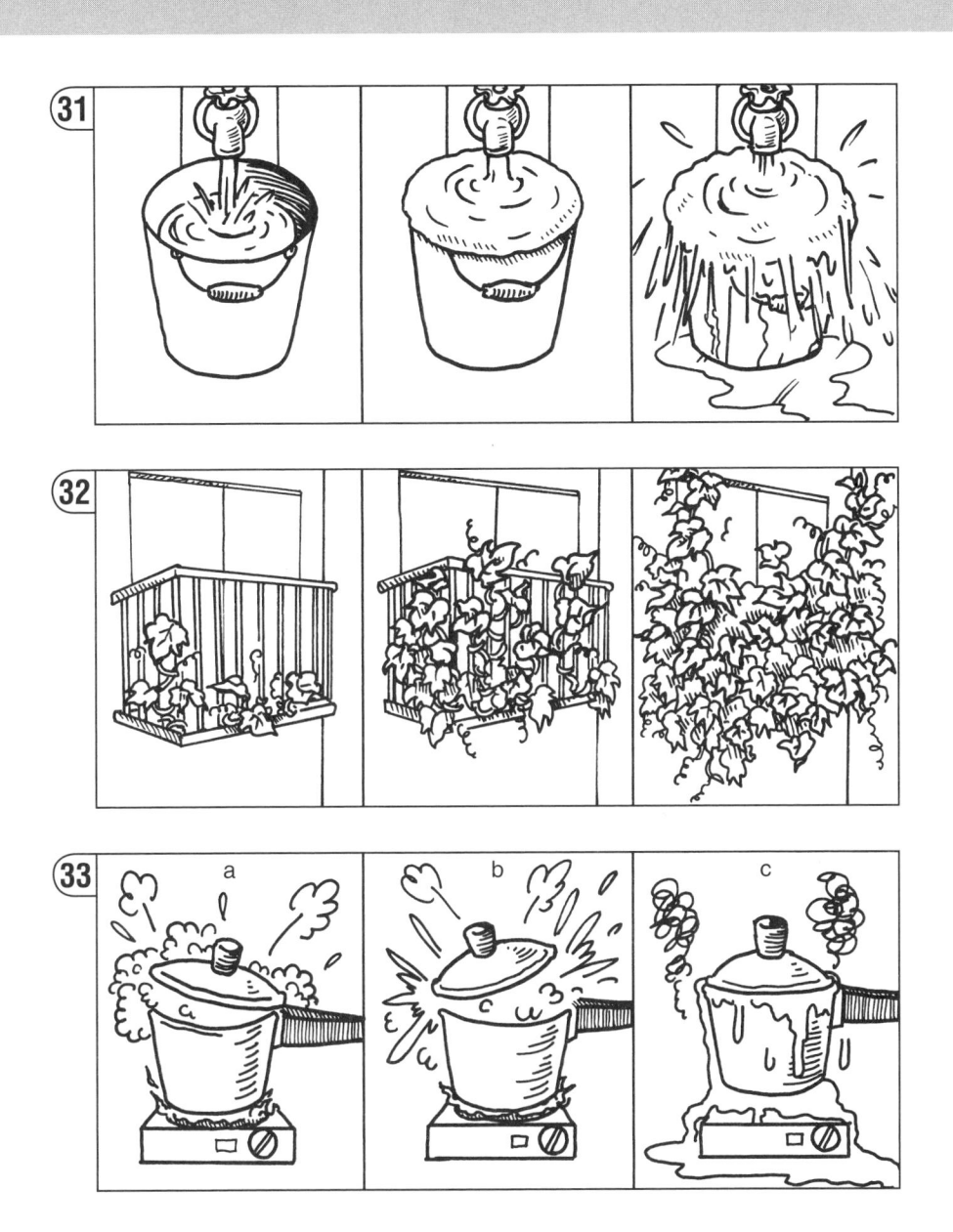

31　The water is spilling over the top of the bucket.
32　c. The ivy is draped over the railing on the balcony.
33　a, b. The soup is boiling over.　c. The soup (has) boiled over.

120 ... over：線と見る

①越える

34 c. Tim is over 90kg.
　　c. Tim's weight is over/above 90kg.
　　c. Tim weighs over 90kg.

35 The temperature is over/above thirty.

36 c. Olivia's height is over 100cm.

37 It costs over ten dollars.　The price is over/above ten dollars.
38 The old woman has been in bed (for) over five years.
39 Tim ate over 15 pancakes.

②ひっくり返す

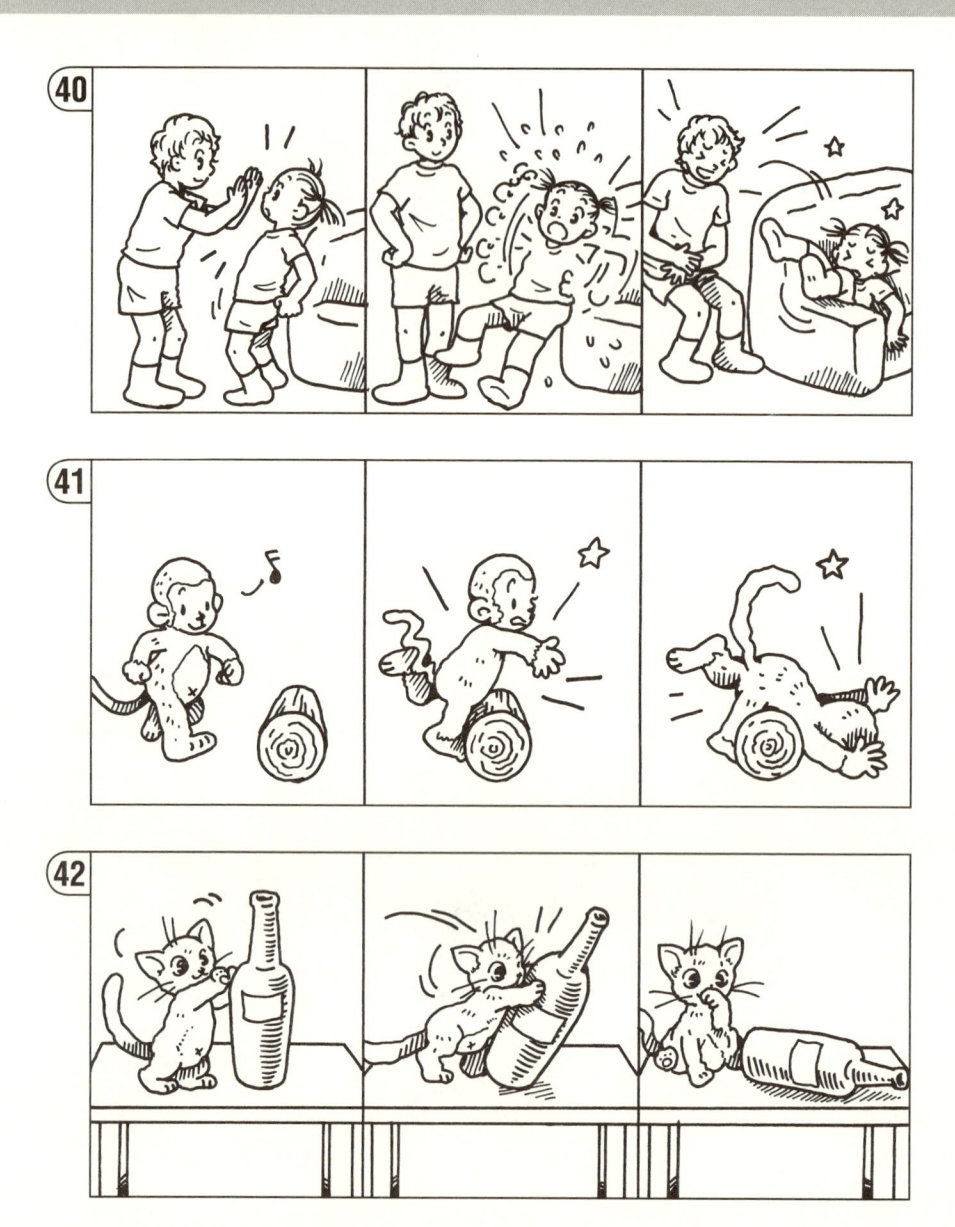

40 Tim pushed Olivia over.
41 The monkey tripped/fell over the log.
42 The kitten knocked the bottle over.
　 The kitten knocked over the bottle.

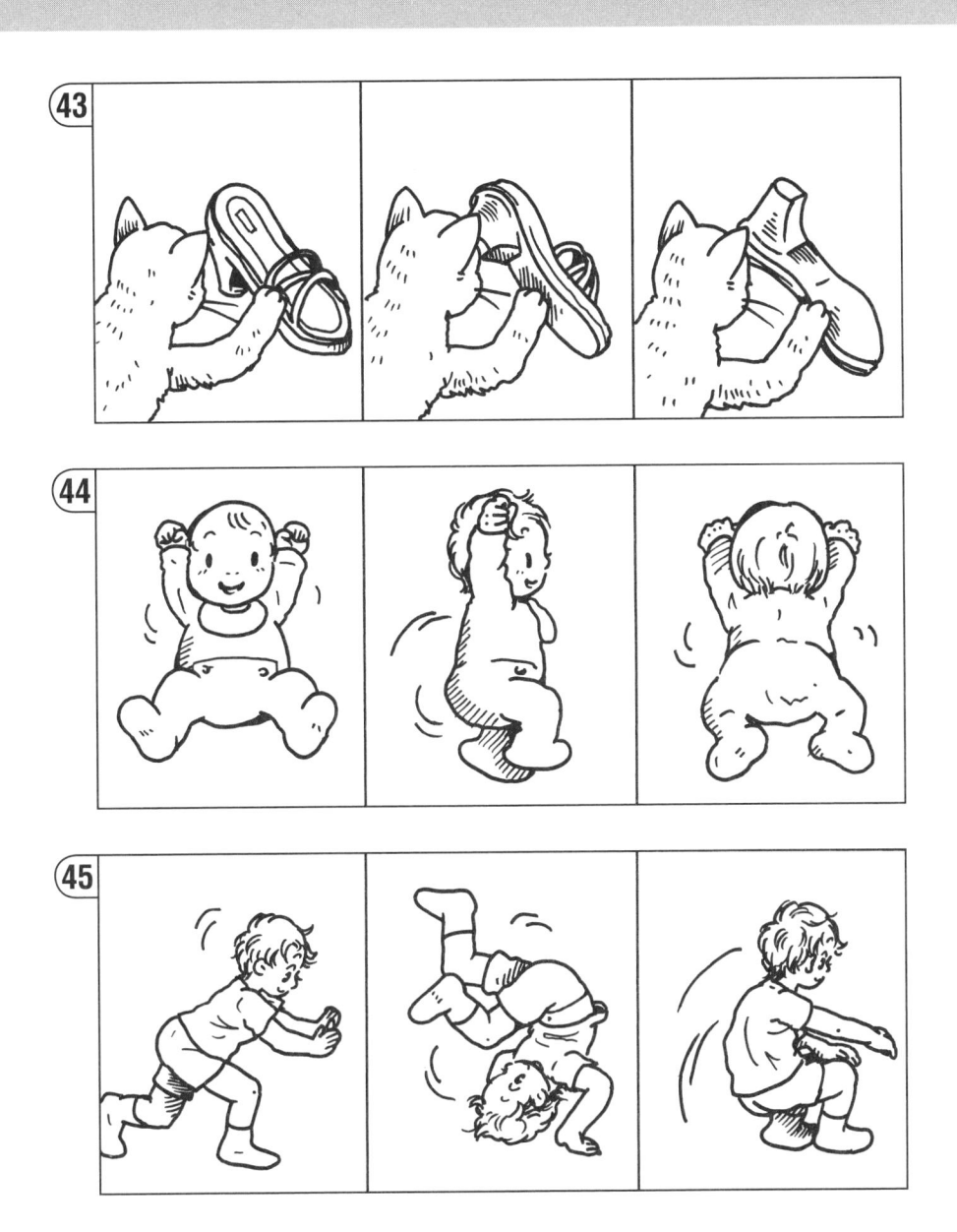

43 The cat turned the shoe over.
　　The cat turned over the shoe.
44 Baby is rolling/turning over.
45 Tim rolled over.
　　Tim did a somersault.

124 ... over：線と見る

③くり返す

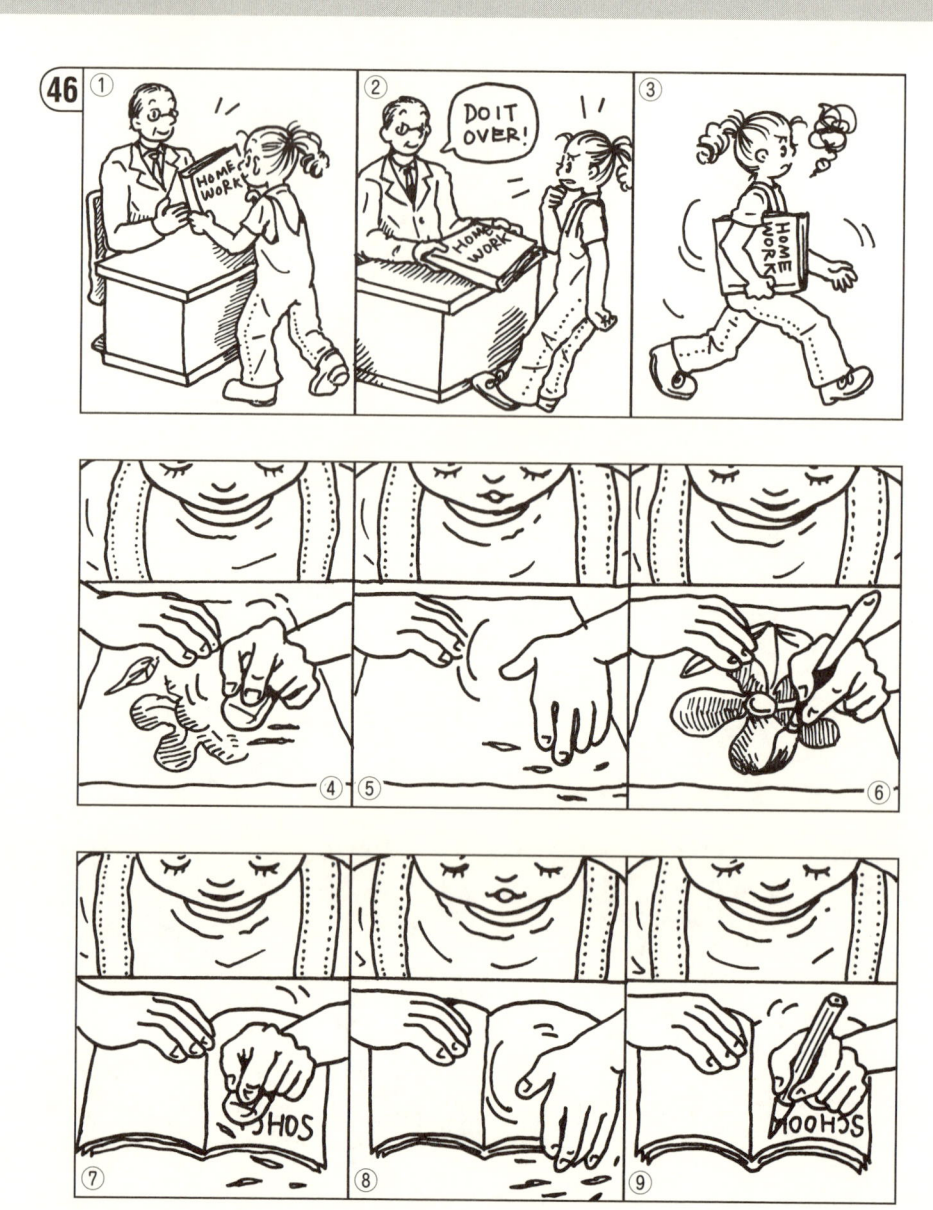

46 ③ Teria has to do her homework over.
⑥ Teria is drawing it over.
⑨ Teria is writing it over.

46　⑫ Teria has to do her homework over again.
47　Teria is drawing circles over and over.
48　Butch wrote the letter over and over.

④終わった

49　The game is over.
50　c. Summer vacation is over.
51　b, c. Teria's work is over for the day.

52　② The time allotted for the test is up.
　　⑥ Candy is not through yet.
　　⑦ Candy is through with the test.
　　⑨ The test is over.

⑤ 視線が越えていく

53 Butch is reading over the man's shoulder.
54 Papa told Teria, "Look over there."
55 Albert asked Sylvia, "Would you put the flowers over there?"

【Ⅱ】連想するイメージ

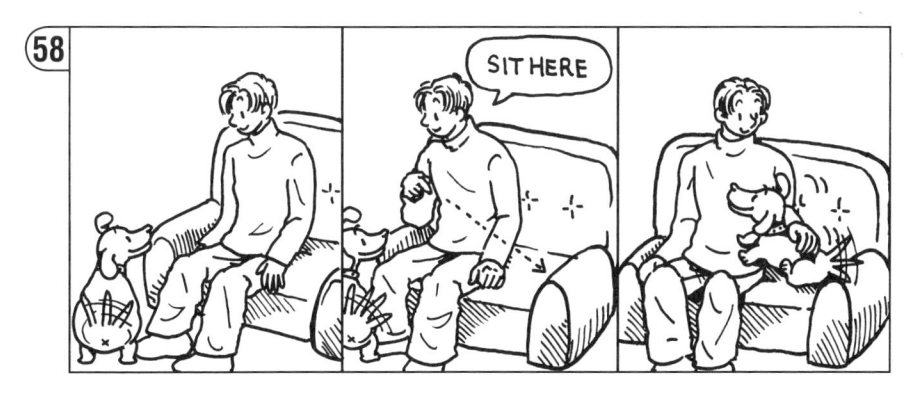

56 Ruby handed the phone (over) to her father.
   Ruby handed (over) the phone to her father.
57 Albert asked /told Sylvia, "Would you please sit over here?"
58 Albert told the dog, "Sit here."

⑤視線が越えていく

across

59　The town is just over the second hill.
60　The town is over the lake.
　　Sylvia lives over the lake.
62　The caravan trekked over the desert to get to the river/to the pyramid.

61　There is a town across the lake.

【Ⅱ】連想するイメージ 131

over / on

63 Ruby and Nautilus are talking over/on the phone.
64 Teria told Olivia, "Come over here."
65 "Come here," Tim said to Puppy.

⑥向こうに目的がある over / across と比べる

66 The puppy is running over the grass to chase a bone. [across, through]
67 Butch is going over/across the lake to buy some shoes.
68 The man is trudging over the sand towards an oasis.

【Ⅱ】連想するイメージ 133

across

across

across

69　The puppy is running across the field.
70　Albert is going across the lake.
71　The travelers are going across the desert.

⑦カバーしている

72 There are clouds over/above the city.
74 There is a bridge over the river.
   The bridge is over Butch's head.
76 There is a chandelier over/above Sylvia and Albert's heads.
73 There is a tarp over/above the picnic table.
75 There is an overpass over the street.
77 There is a tree over Tim.
   There are branches over/above Tim.

【Ⅱ】連想するイメージ　135

78　The helicopter is hovering over the people.
79　There is (some) laundry over/across the alley.
81　There is a bell over/above Teria's head.
80　There is a rainbow over the river.
82　Someone is holding a hat over/above the frog.

… **over**：線と見る

⑦カバーしている

83   all over

84   all over

85   all over

86   a   all over   b   over / on

83   The paint has spilled all over the man.
The paint has spilled on the man's head.

84   Someone has made a mess all over the room.

85   The milk spilled all over the table.

86   a. There are vines growing all over the castle.
b. The vines are even over/on Sleeping Beauty.

87 Grandma has gotten old over the years.
88 Butch looked Sylvia over.
89 Teria read over/through the contract.

over：線と見る

① ジャンプする over と off

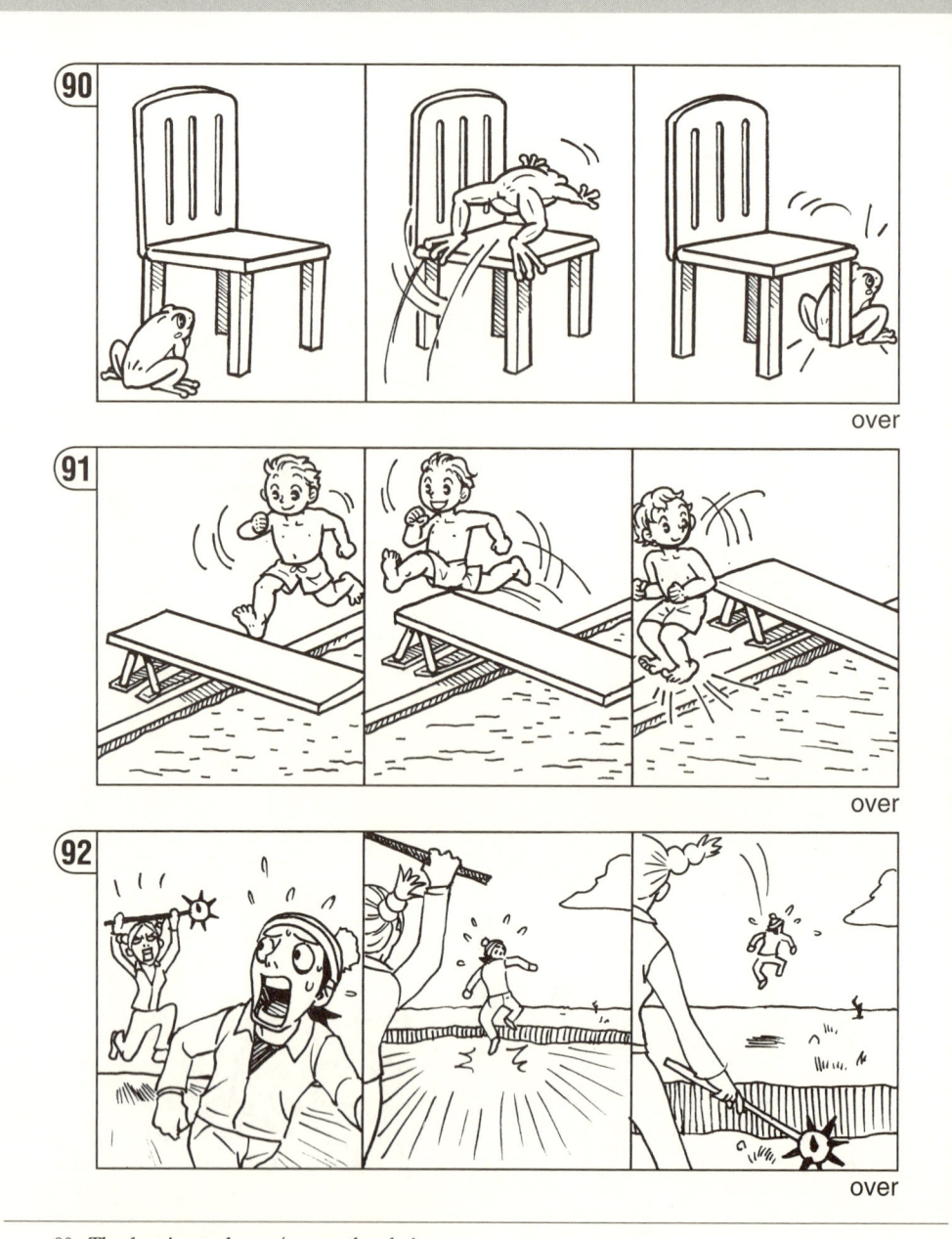

90　over

91　over

92　over

90　The frog jumped over/across the chair.
91　Tim jumped over/across the diving board.
92　Bowsheeman jumped over/across the chasm.

【Ⅲ】イメージを比べる 139

93 a — on b — off
94 a b — off
95 a b — off / over

93 a. Kitten is sitting on the chair.　b. Kitten is jumping off the chair.
94 b. Teria has jumped off the diving board.
95 b. Bowsheeman has jumped off/over the cliff.

②落下している down / over と比べる

knock down

be run down

shoot down

96 Kitten knocked the cup down.
　 Kitten knocked down the cup.
97 Earl was run down by a car.
98 The hunter shot (down) the deer.

【Ⅲ】イメージを比べる 141

knock over

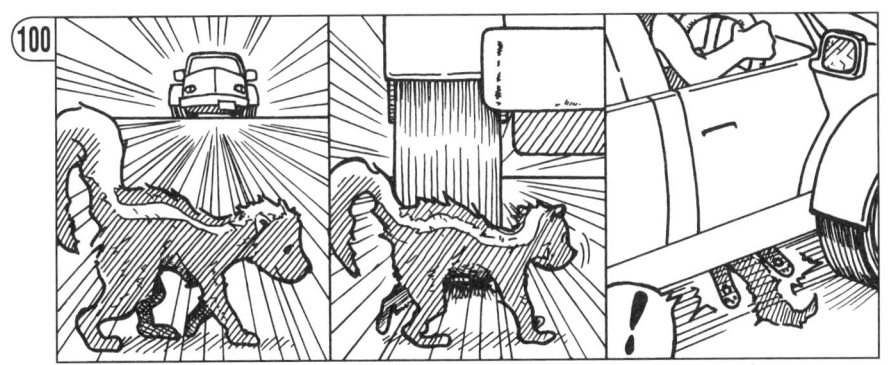

be run over

knock over

99 Dora knocked the cup over.
　Dora knocked over the cup.

100 The skunk was run over by a car.

101 Kitten knocked the bottle over.
　Kitten knocked over the bottle.

142 … over：線と見る

③ひっくり返る **over, down, off**

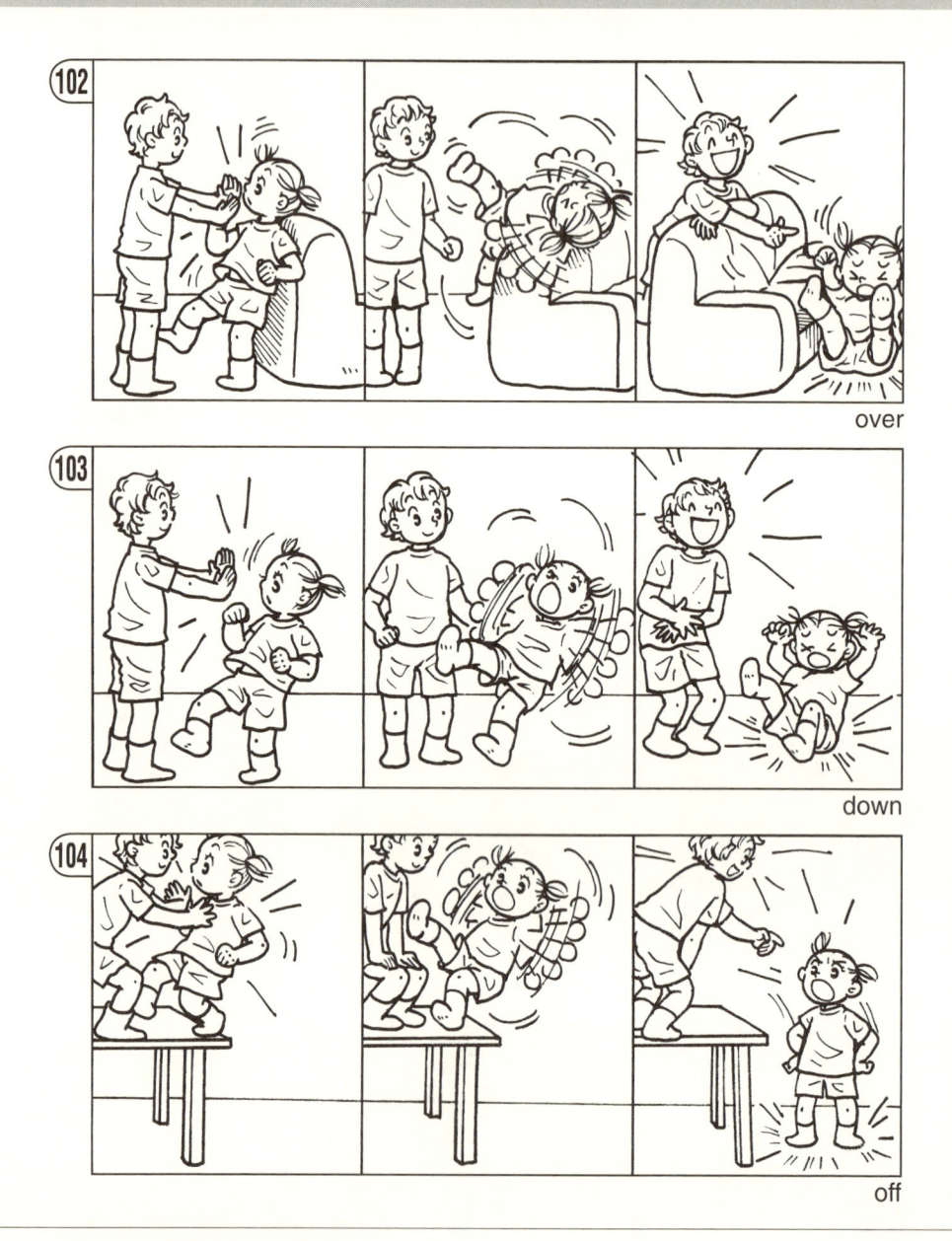

over

down

off

102 Tim pushed Olivia over the sofa.
103 Tim pushed Olivia down.
104 Tim pushed Olivia off the table.

④ころぶ over, down, off

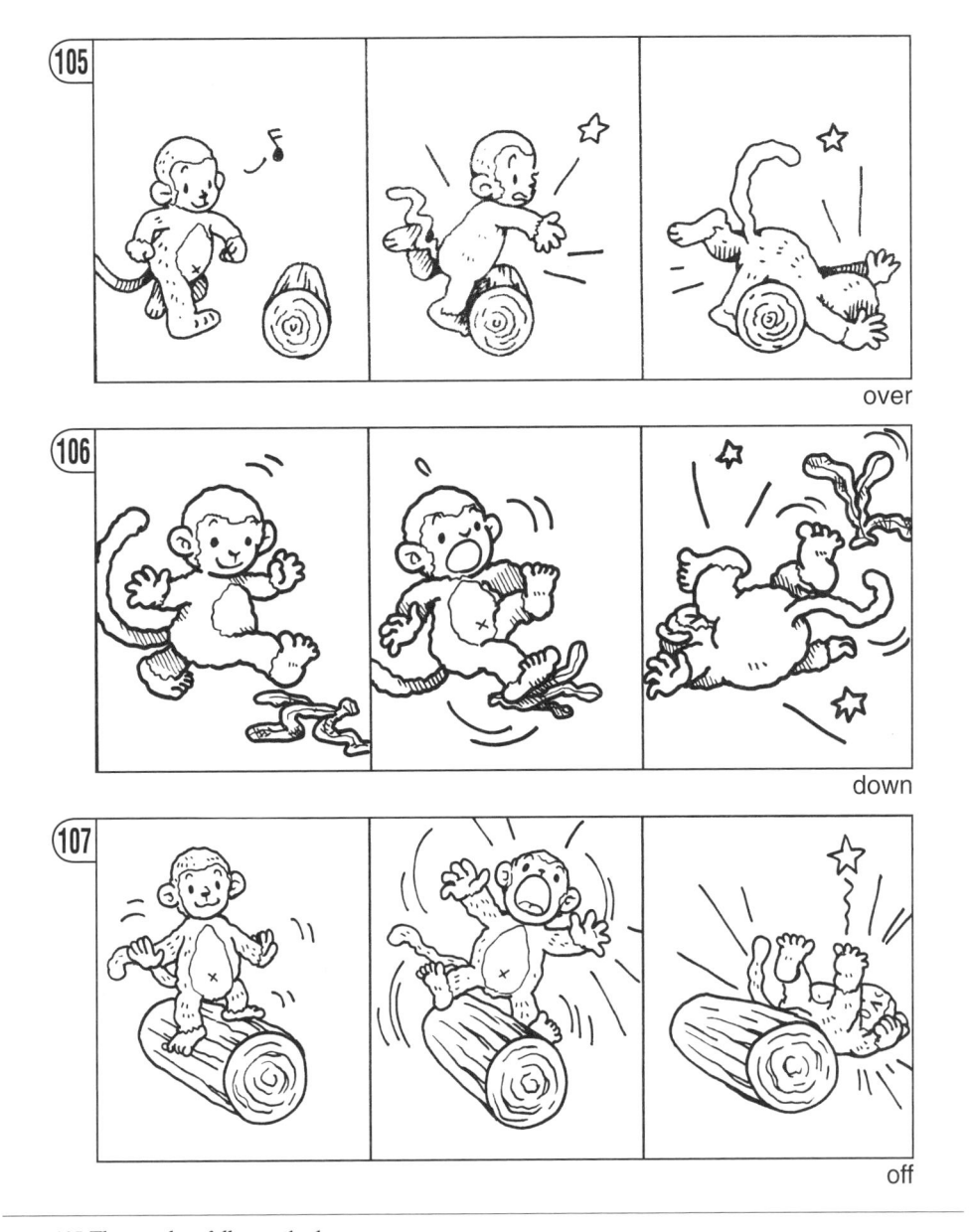

over

down

off

105 The monkey fell over the log.
106 The monkey slipped and fell down.
107 The monkey fell off the log.

over：線と見る

⑤ knock over と knock down

over / down

over / down

over

108 Chicori knocked Fennel over/down.
　　Chicori knocked over/down Fennel.
109 Pooch knocked Olivia over/down.
110 Bakunsai knocked Oton over psychically.

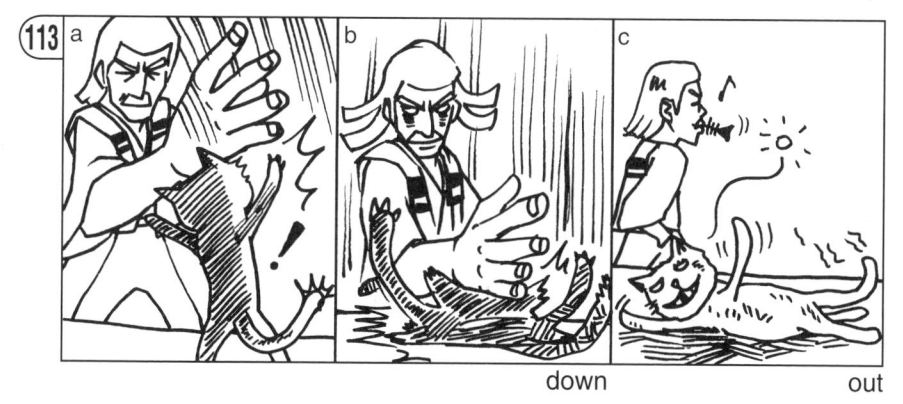

111 Sorel knocked Earl down with his stick.
112 The girl knocked Tim down/over.
   The girl pushed Tim down/over.
113 b. Bakunsai knocked Dora down.   c. He knocked Dora out.

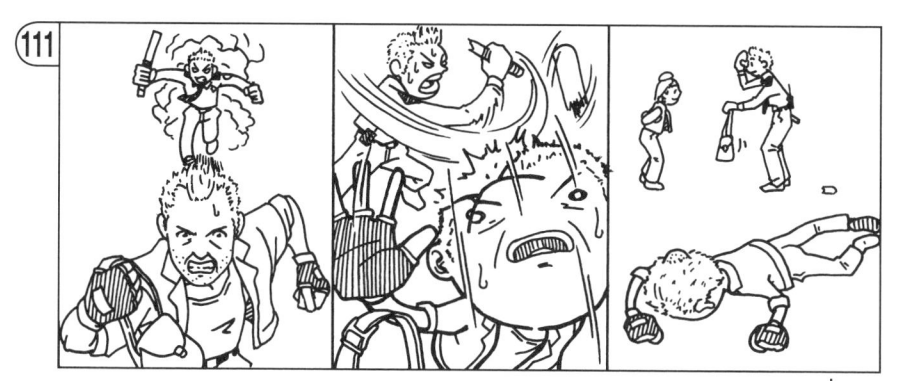

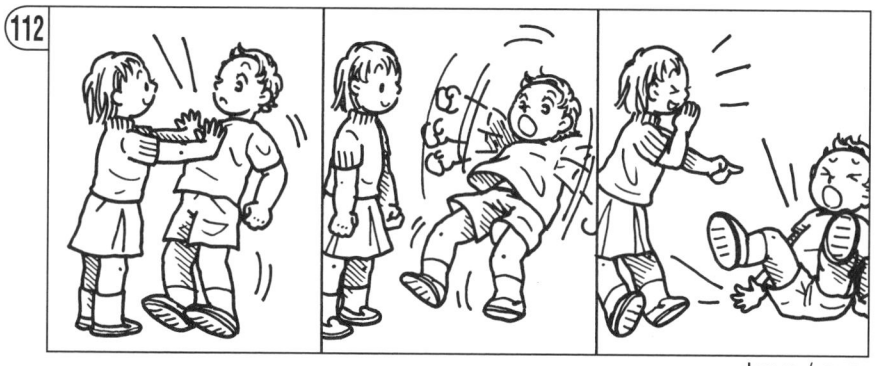

⑥ knock down / over と比べる

114 Baby knocked the blocks down.　　Baby knocked down the blocks.
115 Tim knocked Robo Junior down.　　Tim knocked down Robo Junior.
116 The wind knocked the Eiffel Tower down/over.
　　The wind knocked down/over the Eiffel Tower.

【Ⅲ】イメージを比べる 147

over

over

over

117 Tim knocked the blocks over.　Tim knocked over the blocks.
118 Tim knocked Robo Junior over.　Tim knocked over Robo Junior.
119 Rose turned the picture over.　Rose turned over the picture.

⑦「上に」の over, on, above

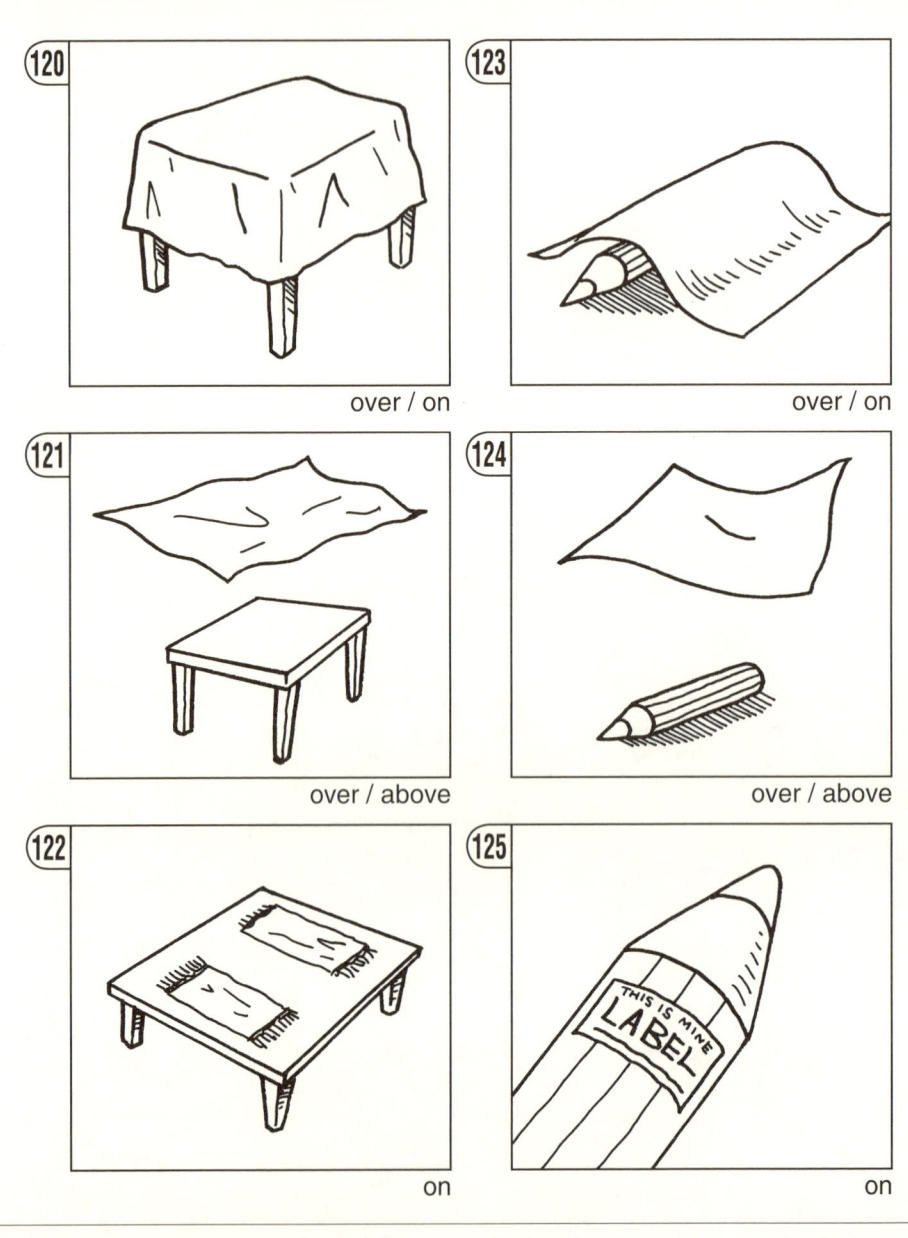

over / on

over / on

over / above

over / above

on

on

120 There is a table cloth over/on the table.
121 There is a table cloth over/above the table.
122 There are two runners on the table.
123 There is a sheet of paper over/on the pencil.
124 There is a sheet of paper over/above the pencil.
125 There is a label on the pencil.

【Ⅲ】イメージを比べる 149

⑫	over / on
⑫	over / on
⑫	over / above
⑬	over / above
⑫	on
⑬	on

126 There are some clouds on /over the mountain.
127 There is a cloud over/above the mountain.
128 There is snow on the mountain.
129 There are 3 bridges over/on /across the river.
130 There is a bridge over/above the boat.
131 There are 3 bridges on the river.

⑦「上に」の over, on, above

132 Papa has a coat over/above his head.
133 There is a coat above Papa's head.
134 Papa has a coat over his arm.
135 Tim is holding his hand/fist threateningly over/above Olivia's head.
136 Sylvia's hands are above/ beyond/out of Butch's reach.
137 Teria's hands are over Olivia's face/eyes.

【Ⅲ】イメージを比べる　151

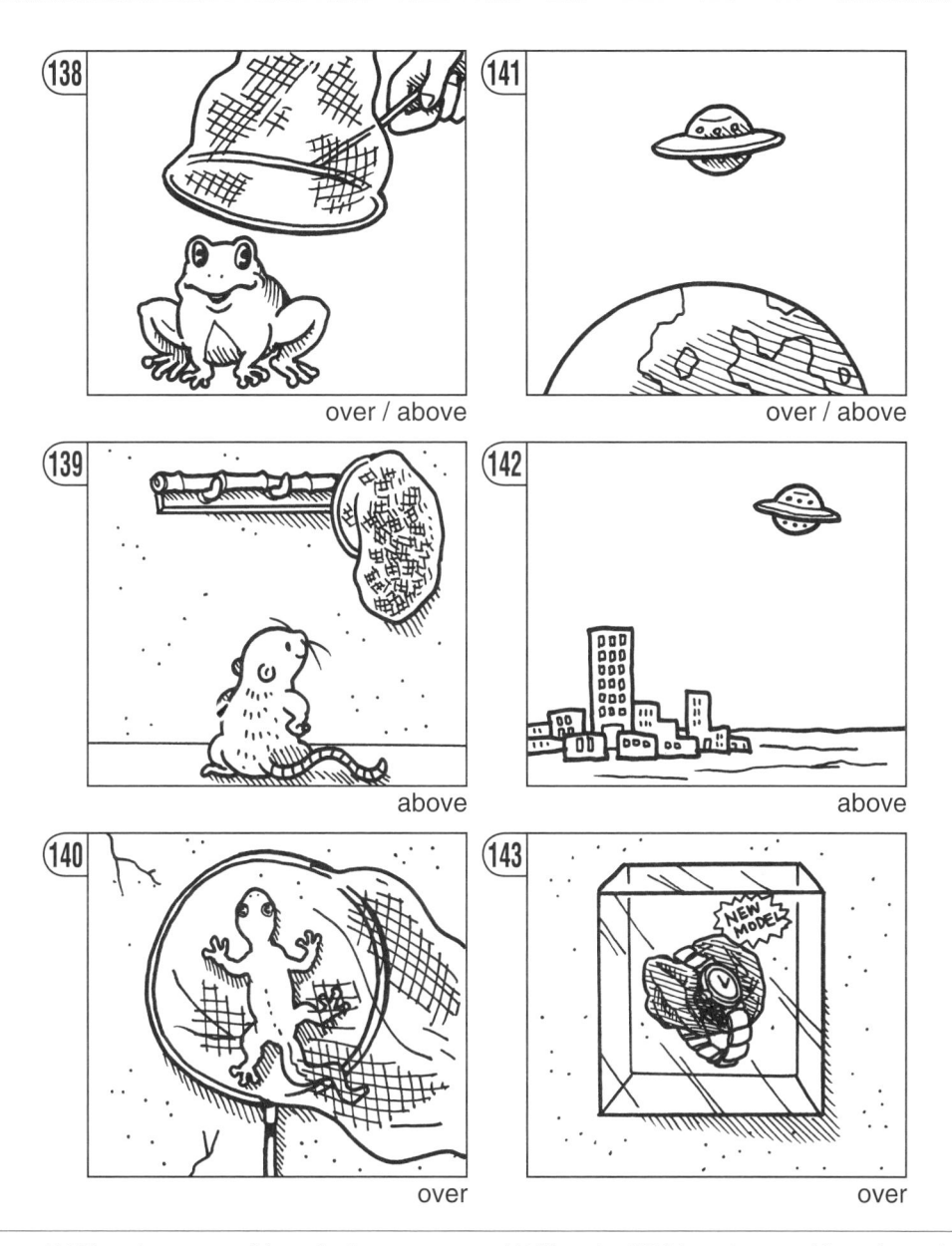

(138) over / above
(141) over / above
(139) above
(142) above
(140) over
(143) over

138 There is a net over/above the frog.
139 There is a net above the mouse.
140 There is a net over the salamander.
141 There is a UFO hovering over/above the earth.
142 The UFO is above the city.
143 A glass box is over the watch.
　　 There is a glass box over the watch.
　　 The watch is in a glass box.

⑦「上に」の over, on, above

144 on / above

145 above

146 on

147 over / above

148 above

149 over

144 The cat is on/above the dog.
145 The rooster is above the donkey.
146 The cat is hanging on the donkey.
147 The moon is over/above Eluca and Leaf.
148 The moon is above Eluca.
149 The moon is over/above the Kobits.

【Ⅲ】イメージを比べる 153

over / above

above / over

above

over

150 b, c. The helicopter is flying over/above the fire.
151 The water is above/over Tim's head.
152 The water is above/beyond the turtle's reach.
153 c. The water is over Teria's head.

①線をくぐる **under**

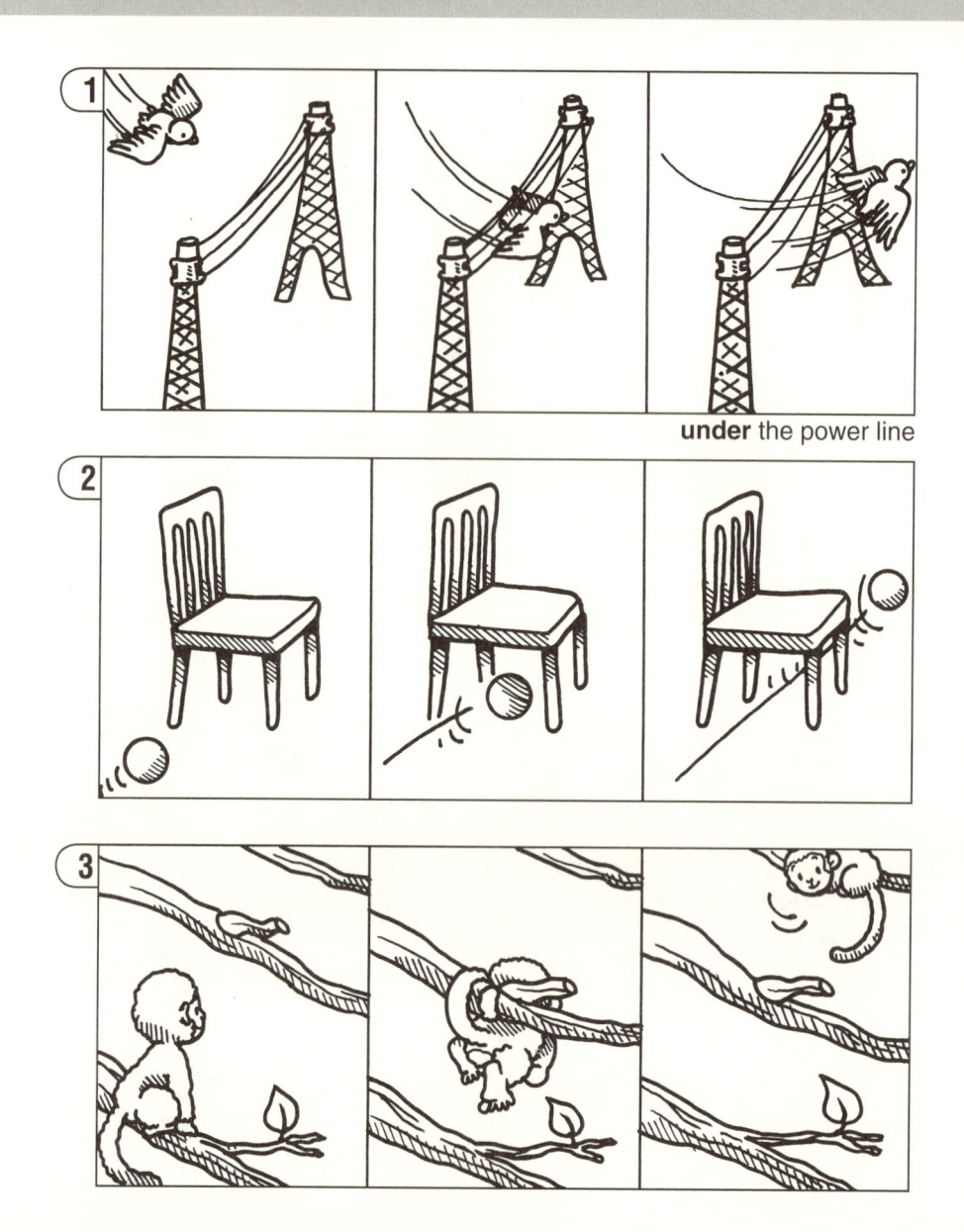

under the power line

1 The bird flew under the power line.
2 The ball went under the chair.
3 The monkey swung under the/a branch.

【Ⅰ】基本のイメージ 155

under the car

through

4　The cat ran under the car.
5　The boat went under/through one of the arches of the bridge.
6　Teria walked through the tunnel.

②線がカバーしている **under**

under an arch

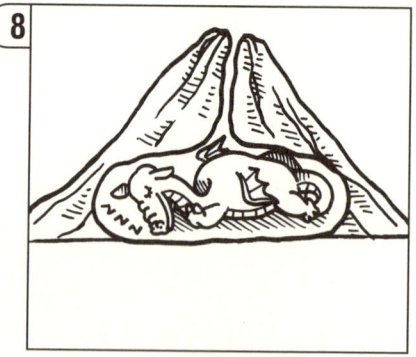

under the mountain

---

7 Pooch's house is under/beneath an arch.
8 The monster lives under/inside the mountain.
9 The river runs under the bridge. [beneath, underneath]
10 Bowsheeman is sitting under a bridge. [beneath, underneath]
11 There is a man sitting under the roof.
12 There is a mouse under the floor.

【Ⅰ】基本のイメージ　157

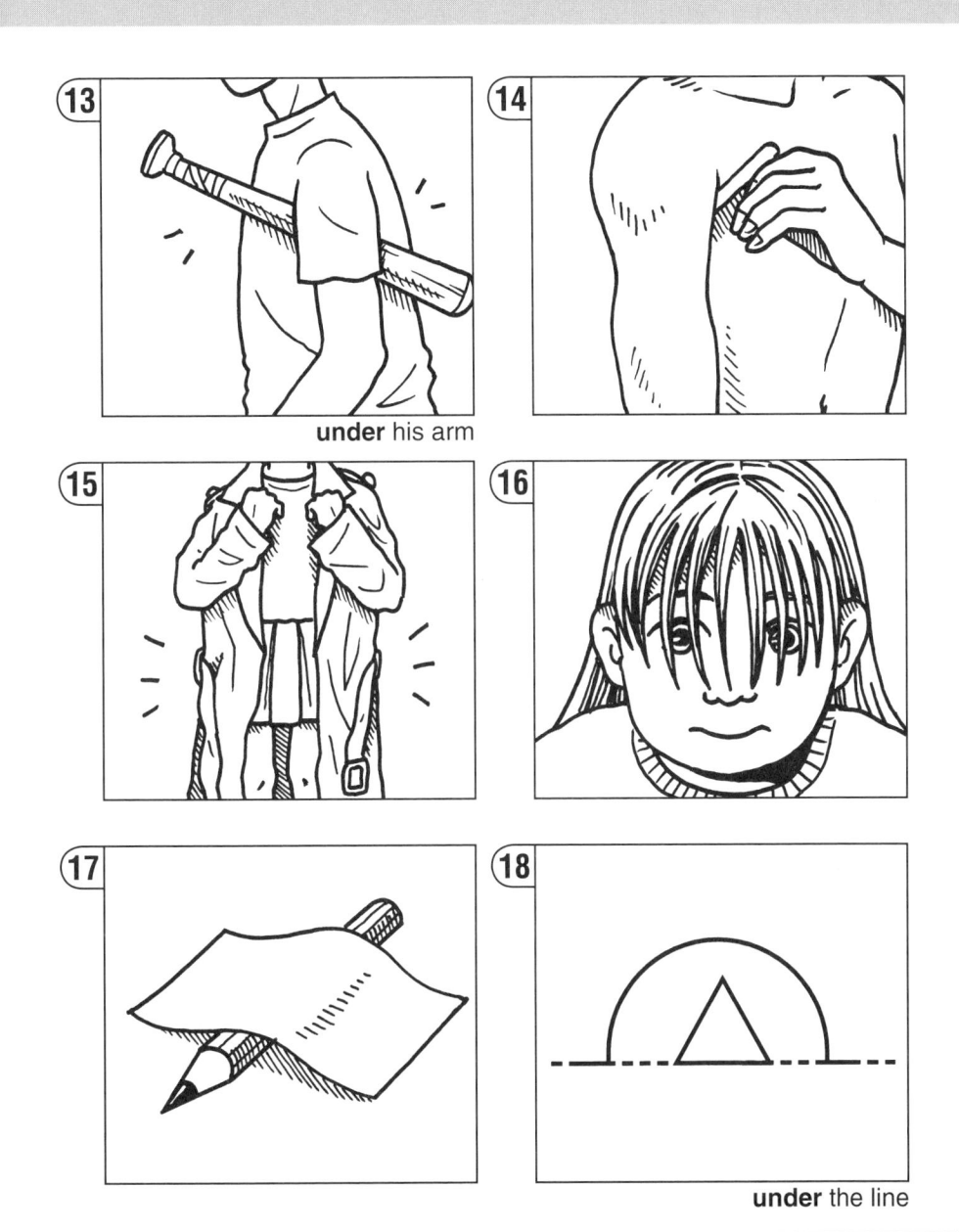

under his arm

under the line

13　The bat is under/beneath the boy's arm.
14　The thermometer is under/beneath the man's arm.
15　She is wearing a mini skirt under her coat.
16　The girl's eyes are under her hair. [beneath, underneath]
17　The pencil is under/beneath the paper.
18　The triangle is under the line/the arch.

③下にいる / ある under

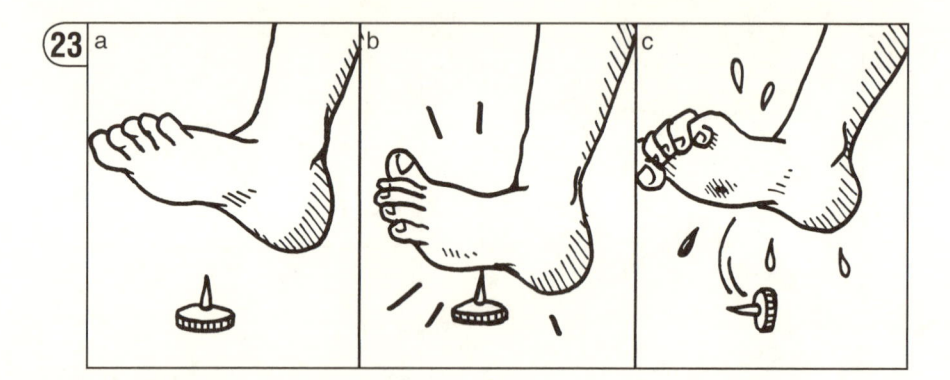

under a cloud

19 The town is under/beneath a cloud.
21 Olivia is standing under the apple. [beneath, below]
23 a, b. The tack is under his foot.
   b, c. He stepped on the tack.
20 Teria and her friend are sitting under a lawn parasol. [beneath, underneath, below]
22 Tim and Teria are (walking) under/ beneath an umbrella.

【 I 】基本のイメージ 159

under the table

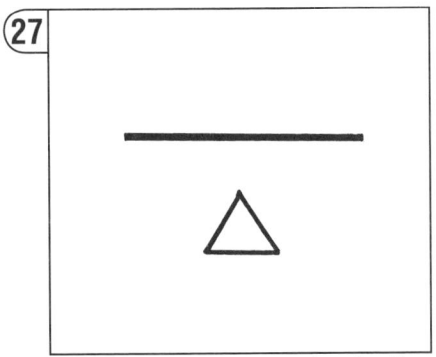

under the line

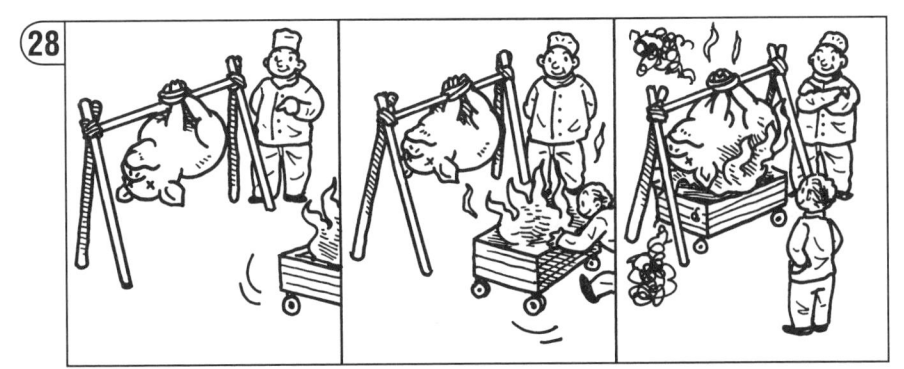

24 The kitten is under the table.
   [beneath, underneath, below]
25 The chick is under Totto.
   [beneath, underneath, below]
26 The table is under the lamp.
   [beneath, below]
27 The triangle is under the line.
   [beneath, below]
28 The man put the fire under the pig. [beneath, below, underneath]

under：線と見る

①下にいる／ある

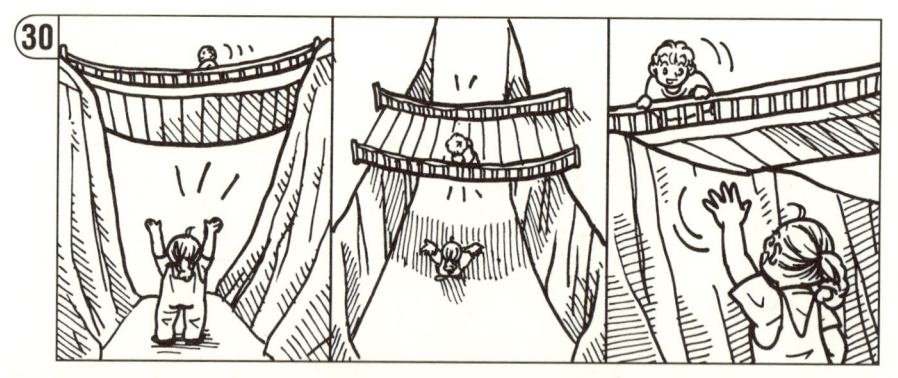

29　Tim hid the magazine under his bed. [beneath, underneath, below]
30　Tim looked under the bridge.
31　Tim's kittens are always underfoot.

32 Olivia is under the required height.
33 The temperature is under/below zero (degrees).
34 The bird's temperature is at zero (degrees).

under：線と見る

① 下にいる / ある

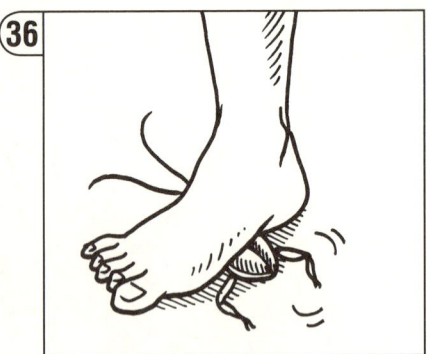

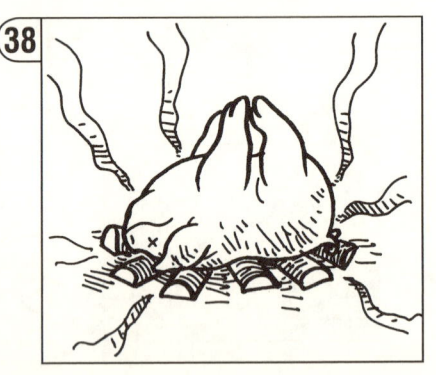

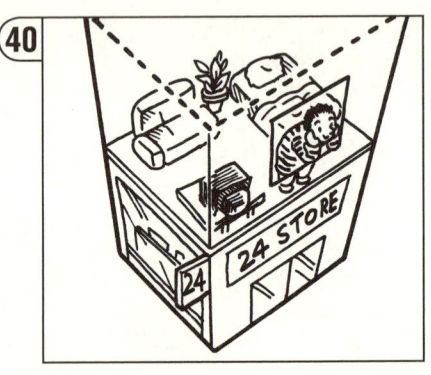

35 The donkey is under/underneath the dog.
36 There is a cockroach under/beneath his foot.
37 The white piece of paper is under the black one. [beneath, underneath, below]
38 The fire is under the pig.
   The pig is on the fire.
39 The hot pad is under the hot dish. [beneath, below]
40 There is a convenience store under/below Butch's room/Butch.

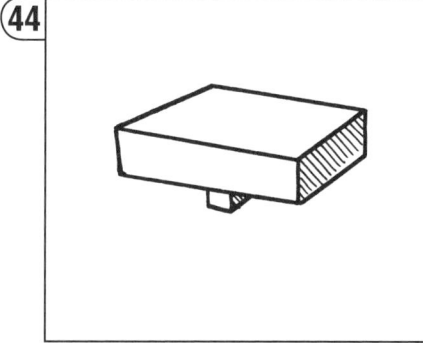

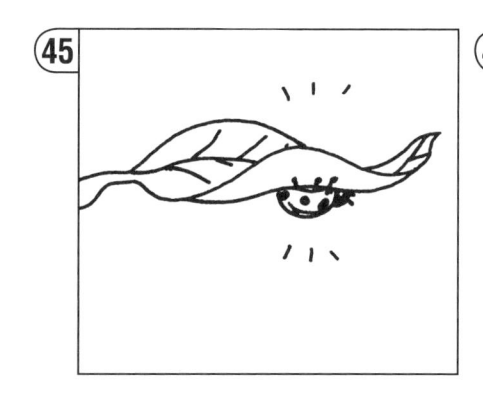

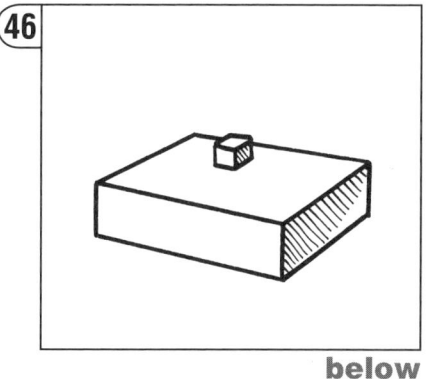

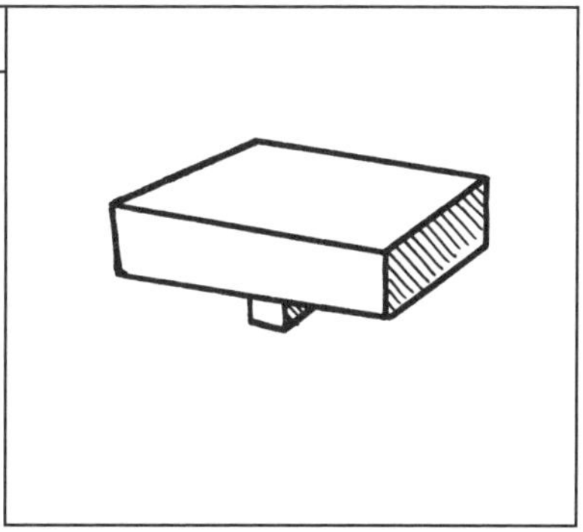

below

41 The book is under/beneath the chair leg.
42 The pole is below/under the elephant.
43 The dress is under Sylvia.
   Sylvia is (standing) on (top of) the dress.
44 The small block is under the big one.
45 There is a ladybug under/on the leaf.
46 The big block is below/under the small one.
   The small block is on (top of) the big one.

164 … under：線と見る

②カバーされている

47 Teria is holding the bottle under her hands.
48 Tim is sleeping under mosquito netting tonight.
49 c. The ants are safe and warm under the leaf.

【Ⅱ】連想するイメージ　165

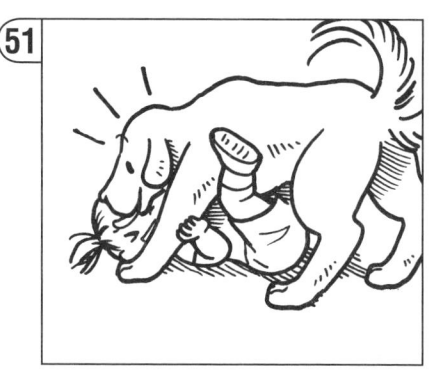

50　Baby is under/beneath the quilt.
51　Olivia is under/beneath Pooch.
52　c. Nautilus and Ruby are under the wings of an angel.
53　The soldier is under fire.

under：線と見る

②カバーされている

54 Bowsheeman is answering nature's call under/beneath the open sky.
55 Sylvia and Albert are kissing under/beneath the stars.
56 The Kobits are dancing under the moon.
57 Sylvia is lying in the sun.
58 The wolfman is howling in the moonlight/at the moon.

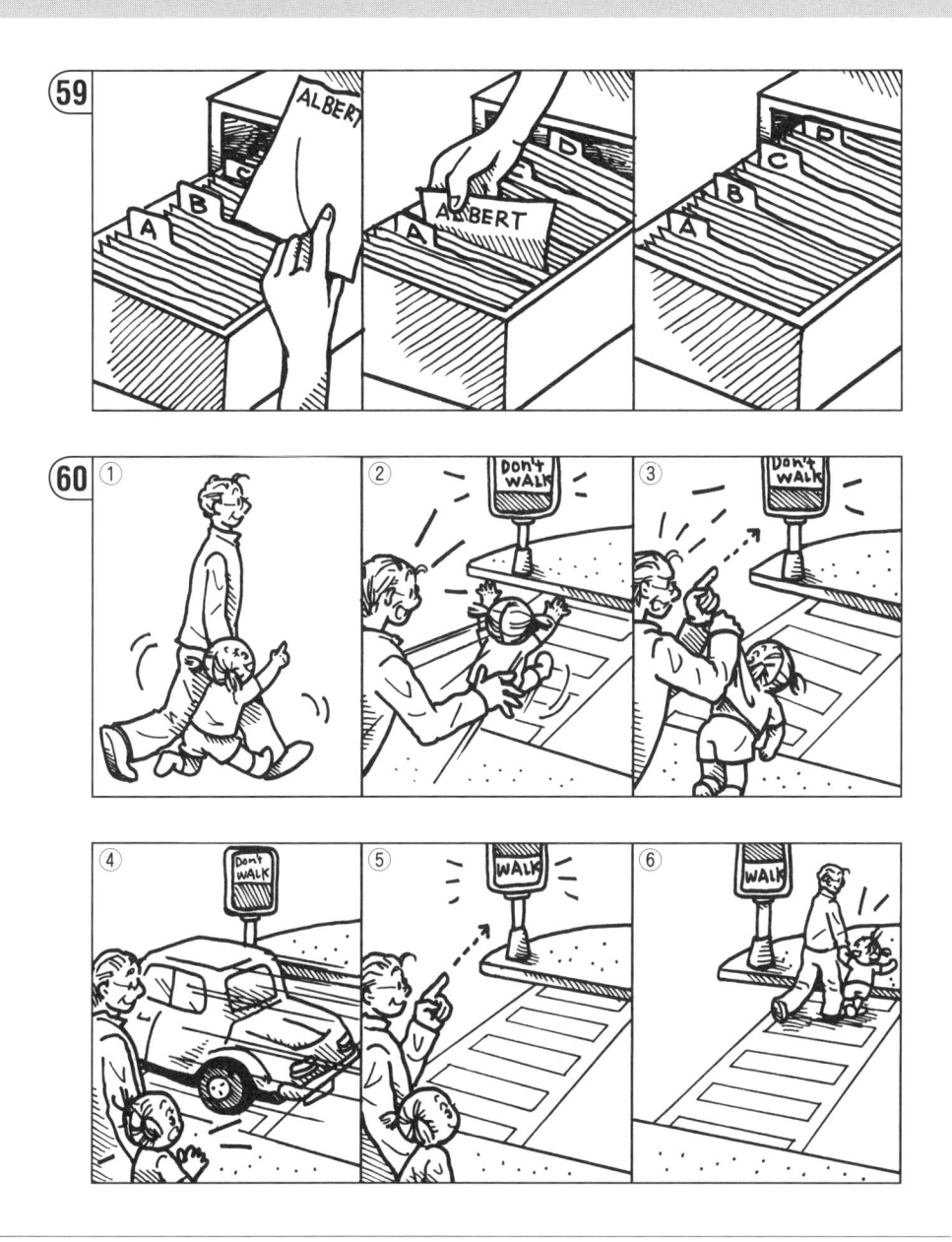

59 You can find 'Albert' under 'A' in the card file.
60 Under traffic law, a pedestrian must wait for the walk signal to cross the road.

③状況下にいる／ある

61 The house is under construction.
62 The sea munchkin is under study.
63 The plans are under discussion.
   The people are in a discussion.

64 Bowsheeman is living under a false name.
65 Olivia was under a false impression.

④かくれている

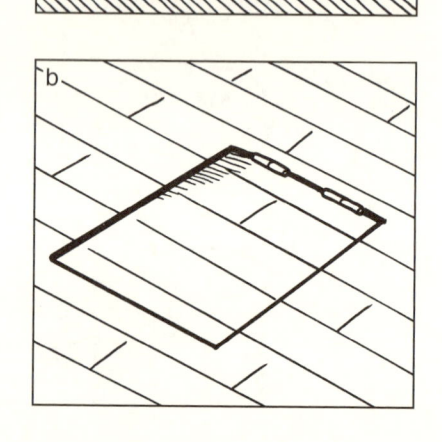

in

66　There is a bug under the leaf.
　　[beneath, underneath]

67　The treasure box/chest is under
　　the ground/the earth.
　　[beneath, underneath] [underground]

68　The treasure is buried under the ground/
　　the surface. [beneath, underneath, below]
　　[underground/in the ground]

69　a. The storage box is in the floor.
　　b. The storage box is under the floor.

【Ⅱ】連想するイメージ 171

70 b, c. Papa's face is under a mask. [beneath, underneath, behind]
71 Under/Beneath Butch's smile, he is actually angry.
72 The man on the left made the payment under the table.

④ かくれている

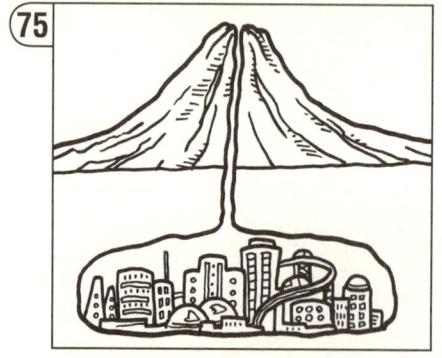

73 a. Pooch buried the bone under the ground/underground. [under/beneath/underneath/below the surface]
   c. Now Pooch is digging the bone out from under the ground.
74 Butch buried the treasure under/in the earth/the ground. [underground]
75 The town is below/under the mountain. [beneath, underneath]
76 The ants live under the ground. [below, beneath]
   The ants live underground.

【Ⅱ】連想するイメージ 173

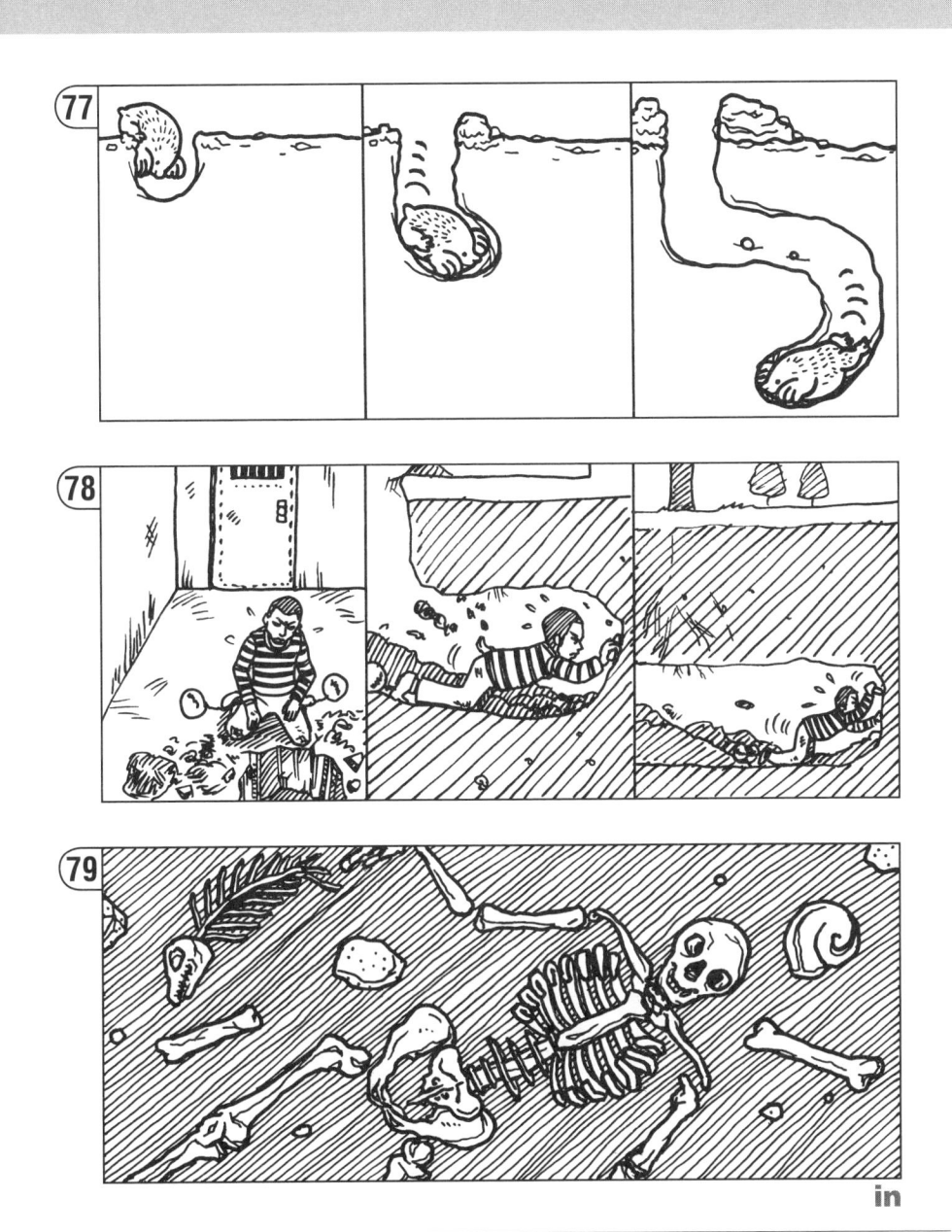

77　The mole is digging under the ground. [beneath, underneath, below, in]
78　The prisoner is digging under (the) ground. [underground]
79　There are bones in the ground.
　　There is a skeleton under/ beneath/in the earth.

④かくれている

walk under the line

80 a. The mermaid is diving into the ocean. b. She is swimming in the ocean. c. She is under the ocean.
81 The mermaid is under/beneath the sea/ the waves. [under water]   82 Mr. T walked under the line.
83 The mermaid is swimming under the surface of the ocean.
The mermaid is swimming in the ocean.

【Ⅱ】連想するイメージ　175

under / in

under / in

in

in

84　Olivia put her hands under/ in the water.
　　Olivia put her hands in the river.
85　b. Olivia is going into the river.　　c. Olivia's legs are in/under water/the river.
86　The children are playing in the sea.　　　　87　Tim is in the river.

176 … under：線と見る

①コントロールの under, over, out of

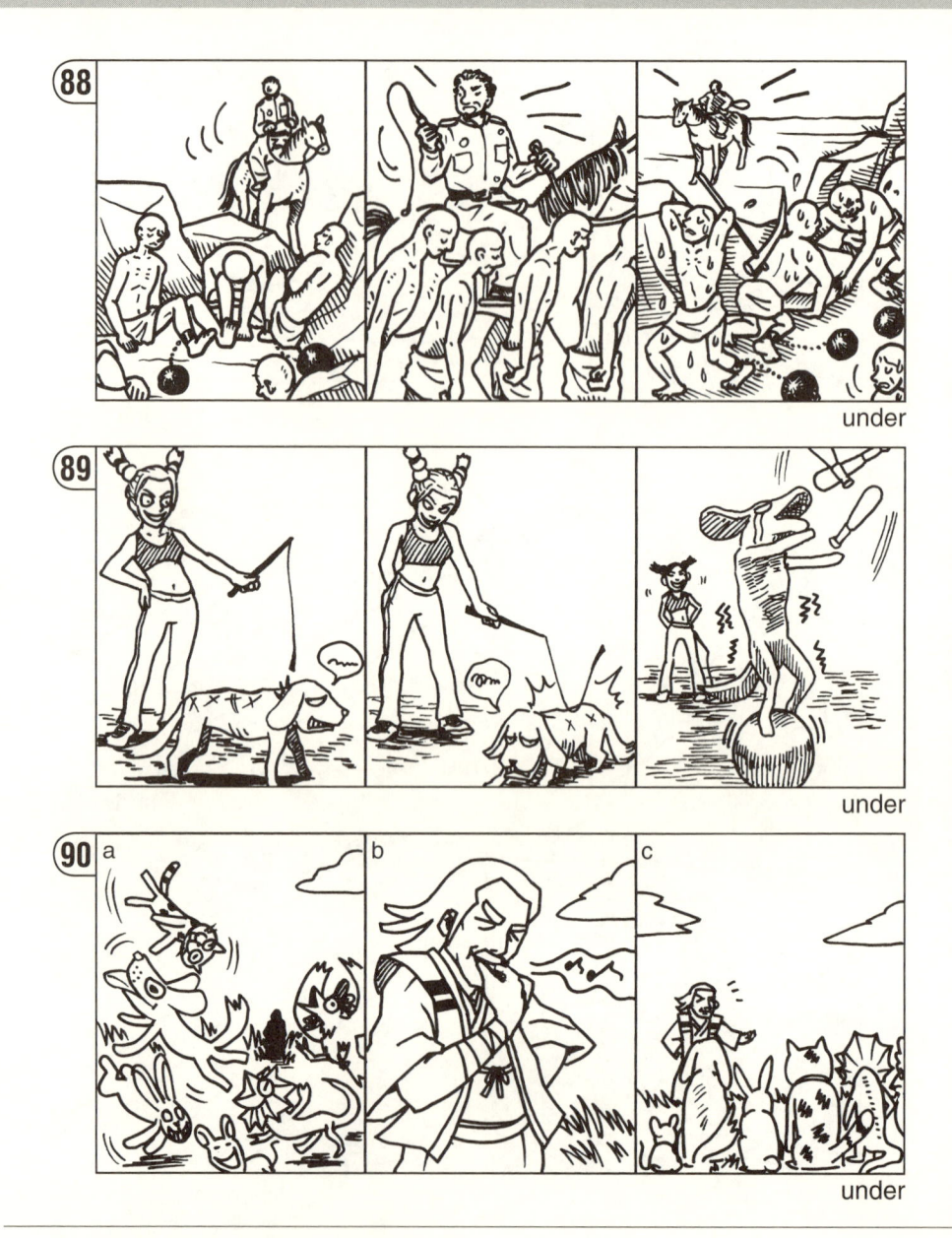

under

under

under

88　The slaves are under their master's control.
89　Doggie is under Candy's control.
90　a. The animals are out of control.
　　b. Now they are under Bakunsai's control.
　　c. Now the situation is under control.

91 Nautilus has authority over the sea munchkins.
92 The captain has control over his men.
   The pirates have control over the prisoner.

178 … under：線と見る

①コントロールの under, over, out of

out of

out of

out of

93　c. Ruby is out of control.
94　c. The Candy robot is out of Dr. Bizarro's control.
95　c. The Candy robot is out of control.

● コラム ①●

under と below の違いって何？

　前置詞に興味を持ち始めた頃、アメリカ人の夫にいろいろと質問をしていました。「テーブルの下に」と言う場合、日本語の「下に」に相当する英語には under, below, underneath, beneath があるので「一体、その違いは何？」と聞いたところ、言語学を学んでいる夫から「There is a dog under/below/underneath/beneath the table. とどれも使えるし、どれも同じような状況だよ。ただテーブルをどう見るかの違いだ」と返ってきました。それなら under だけを使えばいいのだと思い、テーブルがどう見えるのかを追求しないまま終わってしまいました。

　その後、アメリカ大陸をドライブしていたときに突如、山が現れ山のふもとに町があるのが見え、私は思わず "Look at the town under the mountain." と夫に英語で話しかけると、8歳の息子がすかさず「ママ、below the mountain だよ」と訂正するではないですか。えっ？ やっぱり under だけじゃダメなんだぁ。これをきっかけにあらためて前置詞の模索を続けることにしました。

　けれども under, below, beneath, underneath の違いはそう簡単に解決するものではなかったのです。あきらめずに模索を続けてやっと発見したのが under は線のイメージだということ。前述の Look at the town under the mountain. では、under は「山を線と見ろ」と指示しているんですね。だから山の稜線が場になるので、山の稜線の下にある町は山の地中にあることになってしまう。それに対して 639 ページ 29, 30, 31 の 3 枚の絵を眺めているときに発見したのが below は立体のイメージになる、ということ。below the mountain の場合、山は立体のイメージとなり、「山全体の下のほう」とイメージするので、町はふもとにあるか地下に埋もれているという絵になっているのです。こうして 2 つの違いがわかりました。

　そして葉っぱの下に虫がかくれた絵からは underneath は面のイメージだろうと思っていたのですがそうではなかった。2 章 in のグループのことばは「面」とイメージするよりも「境界」とイメージするほうが単純で、共通のイメージになることに気づいたのです。214 ページの in the mirror, in the glasses, in the window ではネイティブスピーカーはそれぞれの枠、フレームを面のイメージとしてとらえていて、鏡や眼鏡や窓の薄いガラスを面としてとらえているのではないのです。そうなると「境界」つまり枠だけならば隠れるというイメージにはならないから underneath は立体のイメージとなる。しかもかくれているということがわかるためには見ている人の存在が必要。だから「3D として見なさい」と指示していることばだとやっと確信したわけです。

　ことばが違えばイメージは異なることを悟った一つの経験です。

along：線と見る

①線に沿って動いている along

along the road

1　Dora is running along the road.
2　The crab is walking up along Butch's body.
3　Indy is walking along the road up the mountain.

along / alongside the train tracks

4 Bakunsai is riding along/alongside the train tracks. [along the road]
5 Ruby and Nautilus are running along/alongside the shore. [along the beach]
6 The Kobits are walking along/alongside the river. [along the riverbank]

along：線と見る

①連れていく take ~ along to と take ~ to

take her along to

take her along to

go along to

7　Sylvia took Olivia along to the beauty parlor.
　　Olivia went along to the beauty parlor with Sylvia.

8　Mama took Olivia along to the supermarket.
　　Olivia went along to the supermarket with Mama.

9　a. Candy is going along to the park with Bowsheeman.
　　b. Bowsheeman is going to the park with his girlfriend.　Candy is tagging along.

【Ⅱ】連想するイメージ 183

take her to

take her to

take her to

10　Mama took Olivia to the restroom.
11　Mama took Olivia to kindergarten.
12　Olivia took Teria to the park.

② follow along と follow after

along

after

take her away

13　c. Pooch is following along behind Grandma.
14　The ducklings are following (along) after/behind their mother.
15　Mama took Olivia away from the toy store.

【Ⅱ】連想するイメージ 185

③寄り添う get along

16　c. Papa and Mama are getting along better now after their fight.
17　b. Kitten and Puppy get along only when they are eating.
18　Olivia gets along with Baby.

186 … along：線と見る

①沿って動いている along / alongside

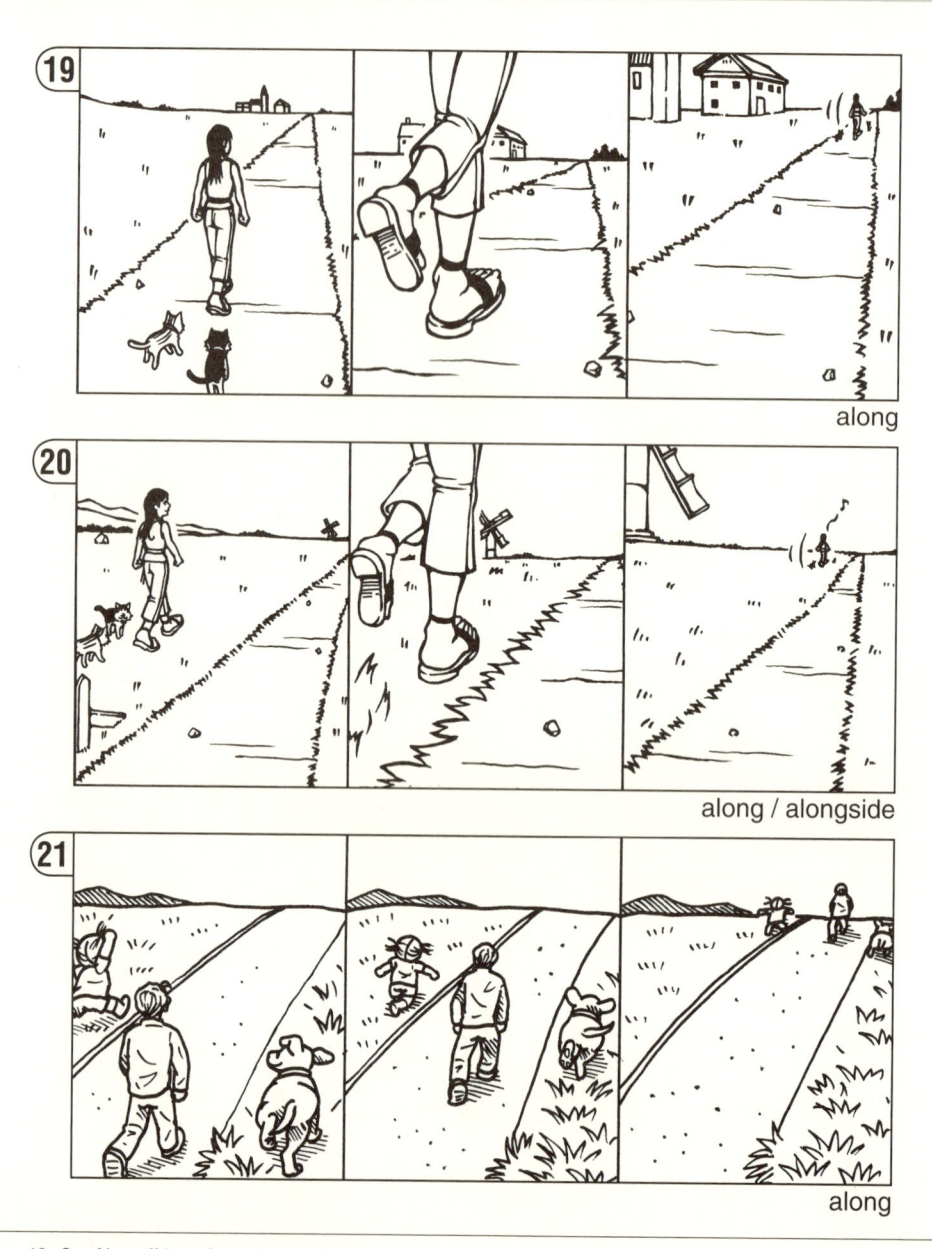

along

along / alongside

along

19　Leaf is walking along the road.
20　Leaf is walking along/alongside the road.
21　Papa, Olivia and Pooch are walking along the road.

alongside : 3Dと見る　【Ⅲ】イメージを比べる 187

alongside / along

alongside

alongside

22 There are some sunflowers along/alongside the road.
23 b. Chicori looked at the sunflowers alongside the road.
24 b. Teria and Bowsheeman happen to be walking alongside each other.

along：線と見る

②そばにいる／ある along, alongside, beside

25 along
28 along / alongside
26 alongside
29 alongside / along
27 beside
30 beside

25 There are some houses along the river.
26 Bakunsai's students are standing alongside him.
27 Dr. Bizarro is standing beside Bakunsai.
28 There are some houses along/alongside the river.
29 There are children playing alongside/along/beside the road.
30 The girls are playing beside the road.

alongside：3Dと見る　　【Ⅲ】イメージを比べる　189

31 along

34 along / alongside

32 alongside / along

35 alongside / along / beside

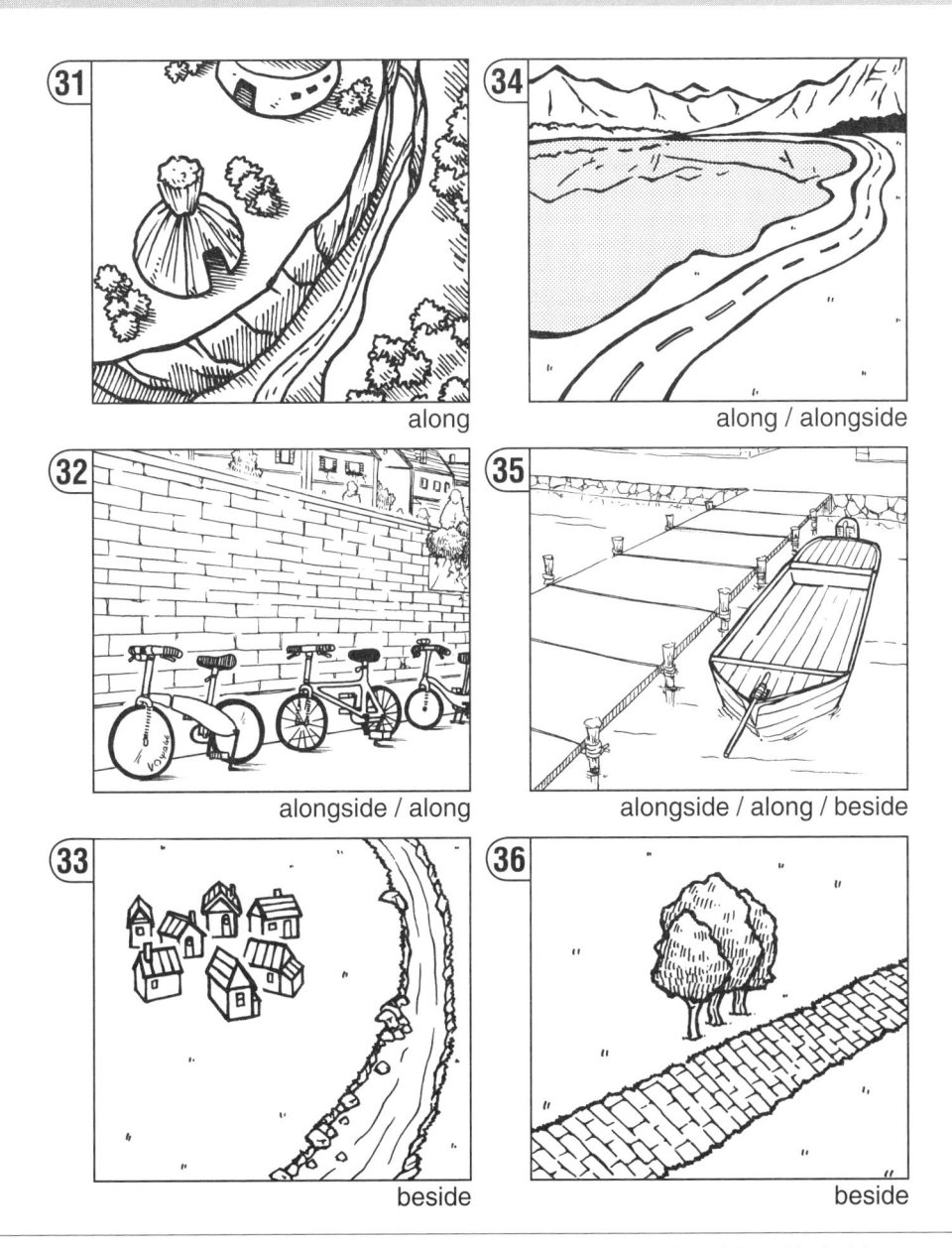

33 beside

36 beside

31　The houses are along the canyon.
32　The bicycles are parked alongside/along the wall.
33　There are some houses beside the river.
34　The road runs along/alongside the lake.
35　The boat is tied up alongside/along/beside the pier.
36　The trees are beside the road.

① 意識だけが向かっている for

for New York

1　Teria is leaving/setting off for New York.
2　Tim left/set off for school.
3　Sylvia has a ticket for Kyoto.

【Ⅰ】基本のイメージ 191

for Mama

fly to

4　Papa has got some flowers for Mama.
5　Papa is buying a teddy bear for Baby.
6　The bird is flying (back) to her nest with a worm for her children.

for：3Dと見る

①意識が向かう

for sale

for the bus

for cars

7　The house is for sale.
8　a, b. Katarina is waiting for the bus.
9　Olivia has to learn to watch out for cars.

【Ⅱ】連想するイメージ 193

for his room

for Teria

for Sylvia

10 Bowsheeman bought a new chair for his room.
11 They saved some cake for Teria.
12 Albert bought a bag for Sylvia.

for：3Dと見る

①意識が向かう

for fun

for her dress

for $100

for his robots

13　Candy fished Bowsheeman's hat off his head for fun.

14　a. Sylvia paid 100 dollars for her dress.
　　b. Sylvia bought a dress for 100 dollars.

15　Dr. Bizarro is famous for his robots.

【Ⅱ】連想するイメージ 195

16 a. Olivia is speaking too softly for Grandma to hear.
   c. Olivia is speaking loudly enough for Grandma to hear.
17 It is difficult for the boy to pick up the beans using chopsticks.
18 It is easy for Bakunsai to catch flies using chopsticks.

② 目的のため

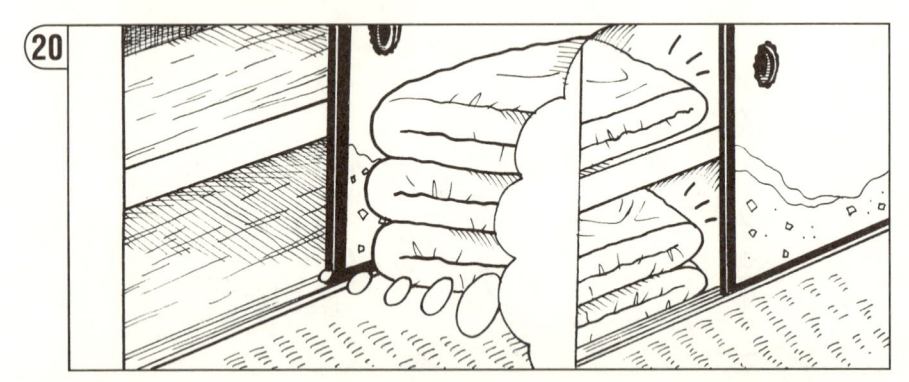

19 The knife is for cutting fish.
20 This closet is for futons.
21 The second cage is for sea munchkins.

【Ⅱ】連想するイメージ 197

for a table

22 Bowsheeman is using a box for/as a table.
23 Mama bought some fish for dinner.
24 Mama rang the bell for dinner.

③サポートしている

25 Oton works for/at the Bizarro Laboratory.
26 The soldiers are for the war, but the students are against it.
27 Albert is fighting for his beliefs.

help Grandma

28 Olivia and Teria are cheering for Butch.
29 Teria lifted the heavy box for Mama.
30 The boys are helping Grandma by carrying her bags for her.

for：3Dと見る

①意識が向かう for と到着する to

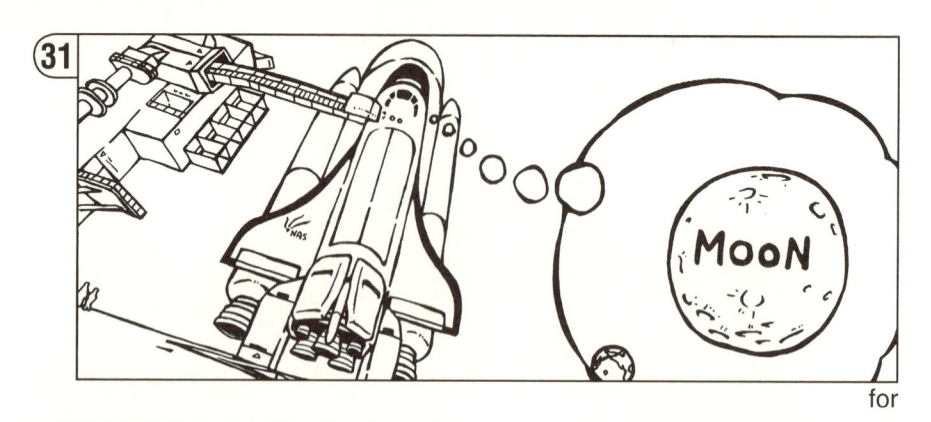

for

for

for

31　The rocket is leaving for the Moon.
32　The train is headed/bound for Bay City.
33　The plane is headed for Bay Island.

【Ⅲ】イメージを比べる 201

to

to

to

34 a. The space ship is flying to Mars.   b. The space ship flew to Mars.
35 Teria walked to the edge of the water.
36 a. The plane is flying to the island.   b. The plane flew to the island.

| 202 | for：3Dと見る

①意識が向かう for と到着する to

37　for Olivia　　to Mama

38　for Olivia　　to Grandma

39　to Sylvia

37　Grandma sent a teddy bear to Mama for Olivia.
38　Mama wrote a thank you note to Grandma for/from Olivia.
　　Olivia sent a thank you note to Grandma.
39　Butch wrote a letter to Sylvia.

② do for と do to

40　Mr. Stone kicked Nautilus for his daughter.
　③ Mr. Stone did something awful to Nautilus.
　⑥ Mr. Stone said that he did it for Ruby.
　⑨ Nautilus did the same thing to Mr. Stone.

204 … against：3D と見る

①はね返っている against / into と比べる

against the window

against

against　　　into

1　Candy is throwing tomatoes against/at the window.
2　Butch is hitting his head against the wall.
3　b. The sun is shining against the mirror.
　　c. Tim is reflecting the sunlight into Kitten's eyes.

【Ⅰ】基本のイメージ 205

into the window

into

against　　　into

4　Ruby threw the stone into the window.
5　Bowsheeman crashed into the truck.
6　b. The sun is shining against Sylvia's face.　c. The sun is shining into Sylvia's eyes.

②逆らっている **against**

against the current

7　The salmon is swimming against the current.
8　Indy is walking against/into the wind.
9　The magnets are pushing against each other.

against parasites

10 Puppy is getting a shot against parasites.
11 People are protesting against nuclear weapons.
12 Ruby's father is fighting against Nautilus becoming her boyfriend.

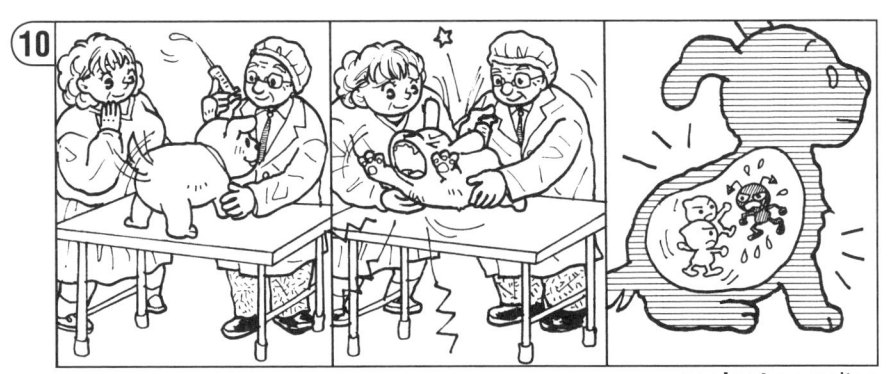

③反している against

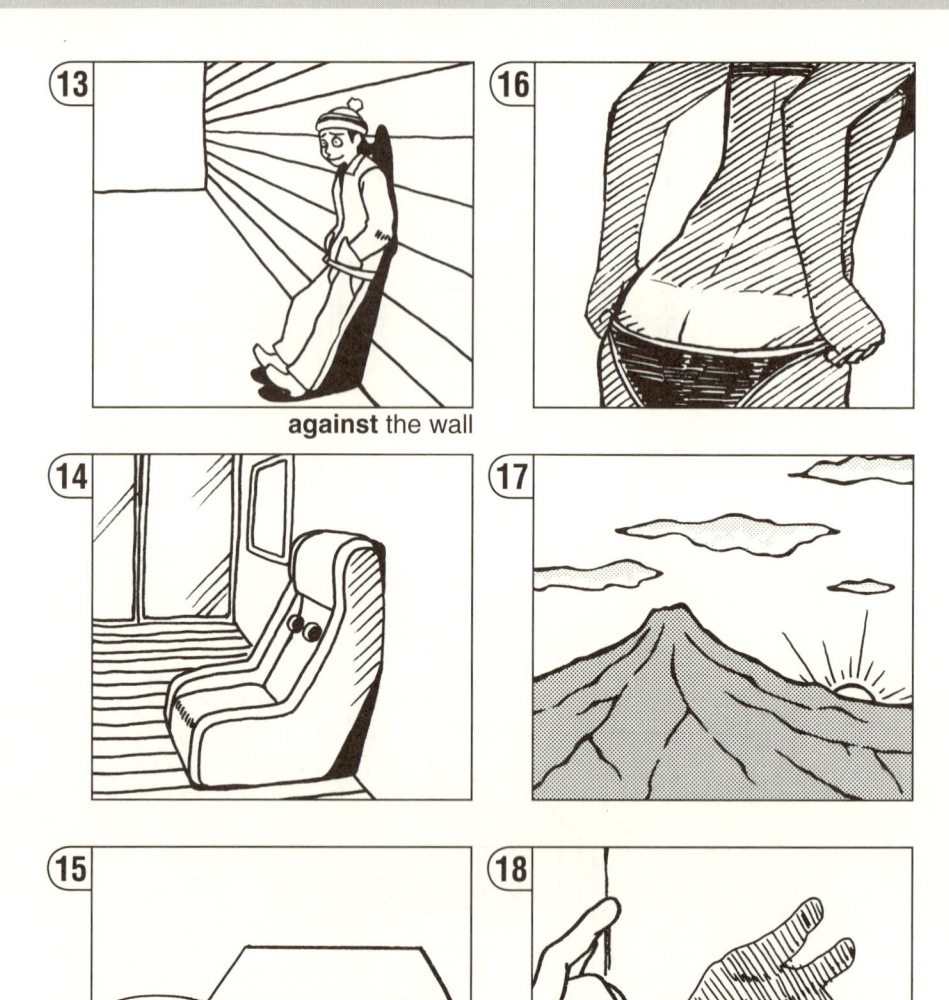

against the wall

13　Bowsheeman is leaning against/on the wall.
14　The chair is sitting/leaning against the wall.
15　The wastebasket is against/next to the desk.
16　Katarina's natural skin color stands out against her dark tan.
17　The mountain is silhouetted against the sky.
18　He is throwing a shadow against/on the wall.

④対称にいる / ある opposite

opposite the south pole

1. The north pole is opposite the south pole.
2. The 'G' marks are opposite each other.
3. The bulls are pulling in opposite directions.
4. Nautilus and Ruby are sitting opposite each other.
5. They are on opposite sides of the line.
6. The teams are opposite/facing each other.

210 … like : 3Dと見る

①似ている like

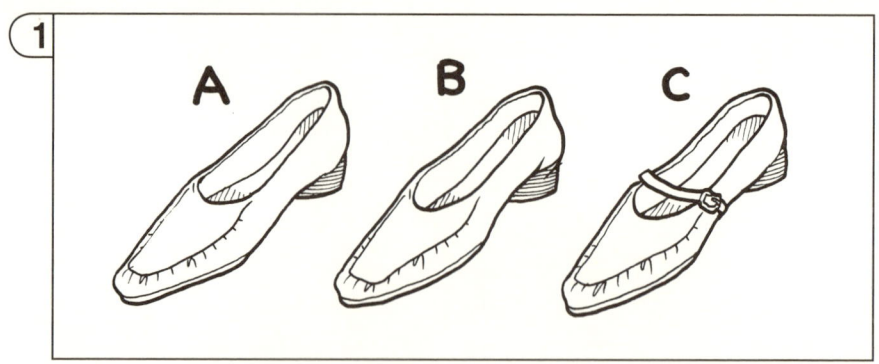

like shoe A

1 Shoe C is like shoe A.
　Shoe B is the same as shoe A.
2 Tim is acting like a monkey.
3 Olivia looks like Teria.
　Olivia and Teria look alike.

②〜のような like

like rain

4　It looks like rain.
5　Do you feel like watching television or playing a game?
6　Butch is good at sports like the rings and the pommel horse.

except
alongside
against
opposite
except for
during

Chapter 2
2次元（面）として見なさい

in
within
into
out of
of
through
throughout
across
around
about
between
among
with
without

214 in：面と見る

①境界内にいる／ある in

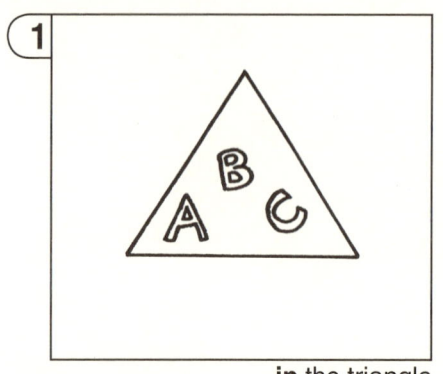

1 in the triangle

2

3

4 Candy is looking at herself in the mirror.

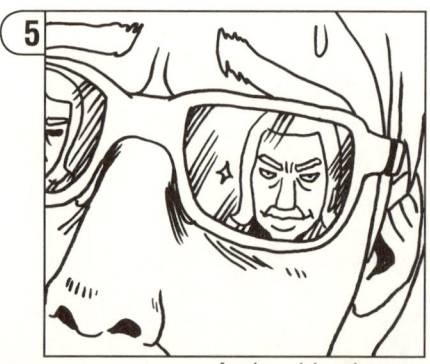

5 in / on his glasses

6 on the building

1　There are some letters in the triangle.
2　There is a picture in the frame.
3　There are sea munchkins in the windows.
4　Candy is looking at herself in the mirror.
5　Bakunsai's face is reflected in/on Oton's glasses.
6　Bowsheeman's shadow is on the building.

【 I 】 基本のイメージ 215

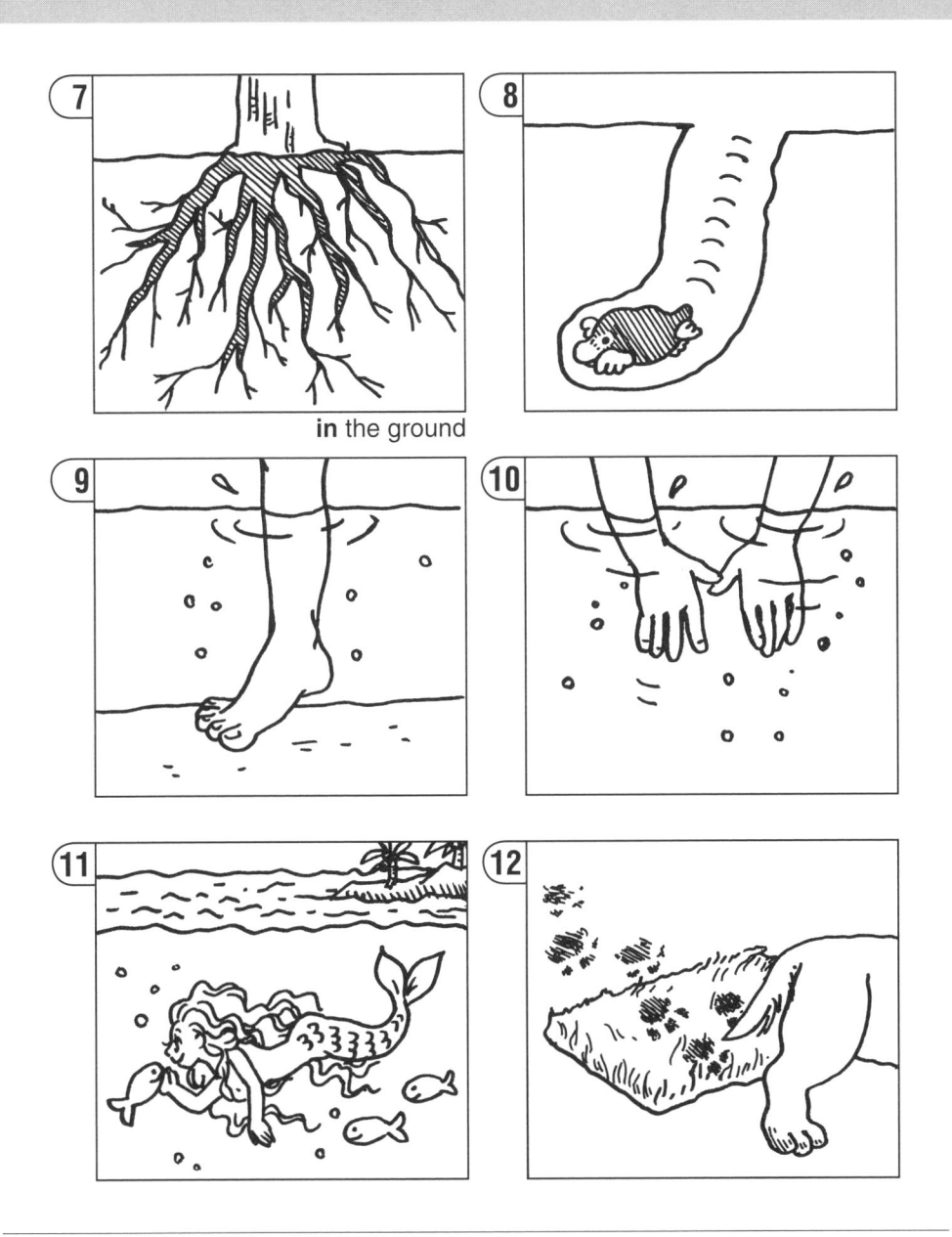

in the ground

7　The tree's roots are in the ground.
8　There is a mole in the ground.
9　His/Her foot is in the water.
10　His/Her hands are in the water.
11　The mermaid is in the sea.
12　There are footprints on/in the rug.

① 境界内にいる / ある in

in the basket

13　Baby is in the basket.
15　There are jewels in the chest.
17　Butch is buried in the sand.
14　There is a baby kangaroo in the pouch.
16　There is a lollipop in Candy's mouth.
18　The children are playing in the sand.

in the circle

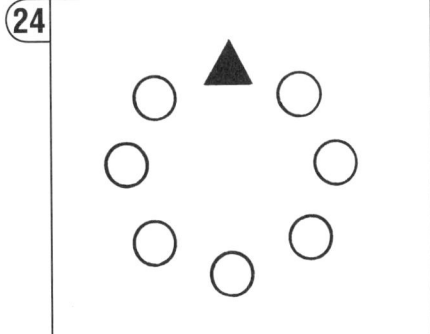

in the circle

19 Teria is in/within/inside the circle.
20 There is a policeman in the intersection.
21 The sumo wrestlers are (still) in the ring.
22 There are several children in the pool.
23 Teria is in the circle.
24 The black triangle is in the circle.

②境界内で動いている in

walk **in** the circle

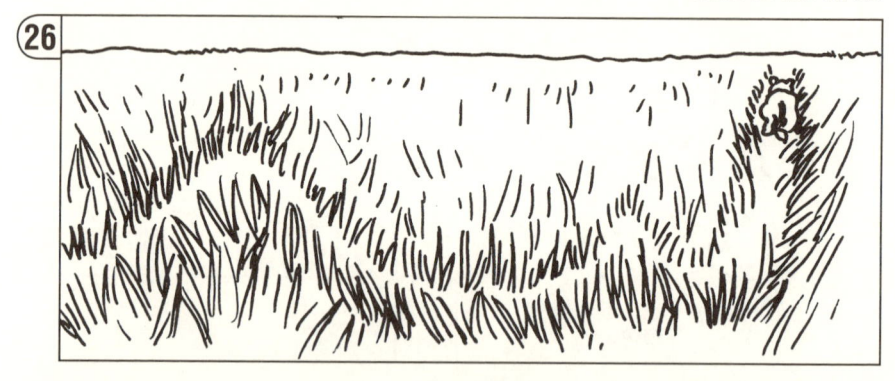

through the grass

25　The sheep is walking in/inside the circle.
26　The dog is walking in/through the field.
27　Sylvia is walking through the grass.

【Ⅰ】基本のイメージ 219

fill **in** the triangle

28 Olivia is filling in the triangle.
29 c. Someone has painted in an eye.
30 Indy is wandering in the fog.

in：面と見る

① 中にいる／ある

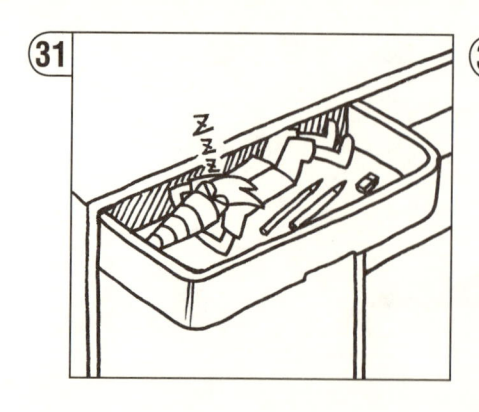

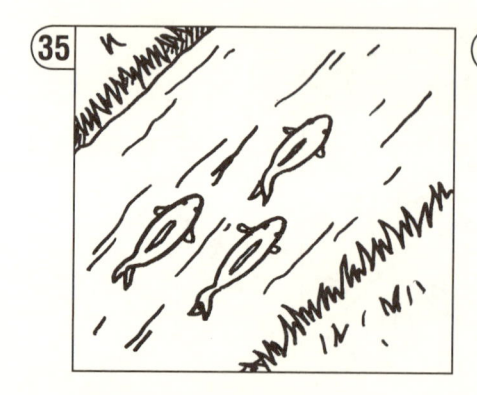

31 The sea munchkin is sleeping in the drawer.
32 There is a carpet in the room.
33 There are berries in the pie.
34 There is a face in the candy.
35 There are some fish in the water/in the stream.
36 There is a cat in the river.

【Ⅱ】連想するイメージ

②入りこんでいる in とついている on

37 There is a flea in the dog's hair.
38 There is a flea on the dog's hair.
39 There are footprints in the snow.
40 There are footprints on the road.
41 There is a wet spot in the mattress/ on the bed.
42 There is water/a puddle on the road.

in：面と見る

②入りこんでいる in とついている on

in / on

in

on

43　c. There is a stain in/on the T-shirt.
44　There is a stain in the T-shirt.
45　a. There is a stain on the sweat shirt.　c. The stain is out.

【Ⅱ】連想するイメージ 223

46　in / on
47　in
48　on
49　in / on
50　in
51　on

46　There is a flower pattern in/on the shirt.
47　There is a whale pattern in the T-shirt.
48　There is a picture of Bowsheeman on the T-shirt.
49　Ken is in/on the chair.
50　The boy is in the chair.
51　Bowsheeman is on the stool.

224　in：面と見る

③囲まれている（in the 〜）（in a 〜）（in 〜）

in the bottle

in a theater

in the fire　　　in flames

52　The mermaid is in the aquarium.
54　There are aliens in the room.
56　The yam is in the fire.
53　The sea munchkin is in the bottle.
55　Bowsheeman and Katarina are in a theater.
57　The city is on fire.
　　The city is in flames.

【Ⅱ】連想するイメージ 225

in the rain

in the hail

in the snow

in the snow

in the sun

in the moonlight

58 Sylvia is standing in the rain.
60 There is a statue in the snow.
62 Sylvia is lying in the sun.
59 The frog is sitting in the hail.
61 Tim is playing in the snow.
63 The wolfman is howling in the moonlight. [at the moon]

in：面と見る

③囲まれている (in the 〜)(in a 〜)(in 〜)

64 in the wind
65 in a blizzard
66 in a tornado
67 in a flood
68 in the light / in the dark

64　Indy is walking in the wind.
65　Katarina is walking in a blizzard.
66　The house is being destroyed in/by a tornado.
67　The houses are being washed away in/by a flood.
68　a. Indy is searching in the dark.
　　　He can see some letters in the light.
　　b. Somebody is lost in the dark.

69　The trees are in bloom.
70　b. The trees are covered in/with snow.
　　c. The town is covered in/with snow.
71　The mail is delivered even when the town is covered in fog.

③囲まれている（in the 〜）（in a 〜）（in 〜）

in a furoshiki

in a fur coat

in a chicken mask

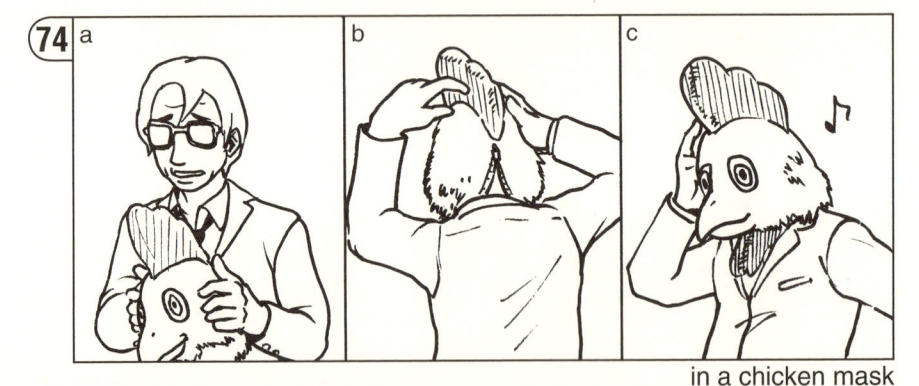

72 She wrapped the box in a furoshiki.
73 c. Sylvia is dressed in a fur coat.
74 c. Oton is dressed in a chicken mask.
　　Oton is wearing a chicken mask.

【Ⅱ】連想するイメージ 229

in black

in uniform

in armor

75 Sylvia is in black.
   Sylvia is in mourning.
76 The girls are in uniform.
77 Bakunsai is in armor.

④状況の中にいる（in a ～）（in ～）（in ～s）

in a panic

in a good mood

in a bad temper

in a fit of jealousy

78　Mama is in a panic.
79　Butch is in a good mood.
80　Butch is in a bad temper/mood.
81　Candy is in a fit of jealousy.
　　Candy is having a fit of jealousy.

in love

in trouble

in danger

82 All 3 couples are in love.
83 Butch is in trouble.
84 Bowsheeman is in danger.

④状況の中にいる (in a ~) (in ~) (in ~s)

in bad health

in good health

in rhythm

85 The boy is in bad health.
86 Tim is in good health.
87 The children are dancing in rhythm.

【Ⅱ】連想するイメージ

in tears

in circles

in droves

88　Candy is in tears.
89　Papa is running in circles.
90　People came to the sale in droves.

⑤ 状況の中にいる（in ～）と場所の（in the ～）

in class

in school

in jail

91　The students are in class.
92　The kids are in school.
93　Goroki is in jail.

【Ⅱ】連想するイメージ 235

in the class

in the school

in the jail

94 Nautilus is in the class.
   There are about 17 students in the classroom.
95 There is a ghost in the school.
96 There is a mouse in the jail.

⑥ 状況の中にいる（in 〜）

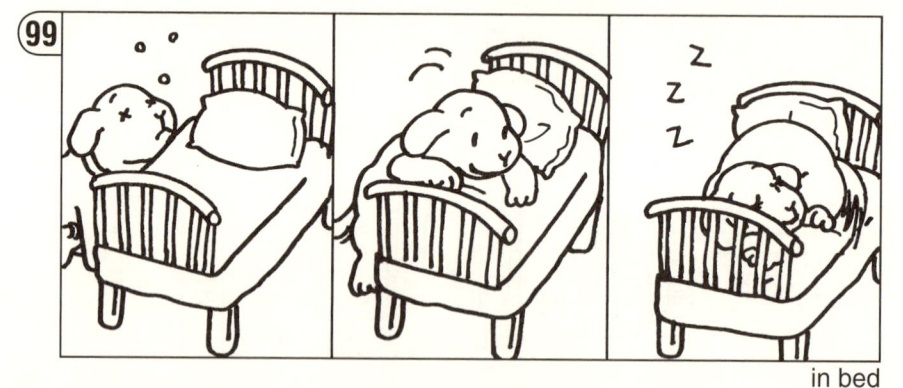

in town

in town

in bed

97 a. The band is in the country (side).　c. The band is in town.
98 a. Okan's family lives in the suburbs.　c. Okan is in town for the day.
99 Puppy is in bed.

【Ⅱ】連想するイメージ

⑦ (in ~)と(in/at/on the ~)を比べる

in harbor

in the harbor

at the harbor

on / in the bed

at the bed

100 Because of the storm, the boat is in harbor.
101 There are some boats in the harbor.

102 The bar is at the harbor.
　　The bar is on the wharf.

103 Pooch is on/in the bed.

104 Pooch is at (the side of) the bed.

⑧境界を意識する

105 The farmer is in the field.
106 Candy lives in the country.
107 Mr. Gold lives in the city.
108 Katarina used to live in this village.

【Ⅱ】連想するイメージ 239

in / on

in the mountains

in the mountain

109 The monster is in the lake.
110 The man is in the desert.
　He is sitting on the ground/sand.
112 There is a ropeway in the mountains.
　There is a ski area in the mountains.

111 Butch, Albert and Sylvia are in the forest.

113 There is a cave in the mountain.

⑧ 境界を意識する

114
115
116

114 The UFO is in the sky.
115 The ship is flying in outer space.
116 There are many kinds of people in the world.

【Ⅱ】連想するイメージ 241

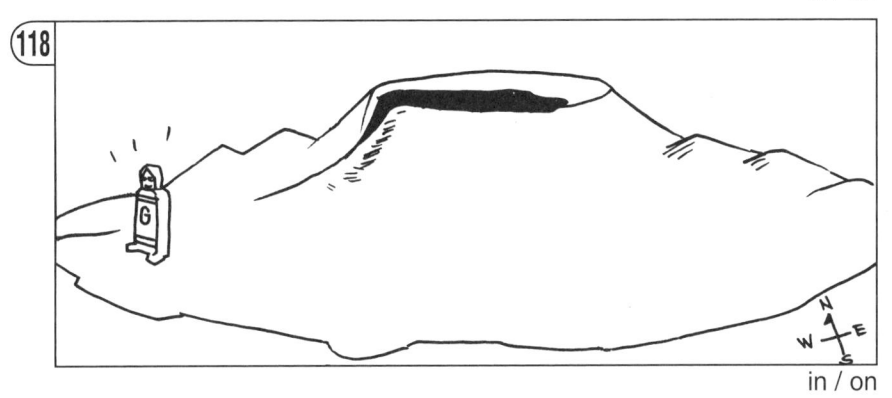

117 Gold Town is in the West.
   Gold town is on the west side of the volcano.
118 The Gold Building is in the West.
   The Gold Building is on the west side of the volcano.
119 The UFO is falling in the West.

242　in：面と見る

⑧境界を意識する

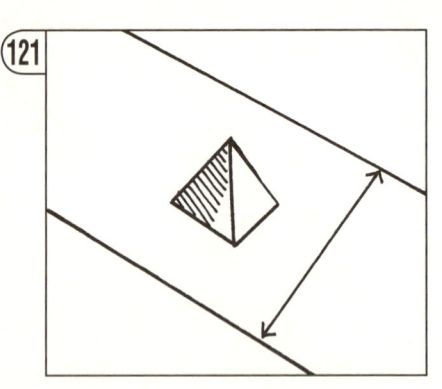

in / on （120〜124）

in / on （125）

120 There is a monkey in the stream.

121 The pyramid is in the space between the two lines.

122 There is a cloud of mosquitoes in the road/on the path.

123 There is a car parked in the parking space.

124 Albert is drawing in/on the street.

125 The circus is in/on the street.

【Ⅱ】連想するイメージ　243

126 c. The car is driving in the center lane.
127 Mama got in the line.
128 The car is parked in/on the street.
129 There are cars on the highway.

in：面と見る

⑧境界を意識する

130 Indy is looking at a camel in the distance.
131 The scenery is best in this direction.
　　The scenery is best to the right.
132 The boys are walking in all directions.

【Ⅱ】連想するイメージ 245

in the center

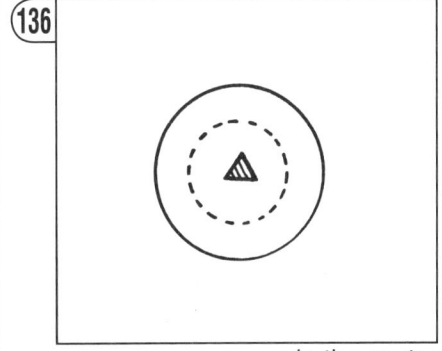

MT. GOLD

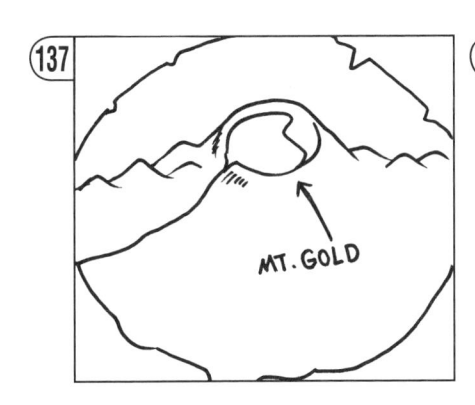

133 The sea munchkin is in the center/in the middle of the turntable.
134 Bowsheeman is standing in the center/in the middle.
135 There are roses growing in the center/in the middle.
136 The triangle is in the center/in the middle.
137 Mt. Gold is in the center/in the middle of the island.
138 The tower is in the center/in the middle of the map.

⑧ 境界を意識する

in the front of

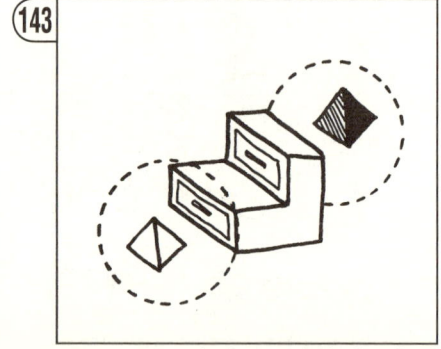

in front of / in back of

139 Katarina is in the front of the car.
　　Her friend is in the back of the car.
140 There is a coffee shop in the front of the building.
141 Tim is in the back of the classroom.
142 The frog is in front of the cat.
143 The white pyramid is in front of the chest.
　　The black pyramid is in back of the chest.
144 The pony is in back of her mother.

in his way

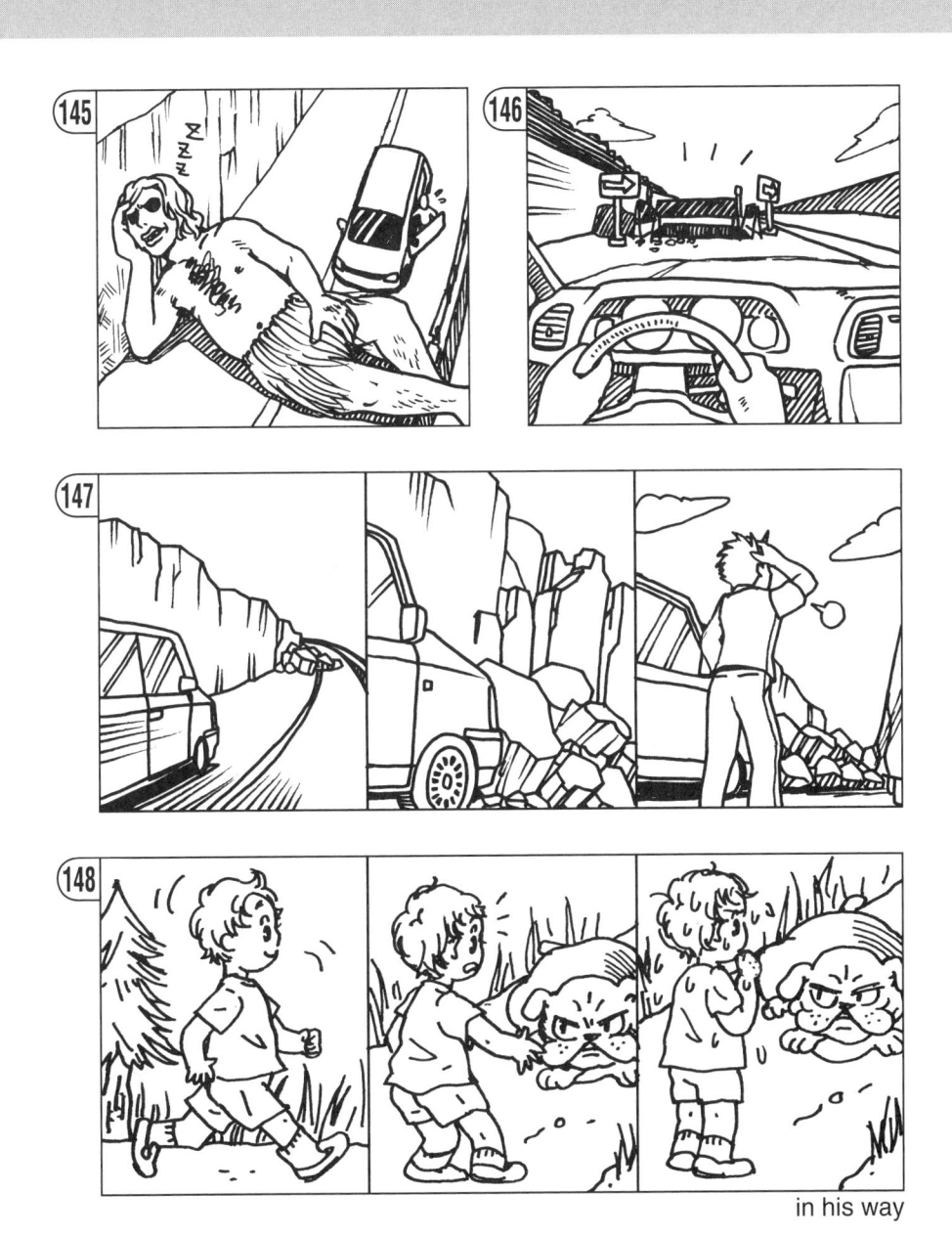

145 There is a giant sleeping in front of the car.

146 There is a road block in front of the car.
There is a road block ahead of the car.

147 There is a pile of rocks in front of the car.
There is a pile of rocks in the way of the car.

148 There is a big dog in Tim's way.

248 ... in：面と見る

⑨境界内に入る

149 b. She is putting in a piece of the puzzle.
150 a. Someone is drawing in one of Bowsheeman's eyes.   b. He has drawn in Bowsheeman's mouth.
   c. He has drawn in Bowsheeman's moustache.
   He has drawn Bowsheeman's face.
151 b. Don't come in!

【Ⅱ】連想するイメージ 249

on

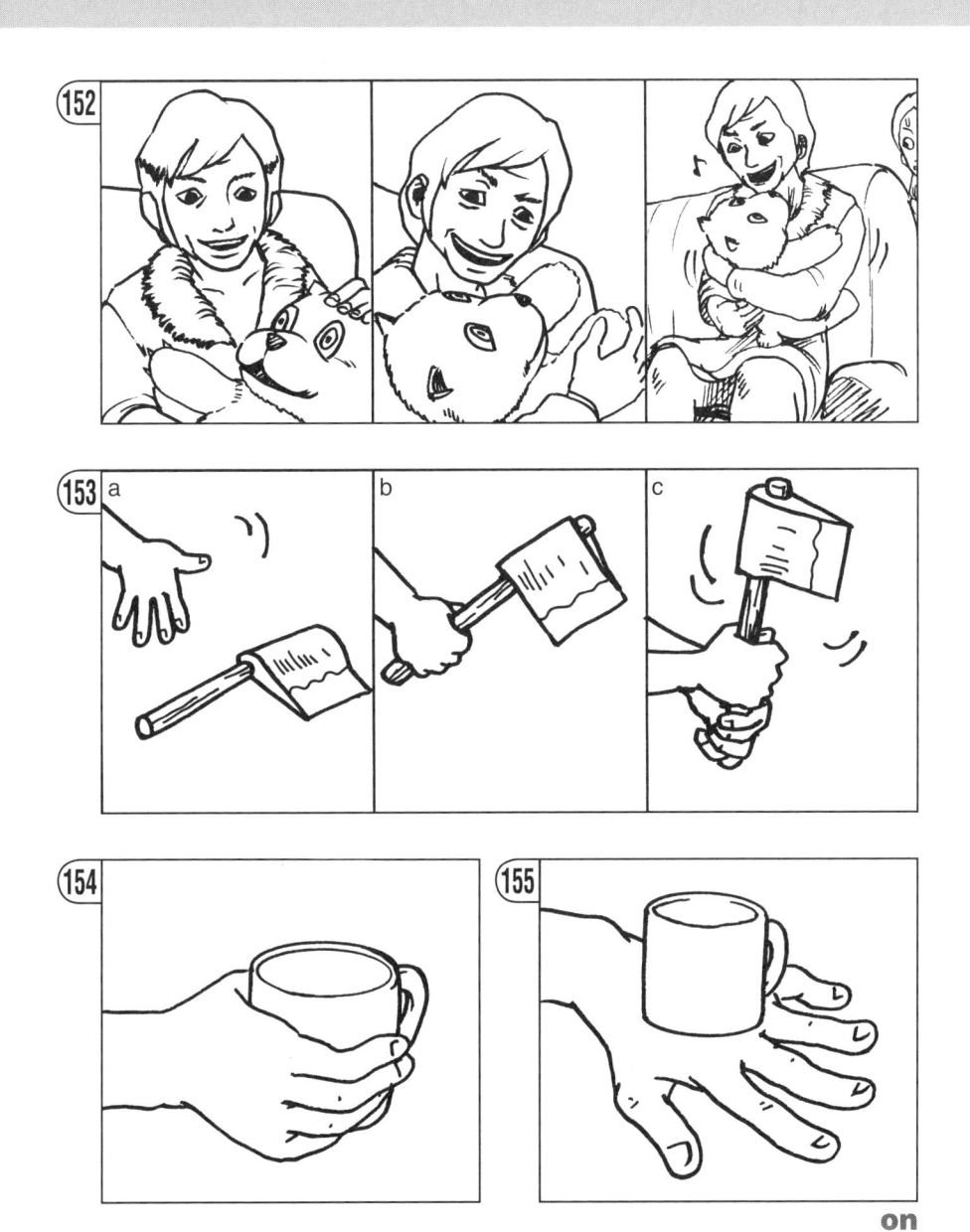

152 Mr. Gold is holding the bear in his arms.
153 c. Someone is holding an axe in his/her hands.
154 There is a cup in his/her hand.   155 There is a cup on his/her hand.

250　… in：面と見る

⑨ 境界内に入る

156 c. The crops are in (the store).
157 Fan letters are pouring in.
158 The tide is in.

159 The hula hoop is in.
160 The camisole (fashion) is in.
161 The Bowsheeman cap is in.

⑩属している (in the ~) (in a ~) (in ~)

in the hospital

in her office

in the library

162 Teria is working in/at the hospital.
163 Teria is working in/at her office.
164 Teria is working in/at the library.

【Ⅱ】連想するイメージ 253

in a hospital

in a laboratory

in a bank

165 Teria works in/at a hospital.
166 Teria works in/at a laboratory.
167 Teria works in/at a bank.

⑩属している (in the ~) (in a ~) (in ~)

in nursing

in advertising

in reference

168 Teria is in nursing.
　　Teria is in the field of nursing.
　　Teria works in the nursing section.
　　Teria works as a nurse.

169 Teria is in advertising.
　　Teria is in the field of advertising.
　　Teria works in the advertising section.

170 Teria works in reference.
　　Teria works in the reference section.

【Ⅱ】連想するイメージ

in business

in music

in education

171 Mr. Gold is in business.　Mr. Gold is in the field of business.
172 Mike is in music.　Mike is in the field of music.
173 Teria is in education.　Teria is in the field of education.

⑩属している（in the ～）(in a ～)(in ～)

174

in the group

175 a b c

in a circle   in the circle

176

in the family

177

in the class

---

174 Bakunsai belongs in/to the group.

175 a. The sea munchkins are dancing in a circle.
　c. The sea munchkin girls are dancing in the circle.

176 There is a baby in the family.　　　　177 There is a monster in the class.
　Baby is a member of the family.

【Ⅱ】連想するイメージ

in a group

in a line

in a circle

in an English class

178 They are traveling in/as a group.
179 The bugs are standing in a line.
181 Ruby is in an English class.

180 Ruby is in a circle of sea munchkins.

⑪ 属している (in a ～) (in ～) (in ～s)

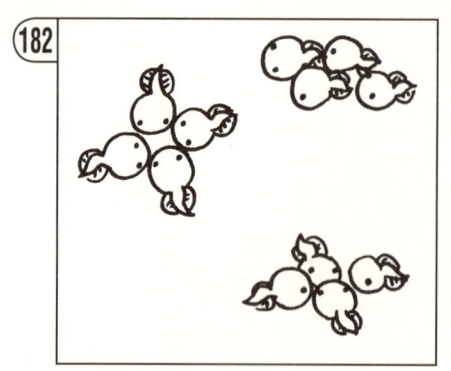

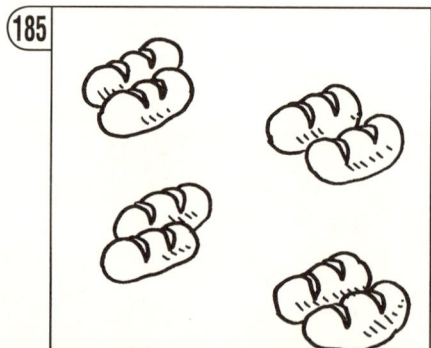

in twos

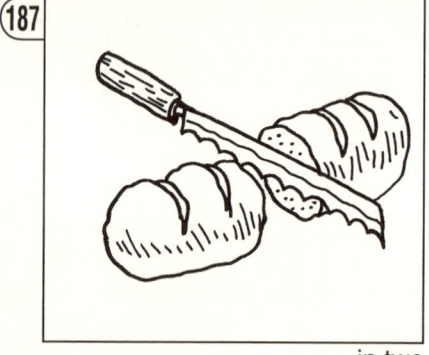

in two

182 The tadpoles are swimming in groups of four.
183 The crop is growing in rows.
184 The sea munchkins are grouped in twos.
　　The sea munchkins are in groups of two.
185 The loaves of bread are grouped in twos.
　　The loaves of bread are in groups of two.
186 The boat is being pulled by sea munchkins in large numbers.
187 The loaf has been/is cut in two.

188 Katarina spoke in English.　Katarina speaks English.
189 Olivia is speaking in a soft voice.
190 Tim and Mama are speaking in loud voices.
191 The pool is 25 meters in length, 10 meters in width and 2 meters in depth.
　　The pool is 25 meters long, 10 meters wide and 2 meters deep.
192 The table is two meters in width, 80 centimeters in depth and one meter in height.
　　The table is two meters wide, 80 centimeters deep and one meter high.

①境界内に入っている in と線上にのっている on

(193) in / on

(194) on

(195) a b into c in

(196) a b onto c on

193 There is a leaf in/on the pond.
194 The sailboat is on the sea.
195 b. The turtle is going into the pond.   c. The leaf is in the water/pond.
　　　The leaf is on the turtle/the turtle's back.
196 b. The leaf is falling onto/into the pond/water.   c. The leaf is (floating) on the pond/water.

【Ⅲ】イメージを比べる 261

197 Puppy is rolling in/on the grass.
198 The girl is in the field.
199 b. Puppy is running into the grass.   c. Puppy is rolling in the grass.
200 b. Tim is putting Puppy onto the grass.   c. Puppy is rolling on the grass.

262 … in：面と見る

② in/on/at the corner

201 in

202 in a corner

203 on

204 on

205 at a corner

201 Kitten is in the corner.
203 Kitten is on the corner of the table.
205 a, c. Teria is at a corner.

202 Teria is in a corner of the yard.
204 Bowsheeman is on the corner.

【Ⅲ】イメージを比べる

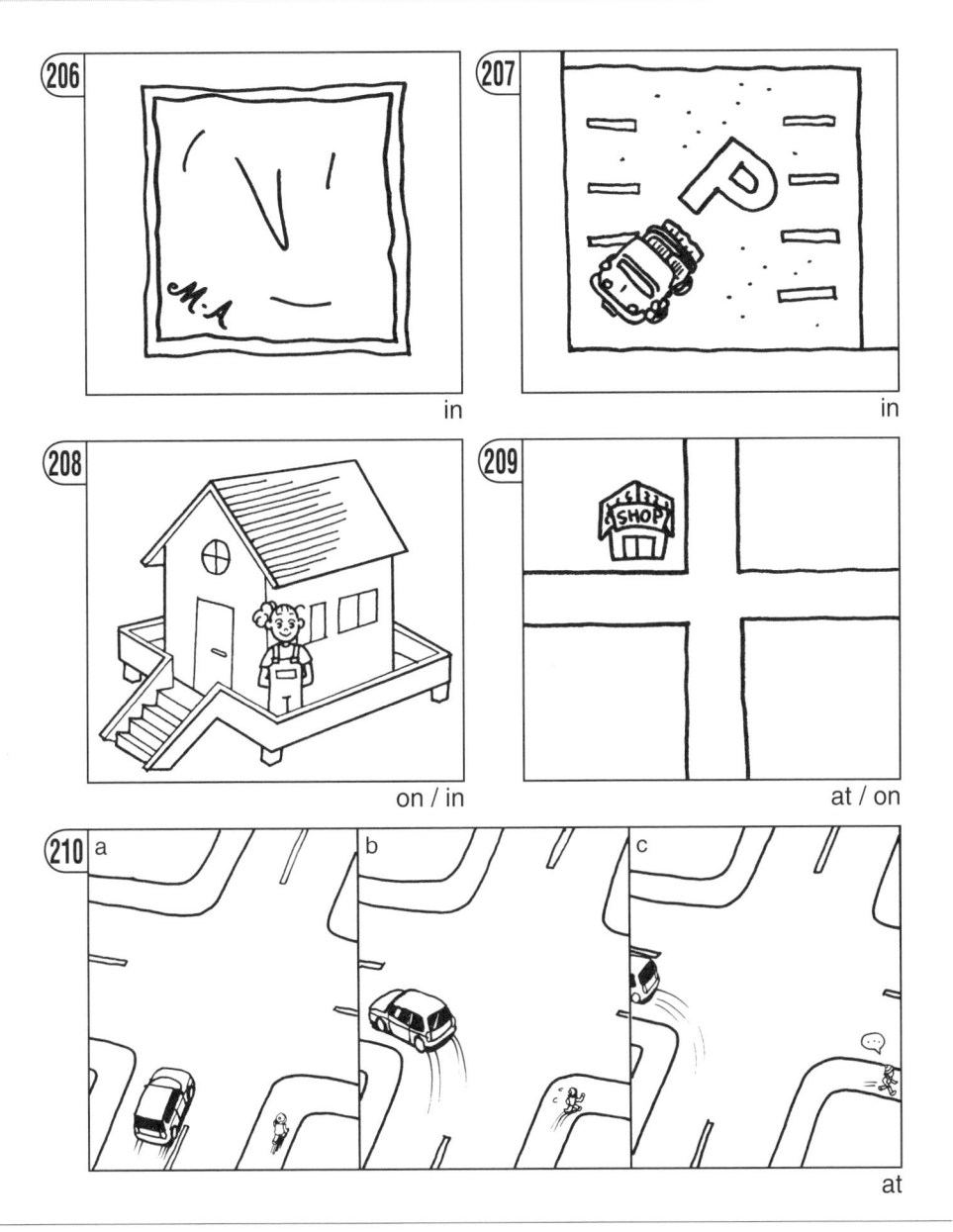

206 ... in

207 ... in

208 ... on / in

209 ... at / on

210 ... at

206 Mari's initials are in the corner.
208 Teria is in/on a corner of the porch.
210 b. The car is turning (at) the corner.

207 There is a car in the corner of the parking lot.
209 There is a shop at/on the corner.
c. The car (has) turned (at) the corner.
The pedestrian turned at the corner.

③ at/on/in the edge of ~

at

at

on

on

in

in

211 Teria, Tim and Olivia are at the edge of the building.
   [near, by, close to, next to, beside]
212 Teria is on/at the edge of the building.
213 The ghost is in the edge of the building.

214 Teria is at the edge of the cliff.
   [near, by, close to, next to, beside, on]
215 Teria is on/at the edge of the cliff.
216 Teria is in the edge of the cliff.

【Ⅲ】イメージを比べる

④ at/on/in the end of〜

㉑⁷

at

㉑⁸

on

㉑⁹

in

217 Indy is at/in the end of the boat.
218 Indy is on/at the end of the boat.
219 There is a hole in the end of the boat.

⑤ 心の中で想像している **in his mind**

in his mind

220 The king's new clothes exist only in his mind.
221 Bowsheeman can fly, but only in his mind.
222 Candy has romance in/on her mind.

⑥ 心から離れない on his mind

on her mind

223 Sylvia has the dress on her mind.
224 Papa has his taxes on his mind.　Papa's taxes are on his mind.
225 Butch has Sylvia on his mind.

268　within：面と見る

①境界をはみ出さない within

within the line

1　Olivia is supposed to draw within/inside the line/circle.
2　The ninja must stay hidden within/inside/in the closet.
3　Ruby is staying within/inside/in the house.

【Ⅰ】基本のイメージ 269

within the hospital

4 Smoking is not allowed within/inside/in the hospital.
5 Drinking is not allowed within/in the office.
　Drinking is not allowed inside this room.
6 Mama wants to keep the secret within the family.

… within：面と見る

① within と in

7　He isn't driving within his lane.
　　He isn't driving/staying in his own lane.
8　Bowsheeman is within the wild woman's reach.
9　Bowsheeman is out of the wild woman's reach.

【Ⅱ】イメージを比べる 271

10 within 11 in

12 within 13 in

14 within 15 in

10 Baby is staying within/in the shade to keep from getting sunburned.
11 Baby is lying in the shade.
12 The girls are within/inside the circle. Teria is within the group of children.
13 Teria is in the circle.
14 (The job will be started) within a month.
15 (The job will be started) in a month.

272 ··· within：面と見る

② in, inside, within

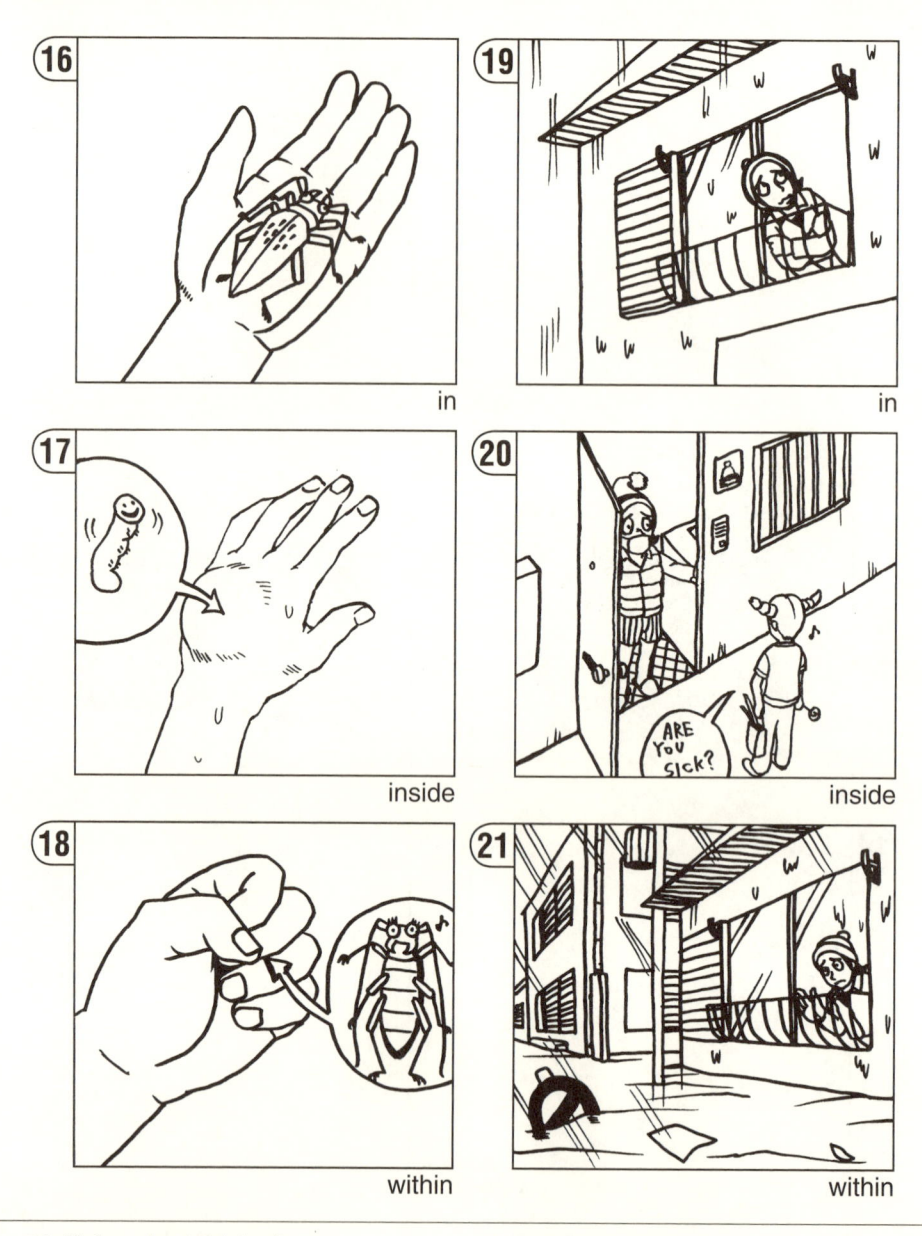

16　in
19　in
17　inside
20　inside
18　within
21　within

16　He has a bug in his hand.
17　He has a bug inside/in his hand.
18　He has a bug within/in his hand.
19　Bowsheeman is staying in/inside the house.
20　Bowsheeman is staying inside with a cold.
21　Bowsheeman is staying within/inside the house.

【Ⅱ】イメージを比べる

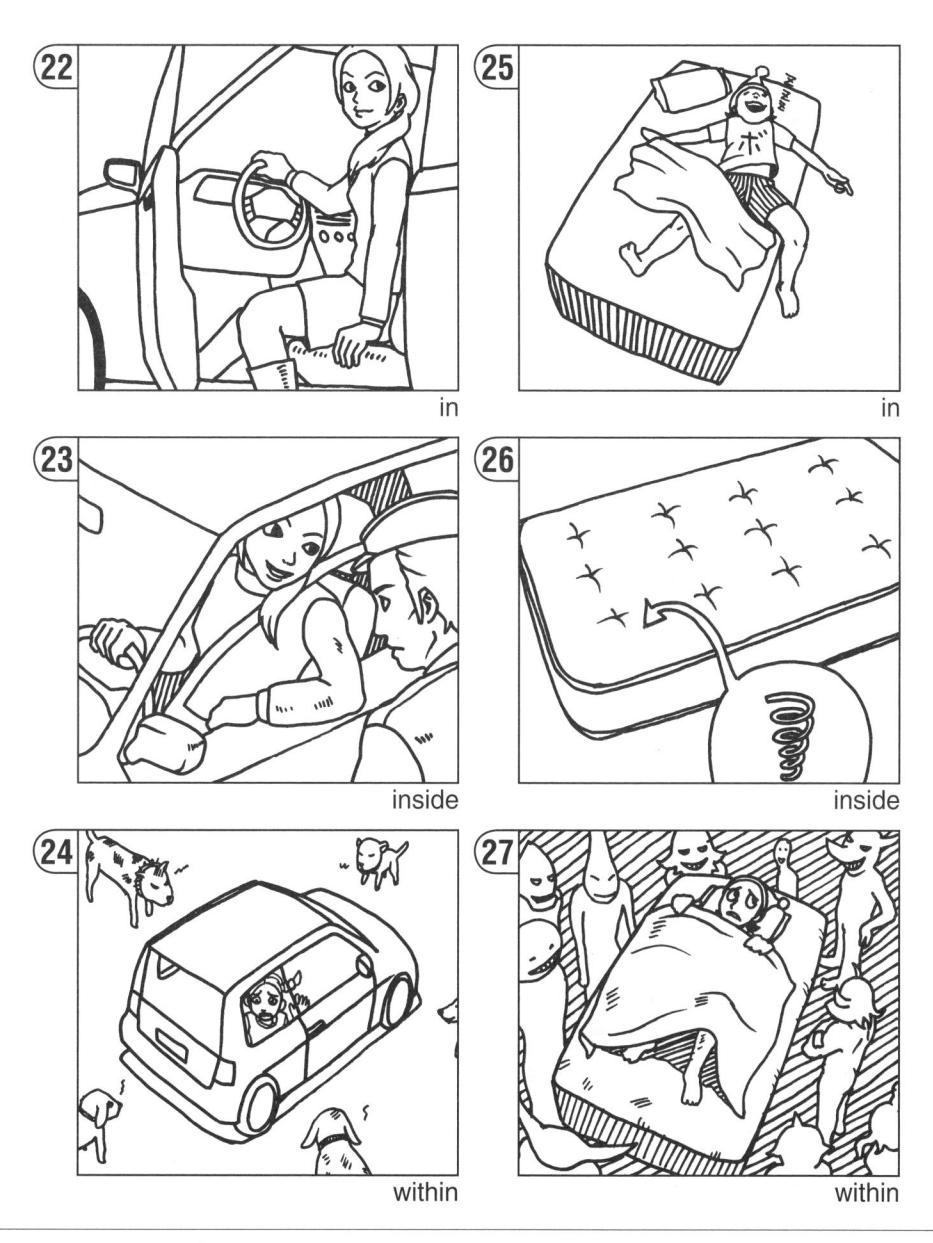

㉒ in
㉓ inside
㉔ within
㉕ in
㉖ inside
㉗ within

22　Katarina is in the car.
23　Katarina is inside the car.
24　Candy is being careful to stay within/inside the car.
25　Bowsheeman is sleeping in/on the bed.
26　There are springs inside the bed.
27　Bowsheeman is keeping his arms and legs within (the edges of) the bed.

274 ... within：面と見る

② in, inside, within

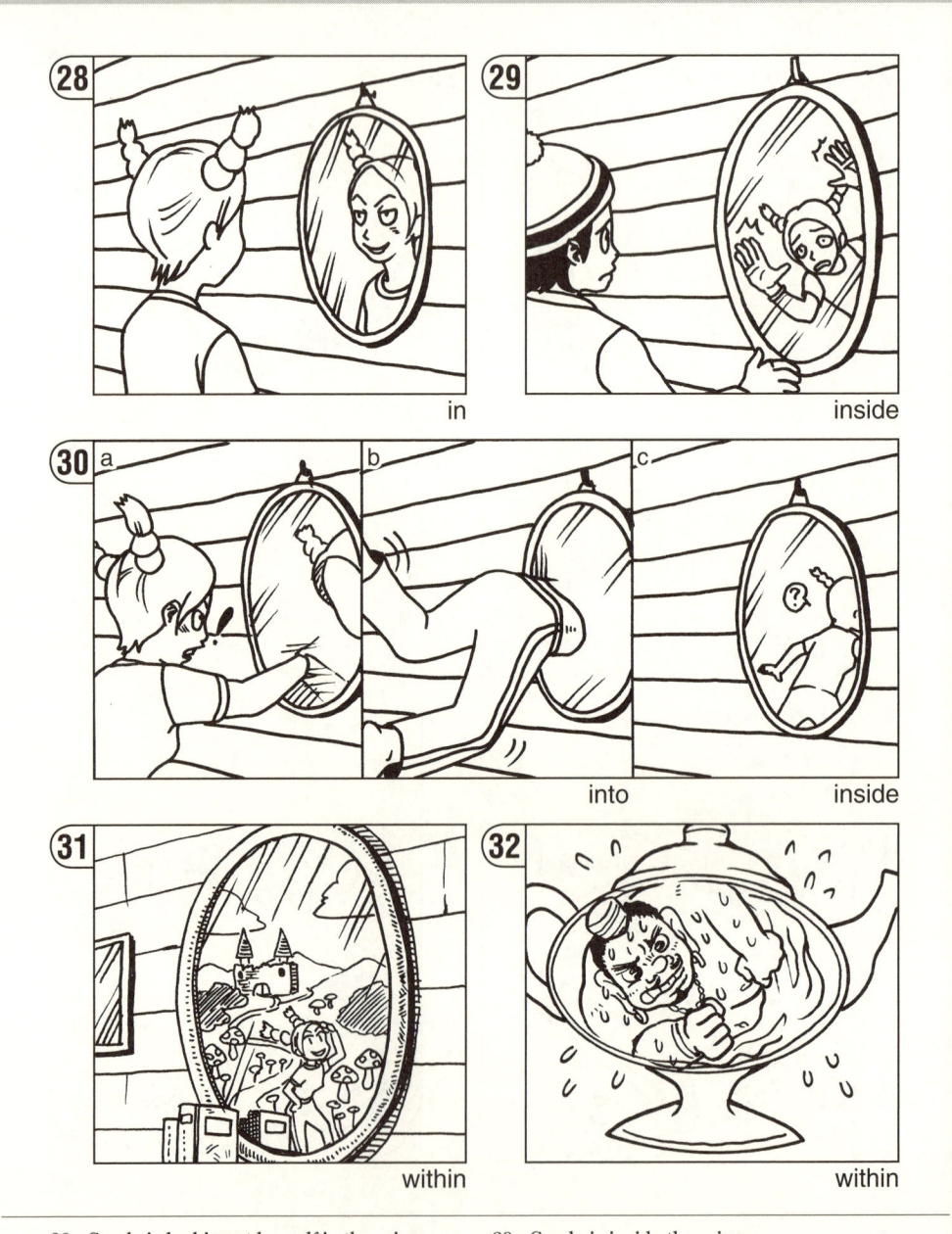

28　in
29　inside
30　a／b　into／c　inside
31　within
32　within

28　Candy is looking at herself in the mirror.
29　Candy is inside the mirror. Bowsheeman is outside the mirror.
30　b. Candy is going into the mirror.　c. Candy is inside the mirror.
31　Candy is within the world of the mirror.　32　The genie must stay within/inside the lamp.

【Ⅱ】イメージを比べる 275

33 The car is stuck in the snow.
35 c. The car is inside the snow.
36 The snowman must stay within the snow.
34 Tim is playing in the snow.
37 The mermaid must stay within/inside/in the water tank in order to breathe.

into：面と見る

①境界内に入っていく into

into the pond

1　a. The puppy is going to jump into/in the pond.
　b. The puppy is jumping into/in the pond.
　c. The puppy is in the pond.
2　b. The man is pushing the boat into the lake.　c. The boat is in/on the lake.
3　b. Ruby is going into her room.　c. Ruby is in her room.

【Ⅰ】基本のイメージ 277

into the vampire's heart

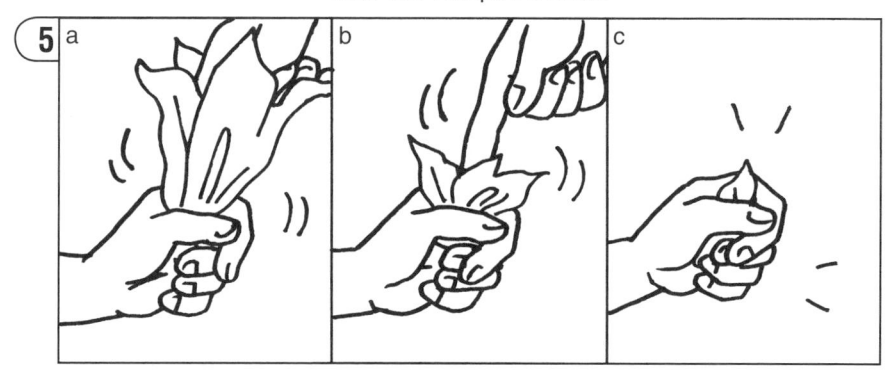

4 b. Indy is pounding a wooden stake into the vampire's heart.
　c. The wooden stake is in the vampire's heart.
5 b. She is stuffing the handkerchief into/in her fist.　c. The handkerchief is in her fist.
6 b. Dr. Bizarro is going into/in the UFO.　c. Dr. Bizarro is in the UFO.

into：面と見る

①中に入っていく into

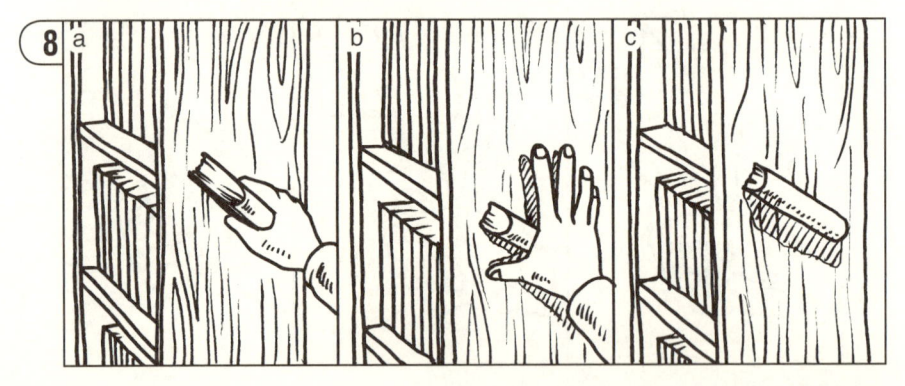

7　The animals are gathering into/in the tent.
8　b. He is putting the book into the bookshelf.
9　a. The train is coming in.
　　b. The train is coming into the station.
　　c. The train has come in.

【Ⅱ】連想するイメージ

②中にいる / ある in

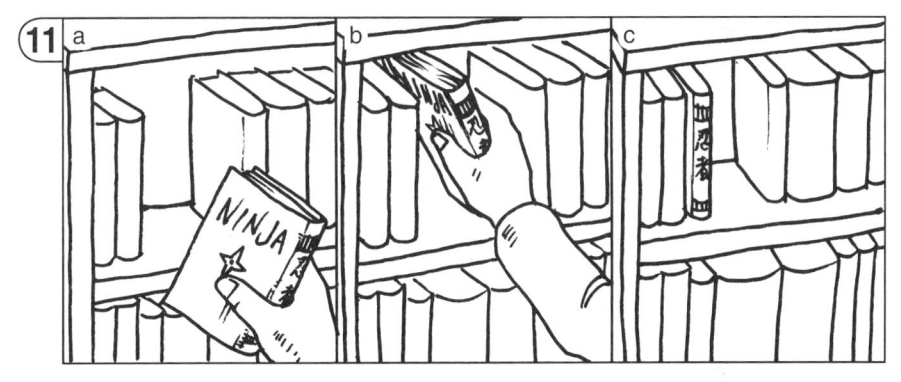

10　The circus trainer is gathering in the animals.
11　b. He is putting the book in/into/on the bookshelf.
12　b. Tim is going into/in the house.　　c. Tim is in the house.

into：面と見る

③突入する

13 Olivia and Tim ran into each other.
14 Bowsheeman ran into a tree.
15 The car ran into a cliff.

④ ばらばらになる

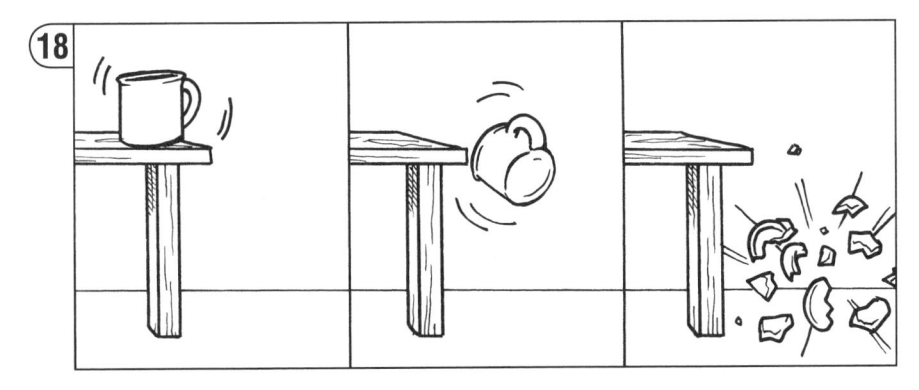

16 He smashed the watermelon into pieces.
17 He sliced the watermelon into halves.
   He sliced the watermelon in half.
18 The cup broke into pieces.
19 The people divided into twos/pairs/couples.
   The people broke into pairs/couples.
   The people are in groups of two.

into：面と見る

⑤ 変身する

20　The frog turned into a prince.
21　The man turned into a werewolf.
22　Leaf grew into a beautiful young woman.

【Ⅱ】連想するイメージ 283

23 Dr. Bizarro turned a man into a cyborg.
24 Sylvia is translating English into Japanese subtitles.
25 She is mixing eggs and flour into batter.

into：面と見る

①変身する into

come into bloom

into / to

into / to

---

26 The trees have come into bloom.
27 Teria changed yen to/into dollars.
   Teria exchanged yen into/for dollars.
28 Kitten broke the aquarium to/into pieces.

②変わっていった to

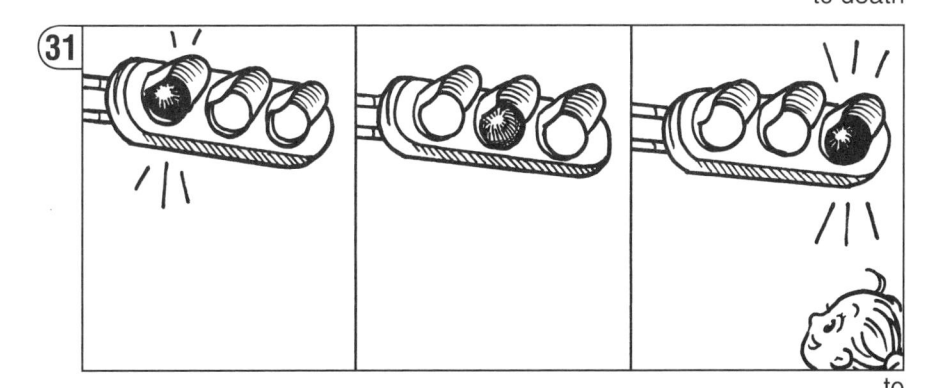

come to life

to death

to

29 The audience came to life when the band began to play.
30 The people beat the octopus to death.
31 The light turned to red.
　The light turned red.

①境界内から外に出る out of

out of the circle

1 b. The sheep is walking out of the circle.　c. The sheep has walked out of the circle.
2 The turtle is coming out of the ocean.
3 Kitten ran out of the cupboard.

【Ⅰ】基本のイメージ　287

out of the water

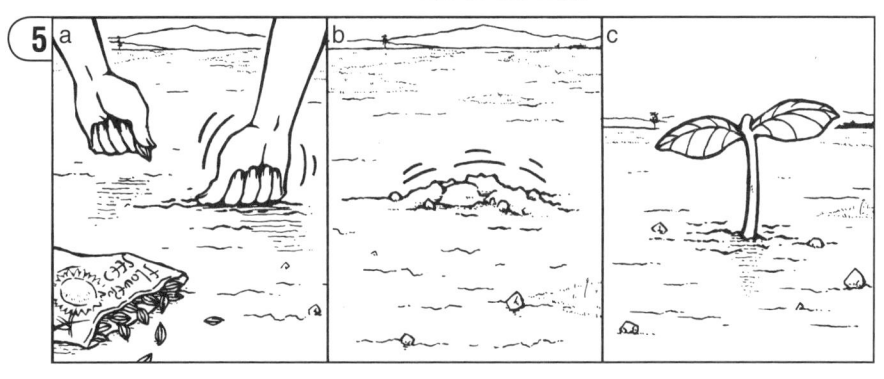

4　b. A dragon is coming out of the water.
5　b, c. The shoots are coming out of the ground.
6　b. The Kobit is coming out of the hole wearing a cat mask.

②境界内から出ている out

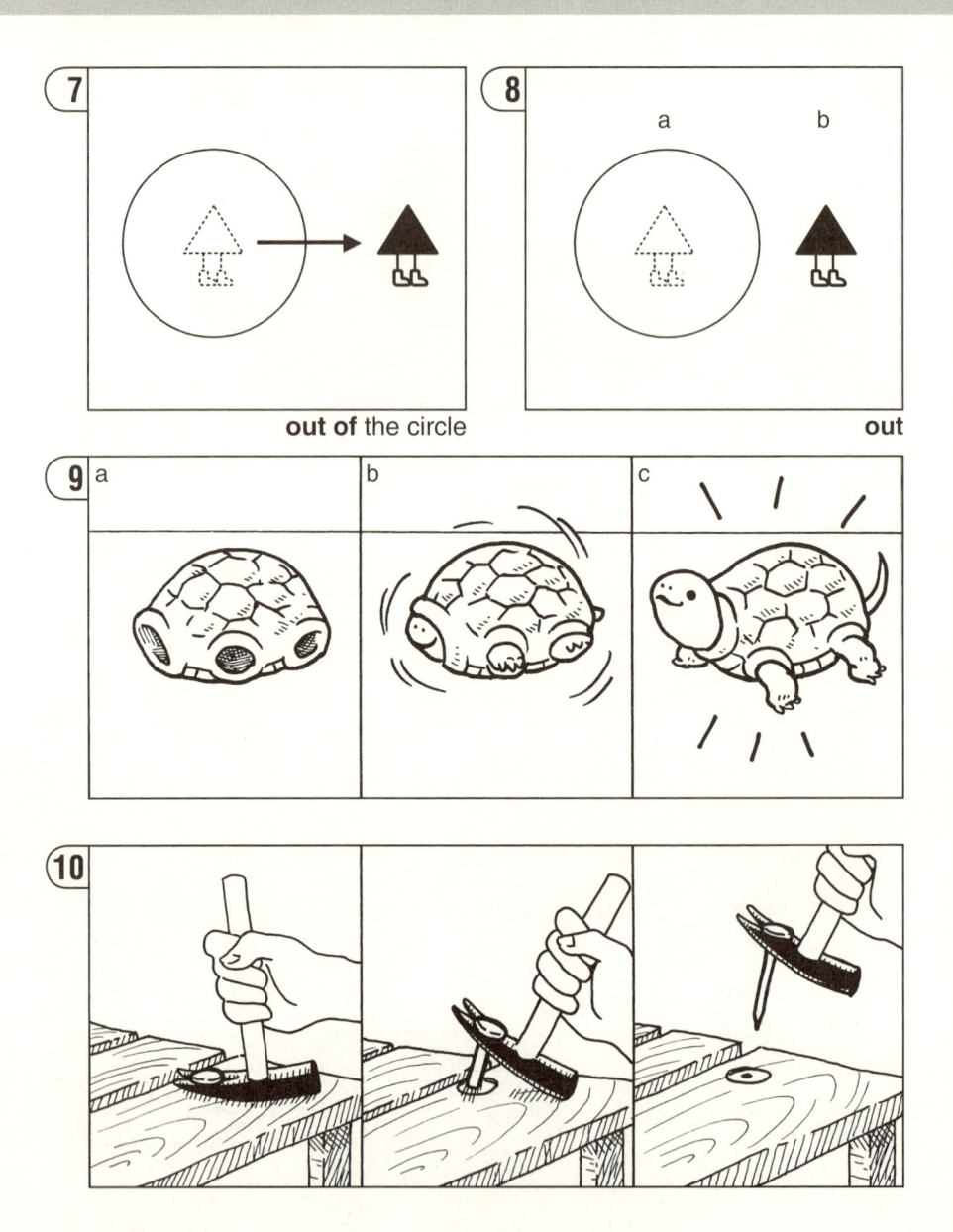

out of the circle

out

7. Mr. T has walked out of the circle.
8. a. Mr. T was in the circle.
   b. Now he is out.
9. c. The turtle poked its head and legs out.
10. Someone pulled out the nail.

11 Okan kept Oton out.
12 Butch was locked out.
13 Borizi is out.

out of：面と見る
①中から外に出る

14　The sea munchkin got out of the box.
　　The sea munchkin escaped from the box.
15　The frog jumped out of Tim's pocket.
　　The frog escaped from Tim's pocket.
16　Teria is coming out of the gate.

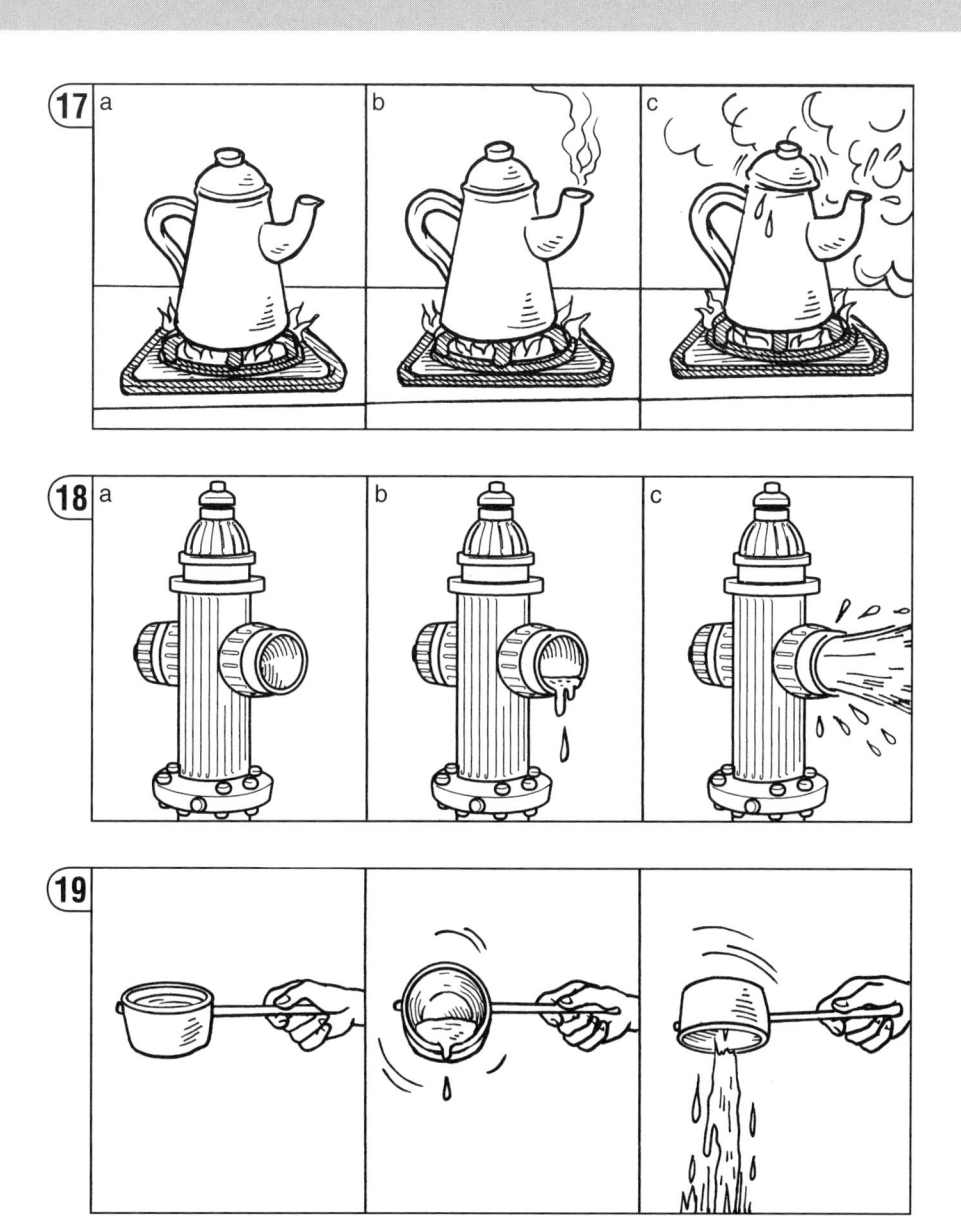

17　b, c. Steam is coming out of the coffee pot.
18　b, c. Water is coming out of the fire hydrant.
19　Someone is pouring water out of/from the ladle.

out of：面と見る

②出している

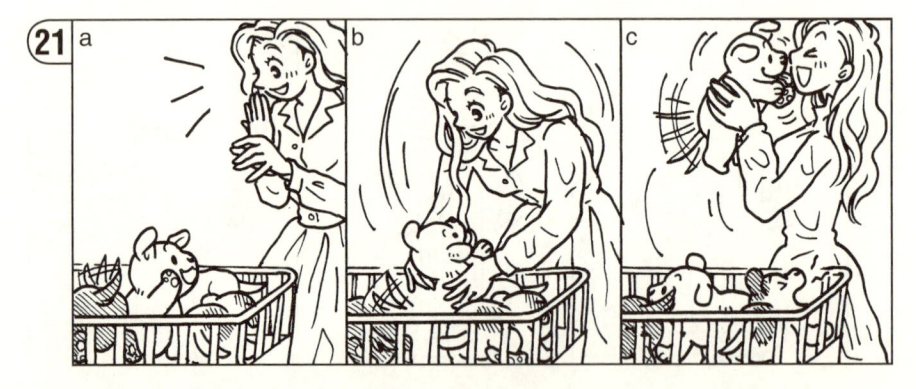

20 The demon is pulling the liar's tongue out.
21 b. Sylvia is taking a puppy out of the pen.
   c. She has just taken the/a puppy out of the pen.
22 b. Chicori is taking the potato chips out of the store.

23　c. Baby is sticking his tongue out (of his mouth).
24　c. Olivia is bleeding out of/from her nose.　　Olivia's nose is bleeding.
25　Mama sent Olivia out of the house.

294 ⋯ out of：面と見る

③なくなってしまう

26　Indy is out of gas.
　　Indy's car ran out of gas.
27　Indy is out of water.
28　Indy is out of food.

29 The cart is driving out of sight.
30 c. The moon is out of sight.
31 Inond sank out of sight.

… **out of**：面と見る

④出ている

32　c. The moon is out.
33　c. The sun is out.
34　b. The stars are coming out.　　c. The stars are out.

【Ⅱ】連想するイメージ 297

out from behind

out from behind

out from behind

35 The moon came out from behind the clouds.
36 The sun came out from behind the clouds.
37 Baby came out from behind Mama.

④ 出ている

38 b, c. The whale is blowing out steam.
39 b, c. The volcano is bursting out in flame(s).　c. The volcano is spewing out lava.
40 c. The long skirt is out (of fashion).

【Ⅱ】連想するイメージ 299

41 Baby is crying out loudly.
42 c. Teria is crying out in pain.　Teria is shouting in pain.
43 Malow is calling out for the waitperson.

out of：面と見る

④出ている

44　b. Butch stands out from the rest of the runners.
45　Leaf stands out from all the others.
46　Sylvia picked out a puppy.

【Ⅱ】連想するイメージ

⑤「（5人）のうちの（2人）」の out of と in

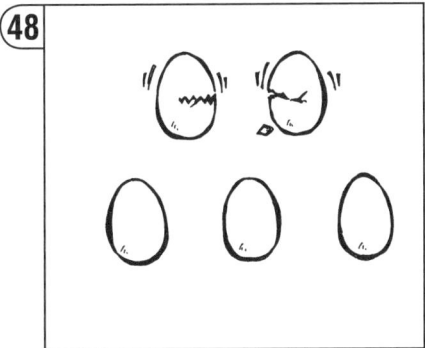

47 He took two (out) of the five sea munchkins.
48 Two (out) of the five eggs are cracked.
49 Two in five sea munchkins are a different color.
50 Two (out) of the five people are tall.
51 Two in five people are tall.

①離れる out of と off

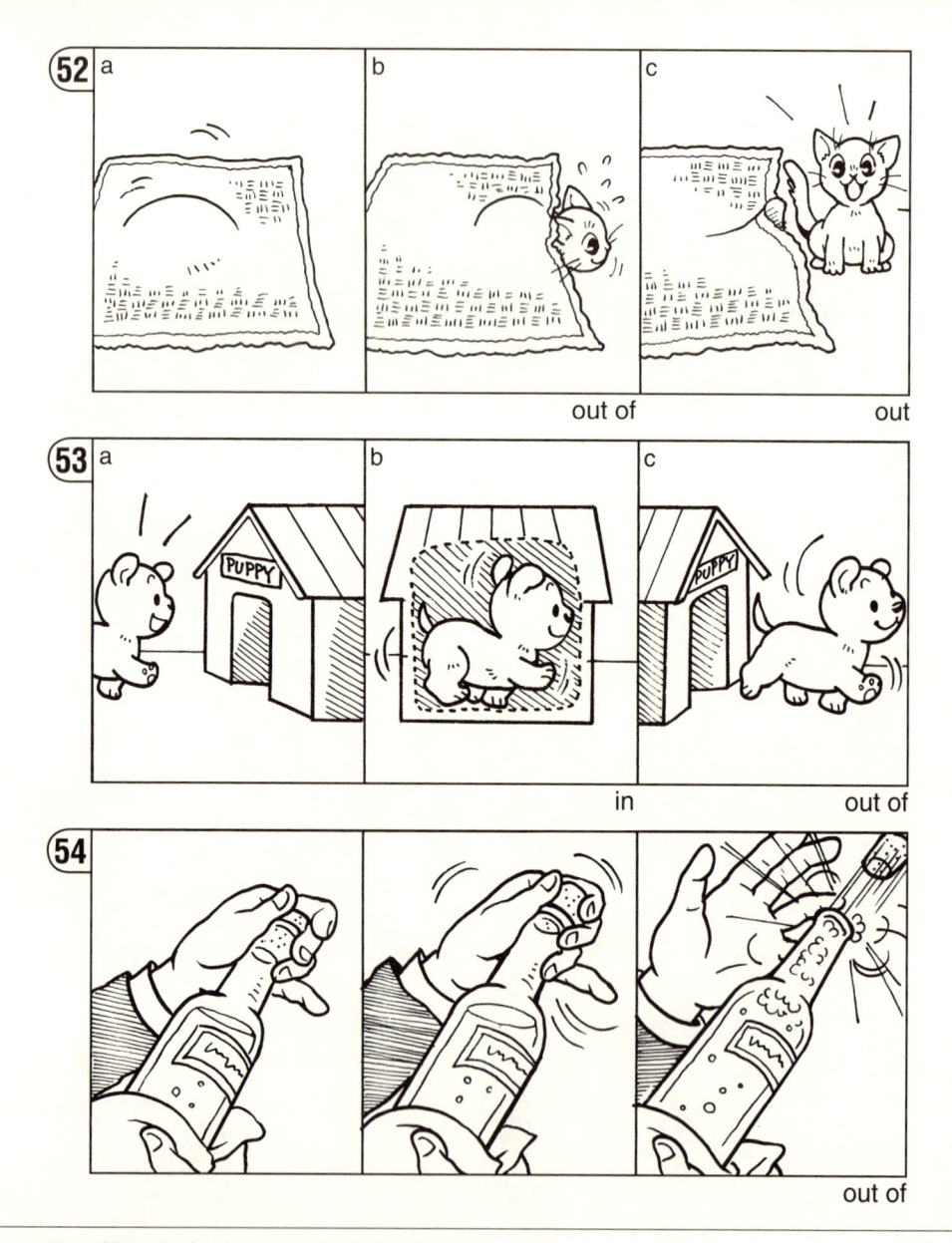

52 a. Kitten is sleeping under/in the blanket.
　b. Kitten is getting out of the blanket.
　c. Kitten is out.

53 b. Puppy is in his house.　c. Puppy came (back) out of his house.

54 Someone took the cork out of the bottle.

【Ⅲ】イメージを比べる 303

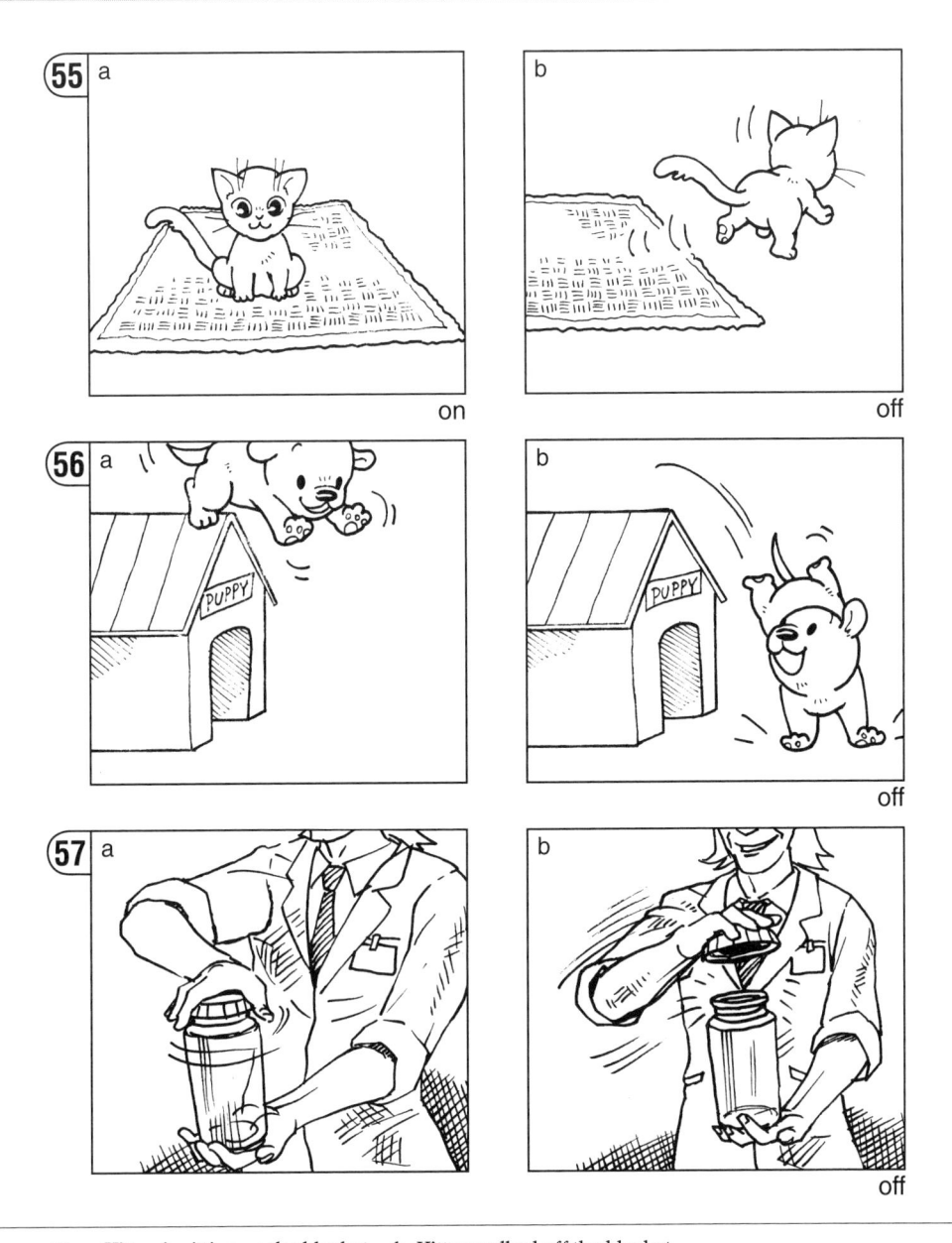

55 a. Kitten is sitting on the blanket.   b. Kitten walked off the blanket.
56 Puppy jumped off the roof of his house.
57 b. Dr. Bizarro took the lid off the jar.

304　out of：面と見る

②離れる out of, off, away (from)

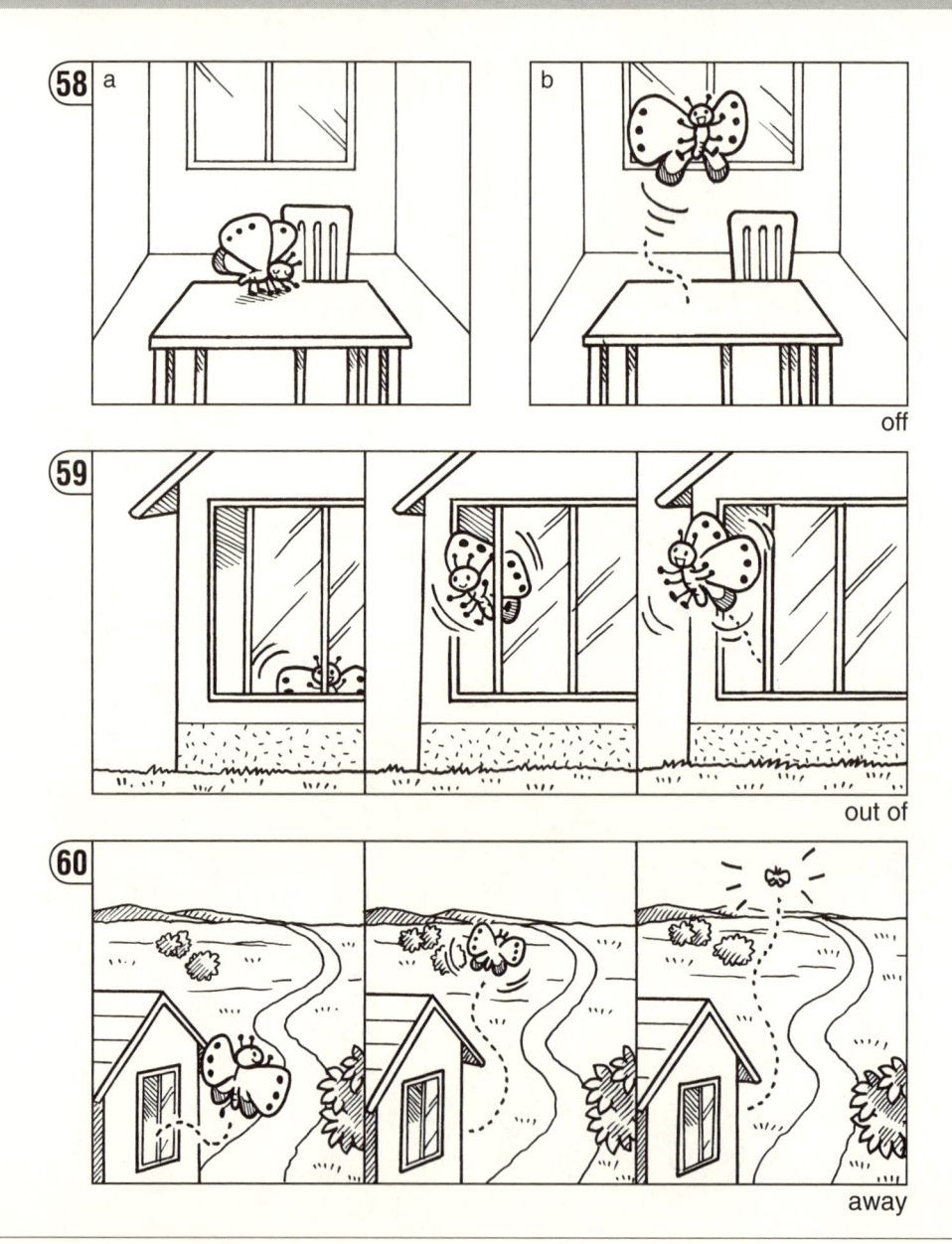

58　b. The butterfly flew off the table.
59　The butterfly flew out (of) the window.
60　The butterfly flew away.

【Ⅲ】イメージを比べる 305

61 a / b
off

62 a / b / c
out of

63
away from

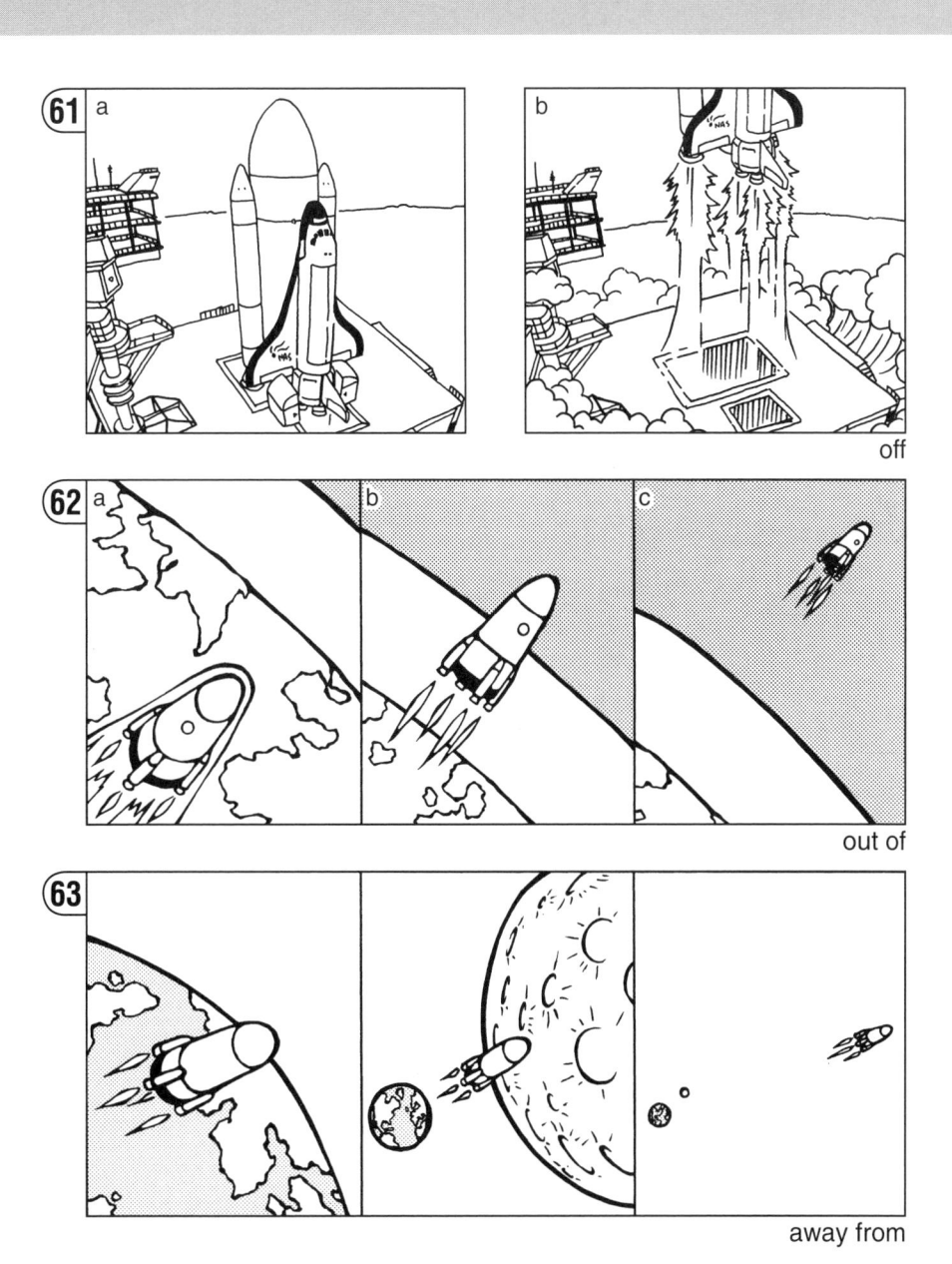

61　b. The rocket is taking off.
62　The rocket flew out of Earth's atmosphere.
63　The rocket is flying away from Earth.

②離れる out of, off, away (from)

off / out of

off

away from

---

64 "Get off/out of my flowers!"
65 Puppy jumped off the patch of grass.
66 Puppy is running away from his house.

【Ⅲ】イメージを比べる 307

out of

off

away

67 Ruby is coming out of her house.
68 Ruby is walking off her property.
69 Ruby has gone away with Nautilus.

308 ··· **out of**：面と見る

②離れる **out of, off, away（from）**

out of

off

away from

70 The mugger came out of a dark alley.
71 Albert backed off (from) the mugger.
72 Albert ran away from the danger.

【Ⅲ】イメージを比べる　309

out of

away

off to

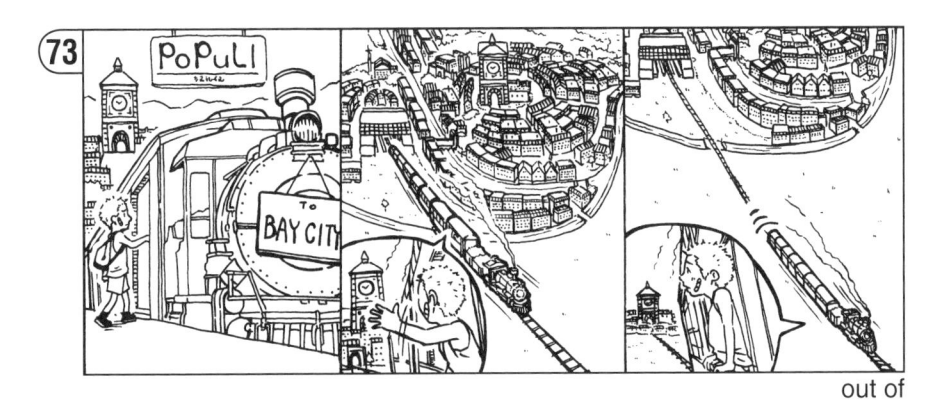

73　The train is coming out of Populi.
74　Eluca went away.
75　Eluca went off to Populi for a few days to visit/see Leaf.

⋯ of：面と見る

①「a of B」でaはBの一部である of

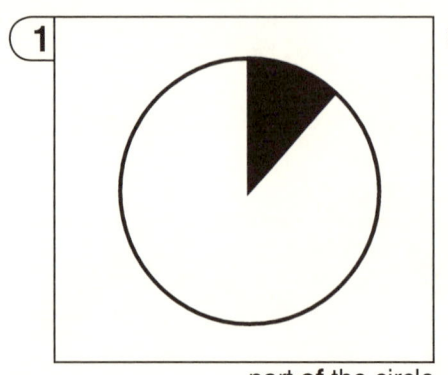

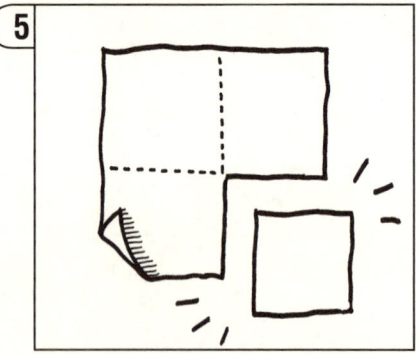

1 part **of** the circle

1. The black wedge/slice is (a) part of the circle.
2. Baby is a member of Teria's family.
3. Bakunsai is a member of a ninja group.
4. a piece of cake
5. a piece of paper

【 I 】基本のイメージ　311

6　6km² **of** land

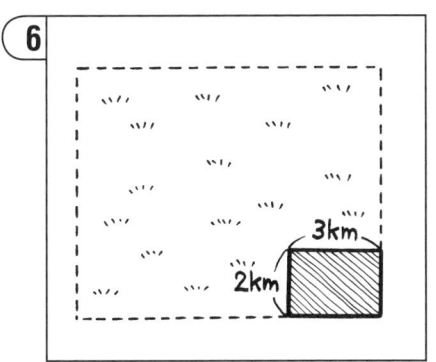

7　one **of** the planets

8

9　Bakunsai

6　The small parcel is 6 square kilometers of land.
7　Earth is one of the planets.
8　Mari is one of Olivia's friends.
9　Bakunsai is one of the ninjas.

312 … **of**：面と見る

②「a of B」の B が強調される

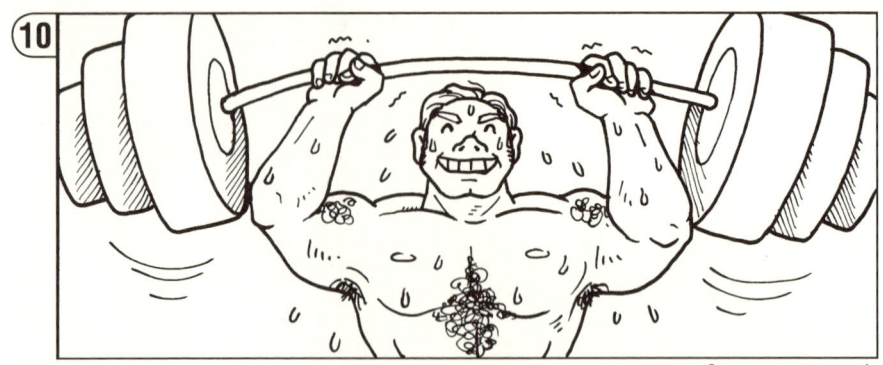

a man **of** great strength

of great use

10　He is a man of great strength.
11　Leaf is a girl of great beauty.
12　The scissors are/were of great use.

【Ⅰ】基本のイメージ 313

③「A of b」でAの中のbを選び出す of

13 
a. Courage   b. Liberty   c. Love
the Statue **of** Liberty

14 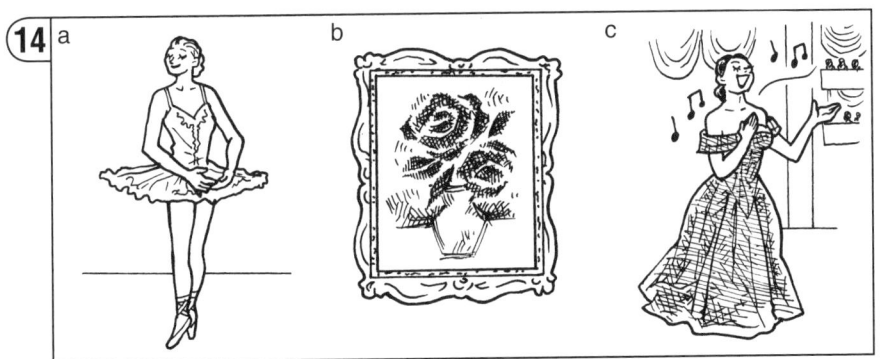
the art **of** painting

15 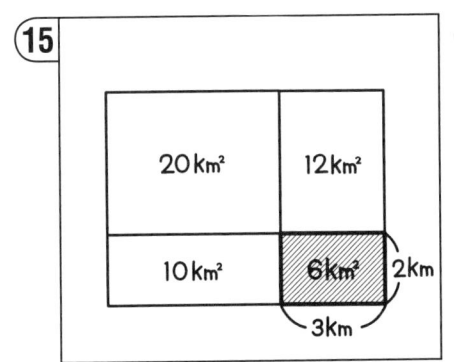
20 km²　12 km²
10 km²　6 km²　2 km
　　　　3 km
land **of** 6km²

16 
the members **of** Teria's family

13　a. The Statue of Courage　　b. The Statue of Liberty is in New York.　　c. The Statue of Love
14　a. the art of dancing　　b. The art of painting is great.　　c. the art of singing
15　This is a parcel of land of 6 square kilometers.　16　These are the members of Teria's family.

314　…of：面と見る

①一部分

17　a glass of milk
18　a bottle of milk
19　a cup of coffee
20　a cup for coffee
21　a box of candy
22　a cage for the lion

【Ⅱ】連想するイメージ

be nice of Teria

23 the lid of the teapot

24 There is a window in one of the walls of the room.

25 the chimney of the house

26 There is a bucket on the floor of/in the room.

27 It's nice of Teria to help Mama.

② 一部分をとり出す

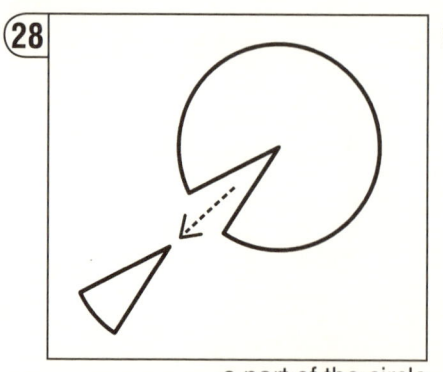

㉘ a part of the circle

㉙ a resident of

㉚ the prairie dog of Mama Zoo

㉛ a. / b. / c. the robot of Candy

28 The wedge/slice was a part of the circle.
29 Nautilus is a resident of Nautilus Island.
30 The prairie dog of/at Mama Zoo is good at dancing.
31 a. The picture of Candy is on the wall.
   b. The robot of Candy looks just like her.
   c. The doll of Candy is sitting on the bed.

【Ⅱ】連想するイメージ 317

32 — a citizen of
33 
34  — a. the city of Osaka — b. the rural part of Osaka
35 — Osaka City
36 — Osaka City

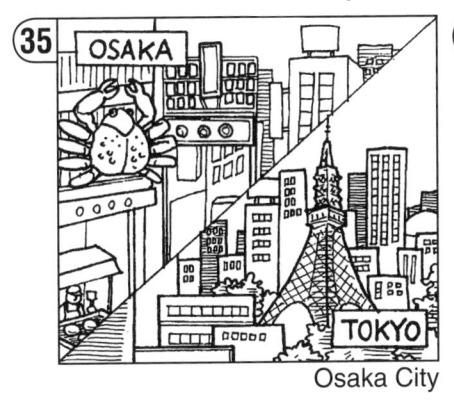

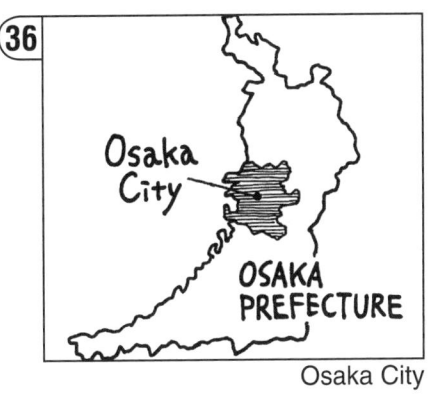

32 Ringo is a citizen of Cold State.
33 One of the tires is off the bicycle.
34 a. The city of Osaka is famous for its food.
   b. Many people don't know about the rural part of Osaka Prefecture.
   Osaka Prefecture includes both Osaka City and a large rural area.
35 Osaka City is smaller than Tokyo City.
36 Osaka City is in Osaka Prefecture.

③ とり出す

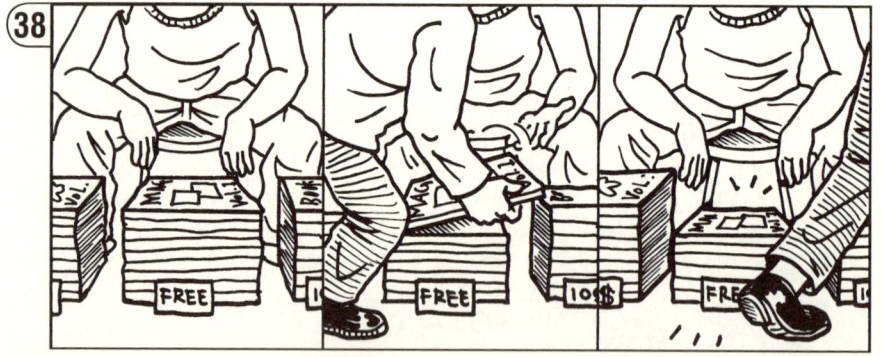

free of toys

free of charge

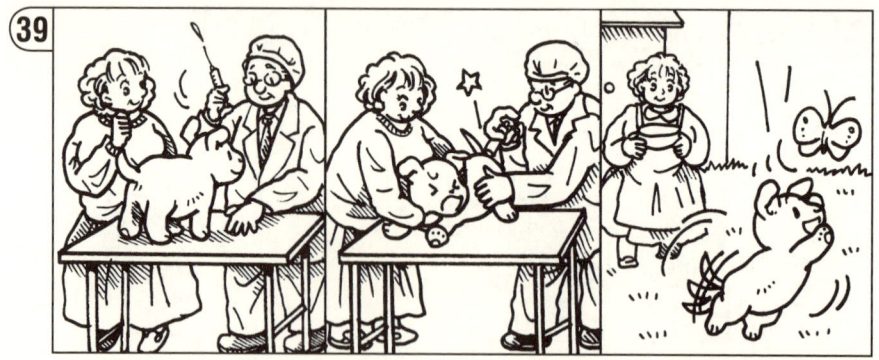

free from disease

37 Mama made the hall free of toys.
   The hall should be kept free of toys.
38 The magazines in the middle pile are free of charge.
39 Puppy has been free from disease since the veterinarian gave him a shot.

【Ⅱ】連想するイメージ 319

get rid of the mice

rob her of her bag

remind him of her birthday

40 They got rid of the mice in the house.
　　The house has been free of mice ever since.
41 The thief robbed Sylvia of her bag.
42 The calendar reminded Papa of Teria's birthday.

① 一部の of, 選ぶ of, 所有の「〜's」

one of her friends

a friend of Olivia's   a friend of Tim's

her friend

43　Mari is one of Olivia's friends.
44　a. Mari is a friend of Olivia's.　b. The boy is a friend of Tim's.
45　Mari is Olivia's friend.

two of his daughters

two of their daughters

his daughters

46 a. Papa has three daughters.   b. Teria and Olivia are two of Papa's daughters.
     c. Sylvia is the other one.

47 a. Teria and Olivia are two of Papa and Mama's daughters.
     b. Baby and Tim are Mama's sons.

48 Teria and Olivia are Papa's daughters.

② B's a と Ba

49 Mama Zoo's ~ 
50 Candy's robot 
51 ~ at Mama Zoo
52 Mama Zoo ~ 
53 the Candy robot  
54 Tokyo sushi

49　Mama Zoo's prairie dog is cute.
50　Candy's robot is her favorite toy.
51　The prairie dog at Mama Zoo is escaping.
　　Mama Zoo's prairie dog is escaping.
52　Mama Zoo prairie dog tastes better than Eno Zoo prairie dog.
53　The Candy robot is bigger than the other one.
54　Tokyo sushi tastes better than New York sushi.

③所有する / 正式な / 子どもっぽい父親

the child's father

the father of the child

a child father

55 The child's father has been taking care of him.
56 The DNA test proved who was the father of the child.
57 The man with the cap is the baby's father.
　 The baby's father is just a young boy.
　 He is a "child father."

④「〜の」はいつも of ではない

58 the door to the restroom

59 the gates to the house

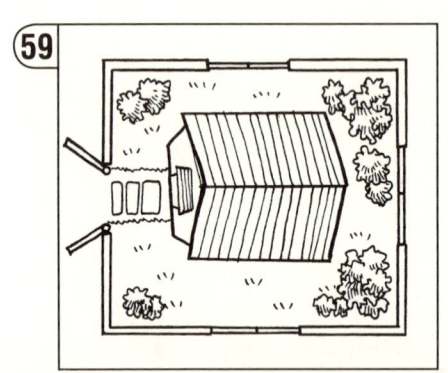

60 the door for the house

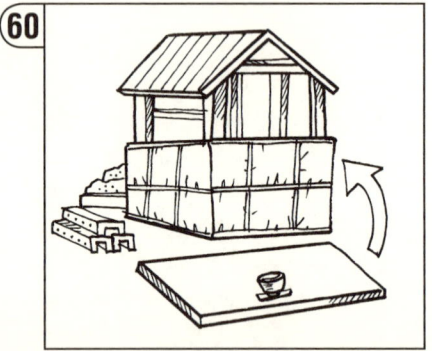

61 the door of the fridge

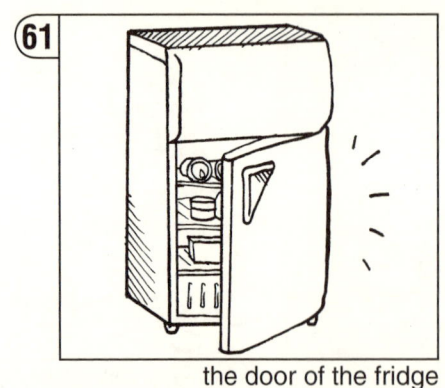

62 a THE HOUSE   b THE GARAGE
the door of 〜

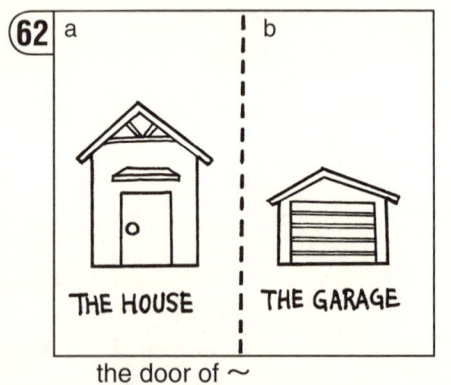

58　The door to the restroom is in the middle.
59　The gates to the house are open.
60　The door for the building/shack/house is on the ground.
61　The door of the refrigerator is open.
62　The door of the house is smaller than the door of the garage.

【Ⅲ】イメージを比べる

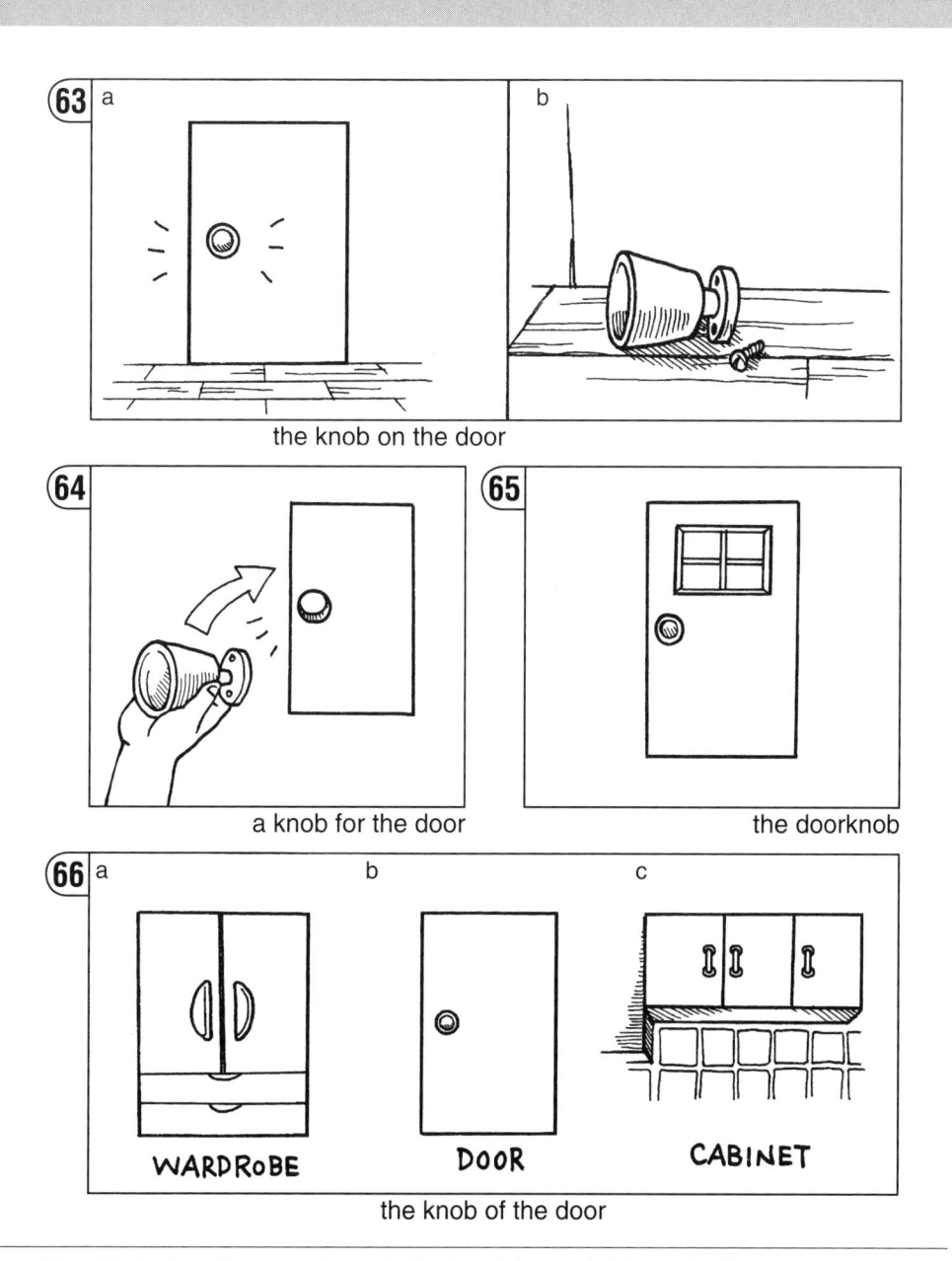

63 a. The knob on the door is shiny.　b. The knob is broken/is lying on the floor.
64　She has a knob for the door.　　　65　There is a window above the doorknob.
66　a. the handles on/of the wardrobe
　　b. the knob on/of the door
　　c. the handles on/of the cabinet

through：面と見る

①境界内を通り抜けている through

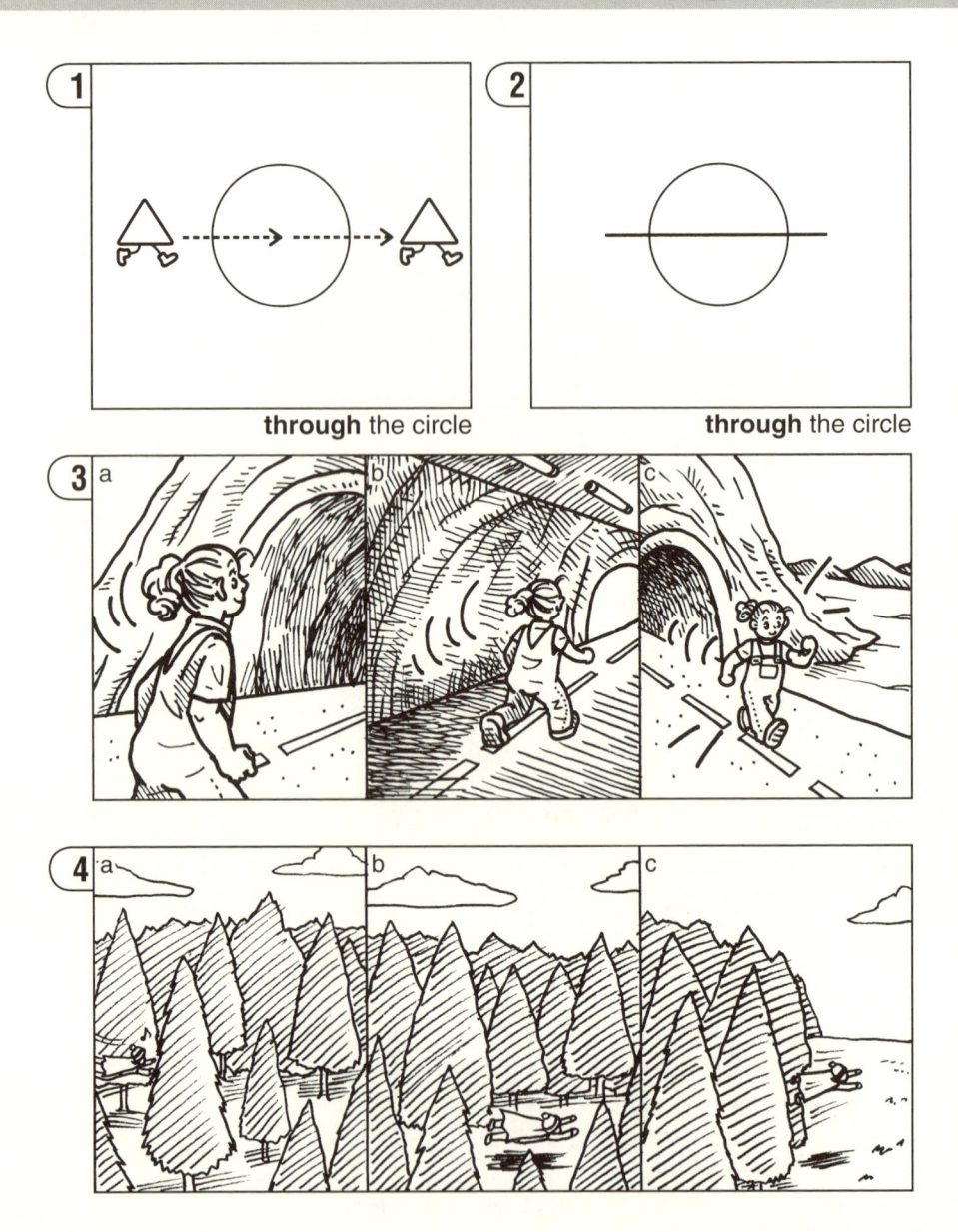

through the circle

through the circle

1. Mr. T walked through the circle.
2. The line is/goes through the circle.
3. Teria went through a/the tunnel.
4. a, b. Bowsheeman is flying through the trees. c. He flew through the trees.

【Ⅰ】基本のイメージ 327

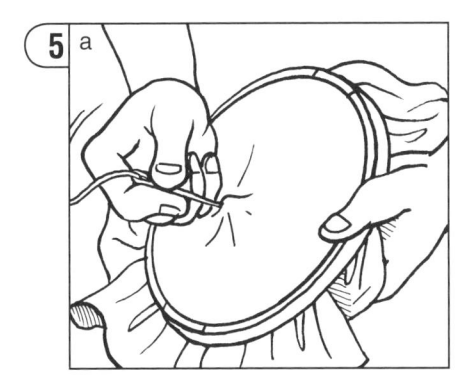

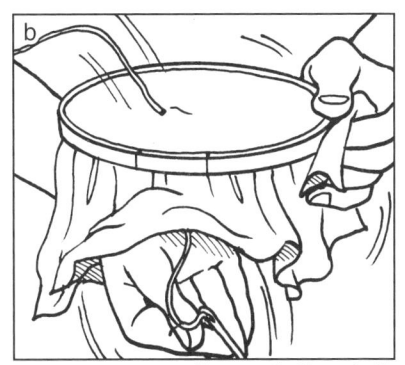

through the cloth

in

5   b. The needle went through the cloth.
6   Ruby threw a stone through the window.
7   The ninja is practicing in the trees.

through：面と見る
①境界内を通り抜けている through

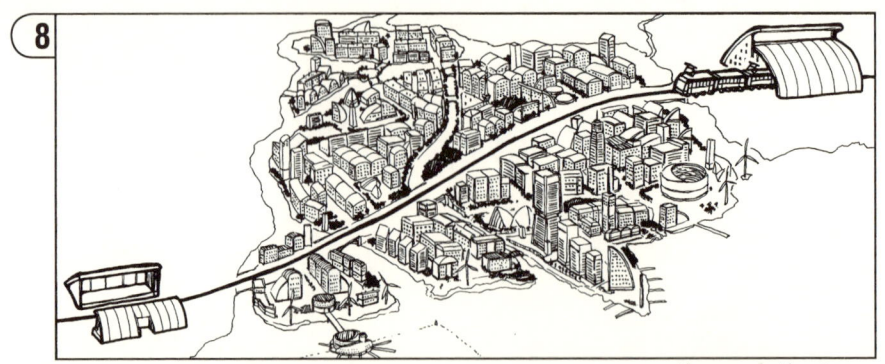

through the town

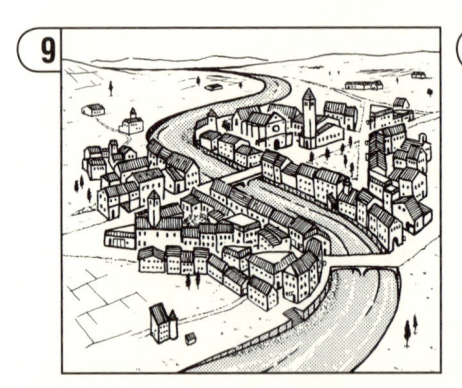

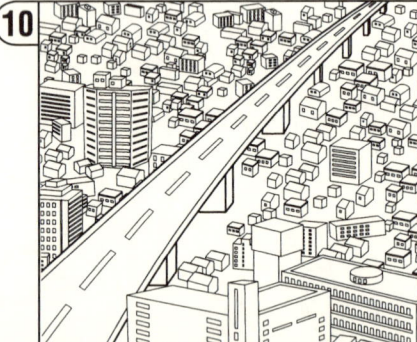

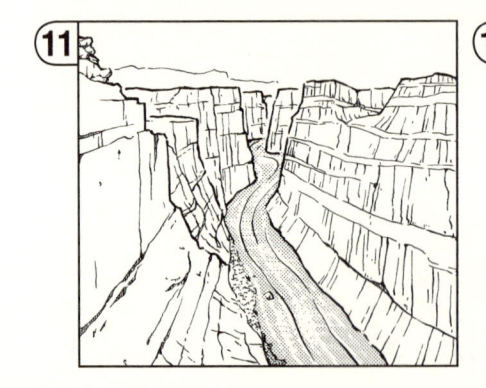

8　The railroad runs through the town.
9　The river runs through the town.
10　The road runs through the town.
11　The river runs through the valley.
12　The river runs through the woods.

【Ⅰ】基本のイメージ 329

through the apple

under

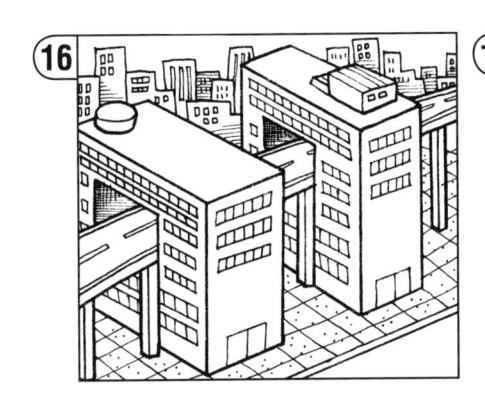

13　There is an arrow through the apple.
15　Bowsheeman ran through the cottage.
16　The road runs through the buildings.

14　There is a tunnel through the mountain.
17　The road runs under the bridge.

… **through**：面と見る

①通り抜けている

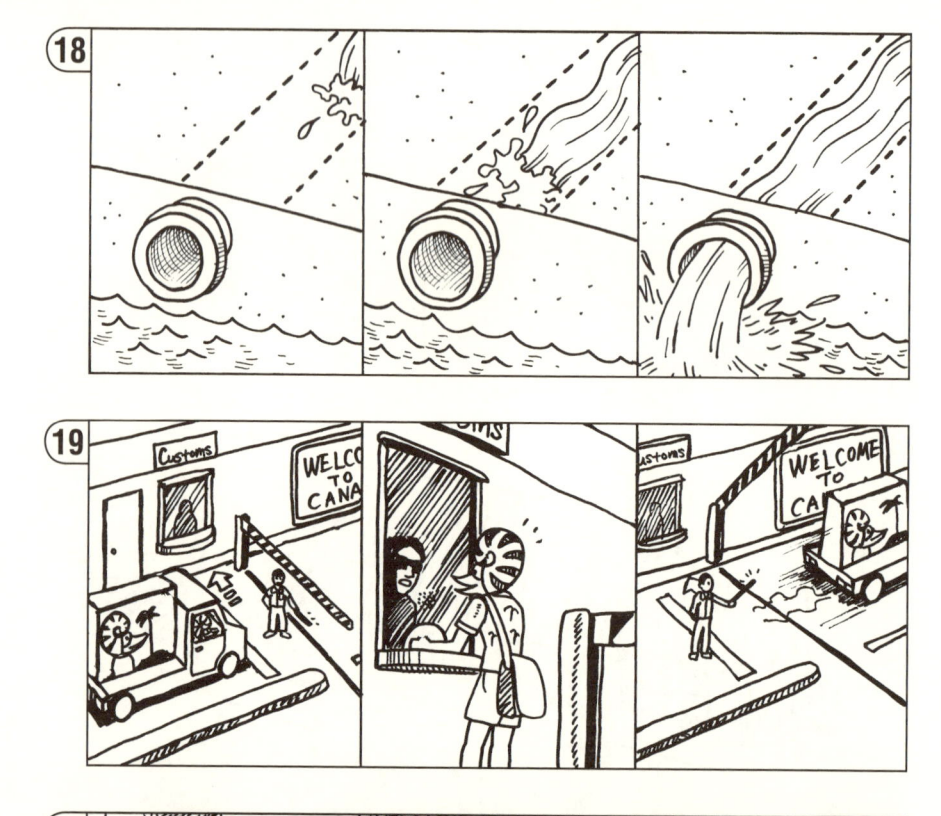

18　Water is running through the pipe.
19　Nautilus went through/across the border. [through immigration]
20　Bowsheeman is going through difficult times.

【Ⅱ】連想するイメージ 331

21 Goroki made a hole through the safe door.
22 The rain soaked through Indy's clothing.
23 Ruby is happy through and through.

through：面と見る
②通り抜けたものを強調する

24 c. Goroki went in through the window.
25 Dr. Bizarro is looking at a sea munchkin through a magnifying glass.
26 Okan is looking through the books for hidden money.

【Ⅱ】連想するイメージ　333

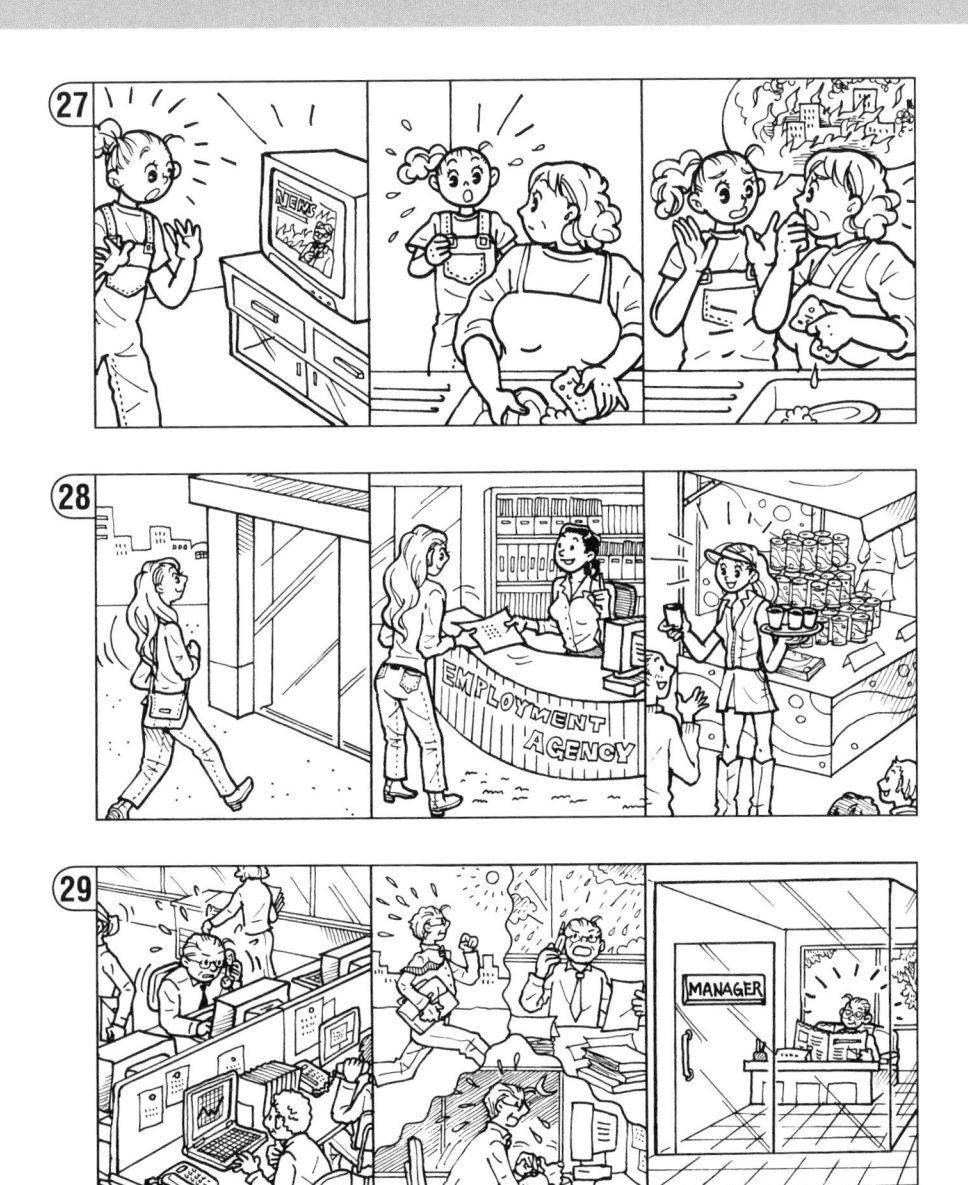

27　Mama found out the news through Teria.
28　Sylvia got the job through an employment agency.
29　Papa got the promotion through hard work.

through：面と見る

③ 始めから終わりまで

30 Bakunsai chopped through the wooden planks.
31 Bowsheeman chopped all the way through the log.
   Bowsheeman chopped through the log lengthwise.
32 Mr. and Mrs. Gold have gone through a marriage together.

【Ⅱ】連想するイメージ 335

33 Tim will be through with elementary school soon.
34 c. Kaede is through with her work for the day.
35 The marriage between Mr. and Mrs. Gold is over.

through：面と見る

① 始めから終わりまでの through

36 Papa is looking through the pictures.
37 Papa read through the pages very carefully.
38 Tim read through the stack of comics.

②カバーする over

over

over

39　The lady is looking over the picture.
40　The lady is looking over the letter.
41　Teria read over the contract.
42　Albert is reading over some books.

through：面と見る

③インフォメーションの through, by と on/in

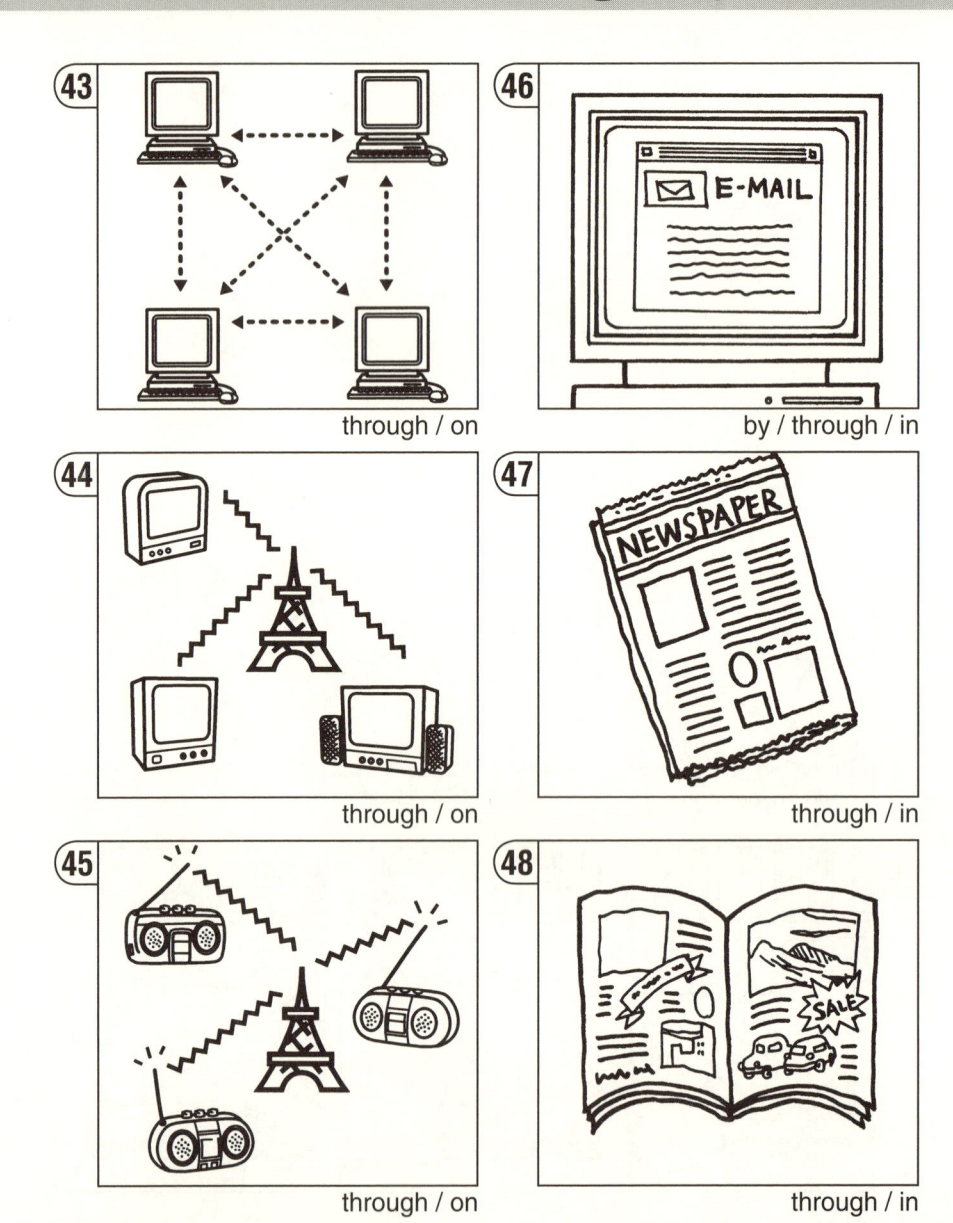

43 through / on

44 through / on

45 through / on

46 by / through / in

47 through / in

48 through / in

43 Teria got the information through/from the Internet. She found it on the Internet.

44 Teria got the information through/from the TV. She found it on TV.

45 Teria got the information through/from the radio. She found it on the radio.

46 Teria got the information through/by E-mail. The information is in the E-mail (message).

47 Teria got the information through/from the newspaper. She found it in the newspaper.

48 Teria got the information through/from a magazine. She found it in a magazine.

【Ⅲ】イメージを比べる 339

(49) through
(50) by
(51) through / in
(52) by
(53) by / on
(54) by

49 Teria got the information from a user group through E-mail.
50 Teria got the information by E-mail.
51 Butch sent the information through the mail. The information is in his letter.
52 The policeman got the information by radio.
53 The group spread the information by telephone. Teria heard it on the telephone.
54 Papa got the information through/from Mama by telephone.

through：面と見る

③インフォメーションの through, by と on/in

55 on

56 through / in

57 on page 18

58 on / in

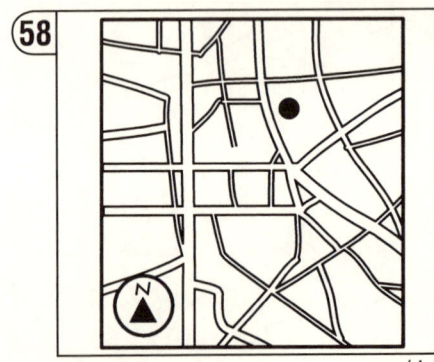

59 at the top of the page

55 The weather news is on the radio/the airwaves.
56 Teria got the information through/from a book. She found it in a book.
57 The explanation of criteria starts on page 18.
58 There is information on/in the map.
59 The picture is at the top of the page.

● コラム ②●

間違った絵から大発見あり！

　本書には膨大な量の絵を載せていますが、ここまで集約するためにイラストレーターはこの3倍以上の量の絵を描いています。なぜならそれぞれの前置詞のイメージが適切に伝わるように描かれているかどうかを何度もネイティブスピーカーのTomとPeterにチェックしてもらっているからです。

　下描きでボツになった絵はもちろん、本描きをした後もそして本が出版された後で描き直した絵もあり、今回新たに加えた絵もあります。しかし私のイメージが間違って描き直してもらった絵からこそ、非常に多くのことを学んでいます。多くの間違いの中からごく一部をお伝えしましょう。

　1つめ。旗がポールに結ばれている絵(p.39-20)で、これをonの例にしようとしたらポールから旗が少し離れているということで、onではなくfromの例の絵となりました。

　2つめ。intoのイメージのために窓に石をぶつける絵を描いてもらったところ、当然石は窓を突き抜ける絵となりました。ネイティブに見せたら石が突き抜けてしまったらintoではなくthroughのイメージだと言うのです(p.327-6)。それでintoのイメージは石が突き抜けないということで描いてもらったのが(p.205-4)の絵。少し不自然な状況ですがthroughとintoの違いを明確にするためにあえて使用しています。

　さらにagainstは波が岩にぶつかりはね返るように、柔らかなものが当たる場合に使えるという。そのためagainstのところでは窓に石はぶつけられず、トマトのような柔らかいものが当たる場合に使うということもわかり、比較した絵(p.204-1)を描いてもらいました。間違った絵からだんだんと核となるイメージが導かれるので、私にとっての間違いはまだ見ぬ発見を秘めた宝物のような価値があります。

　またこういう場合もあります。同じ絵に対して2つ3つの前置詞で表現できるという絵。例えばacrossは日本語で「横切る」、overは「超える」なので違いがありますが、英語ではacrossとoverの両方を使えてしまう絵が何枚もあるのです。試行錯誤の結果、overには「超えるという目的」があり、acrossにはないことがわかりました。前作2巻の出版後に読者から「湖を渡る船の大きさに違いがあることに何か意味があるのか(p.132-67とp133-70)」という質問があったのですが、その質問からacrossは横切る面が強調されることが明確になり、acrossは面と見るように指示している前置詞であることを確信したわけです。

　ほんの一例ですがこのようなプロセスを何度も経て「学習は間違えるところから始まる」ことを、身をもって体験しました。そして当初、間違ったと思った絵は新たな発見や確信を導いてくれるための貴重な資料となり、本書の随所に載って活かされています。

342 throughout：面と見る
①境界内にいきわたっている throughout

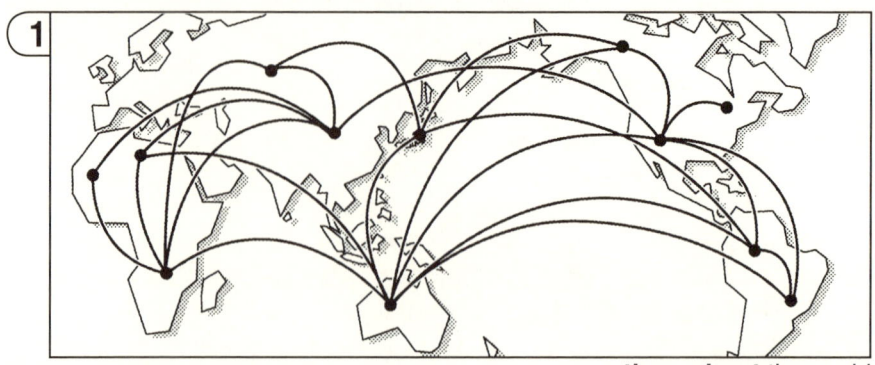

throughout the world

---

1 The Internet has spread throughout the world.
2 The Bowsheeman cap has spread throughout Japan.
3 They are painting throughout the house.

② through, across, in と比べる

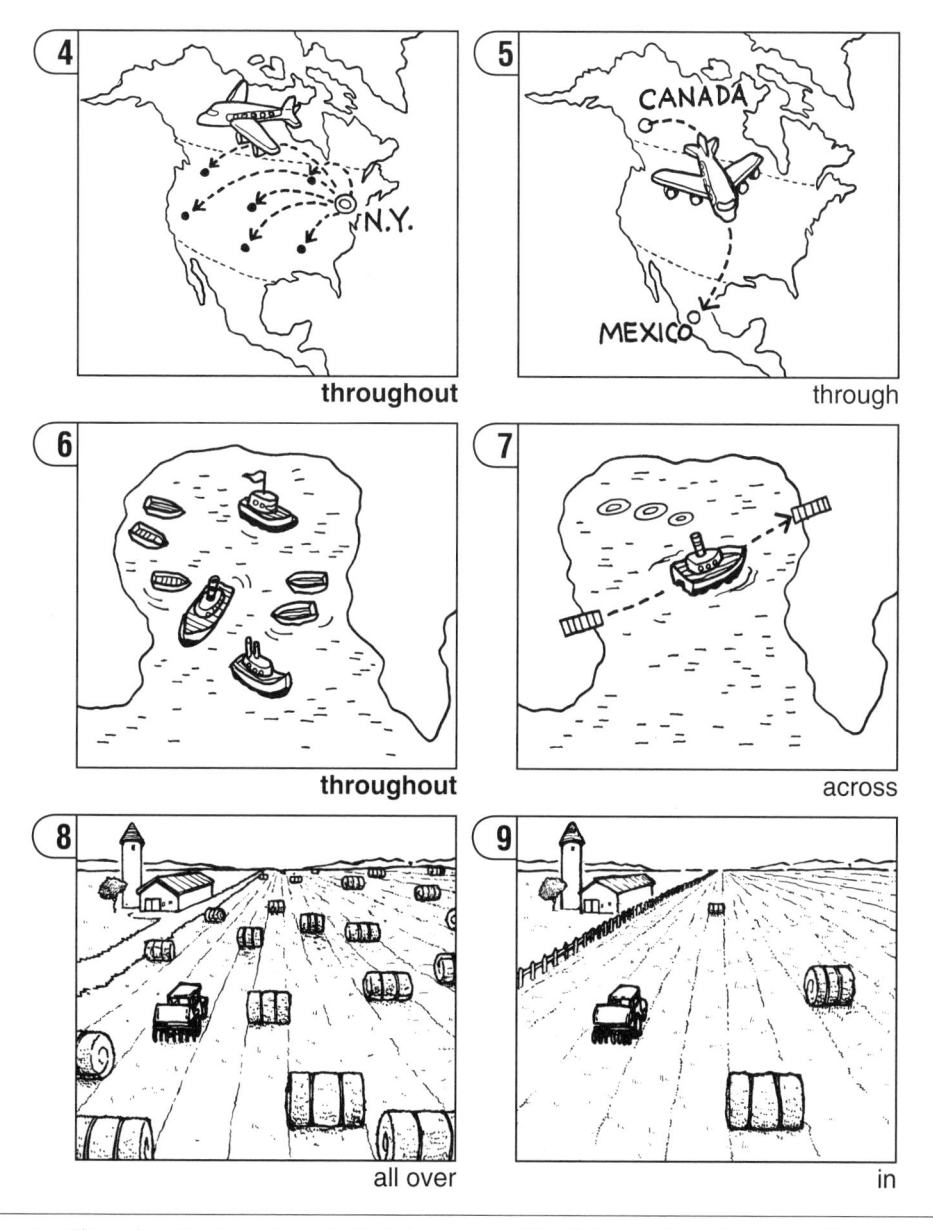

4 throughout

5 through

6 throughout

7 across

8 all over

9 in

4　This airline flies throughout the United States.
5　This flight goes through/over the United States.
6　There are boats throughout Tokyo Bay.
7　The boat is going across Tokyo Bay.
8　There are rolls/bales of wheat all over the field.
9　They are harvesting wheat in the field.

① 境界内を横切っている across

across the wall

walk **across** the circle

across the circle

1 The snail traveled across the wall.
2 Olivia walked across the room.
3 Mr. T walked across the circle.
4 The line is/goes across the circle.

【Ⅰ】基本のイメージ 345

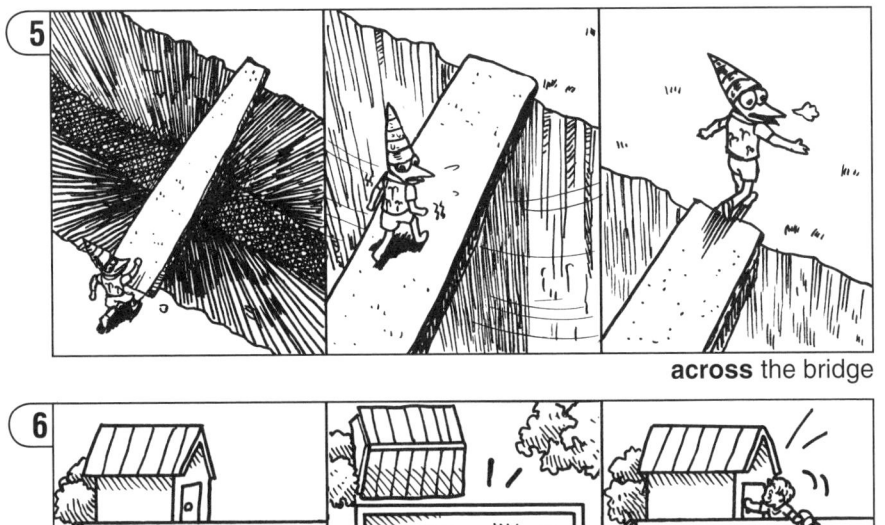

across the bridge

5　The sea munchkin walked across the bridge.
6　Tim cut/walked across the yard.
7　The boat is going across/over the river.

①境界内を横切っている across

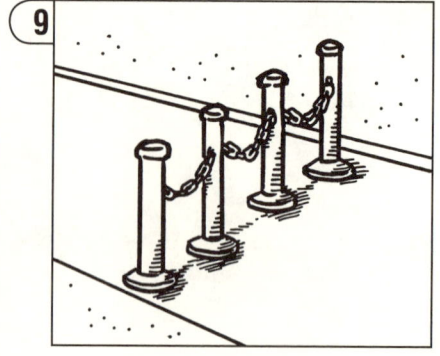

across the street

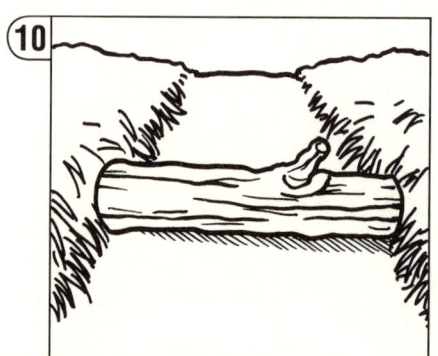

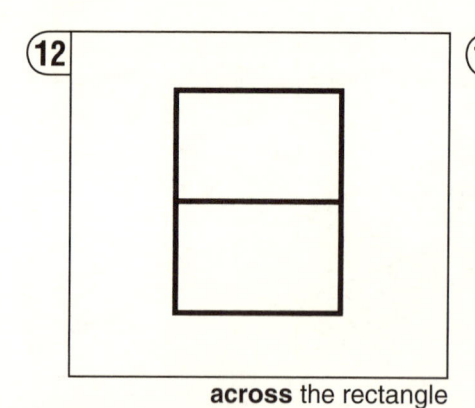

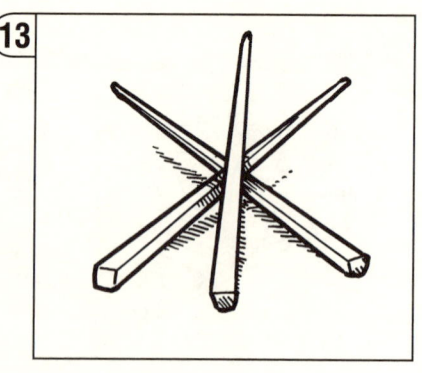

across the rectangle

8 There is a barrier across the street.
10 There is a log across/over the river.
12 There is a line across the rectangle.

9 There is a barrier across the street.
11 Olivia has a bandage across/on her forehead.
13 The toothpicks are lying across each other.

【Ⅰ】基本のイメージ 347

across the block

across / through the rectangle

over

be crossed

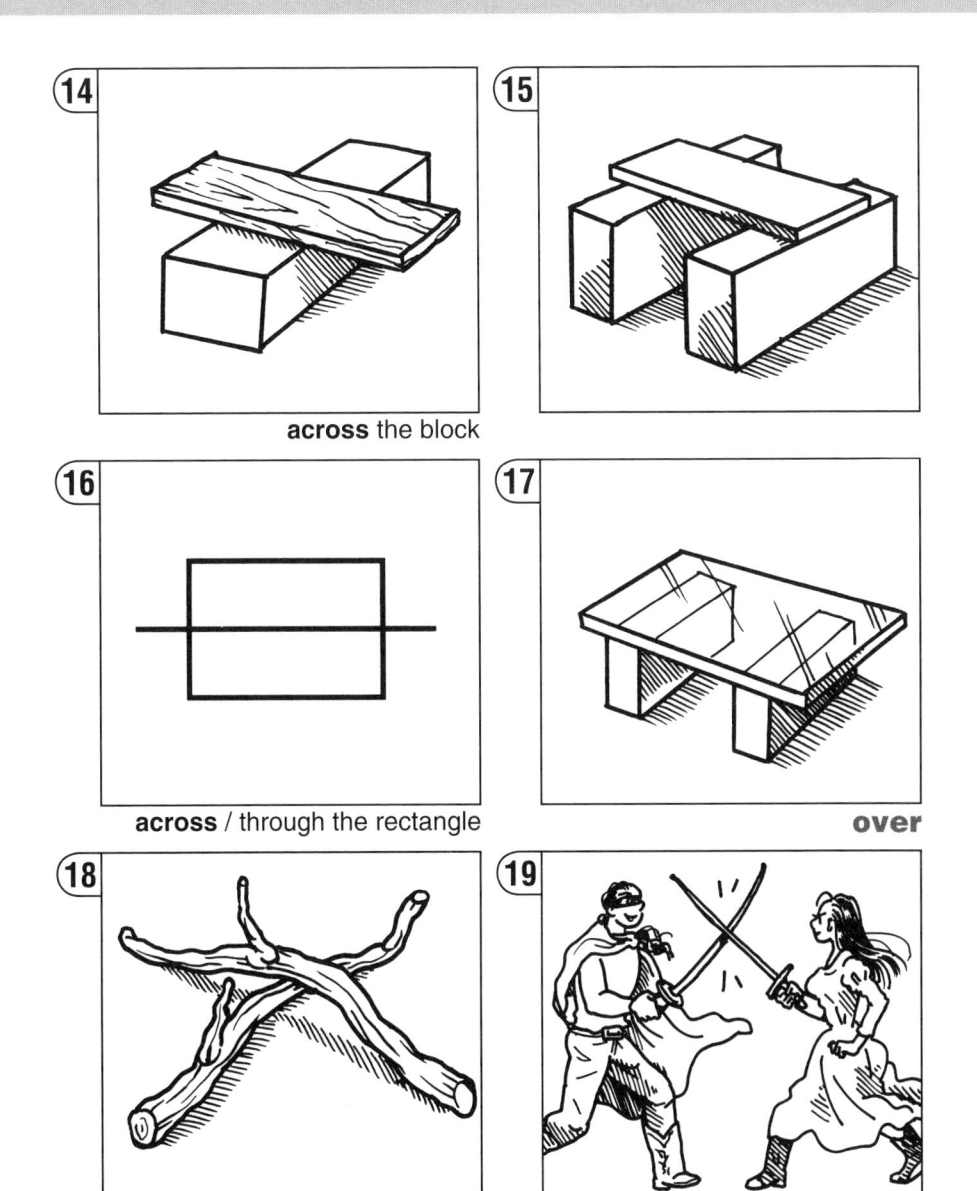

14 The board is lying across the block.
16 There is a line across/through the rectangle.
18 The branches are lying across each other.
15 The plank is lying across the blocks.
17 The sheet of glass/The plywood sheet is over the blocks.
19 Their swords are crossed.

① 横切っている

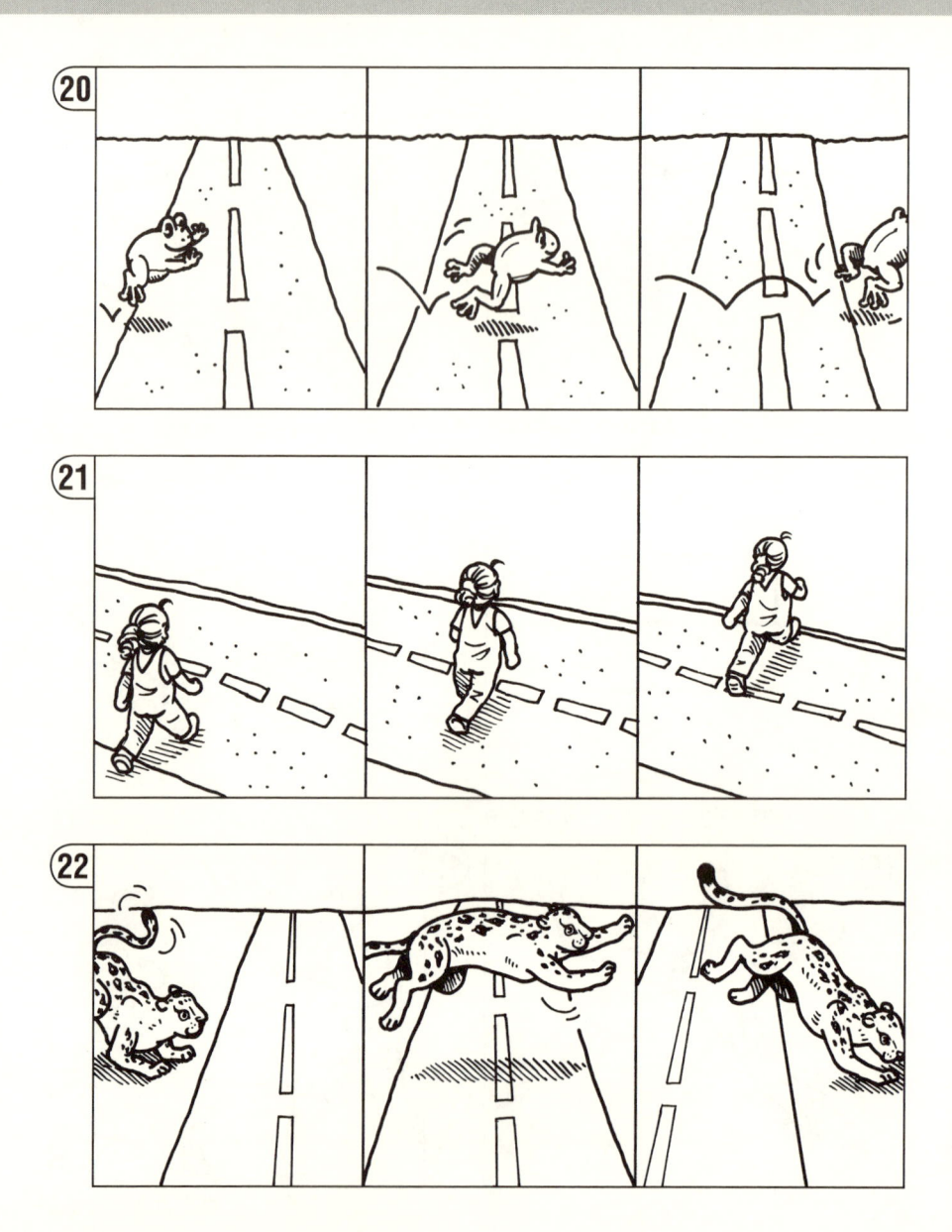

20 The frog hopped across the street.
21 Teria is walking across the street.
22 The leopard jumped across/over the street.

【Ⅱ】連想するイメージ 349

23 Olivia cut/walked across/through the rose garden.
24 The puppy cut/walked across Teria's path.
25 There is a traffic light across the street (from Teria).
26 The restaurant is across the parking lot from the station.

350 ··· across：面と見る

② スペースをはさんで向き合っている

㉗ across the table from each other

㉘

㉙

㉚

㉛ 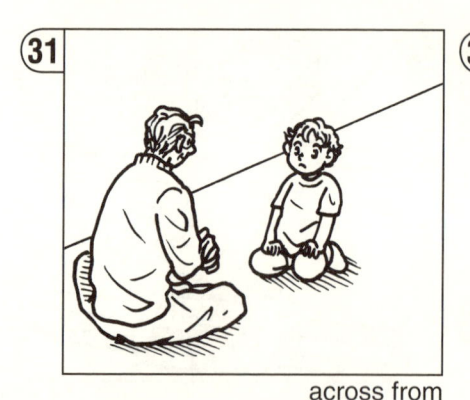 across from

㉜ across from

27 The people are sitting across the table from each other.
28 The pigs are across (the food trough) from each other.
29 The two buildings are across the street from each other.
30 The sofas are across the room from each other.
31 Tim is sitting across from his father.
　 Tim is sitting opposite his father.
32 The TV is across (the room) from the chair.
　 The TV is opposite the chair.

【Ⅱ】連想するイメージ 351

33 across from
34 on either side of the aisle
35 across from
36 side by side
37 across from
38 face to face

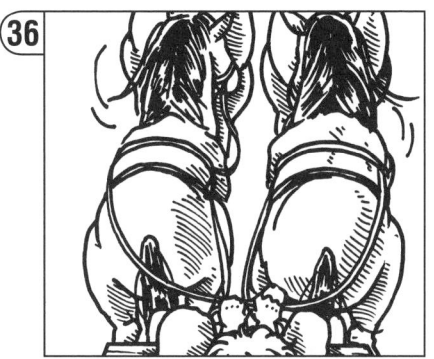

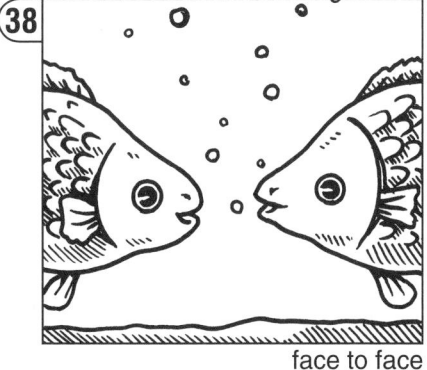

33 The children are sitting across from each other.
34 The people (who are) sitting on either side of the aisle are sleeping.
35 The boys are standing across from/ opposite the girls.
   The boys are standing in a line next to the girls.
36 The horses are side by side.
37 Teria is standing across (a short space) from Tim.
38 The fish are face to face with/to each other.
   The fish are opposite each other.

352 ··· across：面と見る

②スペースをはさんで向き合っている

across the river from

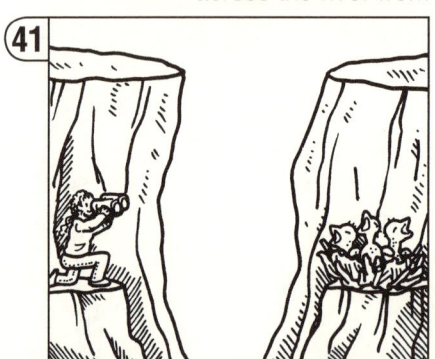

over

39 Sylvia is across the river from Butch.

41 The bird watcher is across the canyon/valley from the bird's nest.

43 The teepees/houses are just across the canyon from each other.

40 Indy is across dangerous waters from the mainland.

42 The stars on the right and left sides are across the galaxy from each other.

44 The neighbors live just over/across the canyon.

【Ⅲ】イメージを比べる 353

① across/on/over/through the border

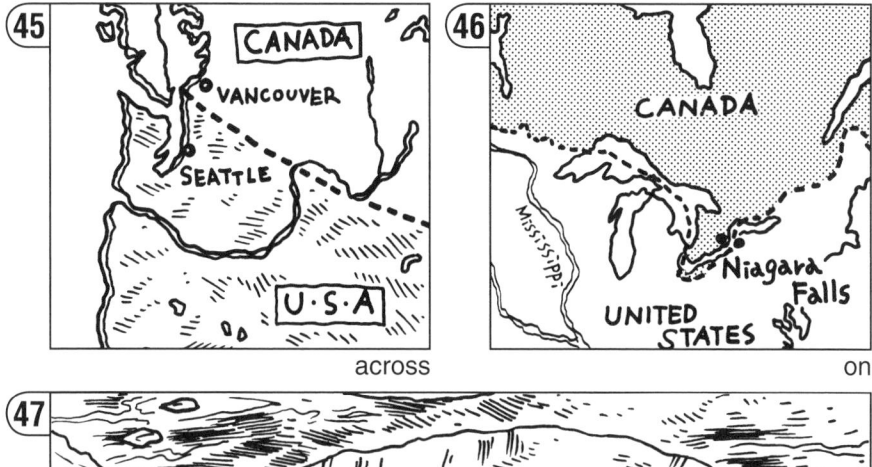

across

on

over

through

45 Vancouver is just across/over the border from Seattle.
46 Niagara Falls is on the border between Canada and the US.
   Canada is across the border from the US.
47 Canada is just over/across the border.
48 Nautilus went through/across the border.

around：面と見る
①境界内の周囲を回る around

around the island

1　The boat is sailing around the island.
2　Baby is crawling around the chair.
3　The car is driving around the mountain.

【Ⅰ】基本のイメージ 355

②まわりにいる / ある around

around his head

in

4　He has a headband around his head.
5　There is a moat around the castle.
6　There is (a) desert around the Bizarro Laboratory.
7　The road goes around the lighthouse.
8　Grandma has her arms around a cat.
9　Bowsheeman is holding Dora in his arms.

③境界内のあちこちをめぐる around

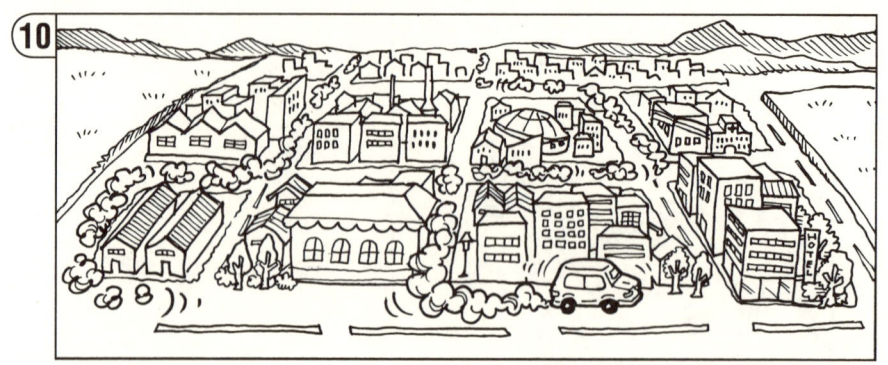

around the town

10 The car is driving around the town.
11 Dora is walking around the neighborhood.
12 The dragonflies are hovering around/about the field.

【Ⅰ】基本のイメージ 357

④境界のあたりにいる / ある around

around / about the boat

around the tree

---

13 The sea munchkins are playing around/about the boat.
14 The cats are playing around/about the house.
15 There is a strange smell around/about the man.
16 The children have made a ring around the tree.
17 The four friends are sitting around the table.
18 There are flowers around the house.

① 自ら回る（1）

358 ··· **around**：面と見る

over

19　Teria is turning around and around.
20　The merry-go-round goes around and around.
21　Baby is turning/rolling over.

②他を回す

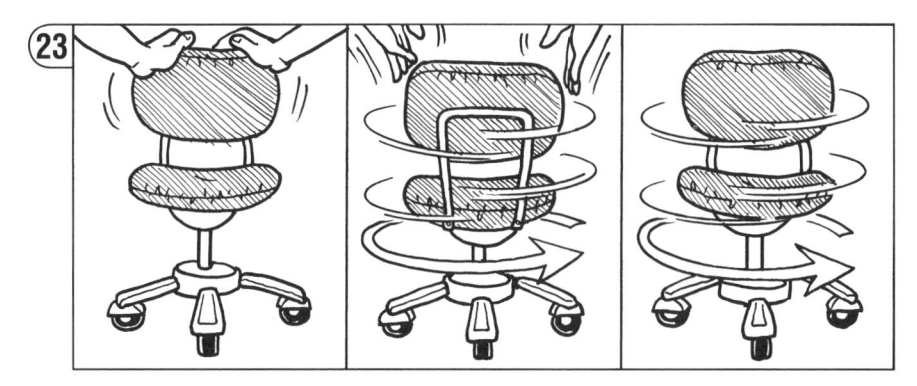

over

22 Albert is spinning/turning Sylvia around.
23 Someone turned/spun the chair around.
   Someone turned/spun around the chair.
24 Baby turned the chair over.

③自ら回る（2）

25 Olivia turned around.
26 Bakunsai turned around.
27 Bowsheeman turned around and ran.

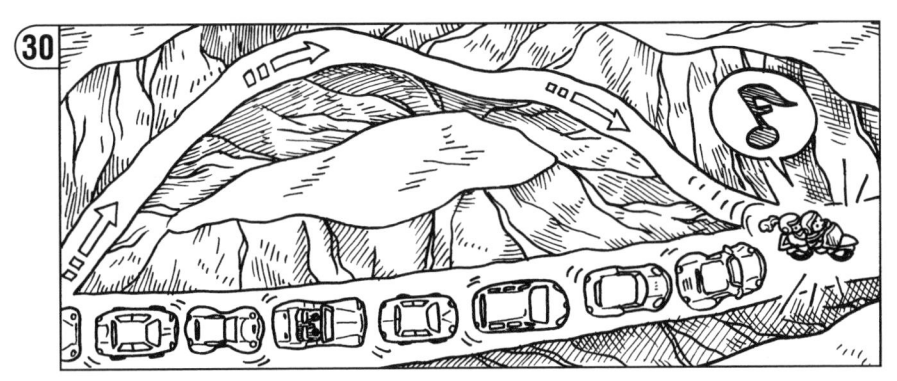

28 The car drove around the corner.
　 The car turned the corner.
29 Pooch and Teria walked around the puddle.
30 They drove around the line of cars.

④「そのあたりのどこかに」

31 The coffee shop is just around the corner.
32 Leaf is somewhere around the clock tower.
33 Leaf is somewhere around the coffee shop.

① around, over, along を比べる

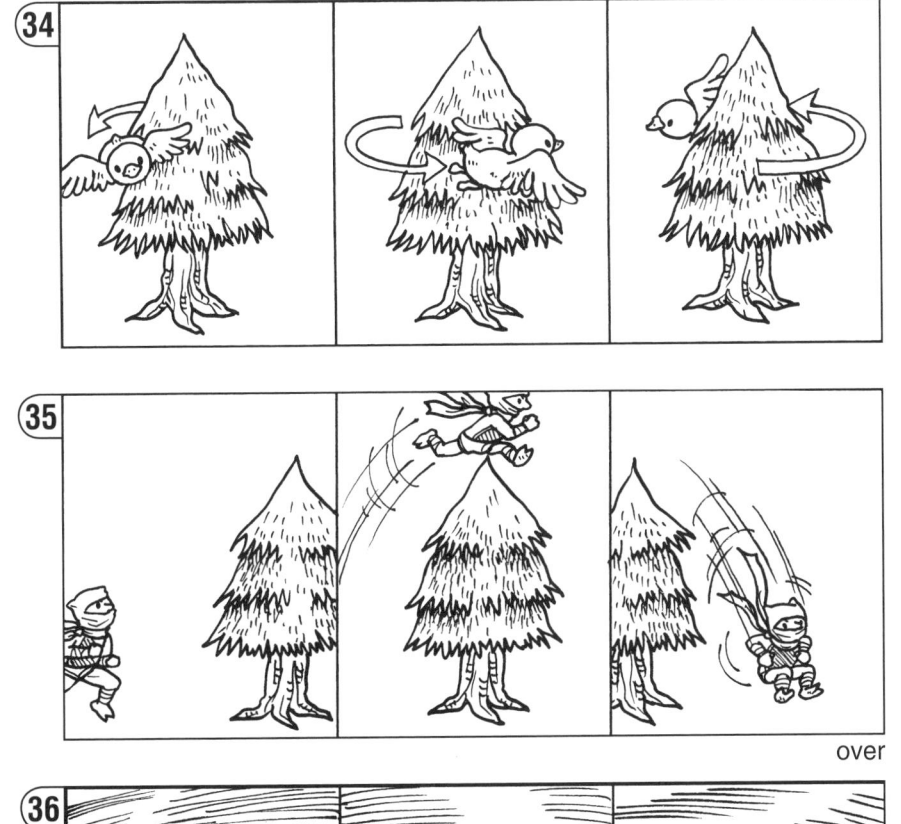

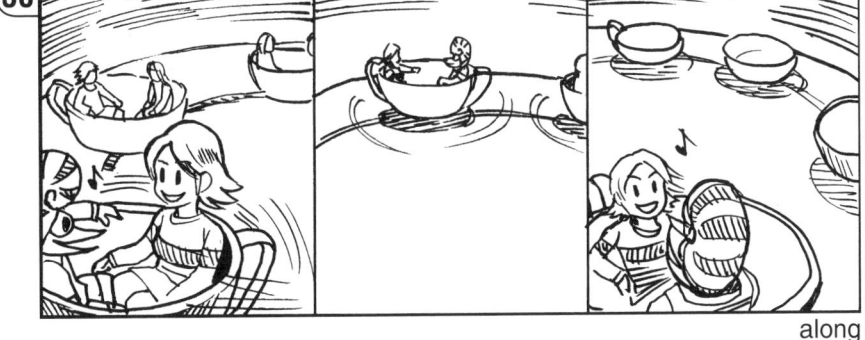

34 The bird is flying around the tree.
35 The ninja jumped over the tree.
36 The cup is turning around as it moves along the edge of the circle.
　 Ruby and Nautilus are turning around as they move along the edge of the circle.

… around：面と見る

②見て回る **look around**

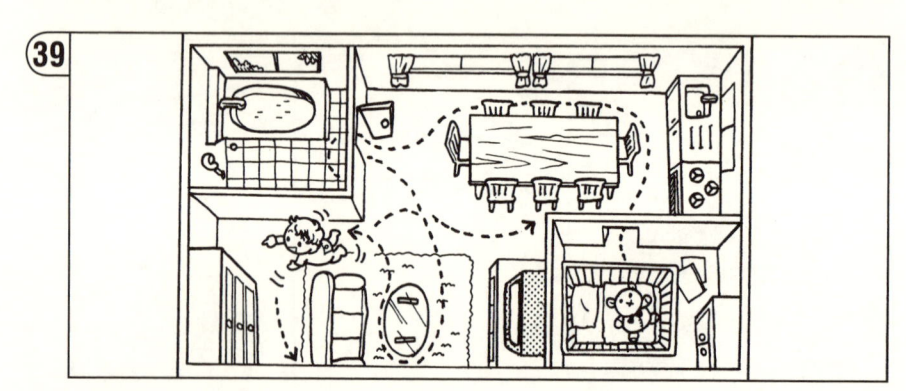

37　Bowsheeman is looking/walking around the house.
38　Bowsheeman is looking around the house.
39　Baby is looking/walking all around the house.

③ 調べ回る look over

40 Goroki is looking the house over.
41 Goroki is looking all over the house.
42 The thief is looking the house over.

about：面と見る

①境界内をあちこち回る about

run **about**

fly **about**

look **about** the table

1　The children are running about.
2　The birds and insects are flying about helter-skelter.
3　Papa is looking about the table for his key.

② around と比べる

run around

fly around

look around the table

---

4 The children are running around.
5 The birds and insects are flying around.
6 Papa is looking around the table for his key.

… **about**：面と見る

③境界内のあちこちにいる／ある **about**

about the table

7　The sea munchkins are standing about the table.
8　The chairs are scattered about the table.
9　Tim has tossed papers about the room.
10　The dolls are sitting about the room.
11　The cars are racing about the room.

④ around と比べる

around the table

12 The sea munchkins are standing around the table.
14 Tim has tossed papers around the chair.
15 The dolls are sitting around the room.
13 The chairs are set around the table.
16 The cars are racing around the track.

① およその about と around

17　About/Around 8:00 AM, Mama and Papa eat breakfast.
18　The tree's shadow is shortest about/around noon.
　　It is shortest at noon.
19　It takes about/around two hours to get there.
20　b. Sylvia is about ready to go.　　c. Sylvia is ready to go.

【Ⅱ】連想するイメージ 371

21 There are about fifteen sea munchkins.
22 There are around fifteen sea munchkins.
23 There are about four mice in the ceiling.
24 There are around four mice in the attic.
25 From his voice the old man sounds about sixty years old.
26 The old man looks to be around sixty years old.

372 ··· about：面と見る
①「およそ〜について」の about（1）

27　They are talking about their robot toys.
28　This is a book about Ms. Flower.
29　This is a book about outer space.

② on, over と比べる

on

over

over

30 Dr. Bizarro is giving a speech on the robot/on his robot project.
31 b, c. Papa is worried over/about his taxes.
   b, c. Papa is worrying over/about his taxes.
32 Albert and Butch are fighting over Sylvia.

③「およそ〜について」の about (2)

33 Teria is talking about her trip around Japan.
34 c. Mama is speaking with Tim about his fight with Olivia.
35 Butch is thinking about/of Sylvia.
   Sylvia is on his mind.

④ of と比べる

36 Albert is talking of/about love philosophically.
37 Speak of Teria and she shows up.
38 Candy is thinking of/about Bowsheeman.
   Bowsheeman is on/in her mind.

376 ··· between / among：面と見る

①2つの間にいる / ある between

1 between Mama and Grandma

2

3 BAY city / BAY Island

4 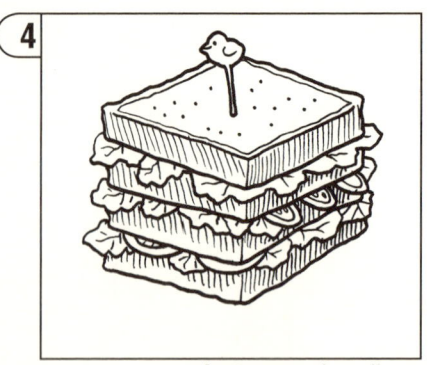 between the slices

5

6

1. Teria is standing between Mama and Grandma.
2. The mouse is between the bottle and the vase.
3. The airplane is flying between Bay Island and Bay City.
4. There is lettuce/are vegetables between/among the slices (of bread).
5. A ninja is peeking between the slats of the fence.
6. There are frogs between the turtles.

② 3つ以上の間にいる / ある among

among the other dolls

among the horses

7　There is a frog doll among the other dolls.
8　Teria is among the crowd.
9　Earth is among the other planets.
10　There are (some) zebras among the horses.
11　There are (some) rotten apples among the good ones.
12　There are (some) houses among the trees.

378 between / among：面と見る

①2つの間にいる／ある

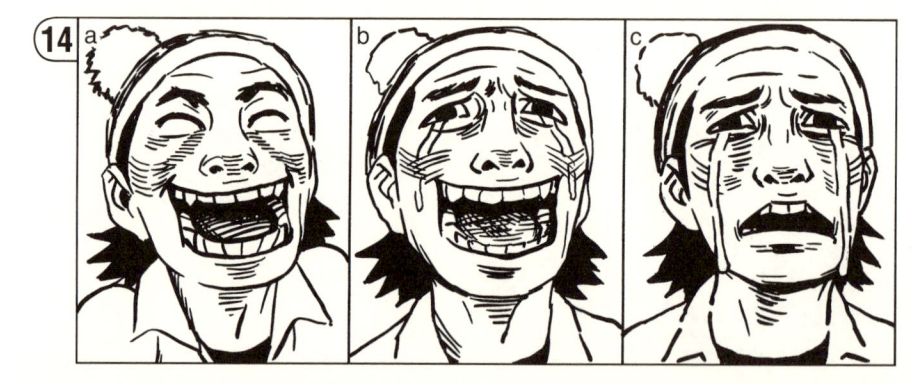

13　Teria is between large and small in size.
14　b. Bowsheeman is between joy and tears.
15　Teria knitted between 8:00 PM and 2:00 AM.
　　Teria knitted from 8:00 PM to 2:00 AM.

【Ⅱ】連想するイメージ 379

16 There is a fight between Butch and Albert over Sylvia.
17 There is great love between Pooch and Kitten.
18 b. Tim and Olivia are keeping a secret (between them).
   There is a secret between Tim and Olivia.
   Tim and Olivia have a secret.

between / among：面と見る

②仲間うちで

19 Some among/of the boys are kicking a soccer ball.
20 A fight has broken out among the ninjas.
   The ninjas are fighting among themselves.
21 Oton divided/distributed the tangerines among the people.

【Ⅱ】連想するイメージ 381

among themselves

among themselves

among themselves

22　The boys are kicking a soccer ball among themselves.
23　The ninjas are fighting among themselves.
24　The musicians are sharing the instruments (among themselves).

between / among：面と見る

③仲間うちで分ける

among themselves

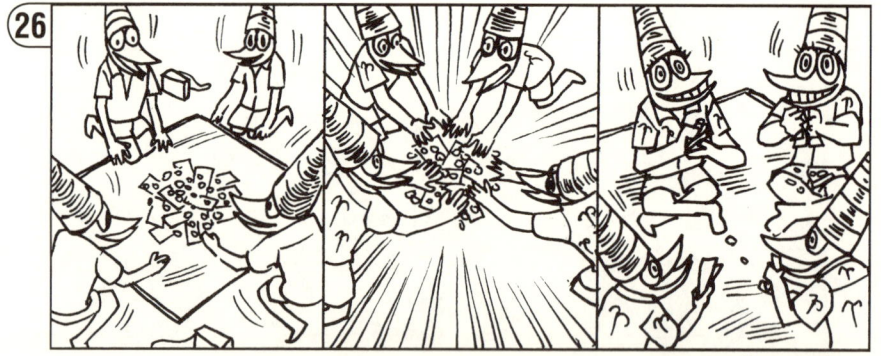

among themselves

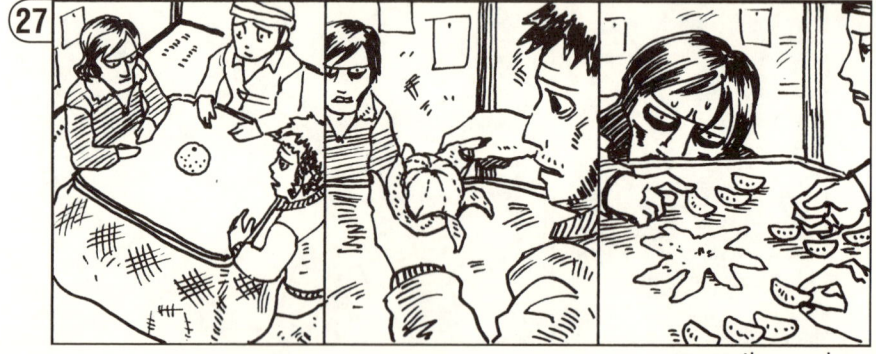

among themselves

25　The monkeys divided the money among themselves.
26　The sea munchkins divided the money among themselves.
27　Bowsheeman and his friends divided a tangerine among themselves.

28 ⑤ Between them, Tim and Olivia had enough money to buy some juice.
   ⑨ They shared the juice between them/themselves.

between / among：面と見る

④異なった力を合わせる

among

among

among themselves

29 The monkeys only made two hundred dollars among them.
   Among them, they only managed to make two hundred dollars.

30 The sea munchkins only made 175 dollars among them.

31 The boys are playing soccer (together), while the girls are skipping rope among themselves.
   The boys are playing apart from the girls.

between   between themselves

together

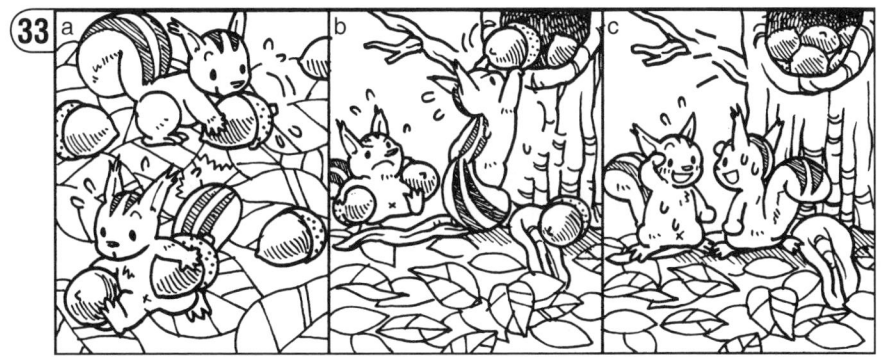

32 ⑤ Between them, the squirrels gathered many acorns.
　 ⑥ They shared the acorns between themselves.

33 a. The squirrels are gathering the acorns together.
　 c. They gathered the acorns together.

between / among：面と見る

①異なった力を合わせる among

among

against

34　Teria's family is camping.
　　Among them, they can manage all the tasks.
35　Teria's family is building a dog house.
　　Among them, they have all the necessary skills.
36　The ninjas and sea munchkins are fighting (against each other).

②一緒に〜する together

37 Together, Teria and her friends managed to roll the boulder off the road.
38 a. The farmers are picking tangerines together.
   c. The farmers have gathered the tangerines together.
39 The three musicians are playing together.

between / among：面と見る
③間にある among と中にある in

(40) among / in

(41) among

(42) in

(43) among / in

(44) among

(45) in

40 There is a house among/in the trees.
41 There is a house among the trees.
42 There is a bird in the tree.
43 There is a village among/in the hills.
44 There is a house among the flowers.
45 There is a bench in the garden.

46 among / in
49 among / in
47 among
50 among
48 in
51 in

46 There is a frog among the turtles.
   There is a frog in the group of turtles.
47 There are (some) frogs among the turtles.
48 There is a frog in the middle/the center of the turtles.
49 There is a keyboard player among the musicians. [in the band, in the group]
50 There are (a couple of) soccer balls among the basketballs.
51 There is a soccer ball in the square.

①境界内で一緒になり共に動いている with

with Tim

1. Olivia is walking with Tim.
2. Teria is playing ball with her friends.
3. Tim is playing with Pooch.

【Ⅰ】基本のイメージ 391

with Sylvia

4　The animals are singing with Sylvia.
　　Sylvia and her animal friends are singing with each other/together.
5　Mama is talking with a neighbor.
6　Grandma is (visiting) with her family.
　　Grandma is visiting (with) her family.

392 ··· with：面と見る

②手と共に動いている with

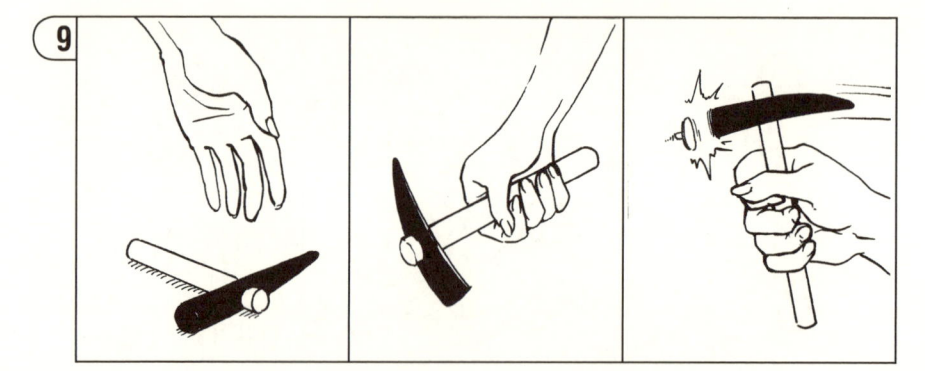

with swords

7　The ninjas are fighting with swords.
8　Sylvia is washing her hair with shampoo.
9　He pounded the nail in with a hammer.

【Ⅰ】基本のイメージ 393

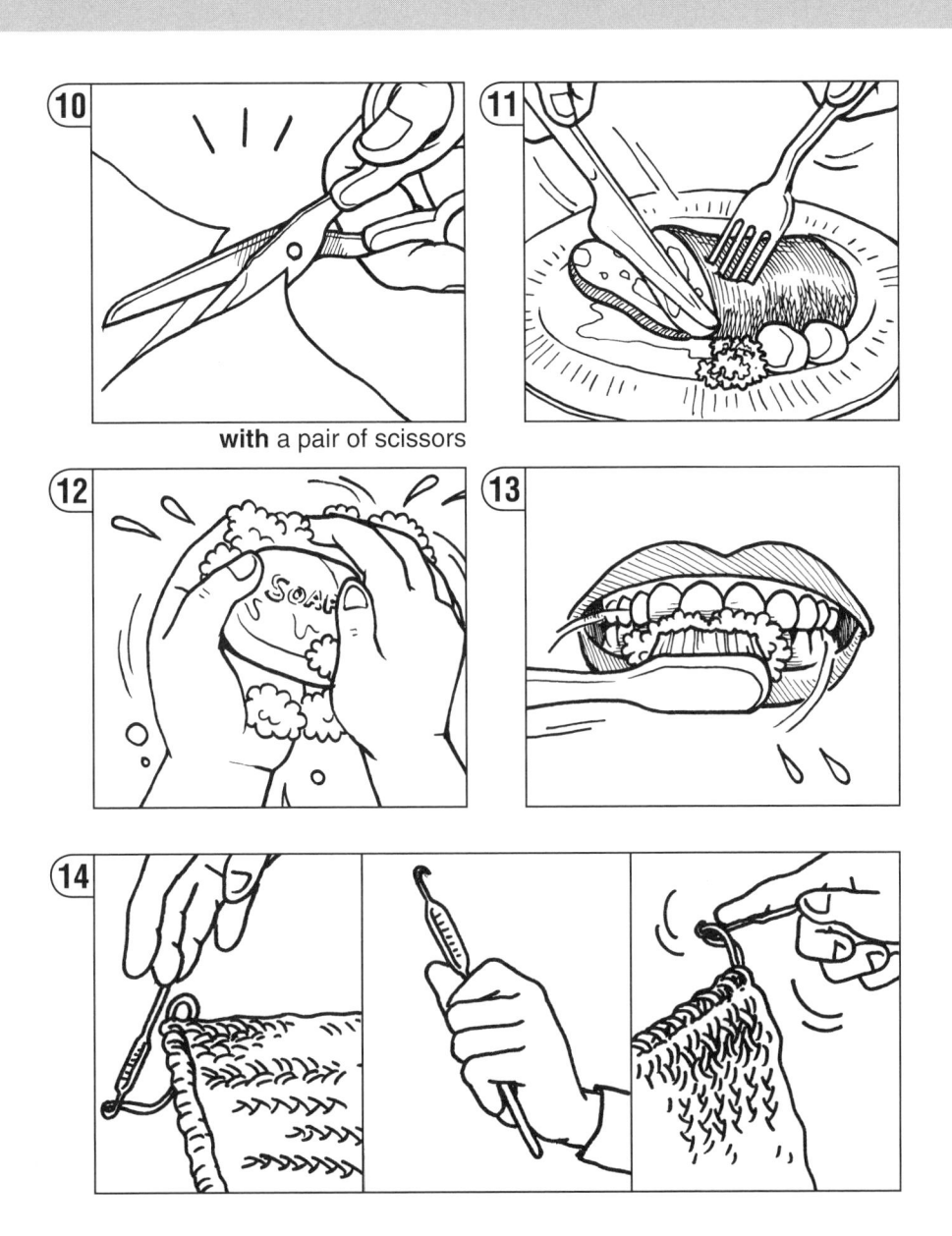

with a pair of scissors

10 He is cutting the paper with a pair of scissors.
11 She is eating with a knife and fork.
12 She is washing her hands with soap.
13 She is brushing her teeth with toothpaste/ a tooth brush.
14 She is knitting with a crochet hook.

① 共に動いている

15 b. Butch is sending his picture with the letter.
　　c. Butch is sending his picture through the mail/by mail.　　His picture is in the mail.
16 Someone is mixing flour with milk.
17 Albert and Sylvia are in love with each other.
　　Sylvia is in love with Albert.

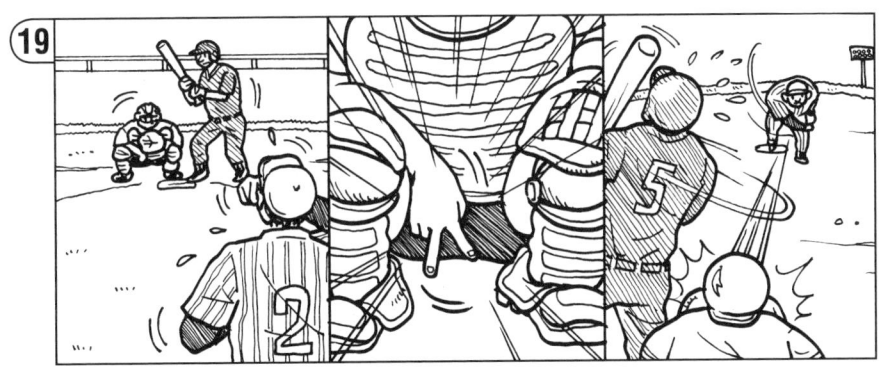

18 Mama always agrees with Papa.
19 The catcher is communicating with hand signals.
20 Something is wrong with Candy.

with：面と見る

①共に動いている

BE GENTLE WITH THE BABY!

21 Dr. Bizarro is being careful with the test tube.
22 Mama told Olivia to be gentle with the baby.
23 c. Teria is pleased with the ring.

【Ⅱ】連想するイメージ 397

with fear

with great interest

with courage

24 Olivia is trembling with fear.
25 Tim and Olivia are watching TV with great interest.
26 The sea munchkins are fighting with courage against the ninjas.

② 共にある

27 She takes her coffee with cream.
   She takes cream with her coffee.
28 Lunch comes with coffee.
29 With a tip and tax, lunch cost 12 dollars.

30 In the room, there is ...
   a ... a curtain with a stain.
   b ... a finger with a bandage.
   c ... a man with glasses.
   d ... a woman with a mud pack.
   e ... a baby with a smile on its face.
   f ... a girl with tears on her face.
      Olivia is in tears.

400　with：面と見る

③共にいる / あるものを強調する

31　b. The bathtub is filling up with sand.
　　c. The bathtub is full of/with sand.　　The bathtub is filled up with sand.
32　c. The room is filled with smoke.
　　The room is full of smoke.
33　Butch is filled with joy/love.

34　The town is covered with snow.
35　c. Kitten is covered with mud.
　　The doormat is splattered with mud.
36　Sylvia is drenched with rain.
　　Sylvia was drenched by the rain.

③共にいる / あるものを強調する

37 Sylvia left Baby with Teria.
38 Tim left a turtle with Mama.
39 Mama left her key with Butch.

【Ⅱ】連想するイメージ 403

compare 〜 with 〜

compare 〜 with 〜

compare 〜 **to** 〜

40 a, b. Olivia is comparing the strawberry shortcake with the muffin.
41 a, b. Butch is comparing the love story with the action movie.
42 Butch compared Sylvia to a rose.

①共に動いている with と逆らう against

43　The boat is moving with the wind.
44　The boat is moving with the current.
45　Bowsheeman is moving along with the crowd.

【Ⅲ】イメージを比べる 405

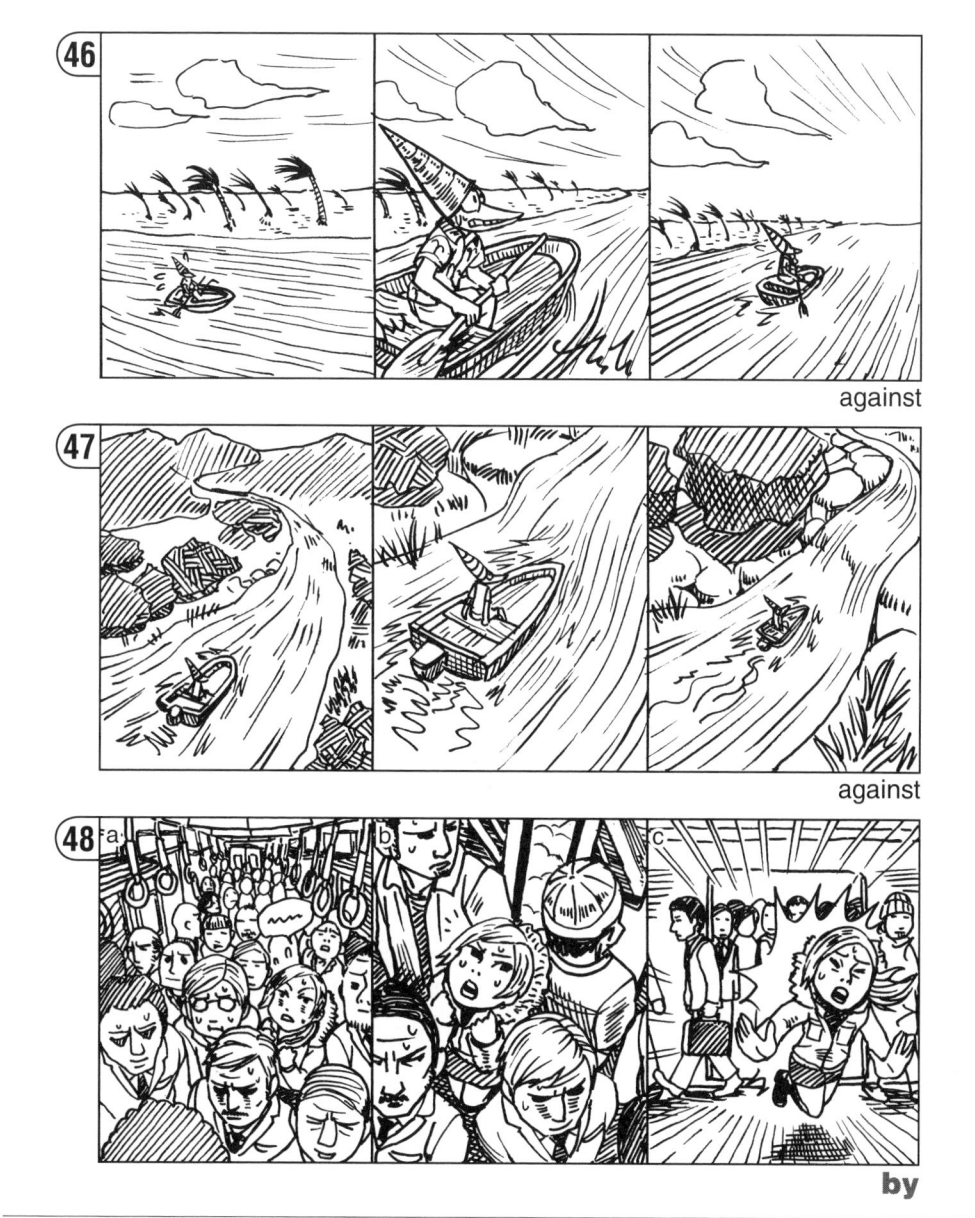

against

against

by

46　The boat is sailing against the wind.
47　The boat is moving against the current.
48　c. Katarina was pushed out by the crowd.

406 ... with：面と見る

②共に動いている with ／ by と比べる

with water

with a hose

with the fire

49 c. Indy flushed out the prairie dogs with water.　The prairie dogs were flushed out by water.
　　Indy is getting rid of the prairie dogs by forcing water into their holes.
50　Indy is getting rid of the prairie dogs by hitting them with a hose.
　　The prairie dogs were hit by the hose.
51　b. Butch is making a fire with branches.　c. Butch is warming his hands with the fire.

【Ⅲ】イメージを比べる 407

by the wind

by the water

by fire

52　The boat is being propelled by the wind.
53　The boat is being moved by the water.
54　They heat their house by fire.

③手段の with, by, in

with

with

by

55 He is drawing graphics with a mouse/his computer.
　 He is drawing graphics by computer.
56 Albert wrote a letter with/using his computer.
57 a. Butch is deciding whether to send his note by E-mail, by fax or by letter.

【Ⅲ】イメージを比べる

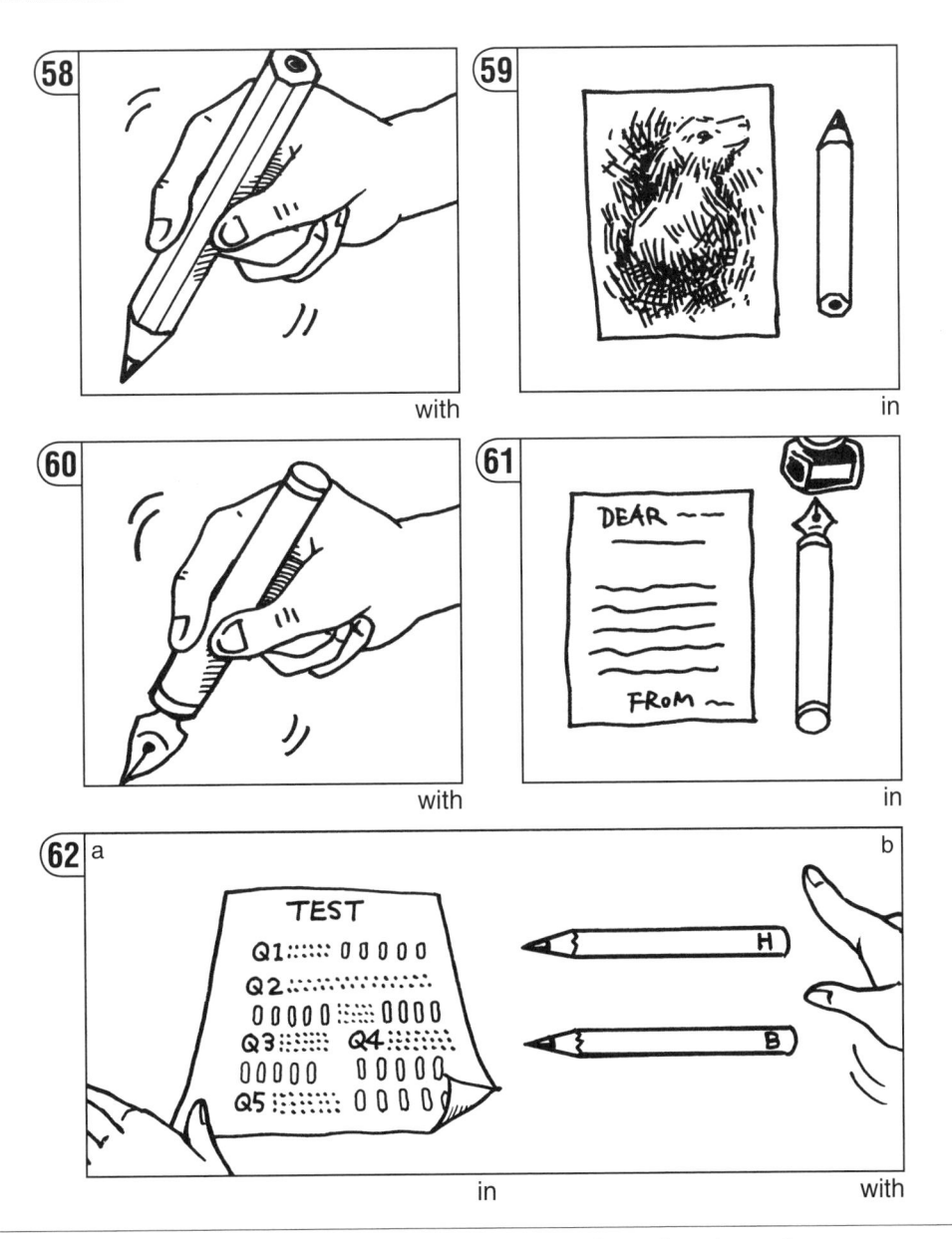

58 with
59 in
60 with
61 in
62 a
   b
   in
   with

58 Someone is drawing/writing with a pencil.
59 The picture is drawn in pencil.
60 Someone is drawing/writing with a pen.
61 The letter is written in ink.
62 a. The mark sheet should be filled out in pencil.
   b. She is going to fill out the mark sheet with a pencil.

① 「〜なしで」の without

without Teria

1 The group is going hiking without Teria.
2 Mama is making soup without meat.
3 The kids are playing without Olivia.

except (for)：線と見る　　【Ⅰ】基本のイメージ　411

①「のぞいて」の except (for)

except (for) Teria

4　Everyone in the group is hiking/climbing except (for) Teria.
5　Mama put everything in the soup except (for) the meat.
6　Everybody is playing except (for) Olivia.

①「異なるものをさらに加えて」の besides

7　Besides/In addition to fish and meat, Albert had a piece of cake for dinner.
8　Besides/In addition to the small robot and the Candy robot, Dr. Bizarro made a cyborg.
9　Besides/In addition to great paintings by Van Gogh and Monet, the Populi Museum has a good coffee shop.
　Besides/In addition to visiting the art museum, they went to a coffee shop.

【Ⅰ】基本のイメージ

besides fish and meat

near

far away

far apart

up

down

Chapter 3
0次元（点）として見なさい

at
to
from
close to
away from
apart from
by
next to

①この時この点にいる／ある at

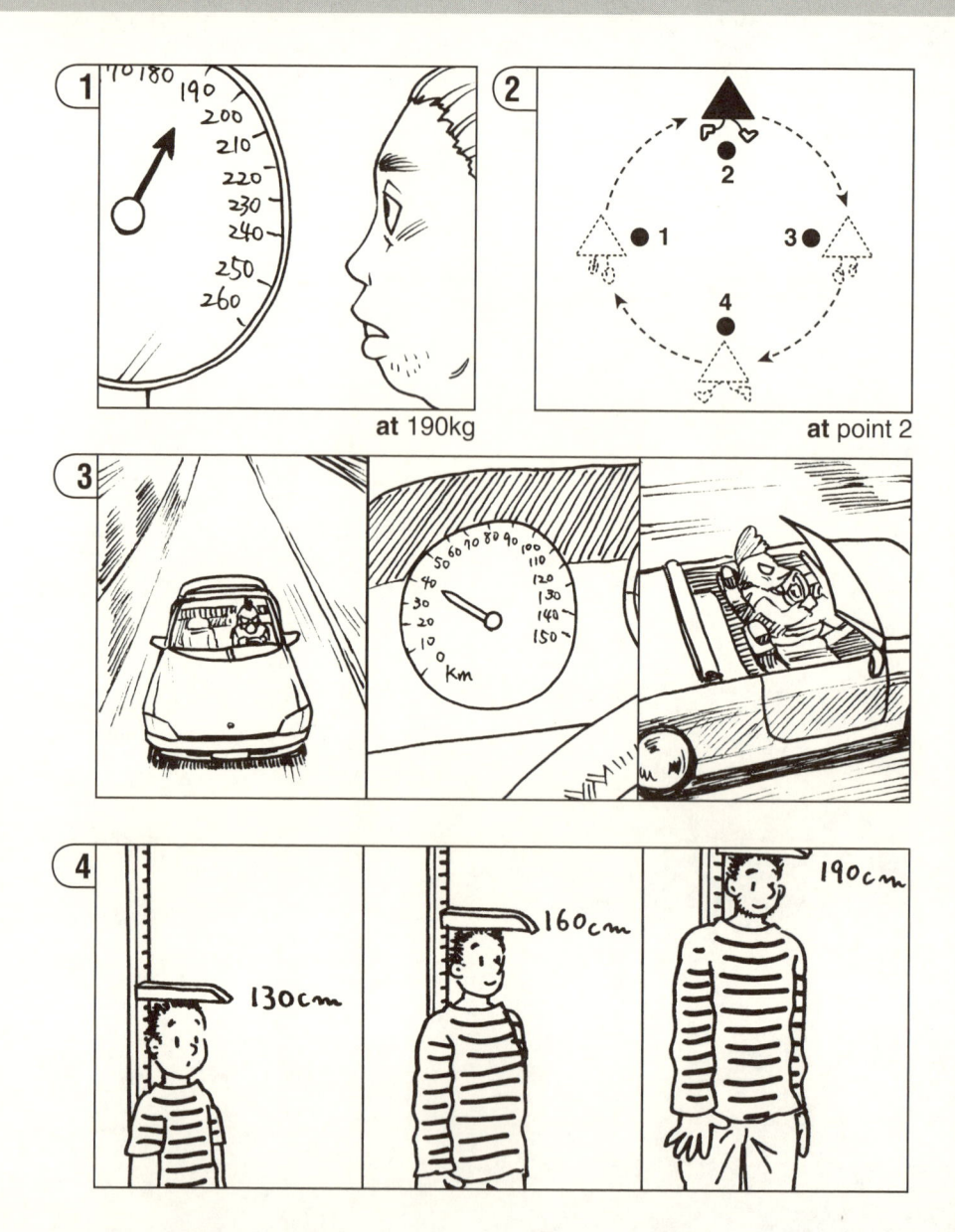

at 190kg

at point 2

1 The scale's pointer is at 190kg.　　2 Mr. T is at point 2.
3 Chickenman (Oton) is driving the car at 40kph.
4 When Butch was six, his height was (at) 130 centimeters, at 12 it was (at) 160 and now it is at 190.

【Ⅰ】基本のイメージ 417

at 20 degrees

at point 1

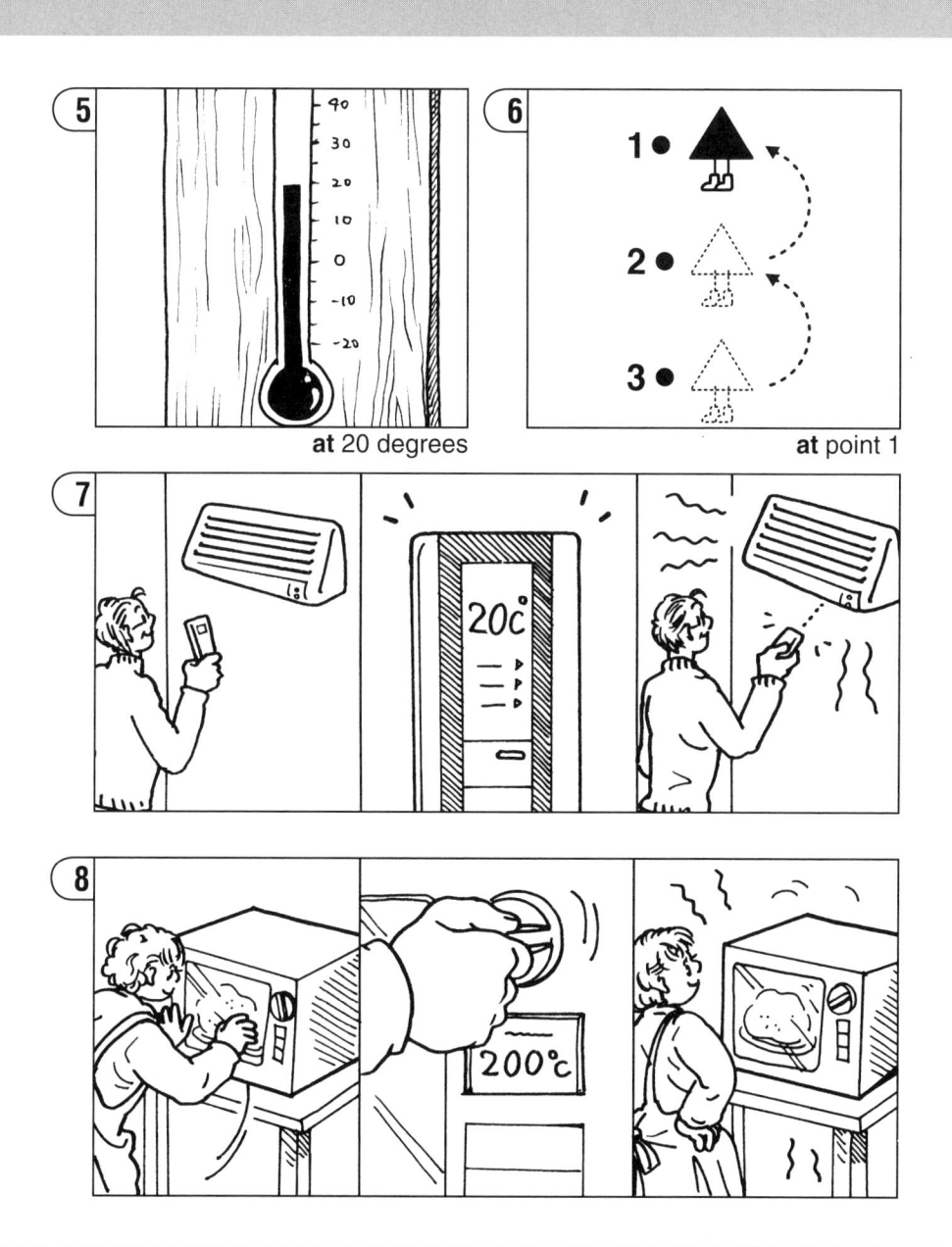

5　The thermometer is at 20 degrees.
6　Mr. T is at point 1.
7　The air conditioner is set at/to 20 degrees.
8　Mama set the microwave (oven) at/to 200 degrees.

②点のあたりにいる / ある at

at his house

9 Doggie is at his house.
10 Doggie is at his house.
11 Doggie is at his house.
12 Bowsheeman is at/under the tree.
13 Bowsheeman is at/under the tree.
14 Bowsheeman is at/under the tree.

【Ⅰ】基本のイメージ 419

at the corner

at the corner

15 Bowsheeman is at the corner.
16 Bowsheeman is at the corner.
17 Bowsheeman is at the corner.
18 Mr. T is at the corner.
19 b. The car is turning (at) the corner.
　　c. The car (has) turned (at) the corner.
　　　The pedestrian (has) turned at the corner.

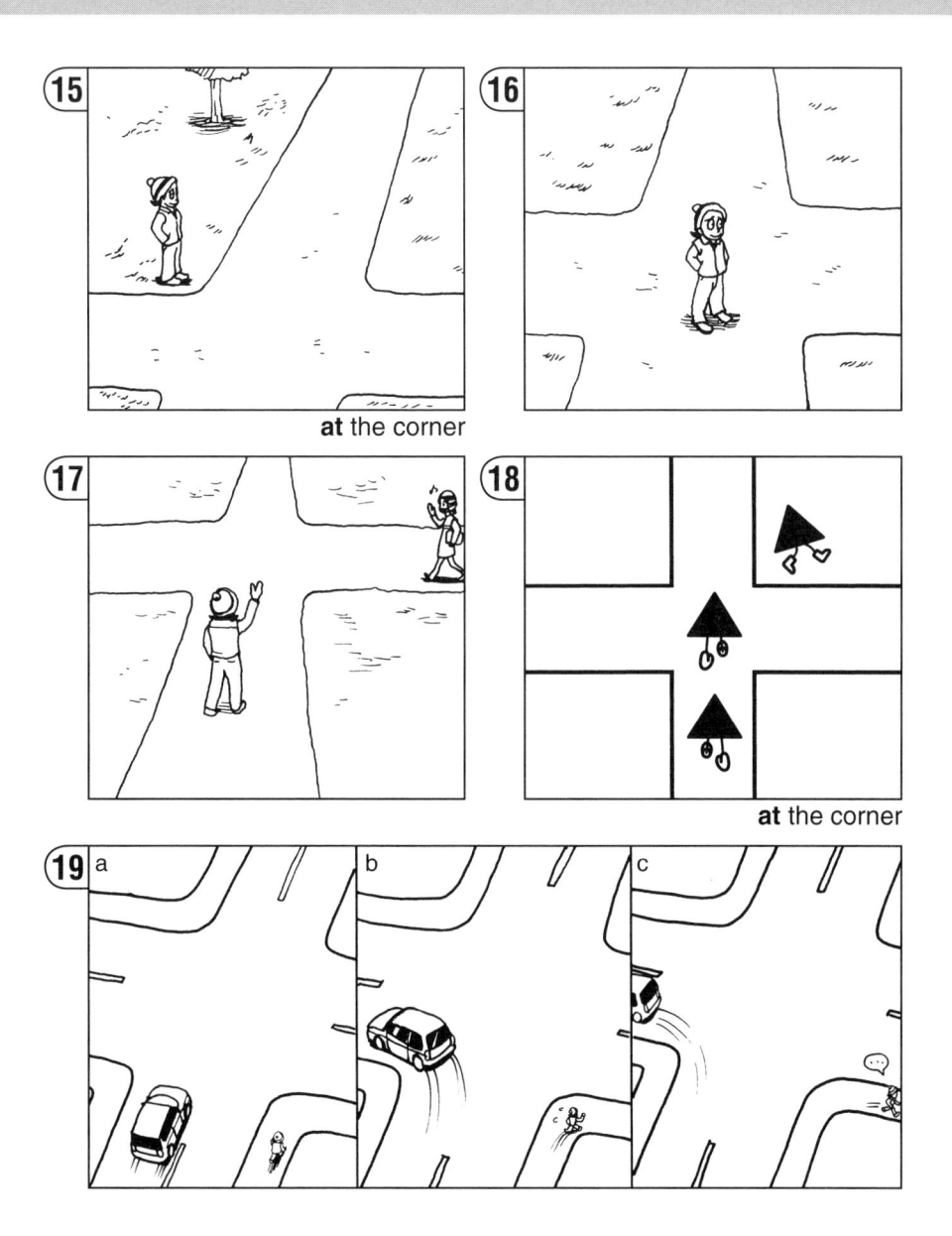

at：点と見る

①この時この点に

20　Teria is at the 50m mark.
21　Teria is almost at the 20km mark.
22　Teria is at point B on the ski slope.

23 The exchange rate is at 100.2 yen per dollar.
24 Sylvia got the flowers at 15 cents each.
25 The house finally sold at $500,000.

①この時この点に

at first

at war

at work

26 ① At first, Tim didn't know how to pay for/buy a turtle.
At first, Tim didn't have enough money to pay for/buy a turtle.
27　The wood munchkins and the sea munchkins are at war.
29　a, b. Bakunsai is hard at work.

at last

at peace

at rest

26 ⑥ At last, Tim was able to afford one.

28 The wood munchkins and the sea munchkins are at peace.

30 c. The ball is now at rest.

424 … at：点と見る

①この時この点に

31 Today Butch is at his best.
32 Bowsheeman is at his best today, too.
33 Jorge is at the top of his class.

34 Today Butch is at his worst.
35 Mr. Gold is at the bottom of his depression.
36 Ken is at the bottom of his class.

② 視線が点にある

37 b. Teria is looking at the old man.　c. Teria looked at the old man.
38 Bowsheeman is staring at the cobra.
39 c. Bakunsai threw his shuriken at the shogun.

【Ⅱ】連想するイメージ 427

point **to**

40 The kids are pointing at Tim.
41 The passengers are pointing at the smelly bum.
42 b. The guard is pointing to Dr. Bizarro.

②視線が点にある

43 Candy is aiming her water pistol at Bowsheeman.
44 b. Mama is running at Papa.   c. Mama is running after Papa.
45 A strange man came at Katarina.
   A strange man came up to Katarina.

46 Tim threw the ball at Olivia.
47 Candy threw a knife at Bowsheeman.
48 The crowd threw rice at the newlyweds.

③心が点にある

49 a, b. Mama is smiling at Baby.
50 Teria is laughing at Tim.
51 Teria is angry at Tim.

52 Bowsheeman is happy at the news.
53 Teria was surprised at Kitten.
54 Teria is embarrassed at being kissed.

③心が点にある

55 In gymnastics, Butch is good at the rings.
56 Bakunsai is skillful at using chopsticks.
57 Teria's boyfriend is pleased at/with/by her reaction.

【Ⅱ】連想するイメージ 433

with

58 Butch is bad at pole vaulting.
59 Yasu is not skillful at using chopsticks.
60 Teria is pleased with the ring.

434 … at：点と見る

④ここに目的がある / by と比べる

61 b, c. Sylvia is at the telephone.
62 b. Papa is at the bus stop.
63 Ruby is at the sea/beach/ocean.

【Ⅱ】連想するイメージ 435

64
- a
- b at
- c

65 TELEPHONE by

66 by

67 by

68 by

64 b. Ruby is hanging the Christmas stockings at the fireplace.
    c. The Christmas stockings are hung at/on the fireplace.

65 Sylvia is by the telephone.
    [near, next to, close to, beside, at]

66 The children's stockings are scattered by the fireplace.
    [around, about, near, close to, beside, at]

67 Nautilus is by/at the sea.

68 Ruby is by the shore/on the beach. [by/at the sea]

436 … at：点と見る

⑤ここに目的がある

69　There are a lot of people at/on the beach.
　　Children are playing at/on the beach.
70　Bowsheeman is at the beach.
71　Ruby is on the beach.
72　Ruby is walking along the shore/the beach.

【Ⅱ】連想するイメージ 437

at school

on

73 Maria is at school.
74 Toby is at the university.
75 Papa is at a picnic.
76 Teria is on a picnic.

438 ... at：点と見る

⑤ここに目的がある

meet at

77　Where shall we meet?
　　Where should we meet?

78 Sylvia met Albert at the museum.
79 Sylvia met Albert at her office.
80 Sylvia met Albert at the subway turnstiles/ticket gate/wicket.

⑥ そこにいる / ある

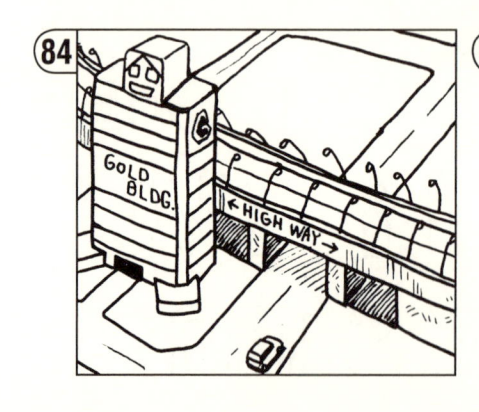

81　Where is the Gold Building?　(It's) at the highway.
82　The theater is on 2nd Avenue at 2nd Street.
83　Gold Books is on 2nd Avenue at 1st Street.
84　The Gold Building is at/next to the highway.
85　The Gold Building is by/behind/next to the highway.

【Ⅱ】連想するイメージ 441

86 Ruby's house is at/on the beach.
87 The Corn Tower is at the lake.
88 The high school is at/on the corner.
89 The Corn Tower is on/near the lake.

on

⑦ そのあたりにいる / ある

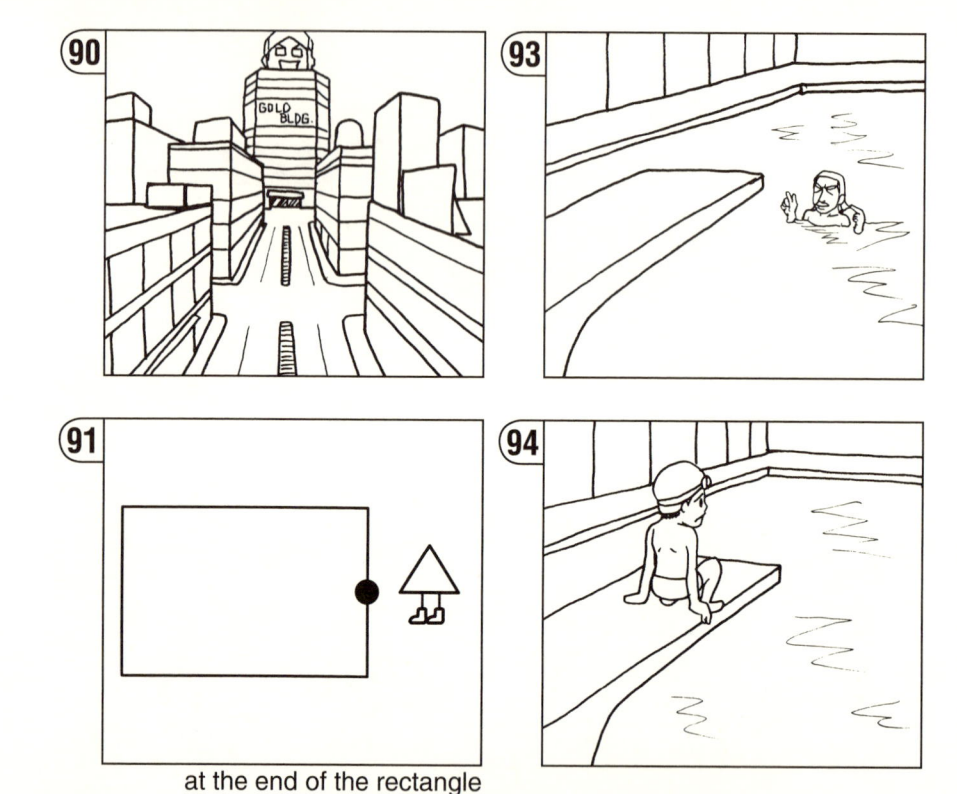

⑨¹ at the end of the rectangle

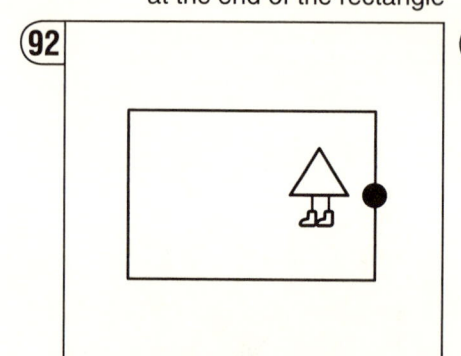

⑨² at the end of the rectangle

90　The Gold Building is at the end of the street.

91　Mr. T is at the end of the rectangle.

92　Mr. T is at the end of the rectangle.

93　Bakunsai is at the end of the diving board. [near, by, close to, next to, beside]

94　Yasu is at the end of the diving board. [near, by, close to, next to, on]

95　Yasu and Bakunsai are at either end of the diving board.

【Ⅱ】連想するイメージ 443

96 Bowsheeman is at the end of the teeter-totter. [near, by, close to, next to, beside]
97 Bowsheeman is at the end of the teeter-totter. [near, close to, on]
98 Candy and Bowsheeman are at either end of the teeter-totter. [near, close to, on]
99 Bowsheeman is at the beginning/end of the bridge. [near, by, close to, next to, beside]
100 Bowsheeman is at the beginning/end of the bridge. [near, by, close to, next to, on]
101 Nautilus and Ruby are at either end of the bridge.

444 … at：点と見る

⑦ そのあたりにいる / ある

102 The house is at the top of the mountain. [near, by, close to]
104 Teria is at/near the bottom of the hill.
106 Bowsheeman is at/by the side of the car.
There are two doors on the side of the car.
103 Teria is at/near the top of the stairs.
105 Teria is at/near the bottom of the stairs.
107 There is a pencil on the paper.
There is an eraser beside/near the paper.
The eraser is at the side of the paper.

【Ⅱ】連想するイメージ 445

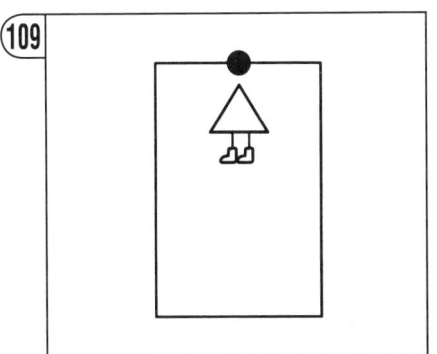

at the top of the rectangle

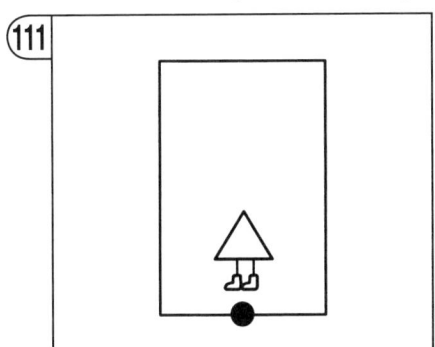

at the bottom of the rectangle

beside

108 The word "SCOOP" is at the top of the page.
110 The rabbit is at the bottom of the page.
112 The bird and the dog are beside Indy.　They are on either side of Indy.
　　 The bird is to Indy's left.　The bird is on Indy's left side.
109 Mr. T is at the top of the rectangle.
111 Mr. T is at the bottom of the rectangle.

⑦ そのあたりにいる / ある

113 a, b. The monkey is at the cookie can.
    c. The monkey has gotten into the cookie can.
114 Papa is washing his car at his house/at home.
115 Papa is at home.

【Ⅱ】連想するイメージ 447

at hand

at hand

on hand

116 Grandma keeps her glasses at hand.
117 Bakunsai keeps his sword at hand.
118 Mama (always) keeps milk on hand.

⑧そのあたりを強調する

119 Bakunsai shot at the bird.
120 The wild dog bit at Butch.
121 Albert shot the gun at/towards the sky.

⑨ at を使わない!

122 Bakunsai shot the bird.
123 The wild dog bit Butch.
124 Teria shot the fireworks into the sky.

450 … at：点と見る

①この時この点にいる arrive at

at

125 b. The airplane is now arriving at Gold Airport.
   It will soon go on to Nautilus Island.
126 b. The train has arrived at Cold Station.
   It is going on to Wood Town.
127 b. Teria arrived at the office at 9:00 a.m.

②着いている場所を強調する arrive in

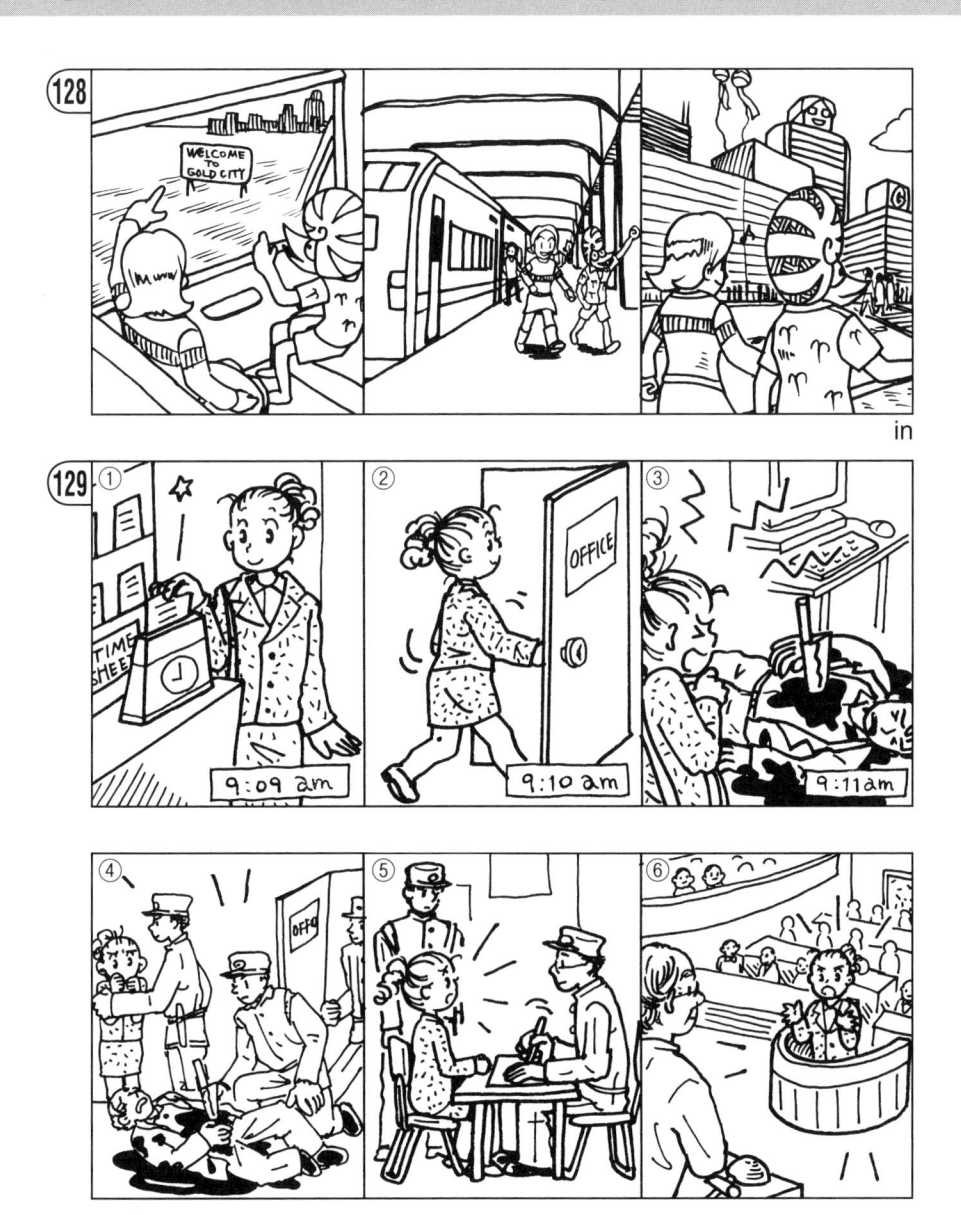

128 Ruby and Nautilus have arrived in Gold City.
129 ⑤⑥ Teria testified that she arrived in the office at 9:10 a.m.

③この時この点にいる work at

at

130 Kaede works at the hospital.　　Kaede works at Gold Hospital.
　　Kaede works for Gold Hospital.
131 Katarina works at an office.
　　Katarina works for Cold Inc.
132 Oton works at the Bizarro Laboratory.　　Oton works for Dr. Bizarro's Laboratory.

④サポートする work for と属する work in

133 Teria works for ABC Hospital.
　　Olivia: Where do you work?
　　Teria: I work at/for ABC Hospital.
134 Teria works for Office Teria.
135 Teria works for ZXY Laboratory.

136 Teria is working in the hospital.
137 Teria is working in her office.
138 Teria is working in the laboratory.

454 ... at：点と見る

⑤ 目的がある at と状況の中にいる in

at the jail

at the church

at the school

139 Goroki's wife is at the jail.
　　Goroki is in jail.
140 c. The wedding was at/in the church.
141 Mama is at the school.

【Ⅲ】イメージを比べる　455

in jail

in / at church

in / at school

142 Goroki is in jail.
143 The people are in/at church.
144 The kids are in/at school.

⑥目的がある at/by と比べる

at

at

at

145 b, c. The mailman is at the door.
146 b, c. Olivia is at the elephant cage.
147 b, c. The family is at the table.

148 Grandma is by the door.
149 Grandma is by the door.
150 There is a baby standing by the elephant.
   [near, next to, close to, beside]
151 There is a baby standing by the elephant.
   [near, next to, close to, in front of]
152 Olivia is by the table.
   [near, next to, close to, in front of]
153 Olivia is by the table.
   [near, next to, close to, beside]

⑦ 目的がある at / in, on と比べる

154 a. Dr. Bizarro is by the table.[near, next to, close to, in front of]
　b, c. Dr. Bizarro is at the table.

155 Some sea munchkins are at the statue (of Nautilus's grandfather).

156 Bowsheeman is at the station.

【Ⅲ】イメージを比べる

157 in

158 on

159 in

160 on

161 in

162 on the platform

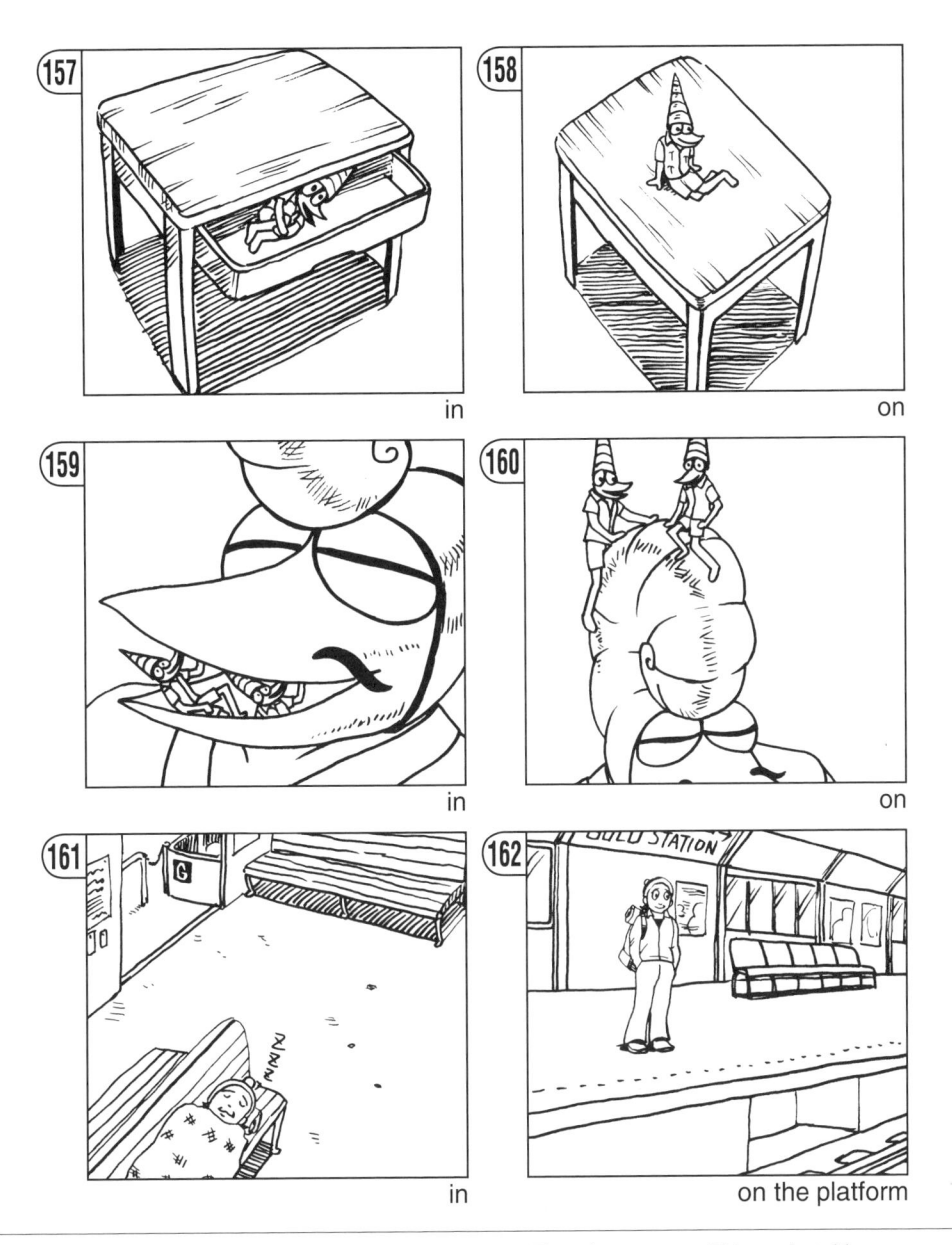

157 There is a sea munchkin in the table.
159 The sea munchkins are in (the mouth of) the statue (of Nautilus's grandfather).
161 Bowsheeman is in the station.

158 There is a sea munchkin on the table.
160 The sea munchkins are on the statue (of Nautilus's grandfather).
162 Bowsheeman is on the platform.

⑧攻撃的な at / to と比べる

run at the matador

talk at

yell at

163 The bull ran at the matador.
164 Everybody is talking at Teria.
165 c. The man/The neighbor is yelling at Tim.

come to the farmer

talk to

yell to

166 The cow came to the farmer.
167 Papa is talking to Mama.
168 c. Grandma is yelling to Baby.

⑨ at と on (1)

at

at

at

169 c. The elephant is at the highest pillar.
170 c. The toy is at the top of the pyramid.
171 c. The snail turned left at the top of the footstool. [when it reached the top of the footstool]

【Ⅲ】イメージを比べる

172 (on)	175 (at)
173 (on)	176 (at)
174 (on)	177 (at)

172 The elephant is on (the) top of the pillar.
173 The toy is on (the) top of the pyramid.
174 The snail is on the top of the footstool.
　　The snail is on the footstool.
175 The sea munchkin is at the top of the pillar/pole. [near, by, close to]
176 The sea munchkin is at the top of the pyramid. [near, by, close to]
177 The sea munchkin is at the top of the footstool. [near, by, close to]

⑩ at/on the top of

(178) at the top of

(179) on (the) top of

(180)

(181)

(182)

(183) on top of

178 The dragonfly is at the top of the pole.
   [near, by, close to]
180 The cloud is at the top of the mountain.
   [near, by, close to]
182 Teria is at the top of the mountain.
   [near, by, close to]

179 The dragonfly is on (the) top of the pole.
   [at the top of]
181 The cloud is on (the) top of the mountain.
   [at the top of]
183 Teria is on top of the mountain.
   [at the top of]

⑪ at と on (2)

184 a. Nautilus is at/near the top of the stairs.　Nautilus is near the stairs.
　　b. Bowsheeman is on/at the top of/near the stairs.
　　c. A sea munchkin is at/near the top of the stairs.
　　d. Dora is on the stairs.
　　e. Candy is at/near the bottom of the stairs.　Candy is on the bottom stair.
　　f. Doggie is at/near the bottom of the stairs.　Doggie is near the stairs.

⑫ at / on / in the bottom of

at

at

at the bottom

185 The cups are at the bottom of the cupboard.
186 The submarine is at the bottom of the sea.
187 Mr. Gold is at the bottom of his depression.

【Ⅲ】イメージを比べる

188 The paper towels are on the bottom of the cupboard.
189 The furnace is in the bottom of the building.
190 There is seaweed growing on the bottom of the sea.
191 The seashell is in/at the bottom of the sea.
192 Bowsheeman is on top of the world.

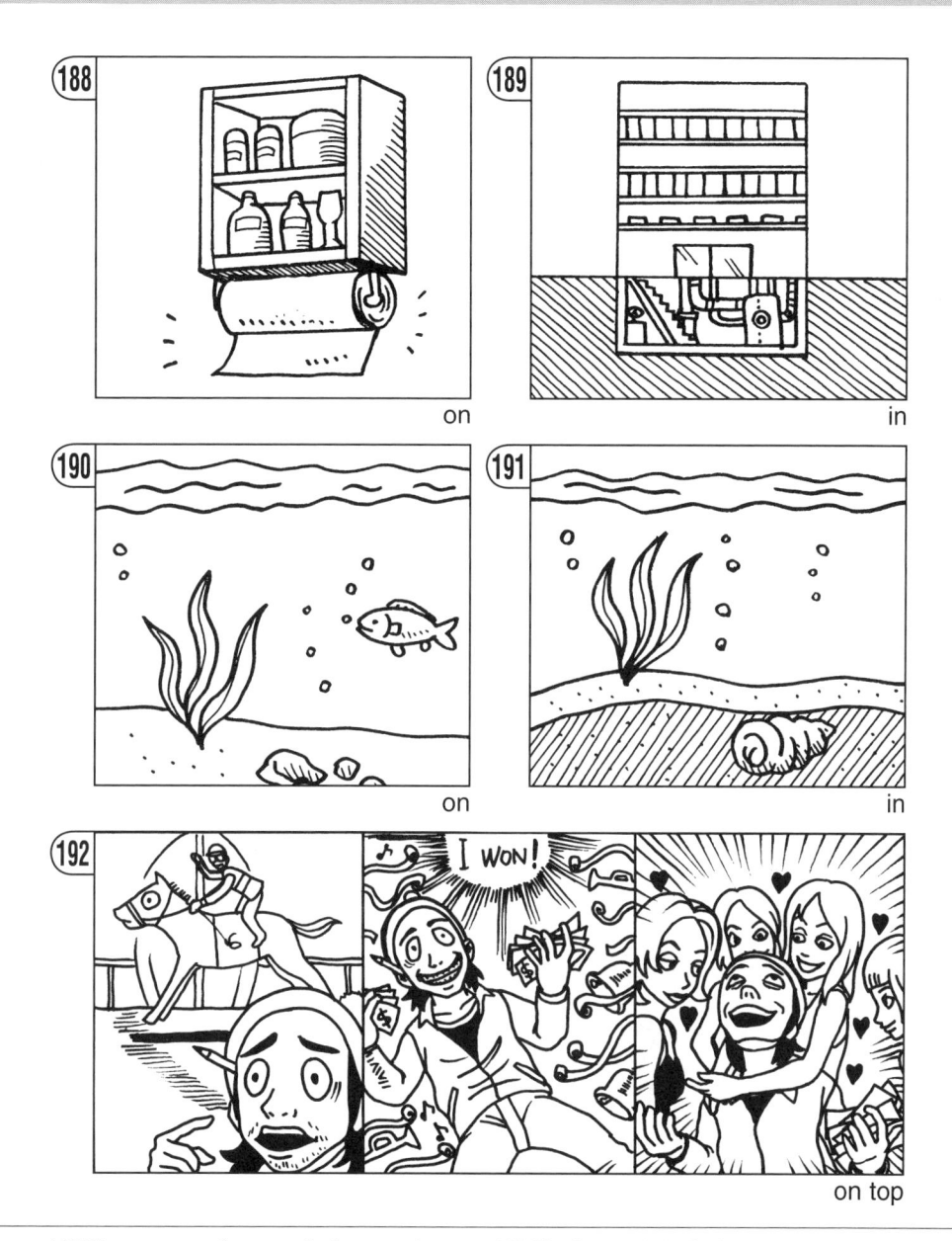

⑬ at / on the side of

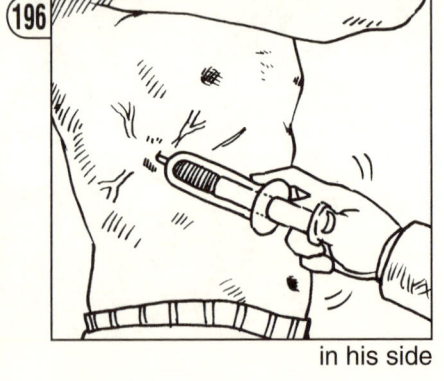

at / on

at his side

on his side

in his side

193 His kiosk is at/on the side of the street.
194 Ruby's picture is always at Nautilus's side.
　　Nautilus keeps Ruby's picture at his side.
195 There is a lizard on Indy's side.
196 The doctor gave Indy a shot in his side.

⑭ at, in, by

【Ⅲ】イメージを比べる 469

197 a. One of the sea munchkins is at Candy's left side.
   One of the sea munchkins is on Candy's left.
   b. There is an arrow in Candy's left side.
   c. There is a trash can by Candy. [behind, in back of, near, close to, next to]

①点に着いている to

to her

1. Teria threw the ball to Olivia.
2. Butch gave some flowers to Sylvia.
3. The space ship flew to Mars.

to the edge of the water

4 Teria walked/ran to the edge of the water.
5 The bird flew to the hole in the tree trunk.
6 The plane flew to the island.

②点へ向かっている to

to school

7 Chicori went to school.
8 Leaf went to Populi.
9 It is 2km to Lorell City.

10 Teria sent a letter to Grandma.
11 The lifeguard came/went to the child's aid.
12 a. Inond is going to the Army.　b. Inond is in the Army.

①〜に着いている

13 Papa ran to Mama.
14 Nautilus walked up to Ruby.
   Nautilus caught up with Ruby.
15 Okan threw a spear to Bakunsai.

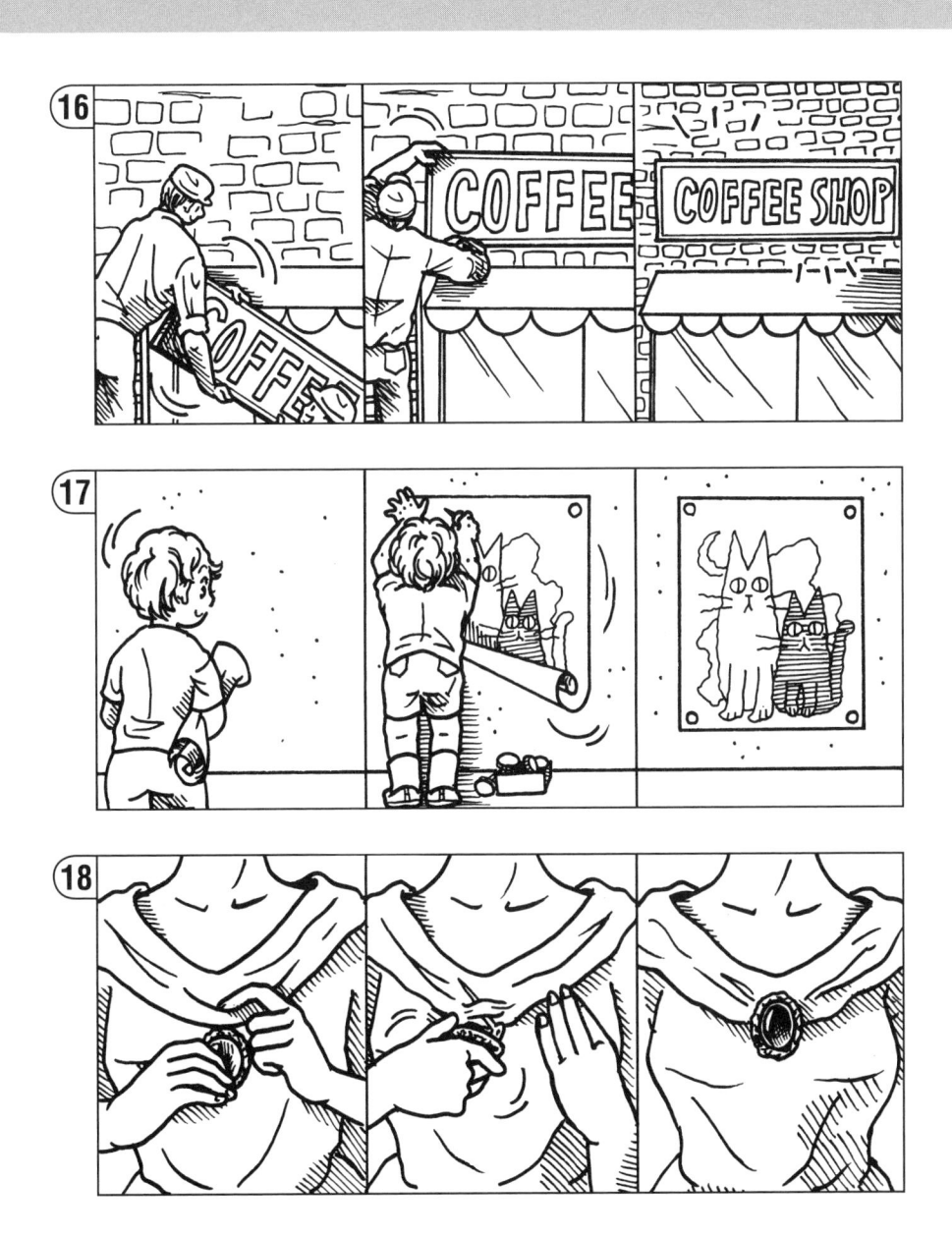

16 The man attached the sign to the wall.
17 Tim tacked the picture to the wall.
18 She fastened the pin to her dress.

②〜に合わせる

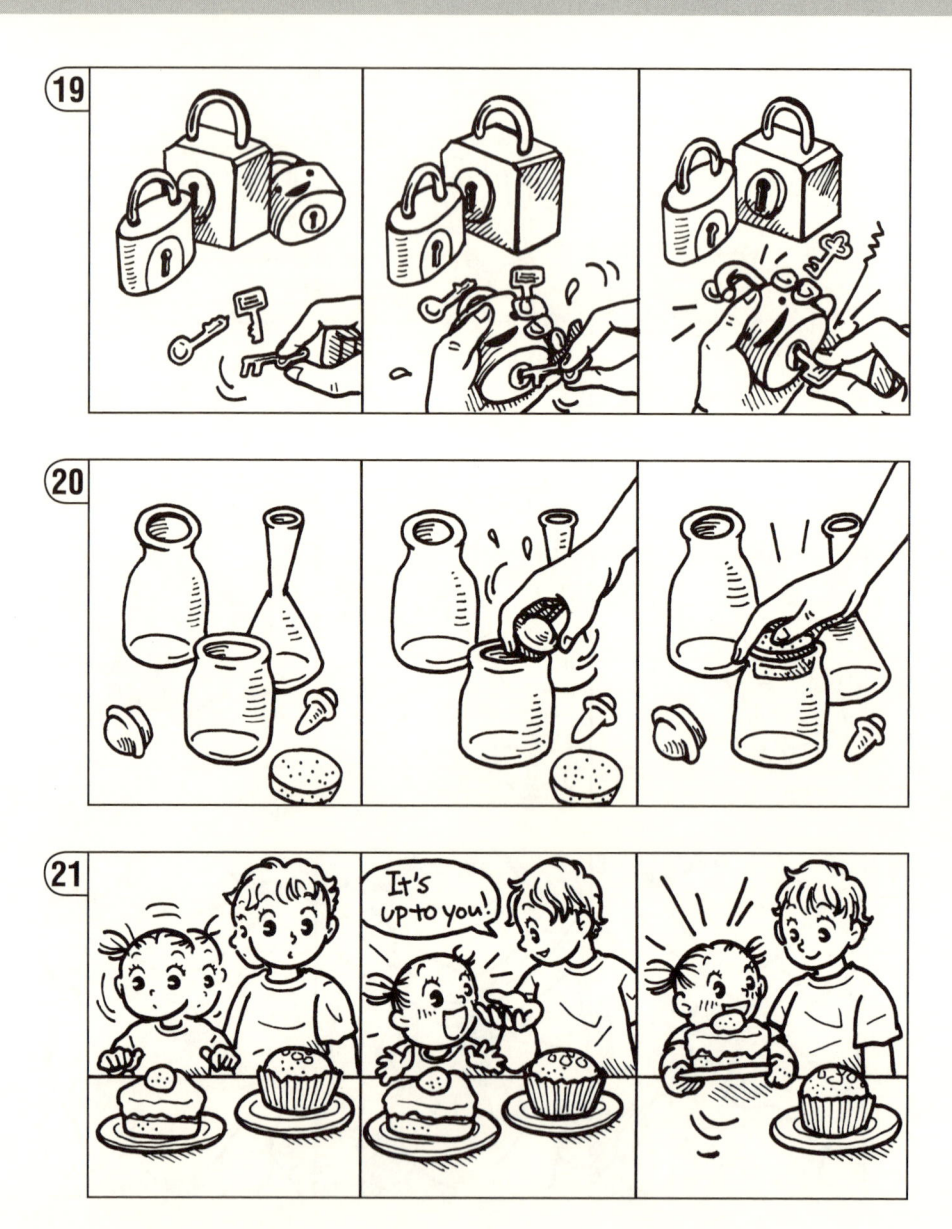

19 He found the key to one of the locks.
20 He found the lid to the short jar.
21 It is your birthday; it's up to you.

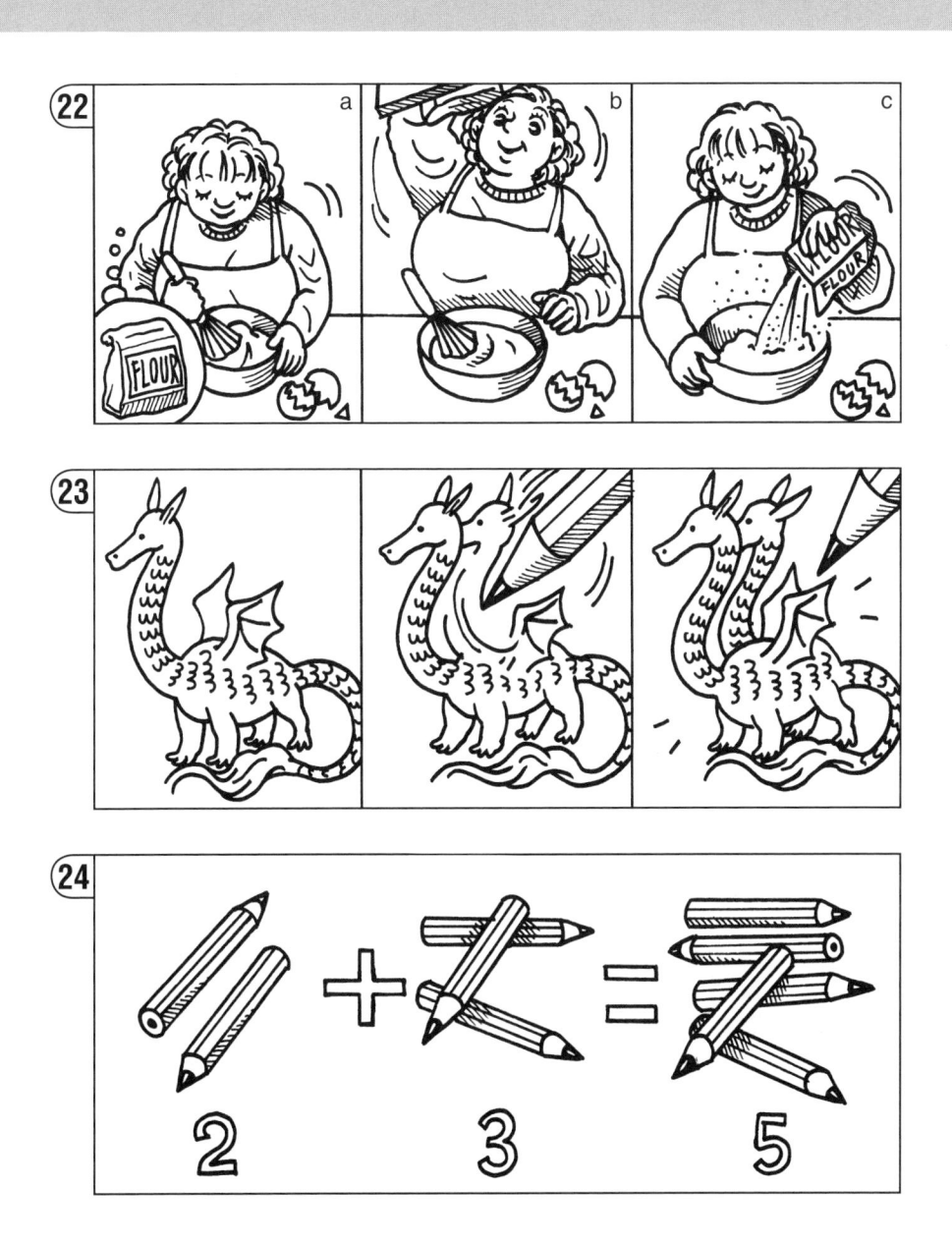

22 c. Mama is adding some flour to the batter.
23 The artist added another head to the dragon.
24 Two added to three equals five.

③最終点に着く

25 The temperature went up to 30 degrees.
　 The temperature reached 30 degrees.
26 The water rose up to Katarina's neck.
27 Tim is soaked to the skin.

【Ⅱ】連想するイメージ

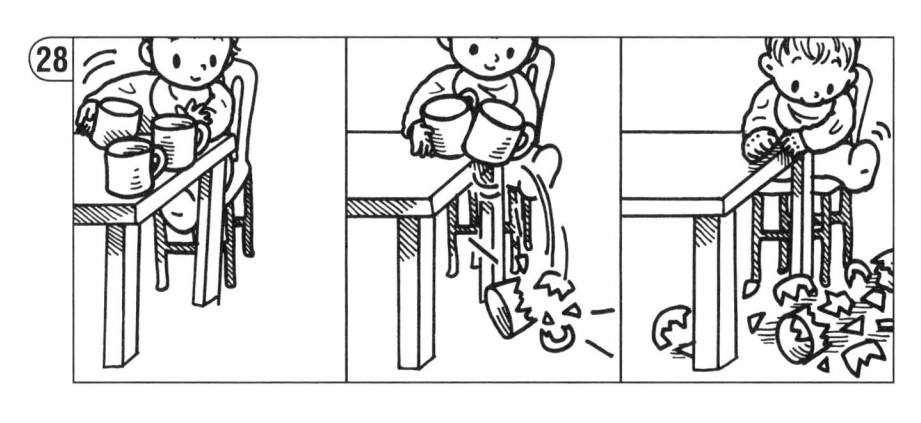

28 Baby broke all the cups to the last one.
29 The horse threw the rider to his death.
30 c. Butch came to consciousness.

④ 〜へ向かっている

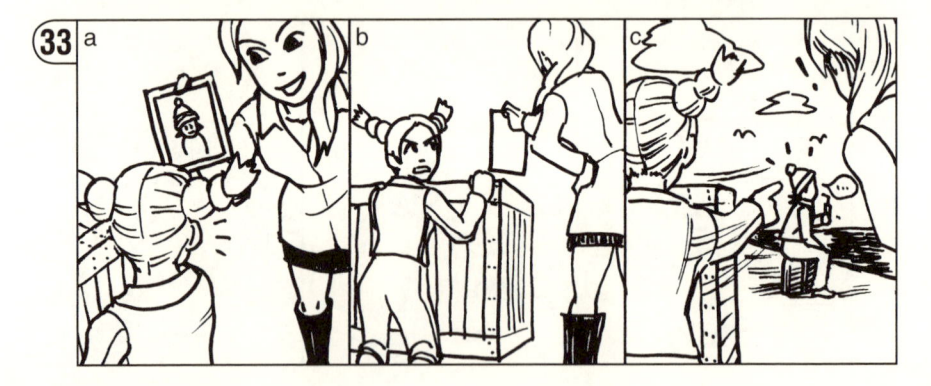

31 c. The monkey is pointing to the apple.
32 c. Albert is pointing to the Big Dipper.
   Albert is pointing out the Big Dipper to Sylvia.
33 c. Candy is pointing to Bowsheeman.
   Candy is pointing out Bowsheeman.

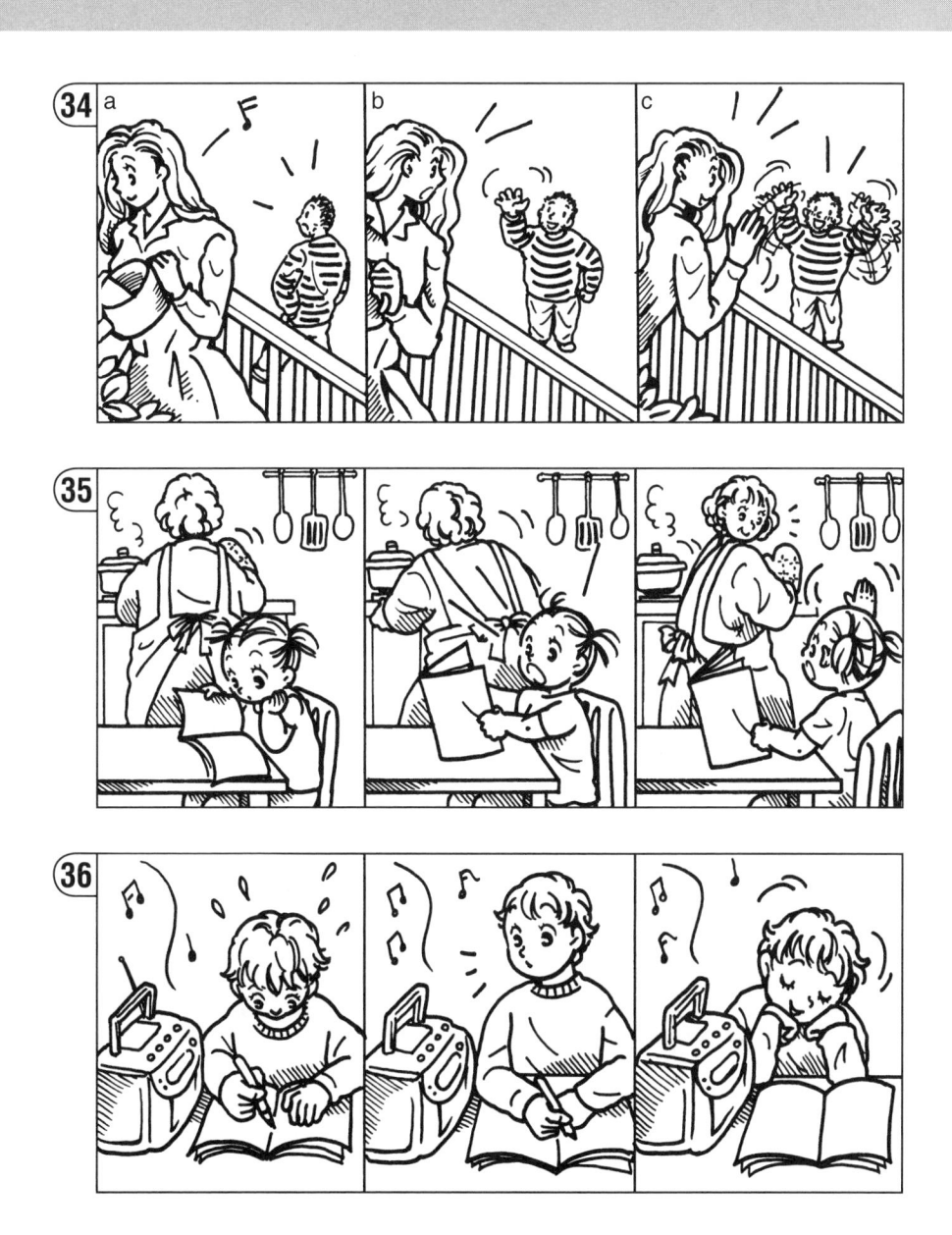

34 c. Sylvia is waving to Butch.
35 Olivia is talking to Mama.
36 Tim is listening to the radio.

④〜へ向かっている

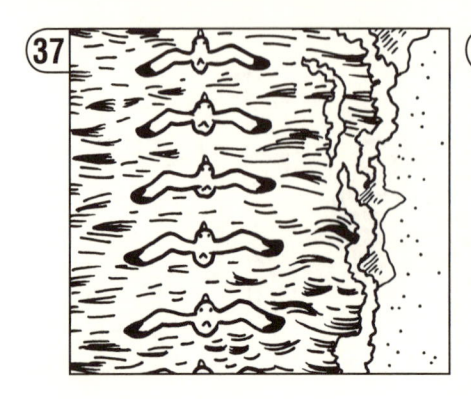

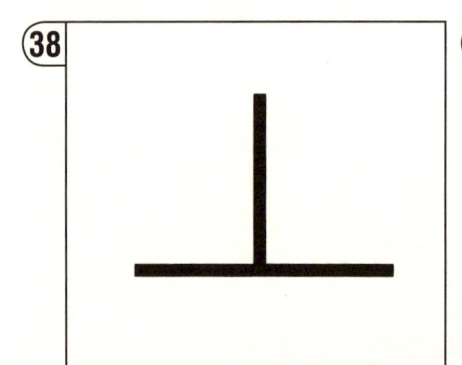

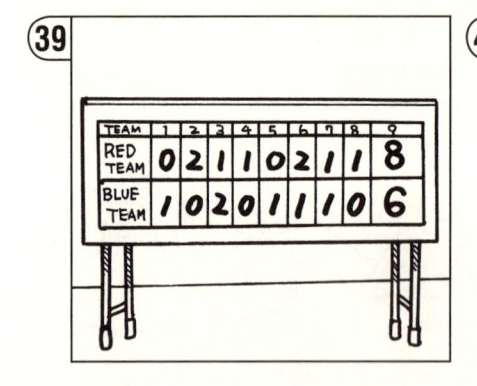

37　The birds are flying parallel to the shore.
38　The lines are perpendicular to each other.
39　The red team won by a score of 8 to 6.
40　Teria and Tim are standing face to face.
41　Teria and Tim are standing back to back.
42　Sylvia and Albert are dancing cheek to cheek.

【Ⅱ】連想するイメージ 483

⑤ 点から点への from ~ to ~

43 The butterfly is going from flower to flower.
44 Sylvia is going from shop to shop.
45 The cat is going from trash can to trash can.

①点から離れていく from

from the middle bottle

1 b. A snake is coming out of the middle bottle.
  c. The snake came from/out of the middle bottle.
2 b. A mouse is coming out of the lunchbox.   c. The mouse came from/out of the lunchbox.
3 b. A bee is coming out of the hive/the nest.   c. The bee came out of the hive/the nest.
    The bee is flying away from the hive/the nest.

from her

from A to B

4 Olivia and Mama received a box of apples from Mama's aunt.
5 Grandma received a letter from Olivia.
6 Teria is traveling from A to B by ship.　　7 Teria is traveling from A to B by train.

②点から出ている from

from the factory

8 Smoke is coming from the factory.
9 Smoke is rising from the fish.
10 Pooch is sitting in the light from the house.
11 The bat is in the beam from/of the flashlight.

【Ⅰ】基本のイメージ 487

from her mother

12 Ruby received a call from her mother.
13 Teria's boyfriend lives 500m from her house.
14 Mama got the potatoes from the garden.

from：点と見る

①〜から出ている

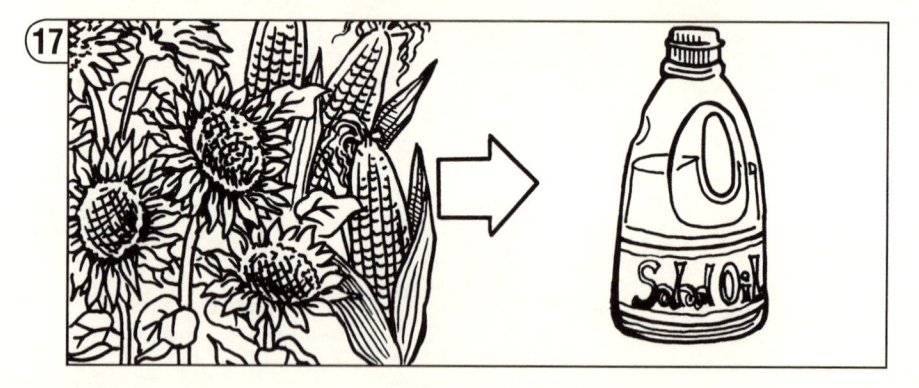

15　Where are you from?
16　Little Green comes from outer space.
17　Sunflower seed oil is made from sunflower seeds.

【Ⅱ】連想するイメージ 489

18 Butch is suffering from a hurt/an injured knee.
19 Butch is suffering from a pain in his stomach.
   Butch is suffering from a stomach ache.
20 Butch is suffering from the cold rain.

from：点と見る

②選べる点から離れていく／out of と比べる

from work

21　Sylvia came (straight) from work.
22　a. The little skiff came from the boat landing.
　　b. The liner came from the marina.

out of the office

23 Papa went out of the office.
24 Sylvia came out of the house.
25 The boat is going out of the harbor.

③選び出している / off と比べる

26 Papa took the picture of Teria from the top of the cabinet.
27 Olivia picked up an apple from the ground.
28 b. Baby took a book from the shelf.

【Ⅱ】連想するイメージ 493

off

off / from

off

29 Mama took the picture of Teria off the wall.
30 Olivia picked an apple (off/from the tree).
31 Mama picked the books up off (of) the floor.

④選び出している

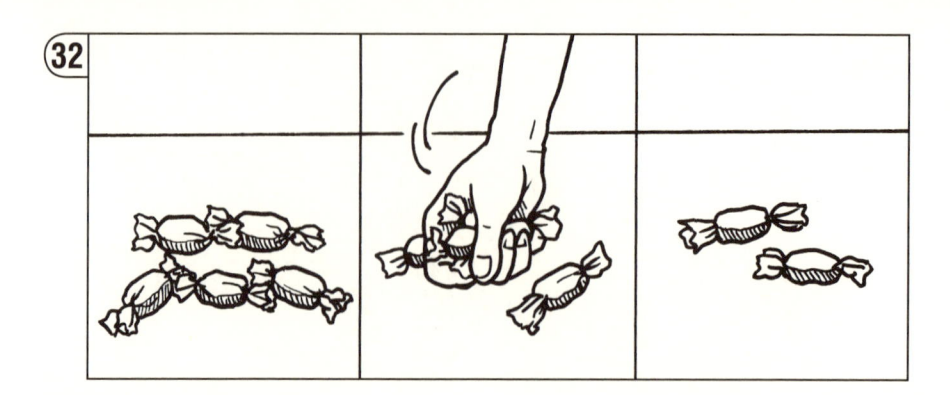

32 3 from 5 leaves 2.
33 A tiger is different from a leopard.
34 A husky is different from a wolf.

⑤ 選び出せない from, off, out of

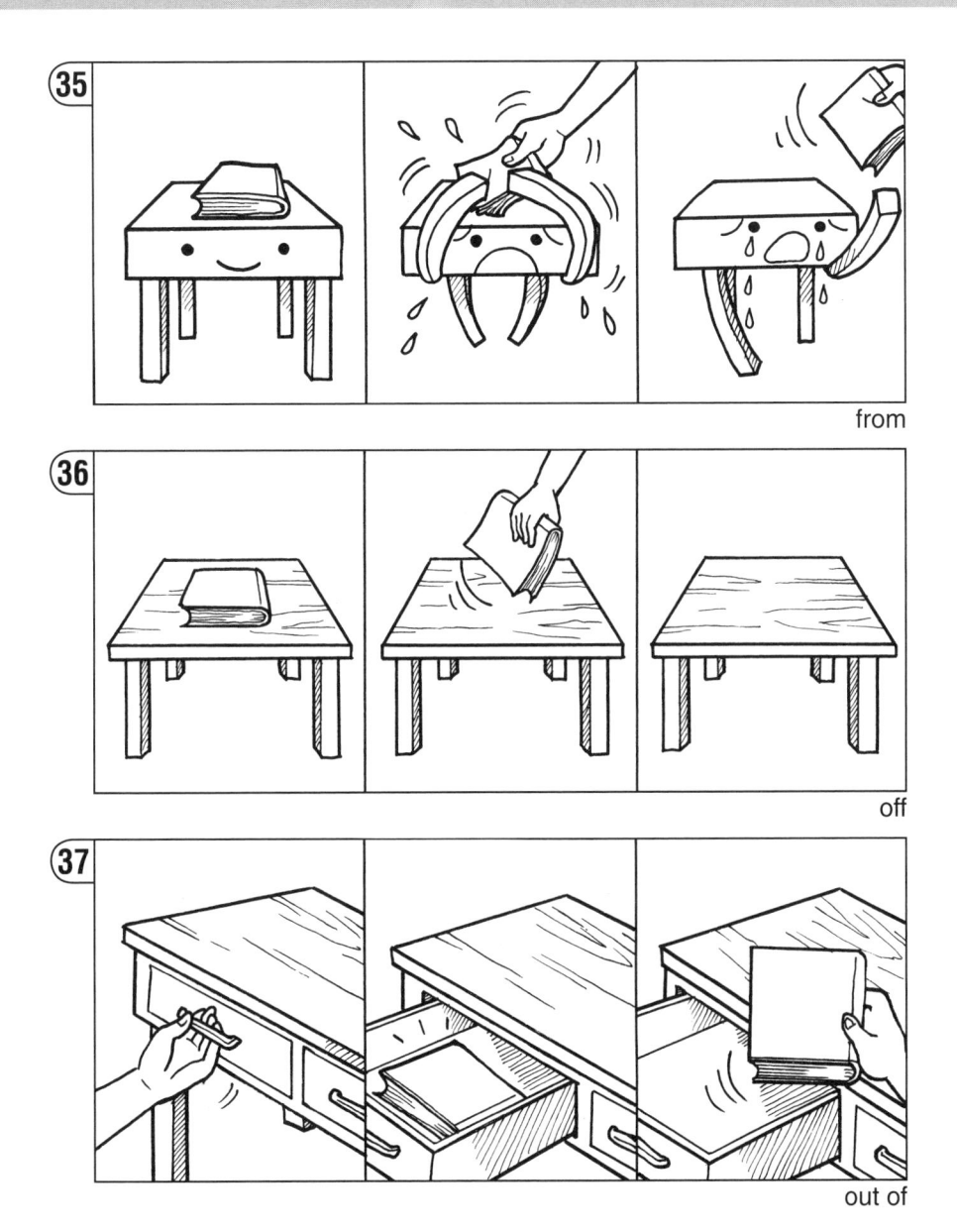

from

off

out of

35 Someone took the book from the table.
36 Someone took the book off (of) the table.
37 Someone took a book out of the drawer.

⑥ 引き離している

38 Katarina took the teddy bear from Mr. Gold.
39 Candy fished Bowsheeman's hat from his head.
40 The man took Sylvia's purse from her.
   The man stole Sylvia's purse.

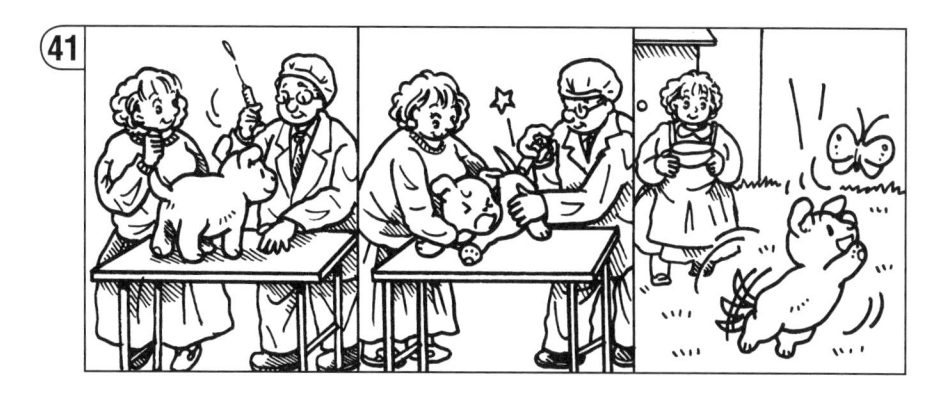

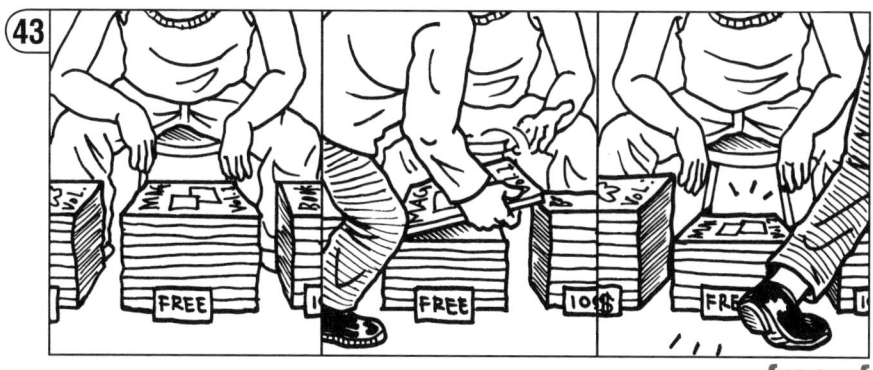

41 The puppy is free from disease.
42 The man was freed from jail.
43 The magazines in the middle are free of charge.

⑦のがれている

44 c. Teria is sheltering from the rain.
45 c. Bowsheeman is hiding from Candy.
46 c. Olivia is hiding from Mama.

free of

47 Butch saved the child from the fire.
48 The bird saved the squirrels from danger.
49 The hall should be kept free of toys.

500 from：点と見る

①起点が原料の from とつくり出す out of

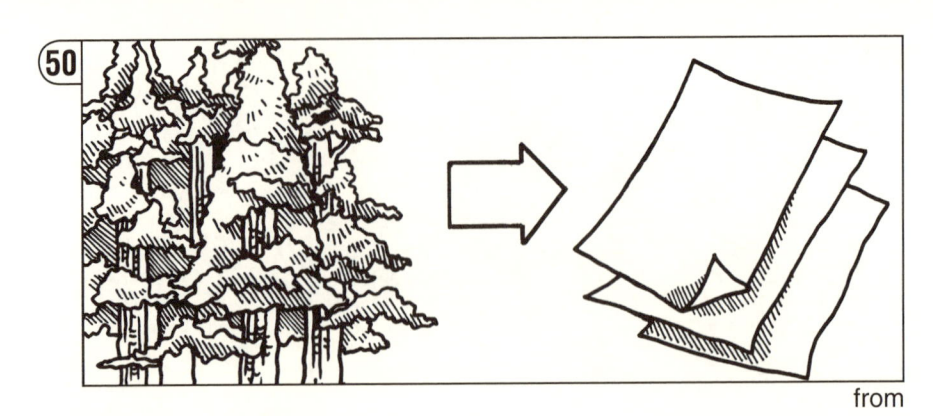

from

from

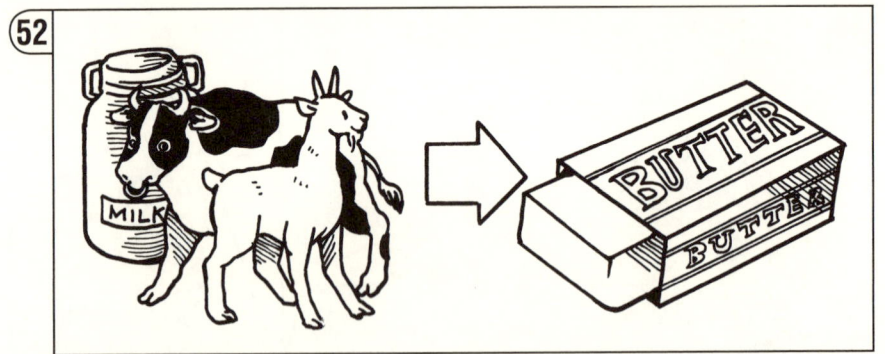

from

---

50 Paper is made from trees.
51 Wool comes from sheep.
52 Butter is made from cow's milk.

【Ⅲ】イメージを比べる 501

out of

out of

out of

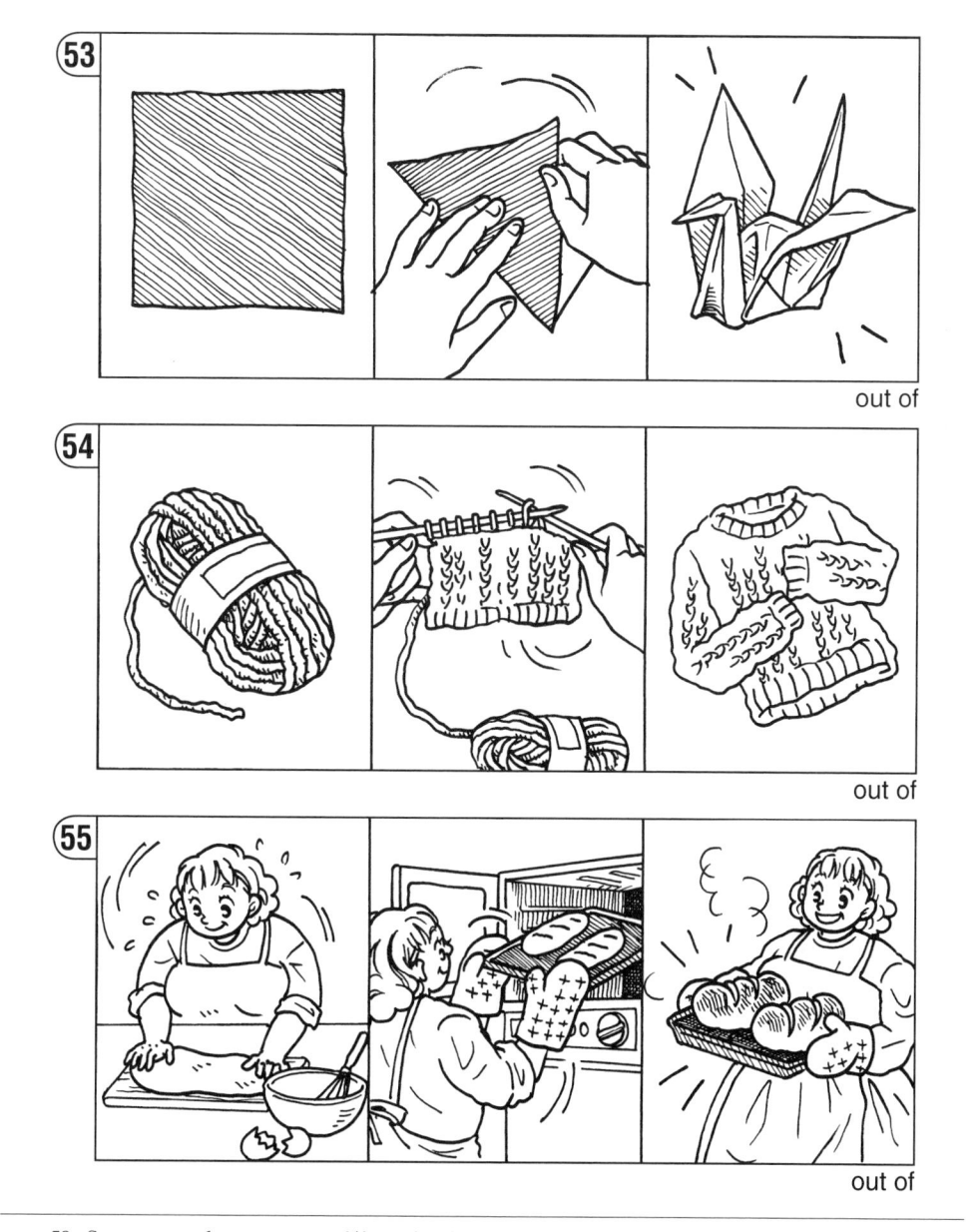

53 Someone made a crane out of/from the sheet of paper.
54 A sweater was made out of/from the yarn.
55 Mama made bread out of/from the dough.

② be made of/from/out of

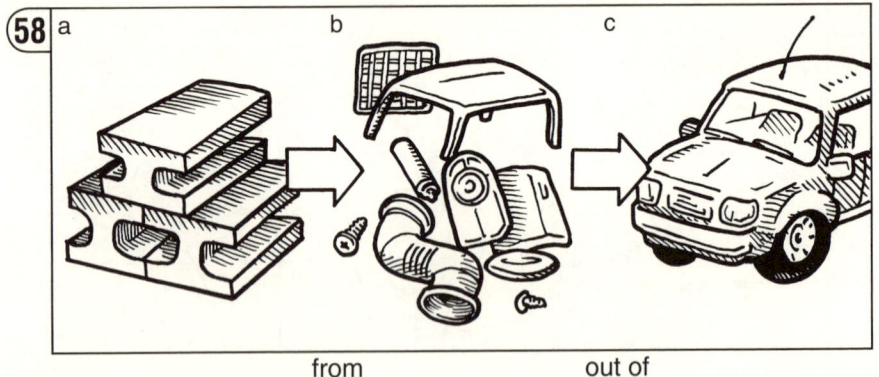

56　The kimono is made of silk, but the sweater is made of wool, and the T-shirt is made of cotton.
57　b. The silk cloth was made from cocoons.　c. The kimono was made out of the silk cloth.
58　a. The I beams are made of steel.
　　b. The pieces were made from the I beams.
　　c. The car was made out of the pieces.

【Ⅲ】イメージを比べる 503

of

from   out of

from   out of

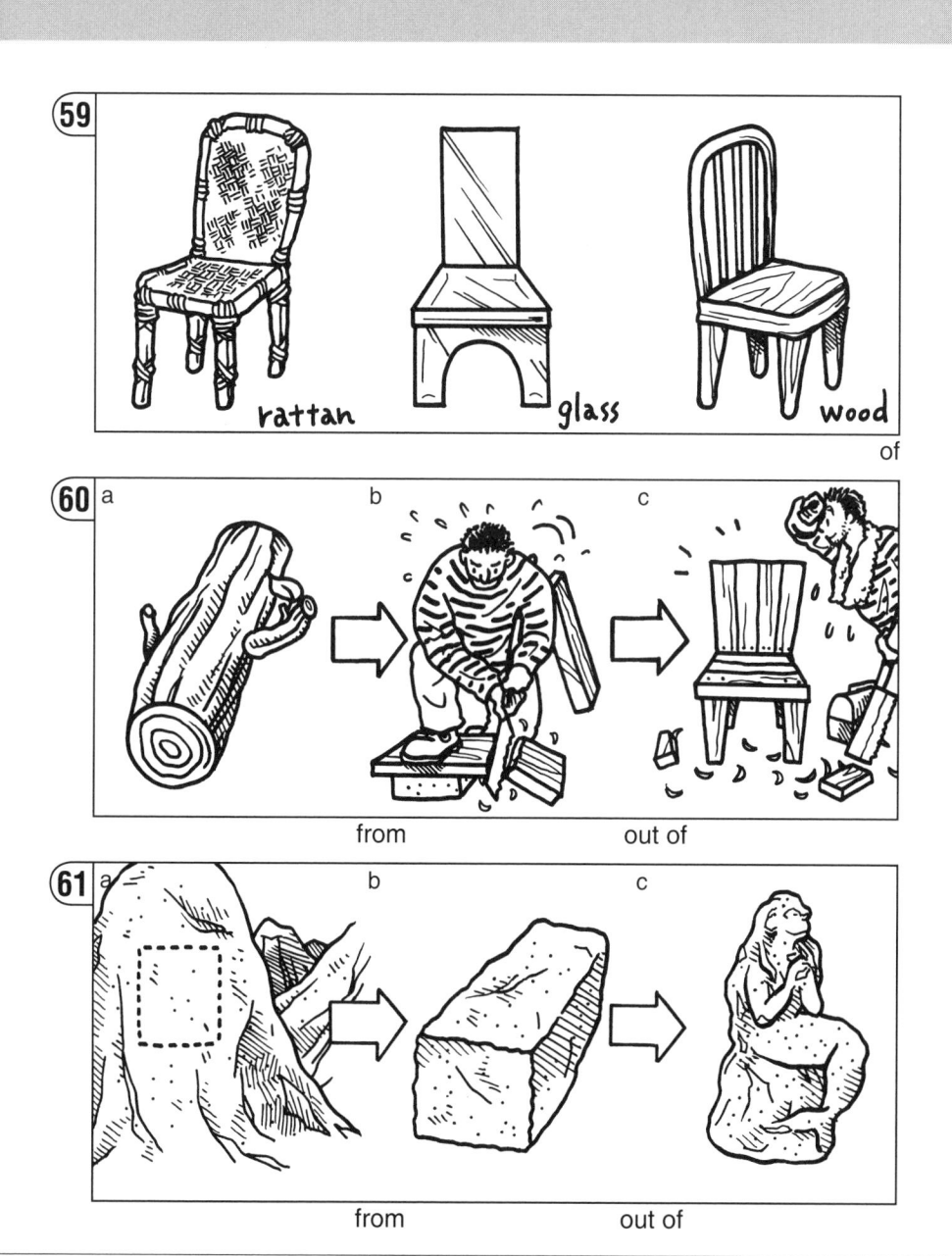

59　One chair is made of wood, another one is made of glass and the other (one) is made of rattan.
60　b. The planks were made from logs.　c. The chair was made out of the planks.
61　b. The block was cut from the stone.
　　c. A statue was made out of the block.　　The statue is made of stone.
　　　The statue was made from the stone.　　The statue is composed of stone.

③疲れる be tired from

62　Tim is tired from running.
63　The illustrator is tired from drawing pictures of sea munchkins.
64　Papa is tired from work.

④ あきる be tired of

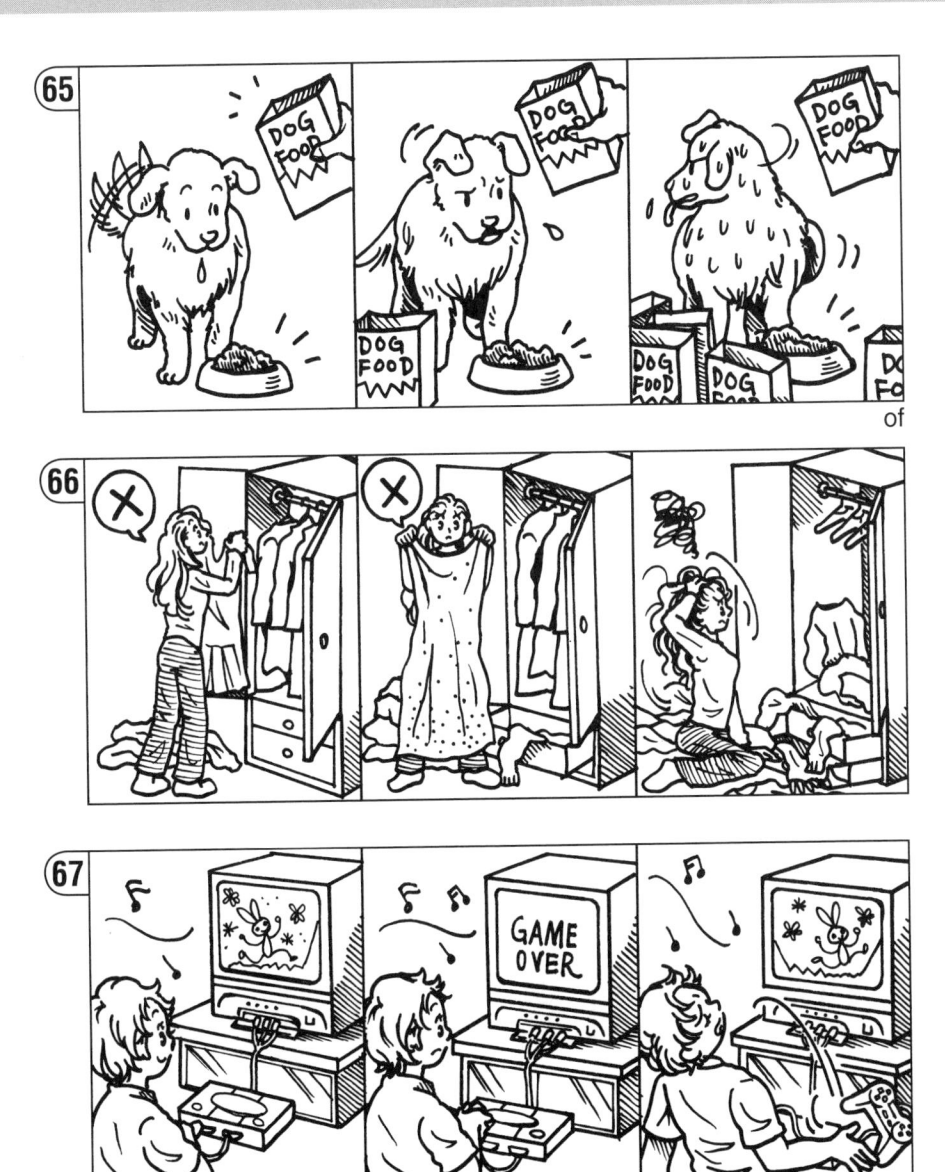

65 Pooch is tired of the same dog food.
66 Sylvia is tired of her clothes.
67 Tim is tired of his video game.

⑤原因となる of, from, by

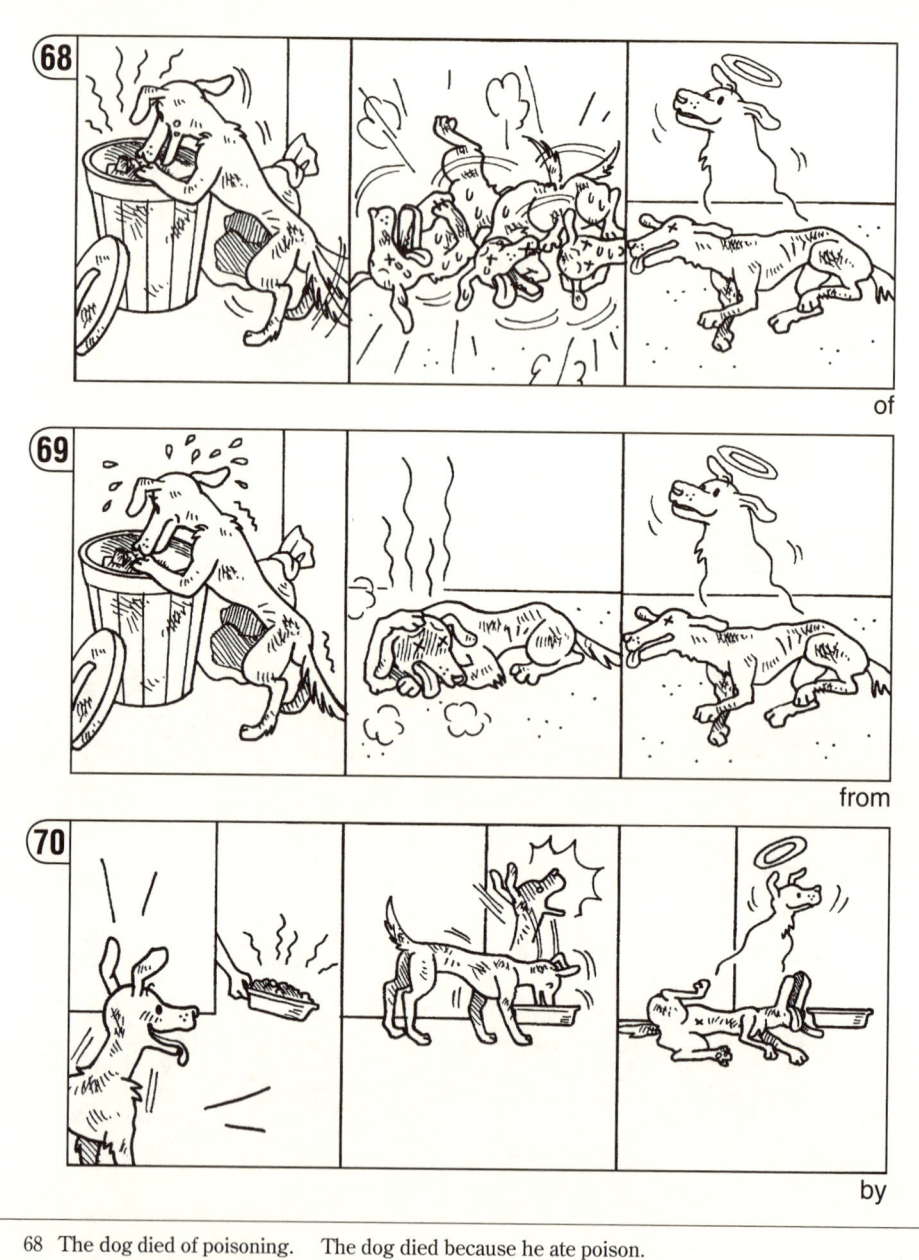

of

from

by

68　The dog died of poisoning.　　The dog died because he ate poison.
69　The dog died from poison.　　The dog died because he ate poison.
70　The dog died by poisoning.　　The dog died because he was poisoned.

【Ⅲ】イメージを比べる

of

from

by

71 The dog died of/because of a high fever.
72 The dog died from/because of a cold.
73 The mouse died by drowning.
   The mouse died because he was drowned.

⑥「〜から」の of と from

74 Mt. Fuji is west of Tokyo.
75 Mt. Fuji is west from Tokyo.
76 The house is within 250 meters of the school.
77 Teria's house is 200 meters from her school.
78 Tim took the book off (of) the desk.

【Ⅲ】イメージを比べる

79 Nautilus is a resident of Nautilus Island.
80 Nautilus is from Nautilus Island.
81 While Mr. Gold was asleep, Katarina took a picture of him.
82 Ruby's father took the picture from Nautilus.
83 Bakunsai is a delegate from the ninjas.

510 … **close to : 点と見る**

①点に近づく close to

close to her

1. The car is close to Leaf.
   The car is following too closely behind the bicycle.
2. The squirrel is close to the rabbit.   The other animals are far behind.
   The rabbit has won the race, but the squirrel is close (behind).
3. a. Olivia is close to her grandmother.   b. Tim is standing near his grandmother.

near：3Dと見る　　　【Ⅰ】基本のイメージ　511

②近くにいる / ある close to と near

close to / near his car

4　Leaf is riding close to/near Borizi's car. [next to, beside, alongside, by]
5　The group is staying close to/near the guide.
6　The family is sitting close to/near the fire. [in front of, by, next to]

③「近い」close to, near と「遠い」far away (from)

7　close to / near　　　far away from

8

9

7　Beach Village is close to/near Bay City.
　　Populi Town is far away from Bay City.
8　Leaf's house is close to/near Herb Village, but it is far away from Populi Town.
9　The brontosaurus is close to/near Fennel, but the Tyrannosaurus Rex is far away (from him).

【Ⅰ】基本のイメージ 513

close to / near   **far away**

apart from

far apart

10 Baby is close to/near Mama; the telephone is far away.
11 Olivia is (sitting) close to/beside/near/next to Baby.
   Papa is sitting apart from Baby and Olivia.
12 The houses are far apart (from each other).
   Leaf's house is three kilometers away from Chicori's.

514 … away from：点と見る

①点から離れていく away from

fly **away**

1 b, c. The bird is flying away (from the tree).
2 c. Bowsheeman is swimming away from the boat.
3 Chicori is walking away from the tree.

【Ⅰ】基本のイメージ 515

move **away from** the TV

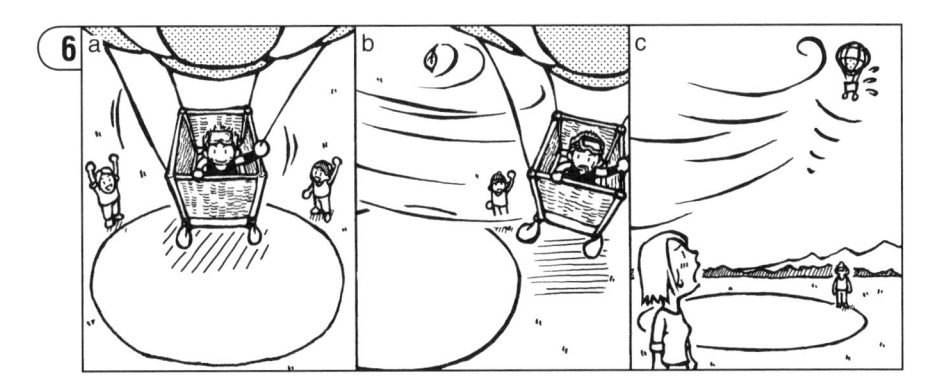

4　Olivia moved away from the television.
5　b. Borizi is taking the bride away from the groom.
　　c. Borizi is taking the bride away (from the church).　They are running off together.
6　b. The balloon took off from the circle.
　　c. The balloon flew away (from the circle).

516 ... away from : 点と見る

①離れていく

7　b. A kidnapper took Olivia away from Mama.
　　c. He took Olivia off somewhere.
8　Bowsheeman's mother told him to get away from her.
9　Bowsheeman is running away from home.

【Ⅱ】連想するイメージ 517

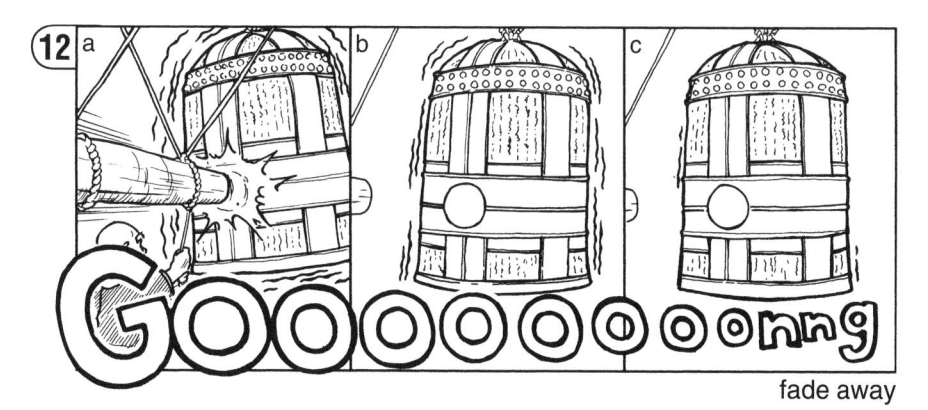

10 The police took her father away.
11 c. The sound of the cat's bell is fading away.
12 c. The sound of the bell is fading away.

518 ... **away from**：点と見る

②時が過ぎ去っていく

13　The water is boiling away.
14　b. Sylvia is talking away.　c. Sylvia talked away the evening.
　　　　　　　　　　　　　　　　Sylvia talked the evening away.
15　Sylvia danced the night away.
　　She danced away the night.

16 The water boiled away.
17 b. Teria is sleeping away the day.   c. Teria slept the day away.
       She slept away the day.
18 Papa worked the day away.
    Papa worked away the day.

③遠ざける

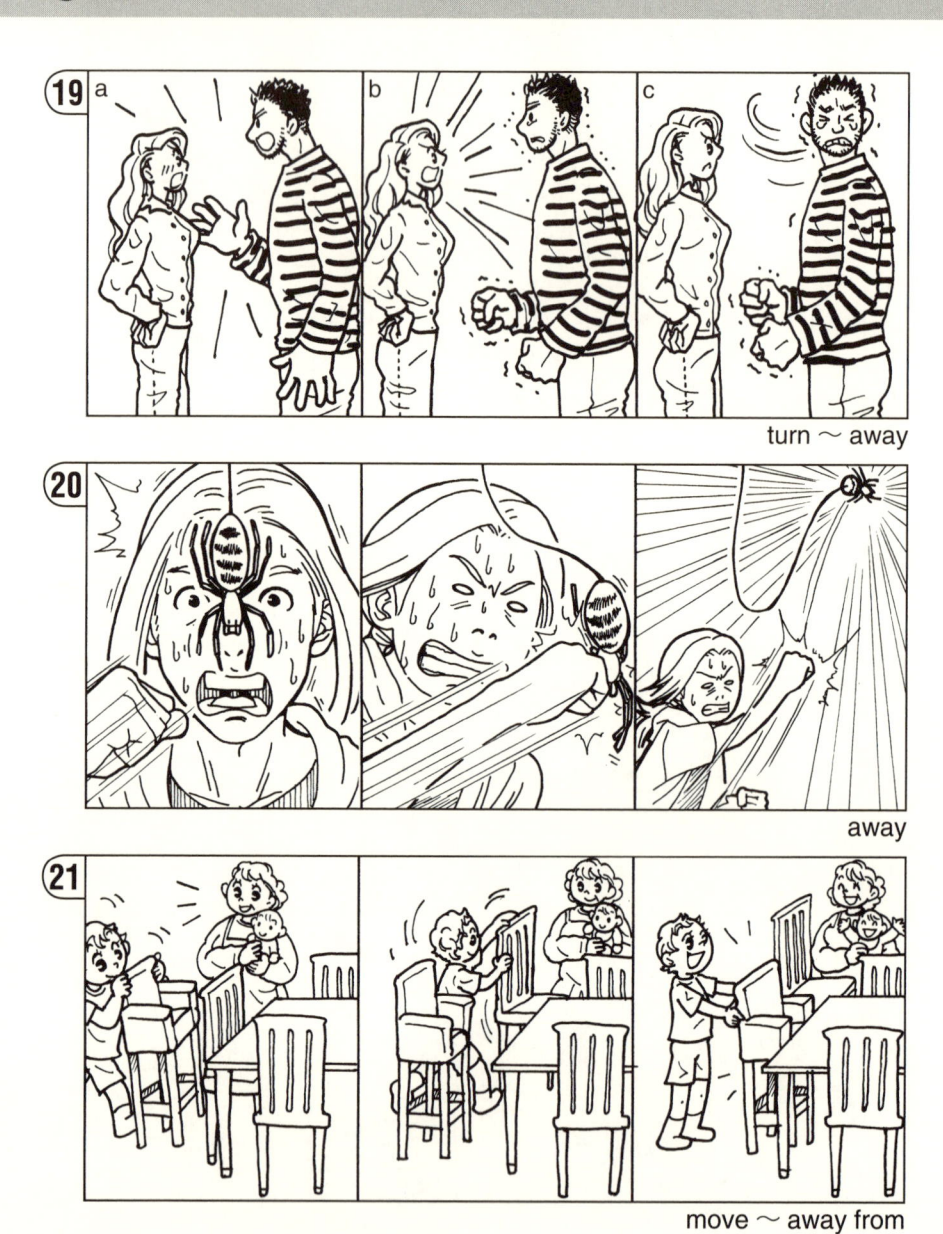

turn ~ away

away

move ~ away from

19 c. Butch turned his face away to hide his tears.
20 Fennel knocked the spider away.
21 Tim moved one of the regular chairs away from the table.

④ away は使わない!

turn ～ on each other

off

move ～ back from

22　Sylvia and Albert turned their backs on each other.
23　b. Chicori slapped the spider off Fennel's back.
24　Mama moved a chair back (away) from the table.

away from：点と見る

⑤ 遠ざけてしまう

25　Mama put the milk away in the refrigerator.
26　b. Olivia is picking her toys up off the floor.　　c. Olivia put her toys away.
27　Albert threw away his old books.

【Ⅱ】連想するイメージ

⑥ みんなあげてしまう

give away

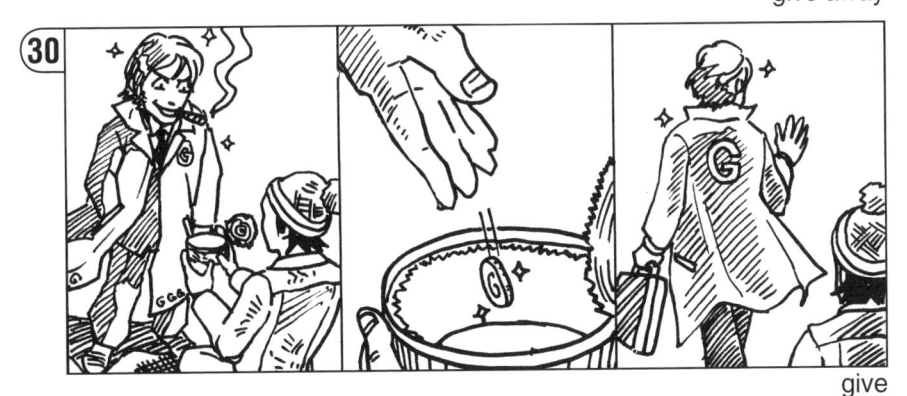

give away

give

28　c. Sylvia gave her clothes away.　She gave away her clothes.
29　Oton gave away all of his money.　Oton gave all of his money away.
30　Mr. Gold gave a coin to Bowsheeman.

① 切ってしまう cut away と cut off

cut away

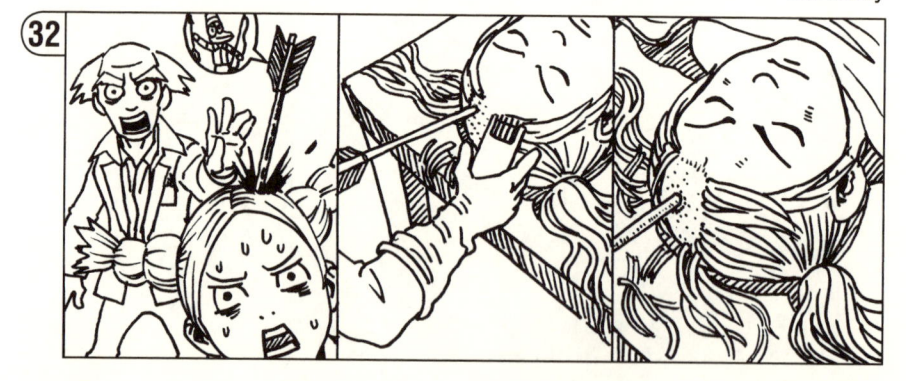

31 Papa cut the branches away.
32 Dr. Bizarro cut away Candy's hair to remove the arrow.
33 b. Inond cut off a branch.   c. Inond cut the trees away.
   Inond cut a branch off.

【Ⅲ】イメージを比べる 525

34 b. Someone cut off the branch.　Someone cut the branch off.
35 b. The barber cut off the man's hair.　The barber cut the man's hair off.
36 b. The beautician cut the woman's hair.

②遠ざけている keep away from

keep him away from

37 Mama is keeping Tim away from the other kids.
38 Children should keep away from fireworks.
39 The guards are keeping the crowd away from the princess.

③分かれている apart (from)

stand apart from

keep them apart

40 c. The girls are standing apart from the boys.
41 The train is keeping the policeman and Earl apart.
42 b. Candy is pulling her doll apart.

528 ··· **by**：点と見る

①点を経由していく **by**

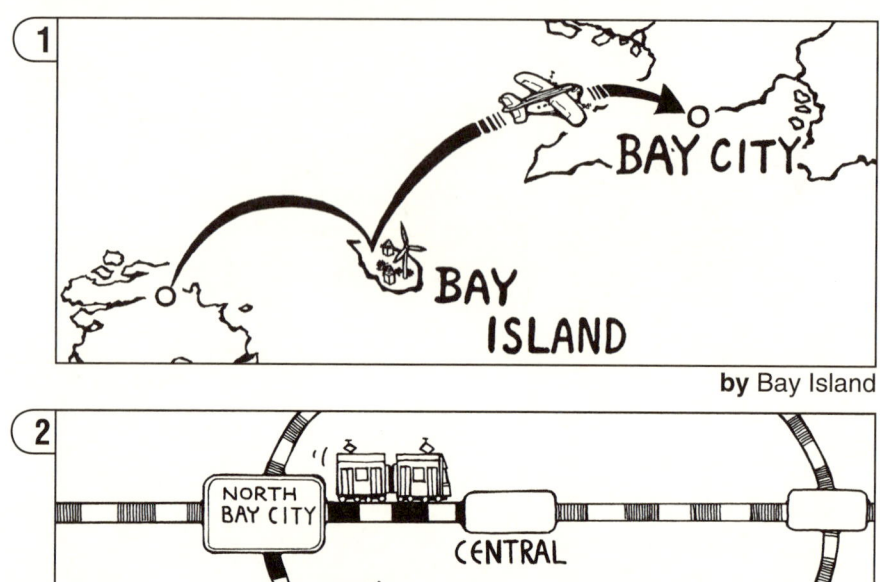

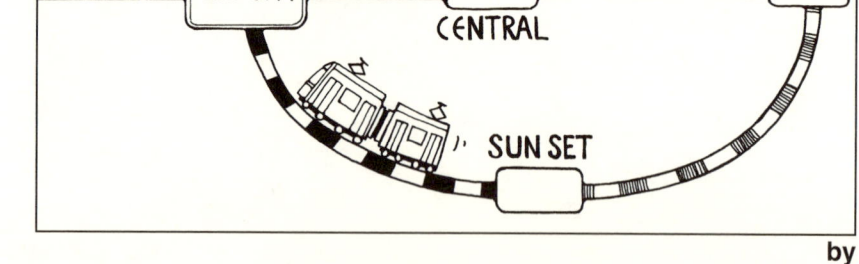

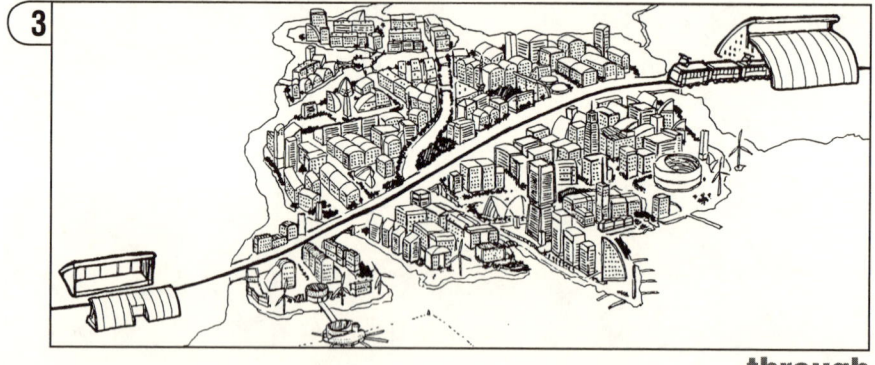

by Bay Island

by

through

1 The airplane goes to Bay City by (way of)/via Bay Island.
2 The train goes from Sunset to Central by (way of)/via North Bay City.
3 The train goes through the city.

【Ⅰ】基本のイメージ 529

by / through the gate

by / through

through

4　Teria went in by (means of)/through the gate.
5　Santa Claus came in by/through the chimney.
6　Goroki went in through/by the chimney.

②点を通過していく by

by / past the gate

by / past

by / past

7 Teria went by/past the gate.
8 The children ran by/past Papa.
9 The train went by/past the platform.

【Ⅰ】基本のイメージ　531

by / past the car

by / past

by

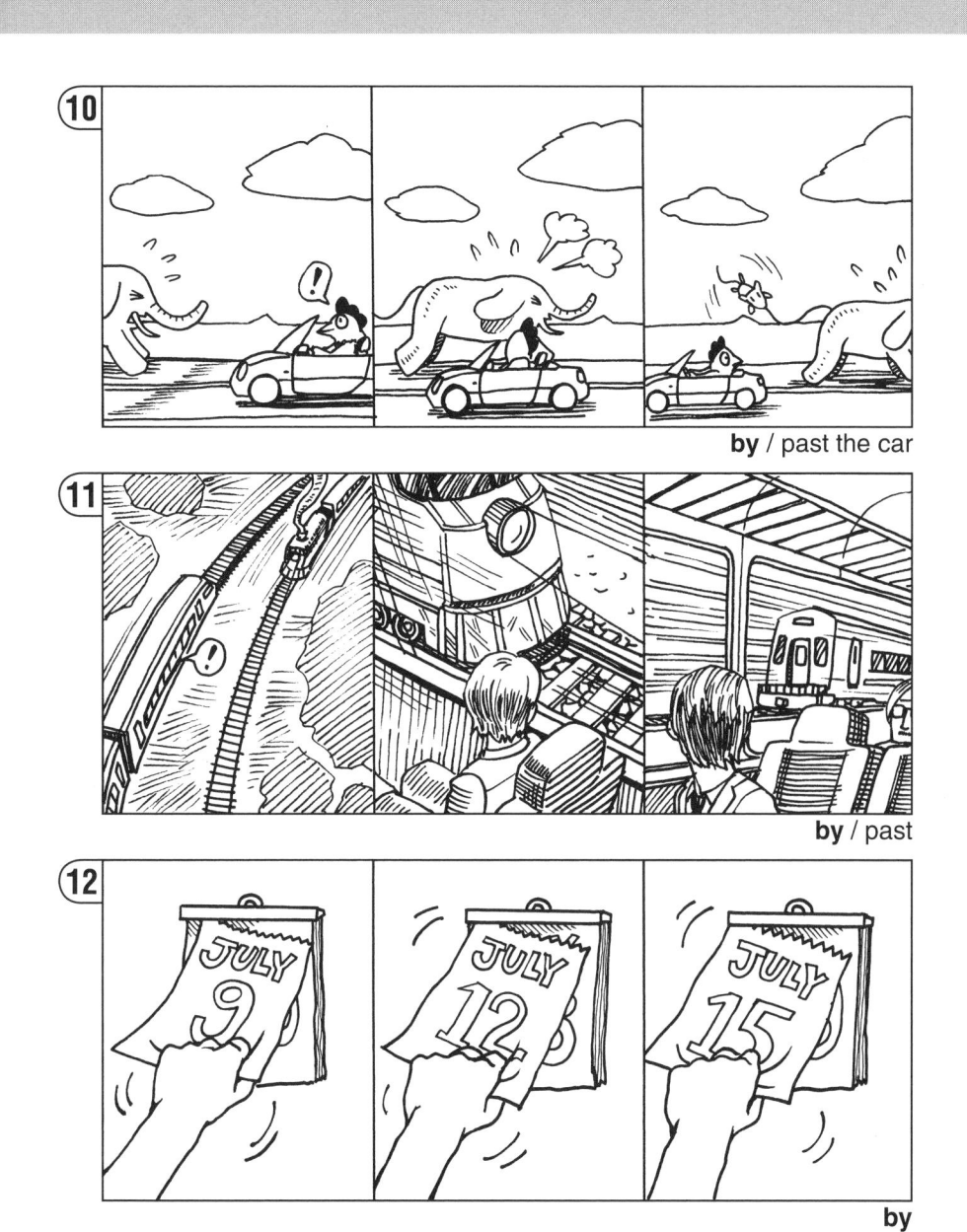

10　An elephant ran by/past the car.
11　The trains are going by/past each other.
　　The trains are passing each other.
12　The days are going by.

③ そばにいる / ある by

by / next to (13)
by / next to (14) 
by / next to (15)
by / next to (16) 
by / next to (17) 
by / next to (18)

13 Baby is sitting by/beside Mama.
 [next to, near, close to, alongside]
14 Butch is standing by/beside Albert.
 [next to, near, close to, alongside]
15 The house is by /beside the river.
 [next to, near, close to, alongside, along]
16 The house is by/beside the lake.
 [next to, near, close to, alongside]
17 There is a pair of shoes by/beside
 the bed. [next to, near, close to, alongside]
18 Grandma is sitting by/beside the window.
 [next to, near, close to, alongside]

【 I 】基本のイメージ

by / near

by / near

by / near

by / near

by / near

by / near

19 The coffee shop is by/near/close to Populi Station. [in front of]
20 The drugstore is by/near/close to the clinic.
21 The house is by/near/close to the lake. [across, beside, next to, alongside, along]
22 The clock tower is by/near/close to the lake.
23 The spaceship is hovering by/near/close to the earth. [next to, alongside]
24 The house is by/near/close to the sea/the beach/the road. [along, alongside]

① 選べる手段を経由している

25　Indy went to Nautilus Island by boat.
26　Bakunsai went to Nautilus Island by airplane.
27　Candy went to Nautilus Island by submarine.

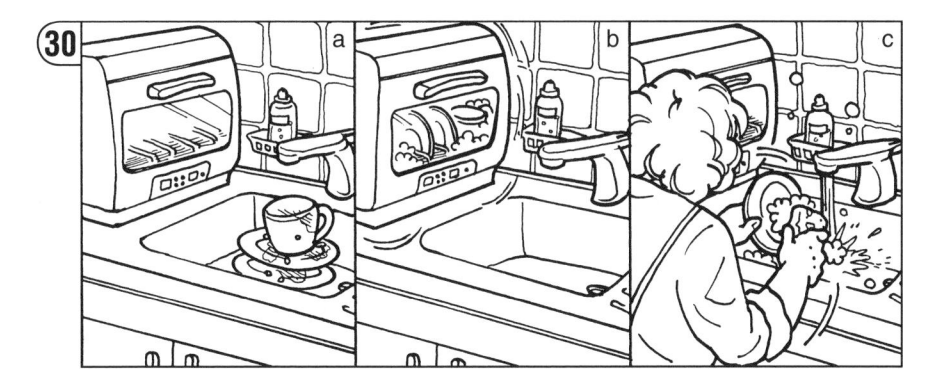

28　a. Bowsheeman is making caps by hand.　　b. The alien is making caps by machine.
29　a. Eluca is washing his clothes by hand.　　b. He is washing his clothes by machine.
30　b.The dishes are being washed by (means of) a machine.
　　c. Mama is washing dishes by hand.　　The dishes are being washed by hand.

②数量を経由している

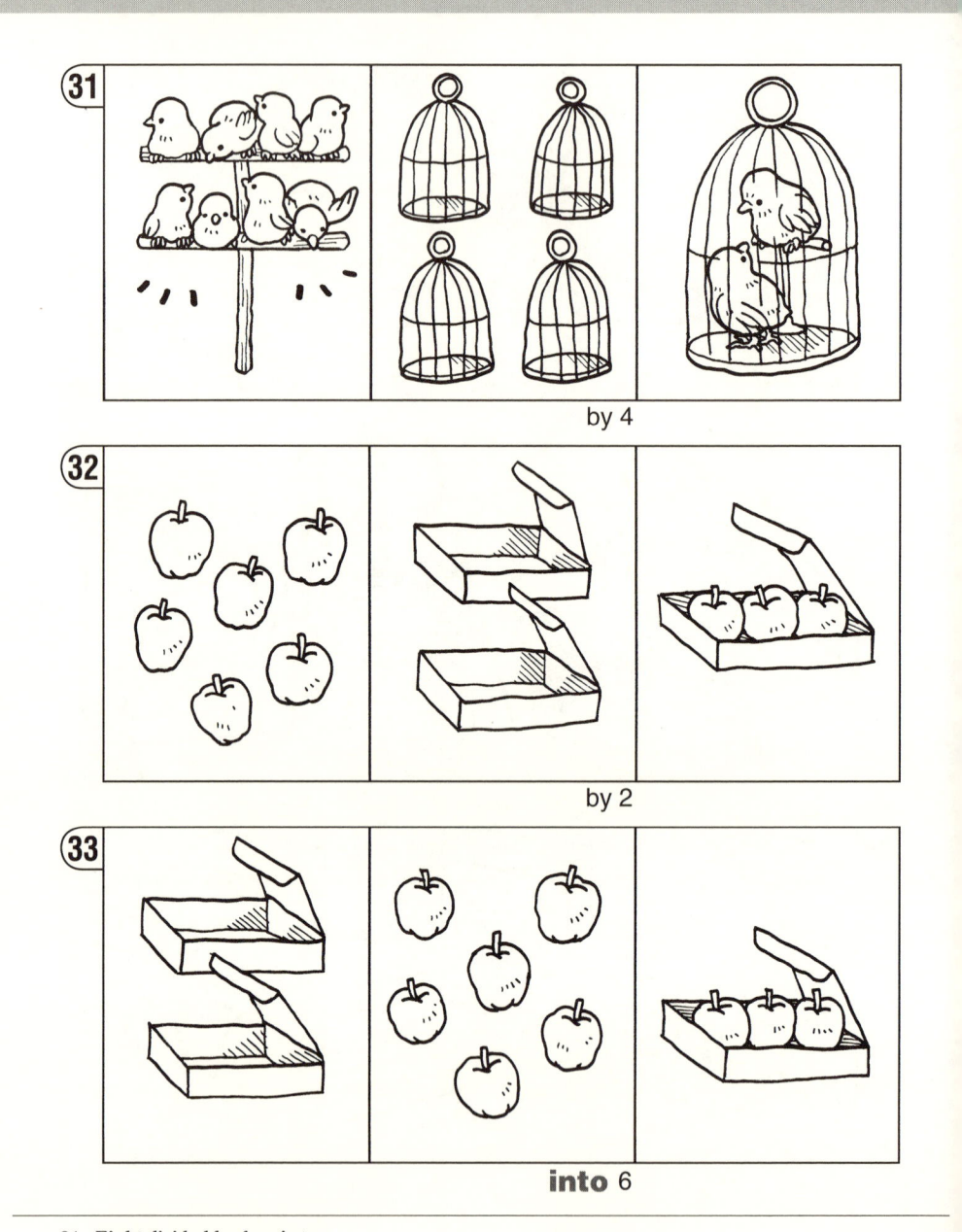

by 4

by 2

into 6

31　Eight divided by four is two.
32　Six divided by two is three.
33　Two divided into six is three.

34 They are selling eggs by the dozen.
35 She is putting sugar in the cup by the spoonful.
36 He is pouring in water by the bucketful.

②数量を経由している

37 Three (multiplied) by five is fifteen.
   Three times five is/equals fifteen.
38 The board is two meters by four (meters).
39 Four (multiplied) by two is eight.
   Four times two is/equals eight.
40 Tim is older than Olivia by almost five years.

【Ⅱ】連想するイメージ

side by side

41 It is getting hotter day by day.
42 Sylvia is paid by the month.
43 The red team won by a score of 8 to 6.
44 The boys and girls are sitting side by side.
   The boys are sitting by/beside the girls.
   [next to, near, close to, alongside]

③経由しているものを強調している

45 The vase was made by Teria.
46 The book was written by Albert.
47 The hole was made by a UFO.

by accident

by the rules

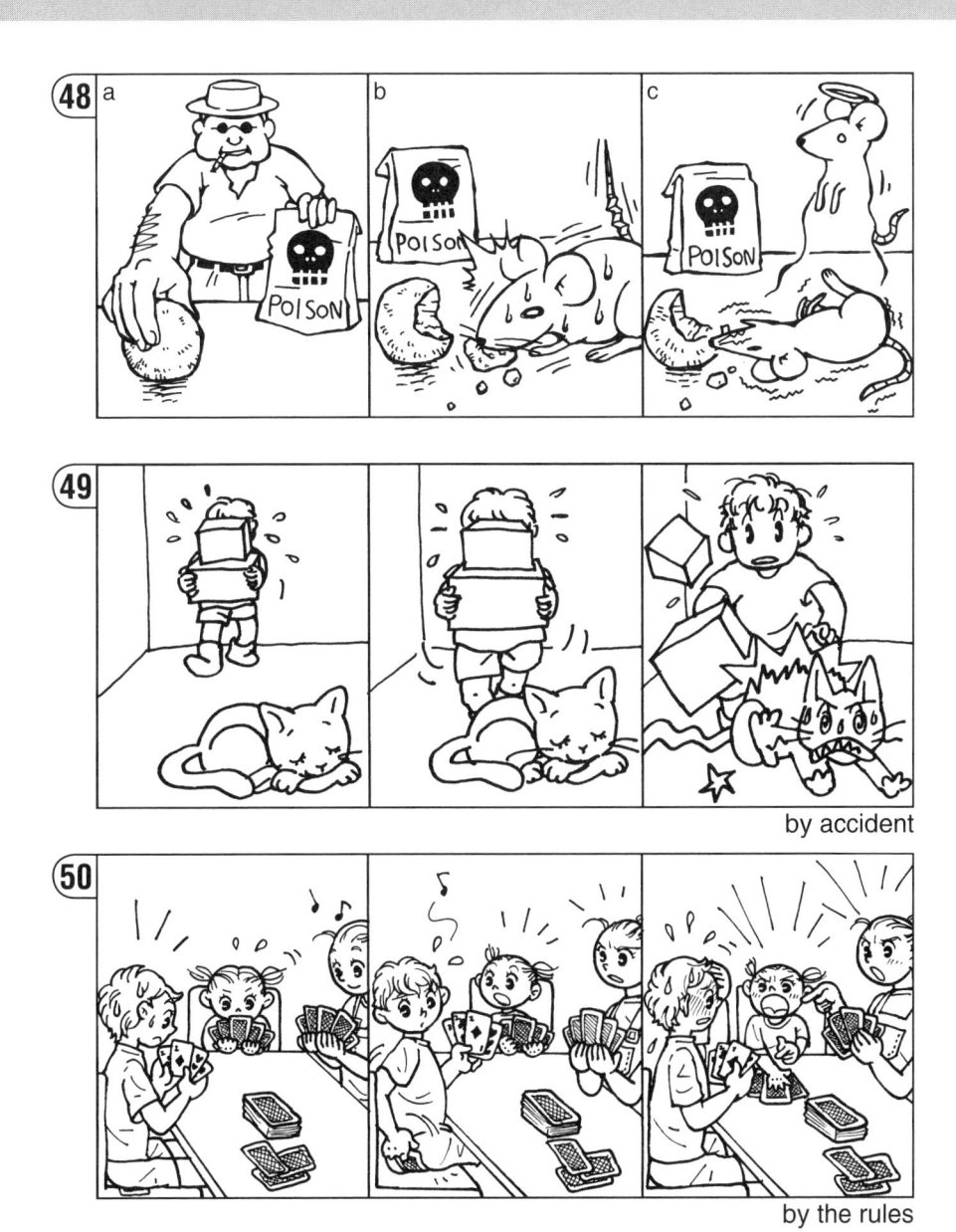

48　c. The rat died by poisoning.
　　　He killed the rat with poison.
49　Tim kicked Kitten by accident.
50　Tim did not play the game by the rules.

by：点と見る

①「そばに」を比べる

51 by / beside
52 by / across
53 by / alongside
54 by / along
55 by / near
56 around

51　The house is beside the lake.
　　[by, near, close to, next to]
52　The tower is across the lake.
　　[by, near, close to, next to]
53　The mansion is alongside the lake.
　　[along, near, close to, next to, by, on]
54　There are houses along the lake.
　　[beside, near, close to, next to, by, on, alongside]
55　The house is near the lake.
　　[by, close to, around, at]
56　There are houses around the lake.
　　[near, close to]

【Ⅲ】イメージを比べる 543

57 Ruby's house is by the beach.
   [near, close to, next to, beside, on, at]
58 Ruby's house is by the sea.
   Ruby's house is along the coast.
59 The playground is by the lake.
   [near, close to]
60 The light house is on the coast/
   the peninsula.
61 b. Ruby's house is at/by the coast.   c. Ruby's house is at the beach.

② **stand by** を比べる

62　Oton, Okan and Bakunsai just stood by without helping.
63　④ The actor is standing by.

【Ⅲ】イメージを比べる 545

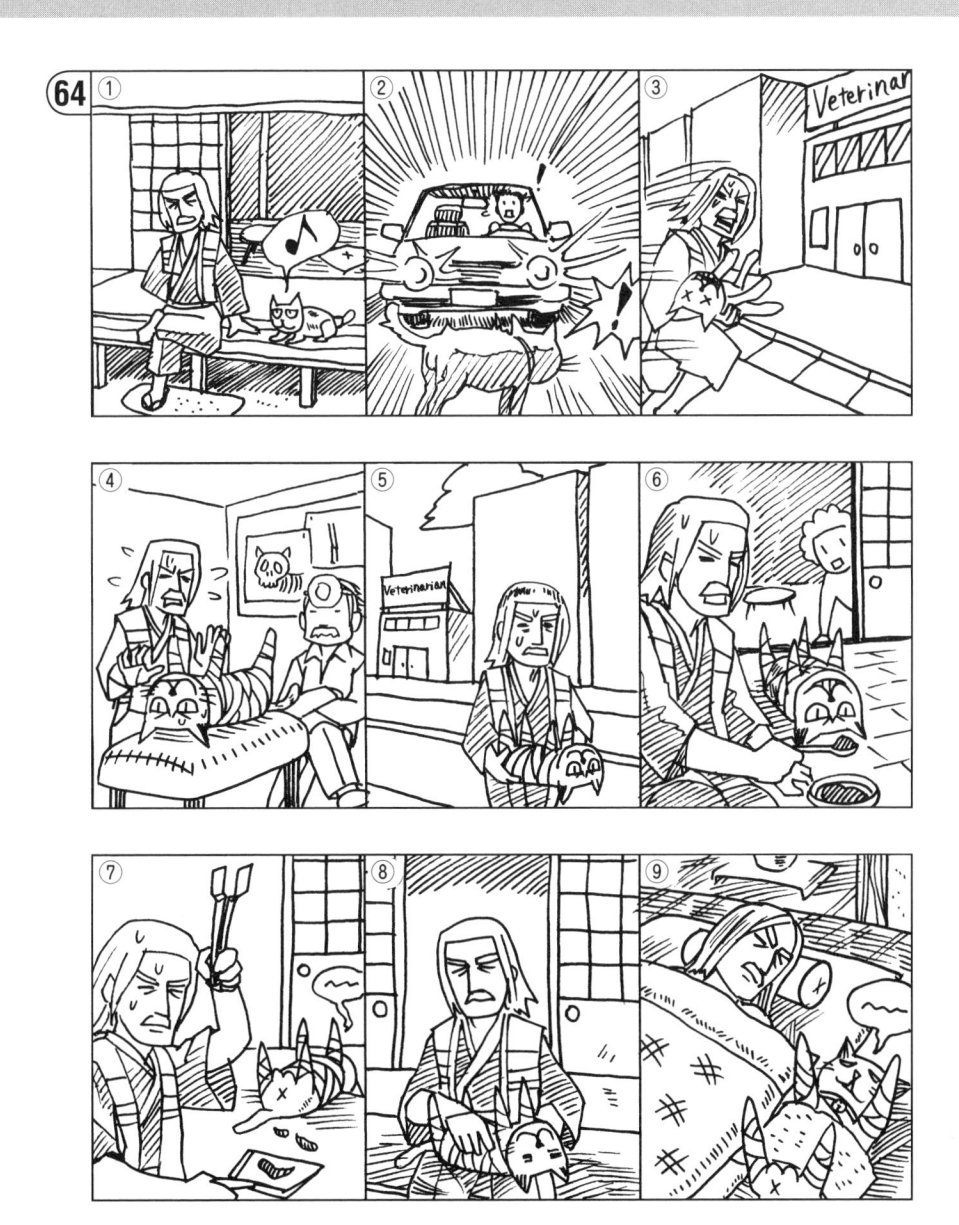

64 Bakunsai always stands by Dora.

① 自ら上がっている up

The sun is **up.**

1 a, b. The sun is rising/coming up.　c. The sun is up.
2 The hot-air balloon is up in the sky.
   The hot-air balloon is rising.
3 b, c. The frog is jumping up from the lily pad.

【Ⅰ】基本のイメージ 547

The flag is **up.**

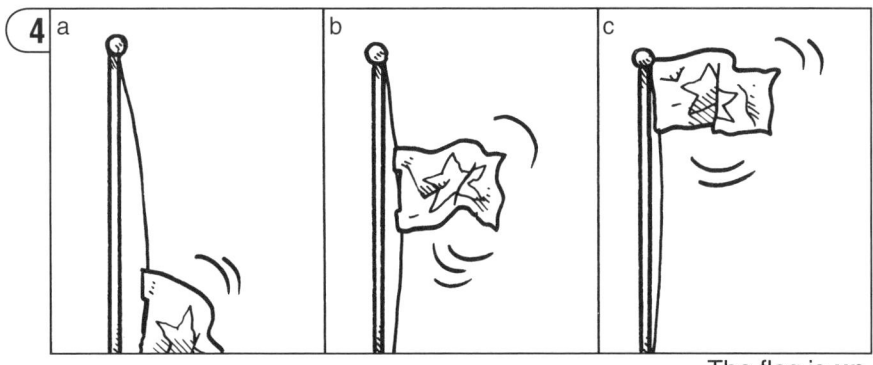

The kite is **up.** (c)

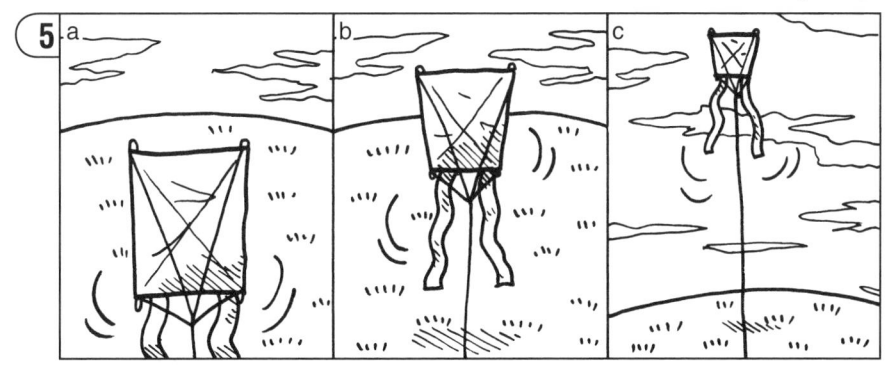

They are pulling it **up.**

4 c. The flag is up.
5 c. The kite is up.
6 The piano is being pulled up.

②他を上げている up

send the flag **up**

7 a, b. Teria is raising the flag.
　c. Teria has sent the flag up.　Teria has raised the flag.
8 Teria is flying a kite.　Teria got the kite up.
9 a, b. The fish is being pulled out of the water.　c. The fisherman is holding the fish up.

put ~ **up** on the shelves

---

10 Tim put the box up on the shelves.
11 Mama put up the koinobori for the holiday.
12 Tim lifted the box up.
   Tim lifted up the box.

①のぼっている

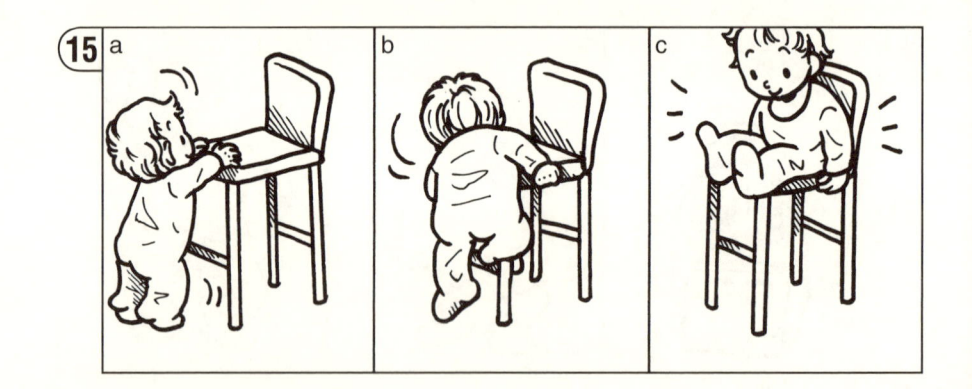

13 Malow is going up the stairs.
14 The fish is swimming up the falls.
15 b. Baby is climbing up the chair.
   c. He (has) climbed up on the chair.
      He is up on the chair.

②到達点までのぼる **up to**

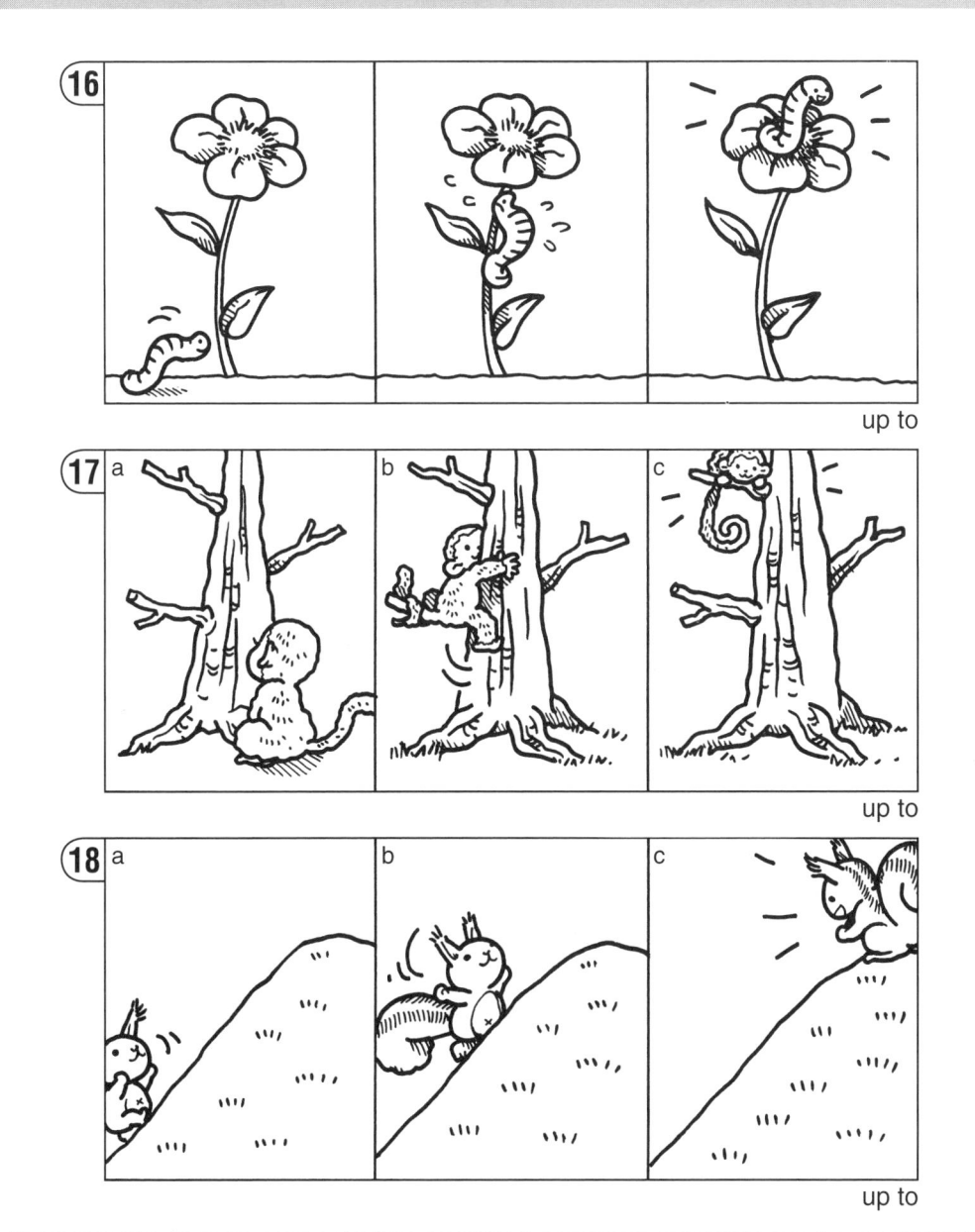

up to

up to

up to

16 The caterpillar climbed up to the top of the flower.
17 b. The monkey is climbing up to a higher branch.
18 a, b. The chipmunk is walking up the hill.
   c. The chipmunk has walked up to the top of the hill.

③自ら大きくしている

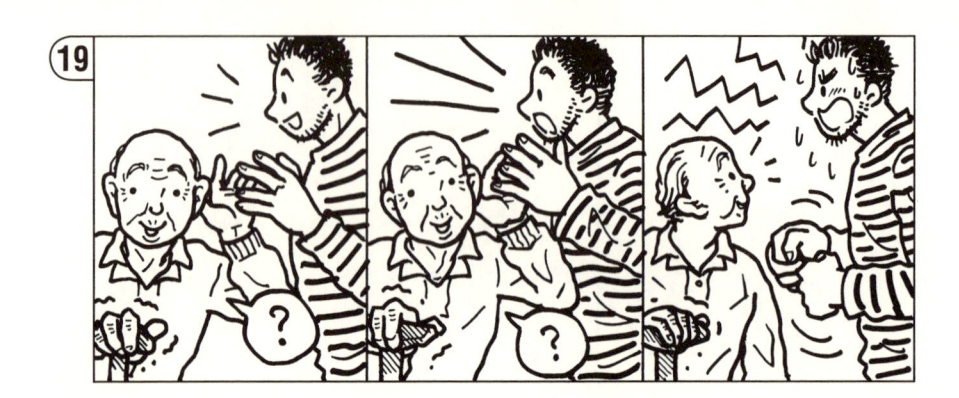

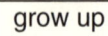

19 The old man asked Butch to speak up.
20 c. Grandma has grown up.   d. Grandma has grown old.
21 The vine is growing (up and up).

④他を強くしている

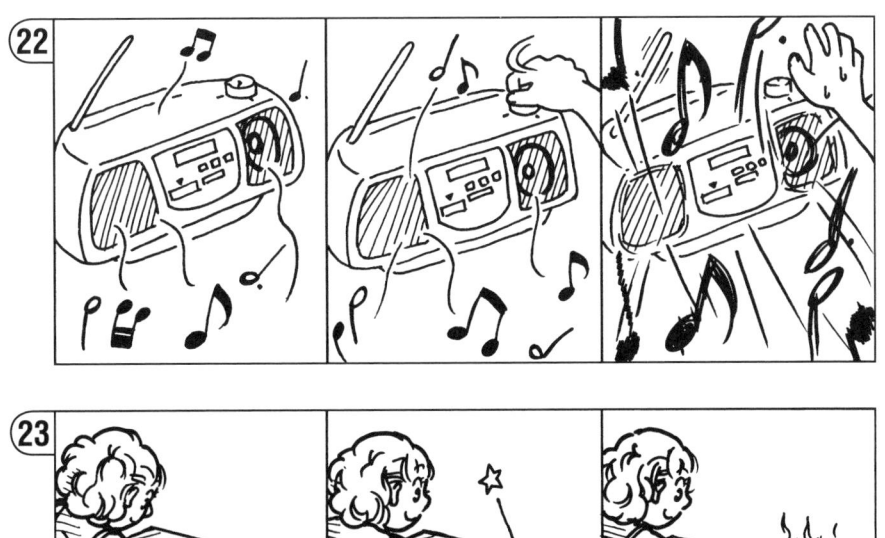

22 The man turned the sound way up.
23 Mama turned the flame up on the stove.
24 a, b. Inond is building up his body.

⑤「近づく」を強調している **up to**

25　The shark came right up to Sylvia.
26　The deer came up (to Teria) and licked her hand.
27　Earl came up to Borizi and held him up.

⑥合わせる up to

28 I don't care; it's up to you.
29 It is your birthday; it's up to you.
30 You choose. This time it's completely up to you.

⑦ 自ら起き上がっている

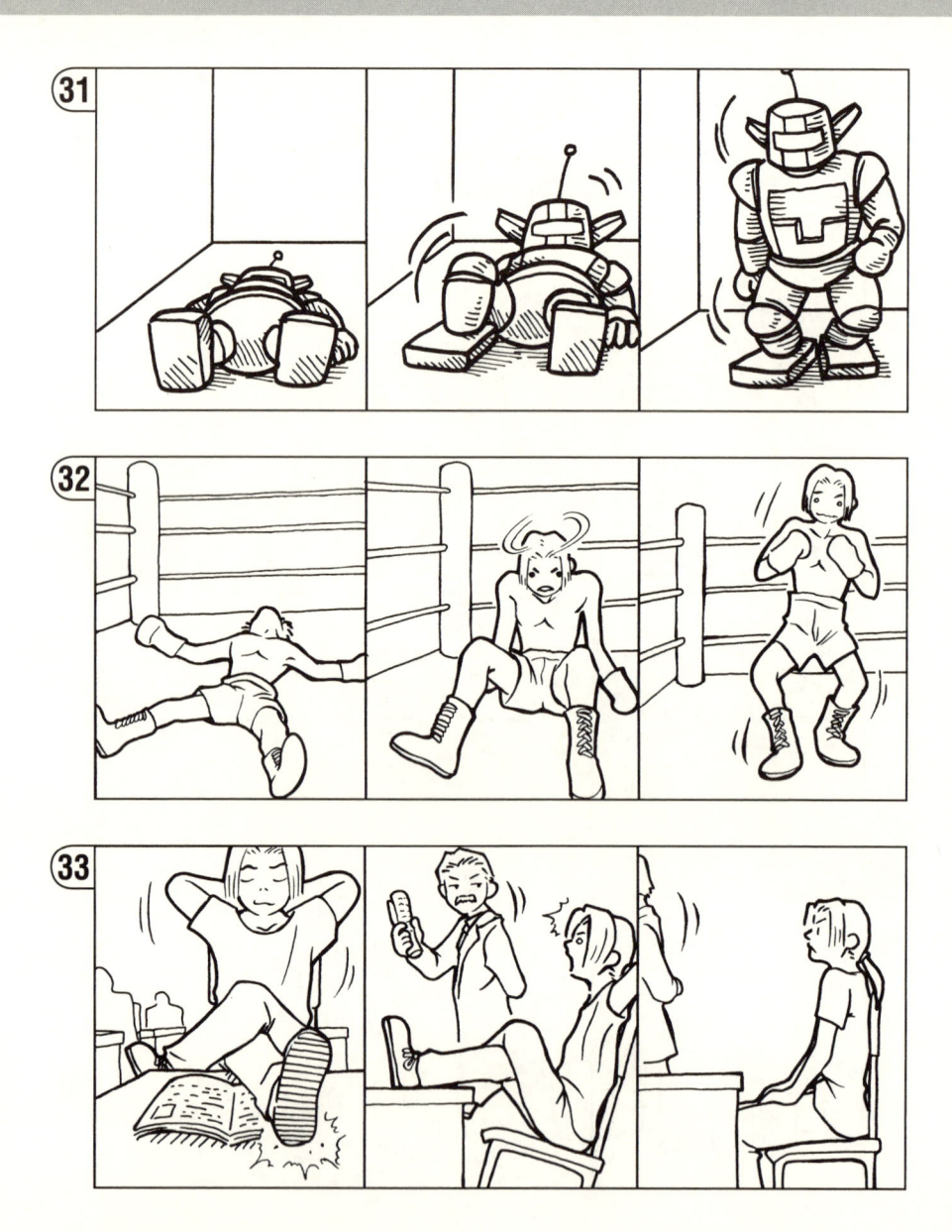

31　Roboman stood up.　He got up.
32　Fennel got up.　He stood up.
33　Fennel sat up.

【Ⅱ】連想するイメージ 557

34　The wolf looked up at the moon.
35　a. Teria woke up.　b. She sat up.　c. She got up.
36　Tim is staying up late tonight.

⑧ 他を起こしている

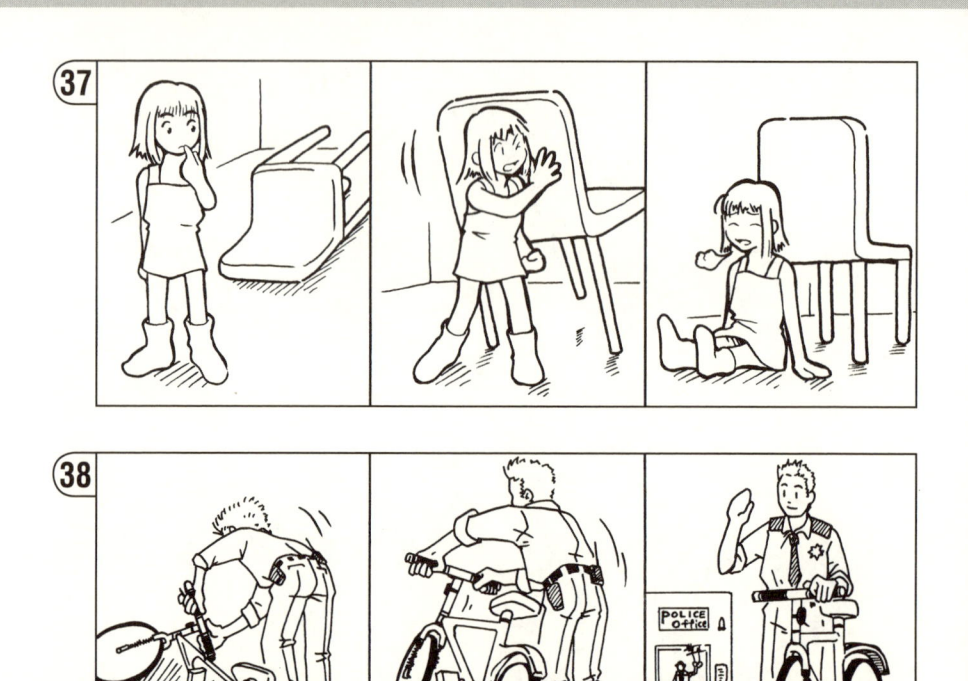

37　Chicori set the chair up/upright.
38　Sorel stood the bike up.
39　Leaf stood the figure up.

⑨「何が起きているの?」の up to

40　Mama, you haven't done anything.
　　What are you up to?
　　Mama is not up to doing her chores today.
41　What are you up to?
42　What are you up to?

560 ... up

⑩ 上げている

hang up the picture

43 Olivia pulled her pants up.   Olivia pulled up her pants.
44 b. Mama is rolling her sleeves up.   Mama is rolling up her sleeves.
45 b. Papa hung up the picture.   He put the picture up.
   c. He moved it/the picture up higher.

【Ⅱ】連想するイメージ

46　b, c. Tim has his hand up.　Tim's hand is up.
　　　　 Tim put his hand up.　Tim raised his hand.
47　c. Teria's leg is up in the air.　Teria put her leg up.
48　Earl held up the bank clerk.　The bank clerk put her hands up.

⑩ 上げている

pick up the phone

49 Teria is picking the phone up.   Teria is picking up the phone.
50 Mama picked the kitten up.   Mama picked up the kitten.
51 Someone picked the flower up.   Someone picked up the flower.

⑪ **up** は使わない!

set it down　　hang on the phone

pick it

pull it out

52　b. Sylvia set the phone down.　Sylvia set down the phone.
　　c. Butch is hanging on the phone.
53　Someone picked the flower.
54　She pulled the flower out (of the ground).　Someone pulled out the flower.
　　She pulled the flower up.　She pulled up the flower.

564 ... up

⑫し上げている

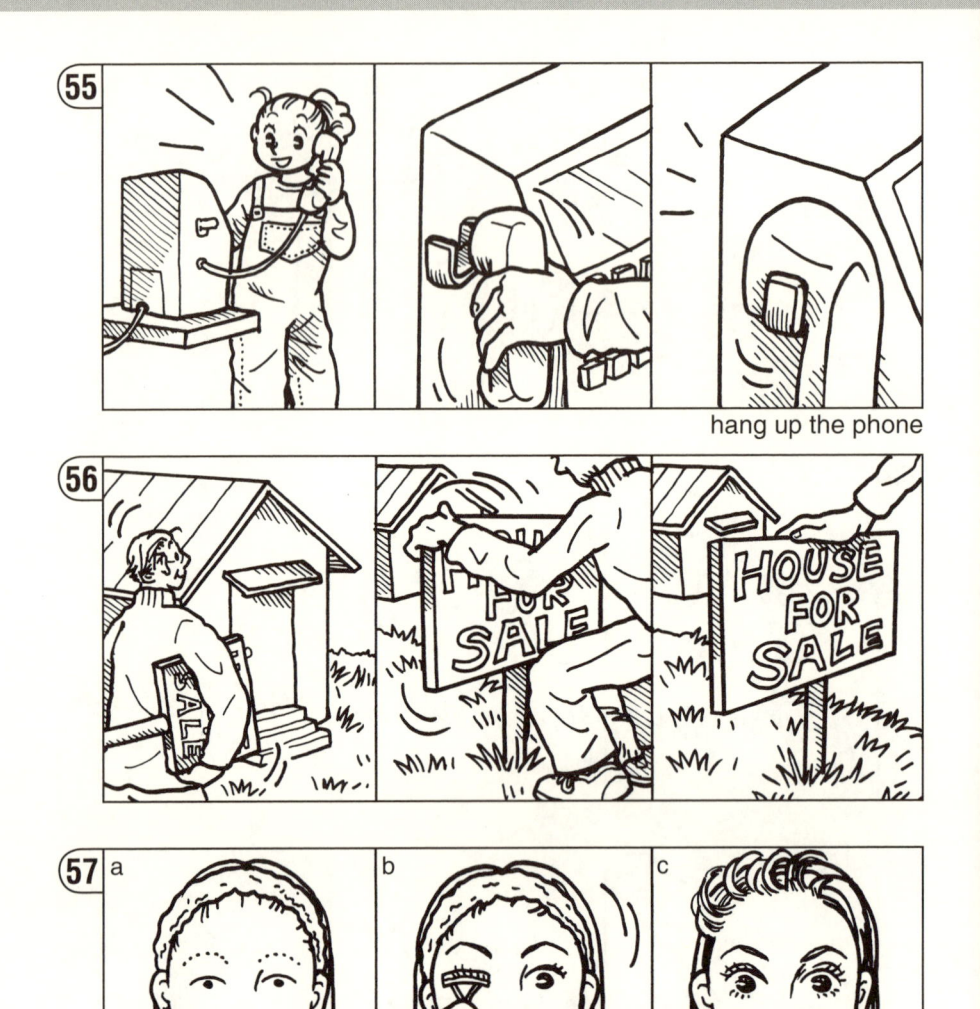

hang up the phone

55 Teria hung up the phone.
56 Papa put up a 'for sale' sign.
57 b. The girl is making up her face.

【Ⅱ】連想するイメージ

make up a story

58 b. Inond is putting a tent up.　Inond is putting up a tent.
　　c. Inond put the tent up.　Inond put up the tent.
59 a, b. Inond is putting a house up.　Inond is putting up a house.　Inond is building a house.
60 c. Papa made up a story.　Papa told a lie.

⑫し上げている

61 ② Dr. Bizarro is tightening the lid.
62 ③ Even though Sorel tied Earl's hands, he managed to escape.
63 ③ Malow locked the door.

【Ⅱ】連想するイメージ

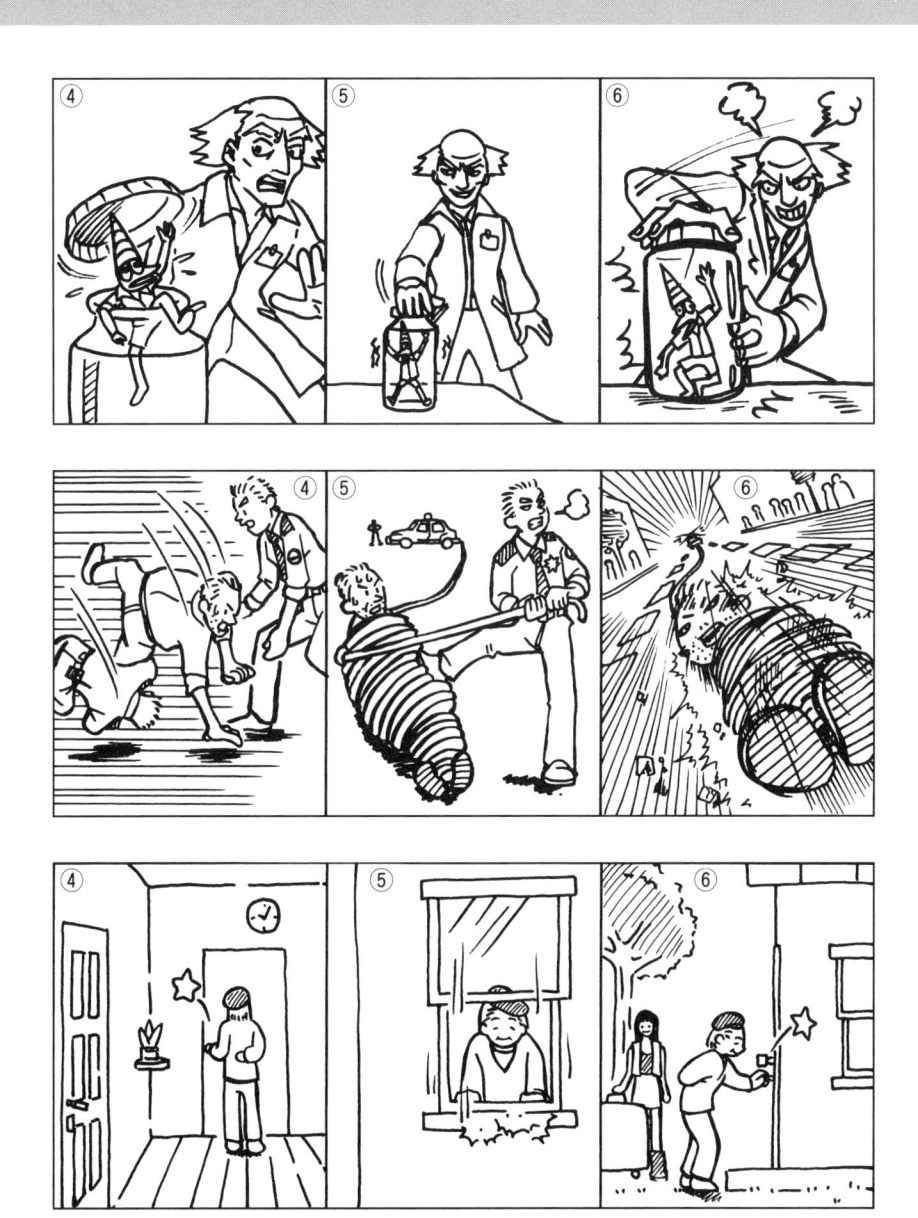

61 ⑥ This time, he is really tightening it up/down.
62 ⑥ This time, they have really tied him up.
63 ⑥ Malow locked up the house.

⑬ 終わりに達している

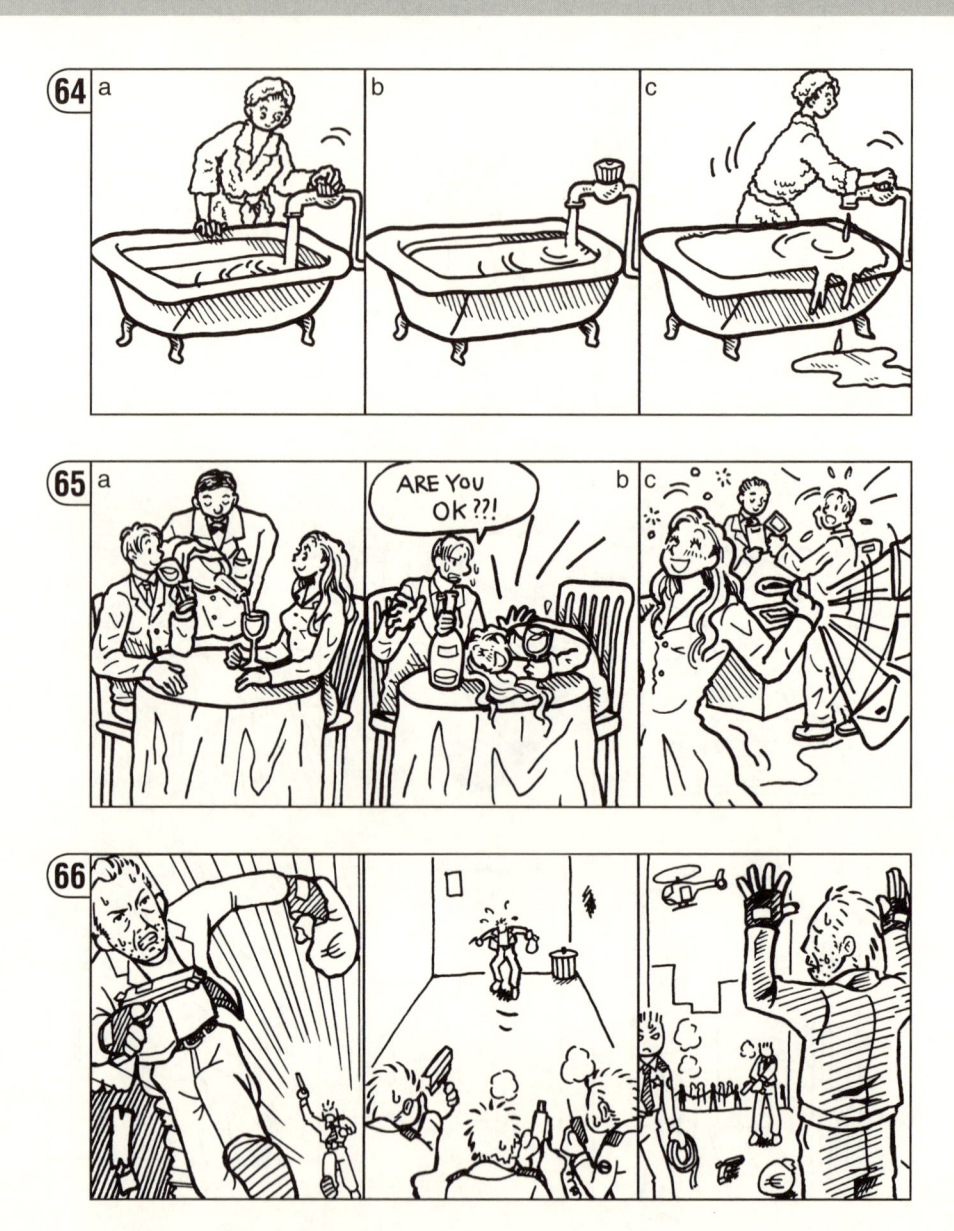

64 c. The tub is filled up (with water).
65 a. The waiter is filling up their glasses.   c. Sylvia ended up drunk.   Her spirits are up.
66 Earl gave (himself) up.

【Ⅱ】連想するイメージ 569

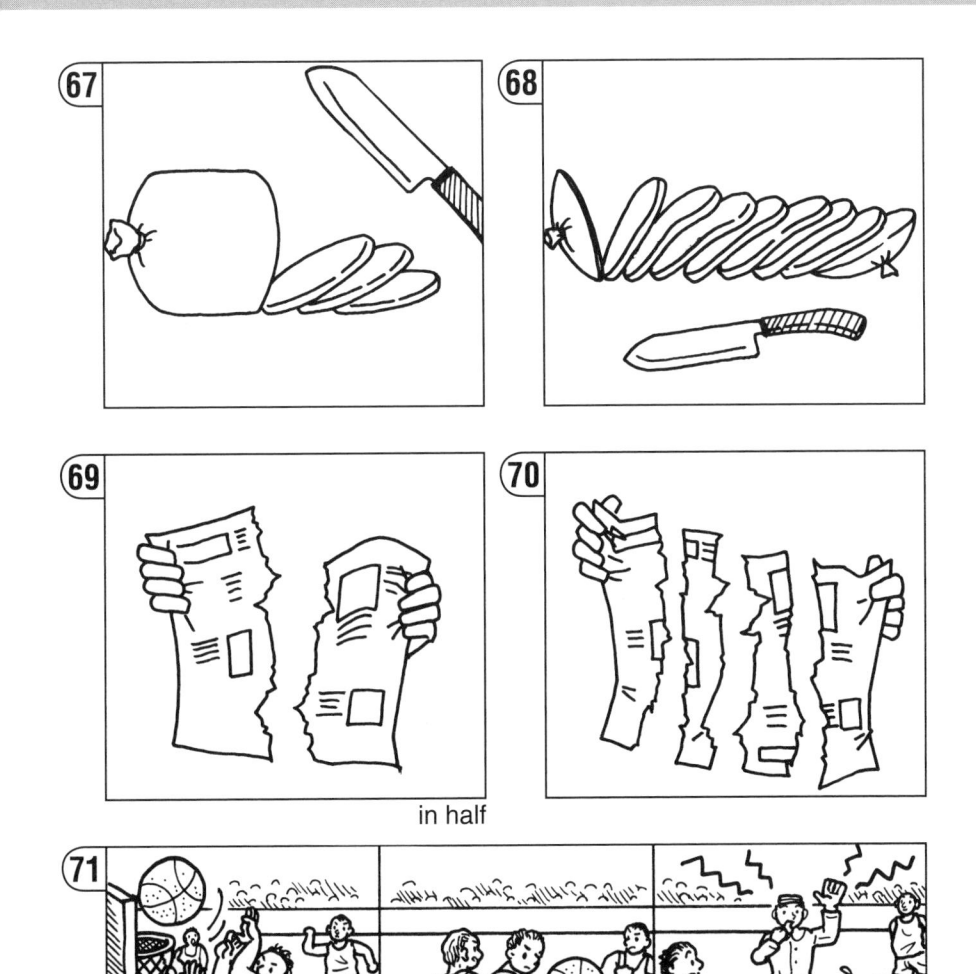

in half

67 Someone sliced/cut three pieces of sausage.
68 Someone sliced/cut up the sausage.
69 Someone tore the newspaper in half.
70 Someone tore up the newspaper.
71 The time is up.

⑬ 終わりに達している

72 ③ Olivia is eating some cookies.
73 ③ Mama is using some sugar in the jam.
74 ②③ The children are gathering the picnic stuff.

【Ⅱ】連想するイメージ　571

72　⑥ Olivia has eaten them all up.
73　⑥ Mama has used up all the sugar.
74　⑤ The children have gathered it all up.

①自ら下げている / 降りている down

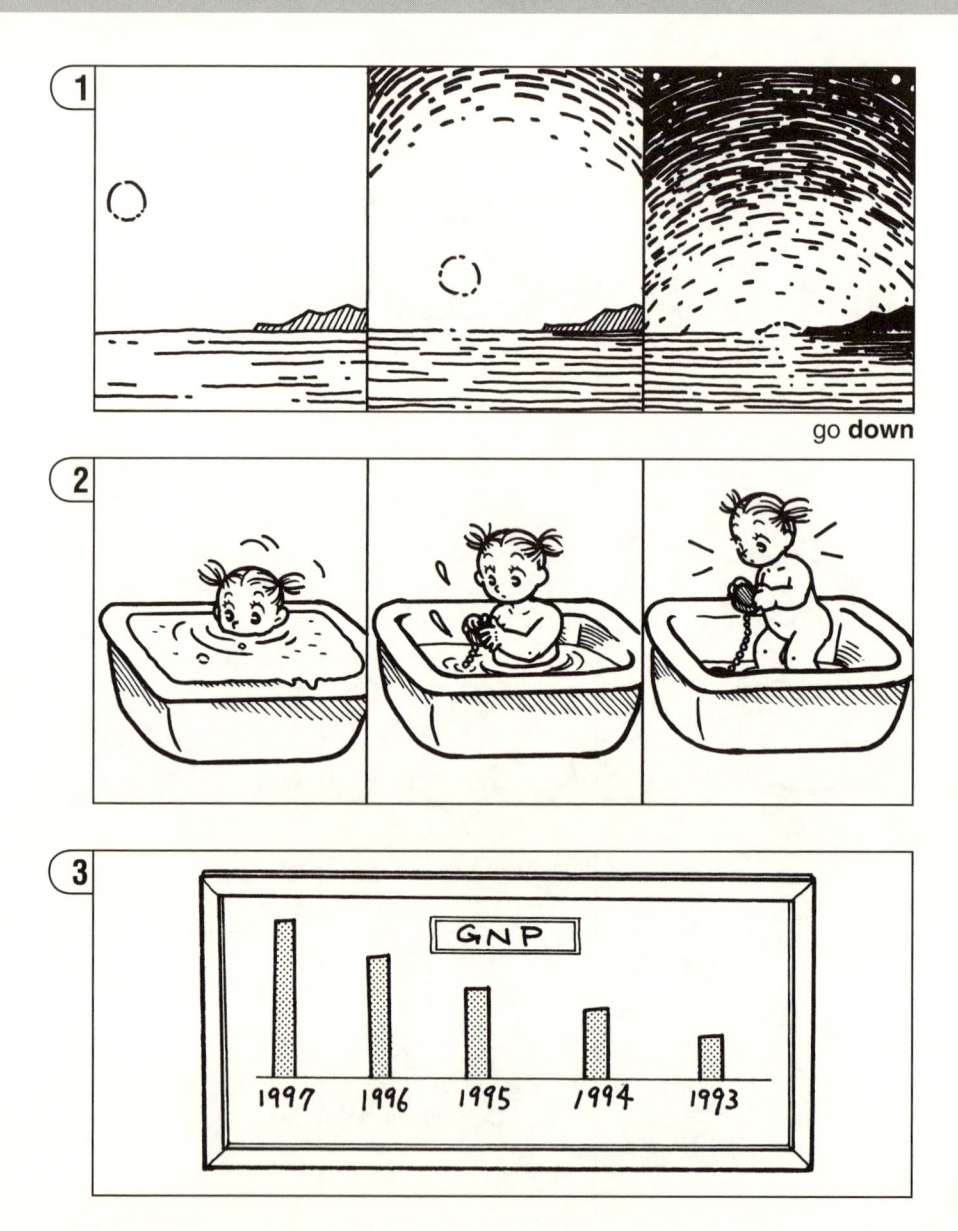

go **down**

1　The sun is going down.
2　The water level went down.
3　The GNP went down.

walk **down**

4　Malow walked down the steps/the stairs.
5　a, b. Ruby is climbing down the wall.
6　The stool/The B.M. is floating downstream/down the stream.

②他を降ろしている **down**

help him **down**

lay her **down**

7　The giraffe helped the koala down.
8　Olivia laid the teddy bear down.
9　Mama laid/put Baby down.

【Ⅰ】基本のイメージ 575

take 〜 **down**

put 〜 **down**

10　Papa took the box down.
　　Papa took down the box.
11　Eluca put the suitcase down.
　　Eluca put down the suitcase.
12　Eluca put the vase down on the table.

down

① 自らを下げている

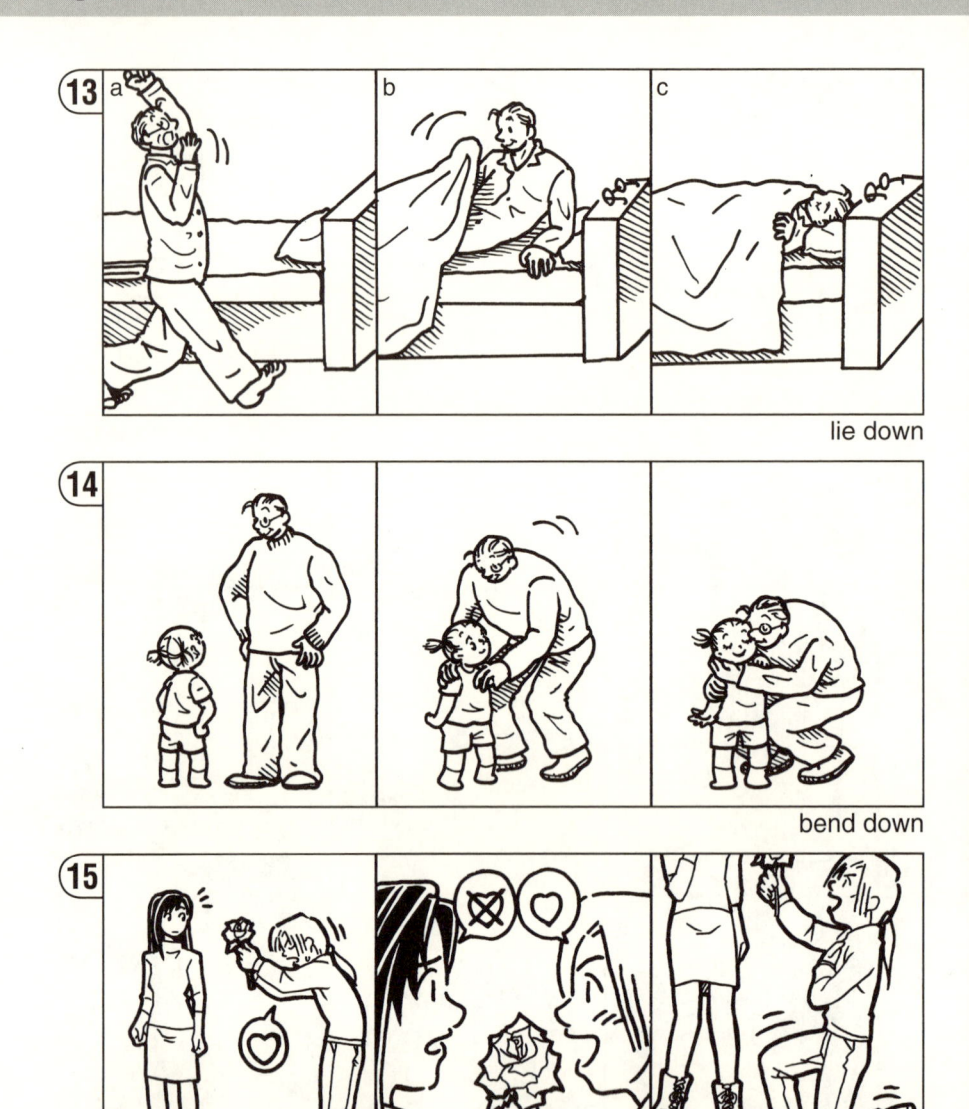

13 lie down

14 bend down

15 kneel down

13 b. Papa is lying down.　c. Papa is lying down.　Papa lay down.
14 Papa bent down to give Olivia a kiss.
15 c. Fennel is kneeling down to propose.

【Ⅱ】連想するイメージ 577

look down

write ～ down

16 Leaf is looking down.
17 The big sumo wrestler is staring down at the smaller one.
18 The big sumo wrestler is staring down at the smaller one.
19 Papa wrote down the message.
　 Papa wrote the message down.

② 落下している

fall down

fall down

fall

20 a. Chicori knocked the icicle down.   Chicori knocked down the icicle.
   c. The icicle fell down.
21 The alarm clock fell down.
22 The meteorite fell from the sky.

【Ⅱ】連想するイメージ

burn down

break down

23 The monkey fell down.
24 The house burned down.
25 The car broke down.

down

③弱くしている

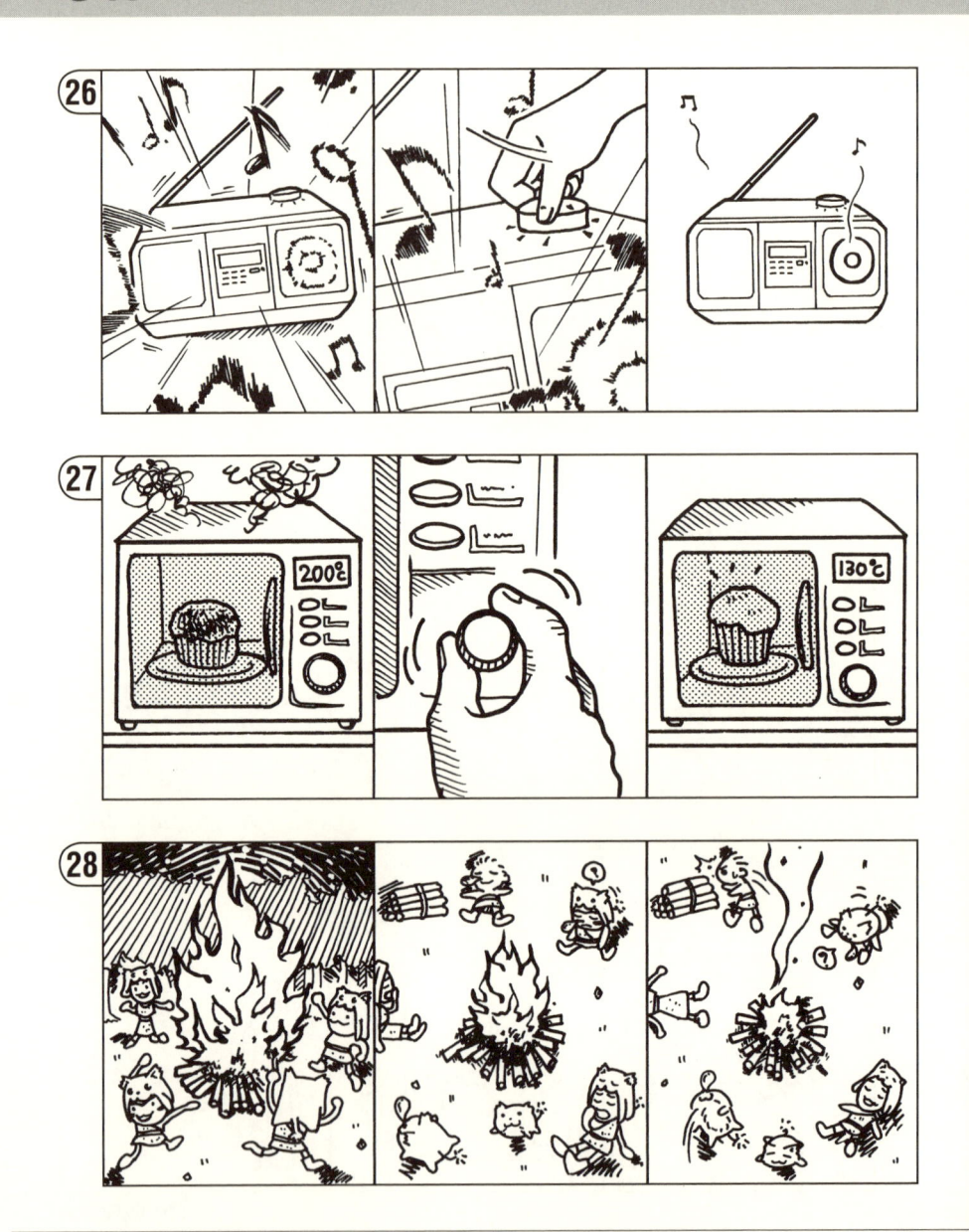

26 Someone turned the music down. He turned the radio/the volume down.
   Someone turned down the music. He turned down the radio/the volume.
27 She turned the oven down.
   She turned down the oven.
28 The fire burned down.

【Ⅱ】連想するイメージ 581

29 b. Papa quieted the children down.
　　Papa quieted down the children.
　　c. The children quieted down.
30　Leaf turned Fennel down.
　　Leaf turned down Fennel.
31　Leaf brought Fennel down.

① 上る up と下る down

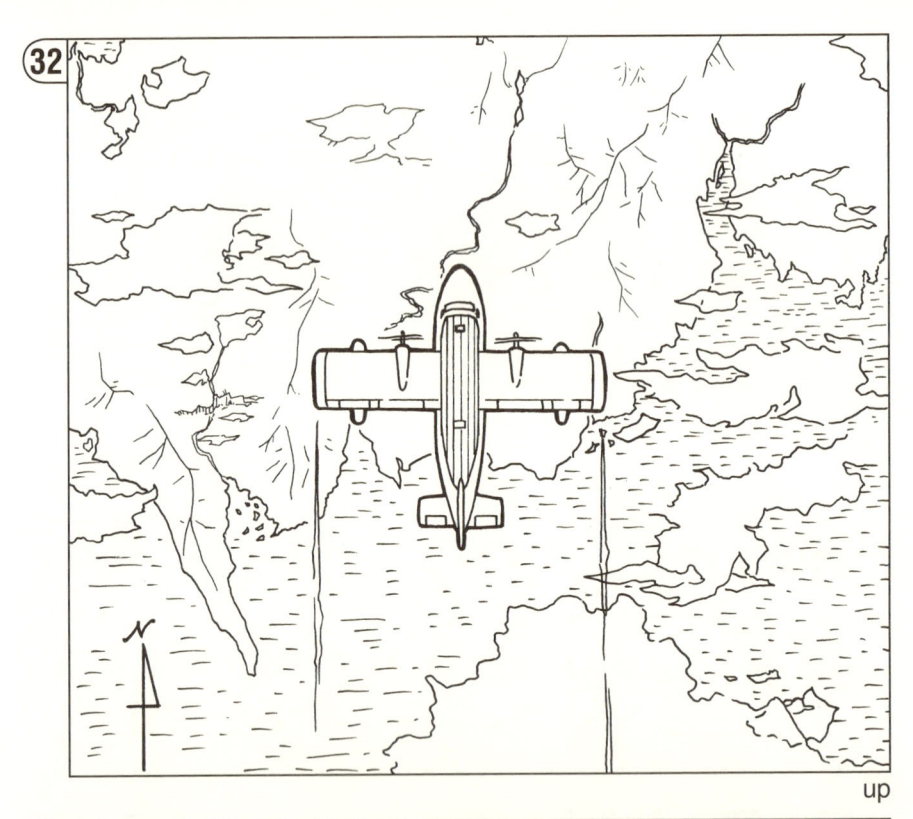

up

32　The plane is flying up North.　　The plane is flying to the North.
33　a. Leaf and Borizi live on the top of the hill.
　　b. Leaf's grandmother, Malow lives down the hill from them.
　　　 Malow lives up the hill from Leaf's friend.
　　c. Leaf's friend also lives down/on the hill.

【Ⅲ】イメージを比べる 583

down

down

down

34　The airplane is flying down South.　The airplane is flying (to the) South.
35　The train is going down South.
36　They are driving down the coast.

②前方の up と down

㊲

up / down

㊳

up / down

㊴

up ahead

37　Let's walk up/down to the post office.
38　How far shall we go?　　Let's walk up/down to the drugstore.
39　The road is under construction just up ahead.

③ up and down

up and down

40 Olivia is jumping up and down on the bed.
41 The bear is walking up and down his cage.
42 The tourists are walking up and down the street.

aside

in front of

in back of

backwards

forwards

ahead of

Chapter 4
3次元（立体）として見なさい

beside
behind
after
before
toward(s)
beyond
above
below
underneath
beneath

①立体の横にいる / ある beside

1 beside / next to the van

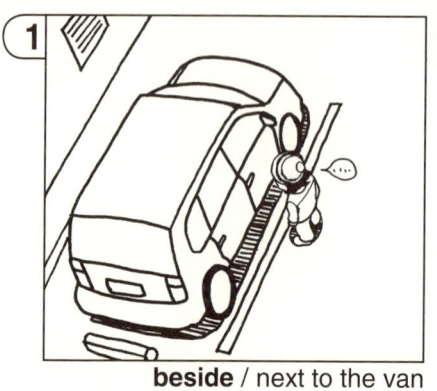

1. Bowsheeman is standing beside/next to/at the side of the van.
2. Doggie is lying beside/next to/at the side of his house.
3. The coffee shop is next to/beside the cheese shop.
4. Kitten is lying next to/beside the tree.
5. The orange is next to/beside the apple.
6. The tulip is next to/beside the sunflowers.

The coffee shop is located to the side of the cheese shop.

next to：点と見る 【Ⅰ】基本のイメージ

② 点のとなりにいる / ある next to

7 next to / in front of Teria

10 next to / under

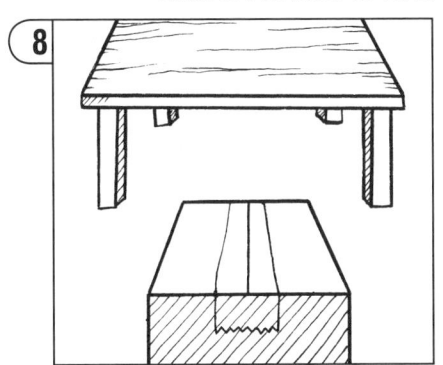

11

12

7　Baby is next to/in front of Teria.
8　The box is next to/in front of the table.
9　Olivia is next to/behind/in back of the chair.
10　Tim is next to/under the tree.
11　The chopsticks are next to the bowl.
12　The tea shop is next to/in front of the bakery.

③横の beside と、となりの next to

beside / next to the washing machine

13 Teria put the laundry beside/next to the washing machine.
14 Tim put the turtle down beside/next to the rock.
15 The deliveryman put the box down beside/next to the table.

④「脇へ」の aside

put her handbag **aside**

move **aside**

16 Sylvia set/put her handbag aside/down.
17 Kitten moved aside for the big cat.
18 Olivia and Baby moved aside to let the car go by.

⑤立体の中— inside 外— outside

inside the house   outside the house

in   out of

1 a. Olivia and Baby are playing inside (the house).
   b. Olivia and Baby are playing outside (the house).
2 a. Ruby is outside the shower.   c. Ruby is inside the shower/bathtub.
3 b. Ruby is in the shower.   c. Ruby is out of the shower.

【Ⅰ】基本のイメージ 593

outside the store　　　　　　　　**inside** the store

on

on

4　a. There is a sale sign outside the store.　　　c. There is a sale sign inside the store.
　　　The sale sign is outside the store.　　　　　　The sale sign is inside the store.
5　The for sale sign is outside the house.
6　The for sale sign is on (the outside of) the building.
7　The chocolate is inside/in the pastry.
8　The chocolate is on (the outside of) the pastry.

594 behind : 3Dと見る

①立体の向こう側にいる / ある behind

behind the car

1 Candy is standing behind the car.
  [on the other side of]
2 There is a dinosaur behind the house.
  [on the other side of]
3 Ruby's father is behind the newspaper.
4 a. The car is behind Dr. Bizarro.   c. Dr. Bizarro is behind the car.

【Ⅰ】基本のイメージ 595

②影響している behind と場所だけの in back of

behind the driver

in back of the pilot

behind

in back of

behind

in back of

5　There is an alien sitting behind the driver.
7　A girl is hiding behind the tree.
9　The flowers are behind the house.

6　Rose is sitting in back of/behind Inond/ the pilot.
8　The children are running in back of/ behind the tree.
10　The flowers are in back of the house.

③背後にいる behind

behind many people

in back of Olivia

11 Teria is behind many people.
12 Butch is in back of Olivia.
13 The children are following behind Mama.
14 The policeman is coming up behind Earl.

【Ⅰ】基本のイメージ 597

④あとを追う after

after Ruby

15　Ruby's father follows after her everywhere she goes.
16　The ducklings are following (along) after/behind their mother.
17　The policeman is following after Earl everywhere.

598 … in back of：面と見る

①後ろにいる/ある in back of

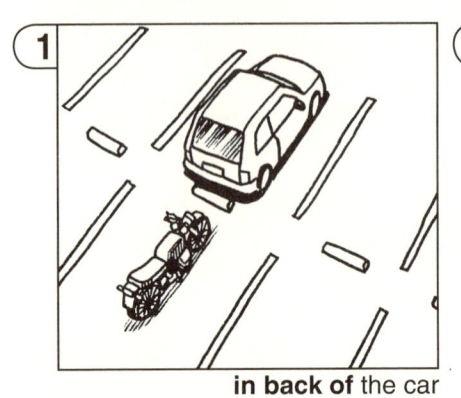

in back of the car

WHERE'S KITTEN?

IN BACK OF THE TREE!

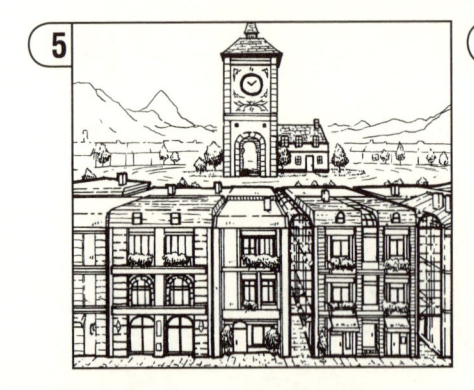

1 The motorcycle is in back of/behind the car.
2 Doggie is in back of /behind Dora.
3 Kitten is in back of/behind the tree.
4 Ruby is in back of/behind Nautilus.
　Ruby is on the back of the motorcycle.
5 The clock tower is in back of/behind the buildings.
6 The windmill is in back of/behind the house.

【Ⅰ】基本のイメージ 599

②後ろの方にいる / ある in the back of

in the back of the car

on the back of

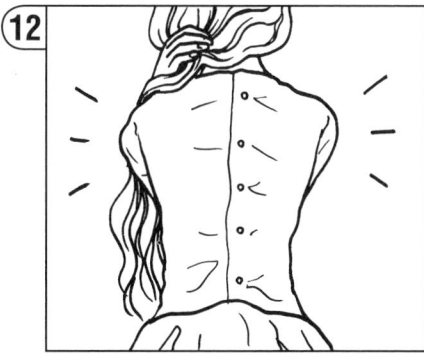

on the back of

7 Bakunsai is in the back of the car. He is in (the) back.
8 Bowsheeman is in the back of the bus.
9 Teria is in the back of the theater.
10 Candy is on the back of the bike.
11 The windmill is in the back of the corral/enclosure.
12 The buttons are on the back of the dress.

①「時間的に前に」の before

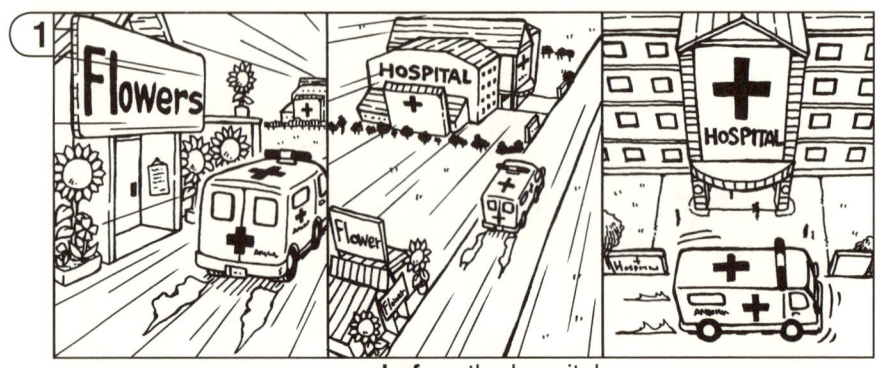

before the hospital

1. The flower shop is before the hospital.
2. There are two gates before the entrance.
3. There are many people before Katarina (in the line).
   There are many people in front of Katerina (in the line).

②「位置的に前に」の in front of

in front of the hospital

4 There is a flower shop in front of the hospital.
5 There are two gates in front of the entrance.
6 There are four people in front of Katarina.

③目の前の before

before him

before his eyes

7　The town is spread out before Inond.
8　A field of flowers lies before Leaf.
9　Majestic mountains stretch out before Eluca.
10　Bakunsai's fingers are right before the ninja's eyes.
11　The accident is happening before Bowsheeman's eyes.
12　There is a burst of light before Bakunsai's eyes.

④ before と in front of を比べる

before (13, 14, 15)

in front of (16, 17, 18)

13 Mama and Papa are fighting bitterly before/in front of Olivia.
14 Tim sits before/in front of the TV all day long.
15 A bear suddenly appeared before/in front of Butch's eyes/Butch.
16 There is a crowd of sea munchkins in front of Dr. Bizarro.
17 There is a crowd in front of Teria.
18 There is a woman with a big hat sitting in front of Teria.

①前にいる / ある in front of

in front of the car

in front of

in **the** front of

1　The bicycle is in front of the car.
2　Teria is in front of Butch.
3　Bowsheeman is in front of the picture.
4　Sylvia is in front of the display window.
5　The park is in front of the hotel.
6　There is a cafe in the front of the hotel property.

②前の方にいる / ある in the front of

in the front of the car

7 The engine is in the front of the car.
8 Inond is in the front (seat) of the airplane.
9 Bakunsai is in the front of the picture.
10 There is a dress in the front of the shop.
11 There is a coffee shop in the front of the building.

toward(s)：3Dと見る

①立体に向かっている toward(s)

toward(s) the north

1 Butch is walking toward(s) the north.
2 Teria is running toward(s) her goal.
3 Icarus flew toward(s) the sun.

【Ⅰ】基本のイメージ 607

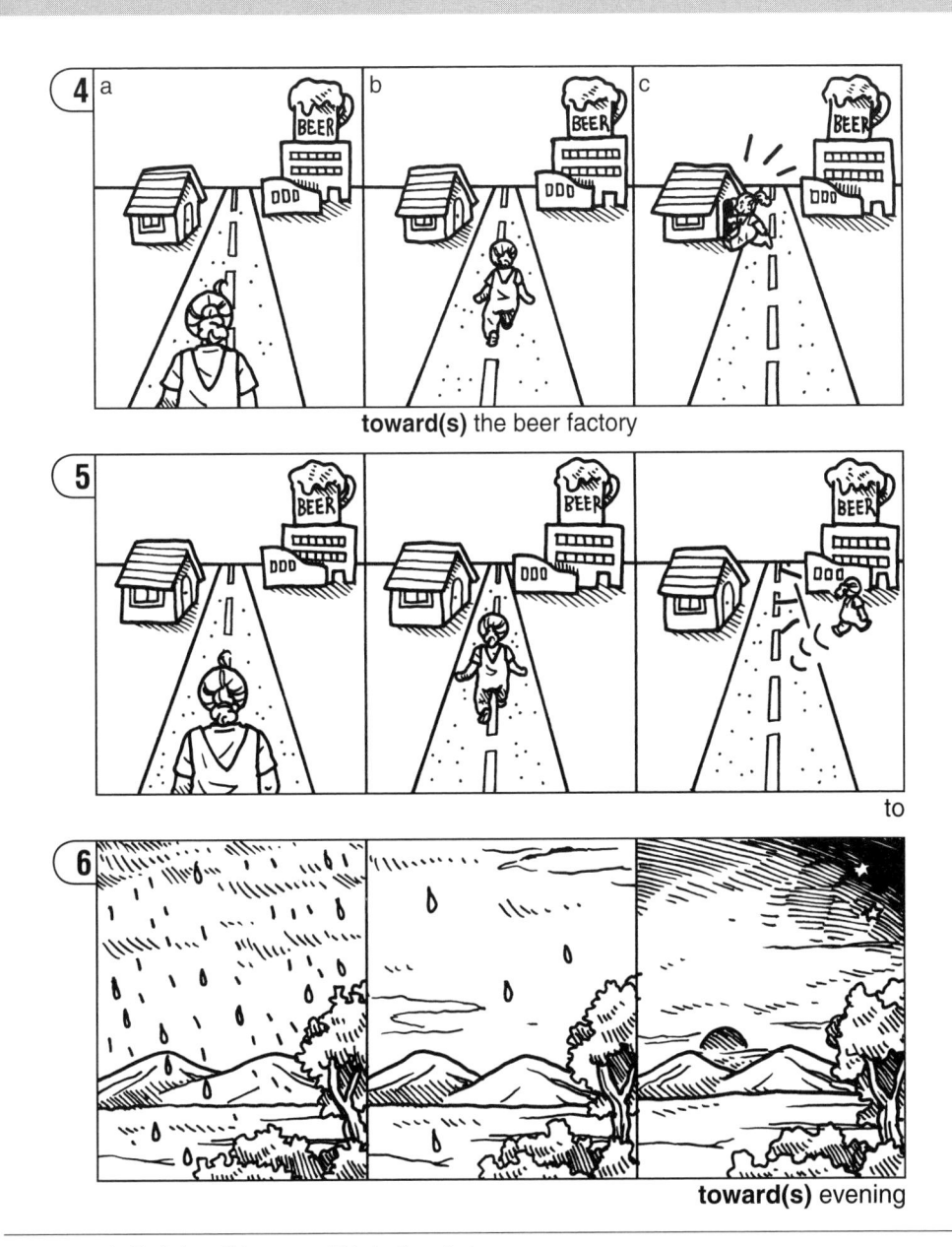

toward(s) the beer factory

to

toward(s) evening

4 a, b. Teria is walking toward(s) the beer factory.
5 Teria is walking to the (beer) factory.
6 The rain stopped toward(s) evening.

toward(s)：3Dと見る

②立体に向いている toward(s)

toward(s) Ruby

7　Nautilus and Mr. Stone are both jumping toward(s) Ruby.
8　b, c. The house is tilting toward(s) the ocean.
9　The sunflower turns toward(s) the sun.

toward(s) the station

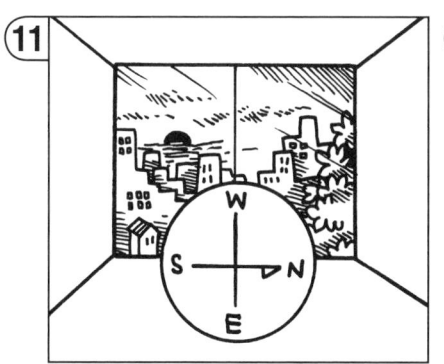

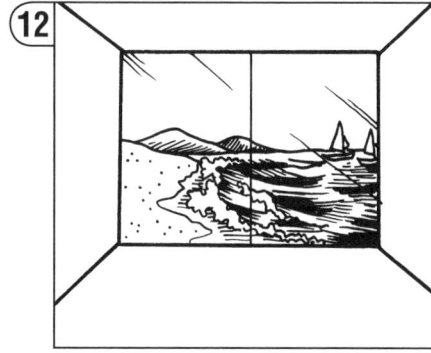

10 The fruit shop faces/is facing toward(s) the station.
11 The window faces toward(s) the west.
12 The window faces/is facing toward(s) the beach/the ocean.
13 The statue's finger points toward(s) the North Star.
14 Sylvia is pointing toward(s)/to the west.

610 toward(s)：3Dと見る
① toward(s) と to

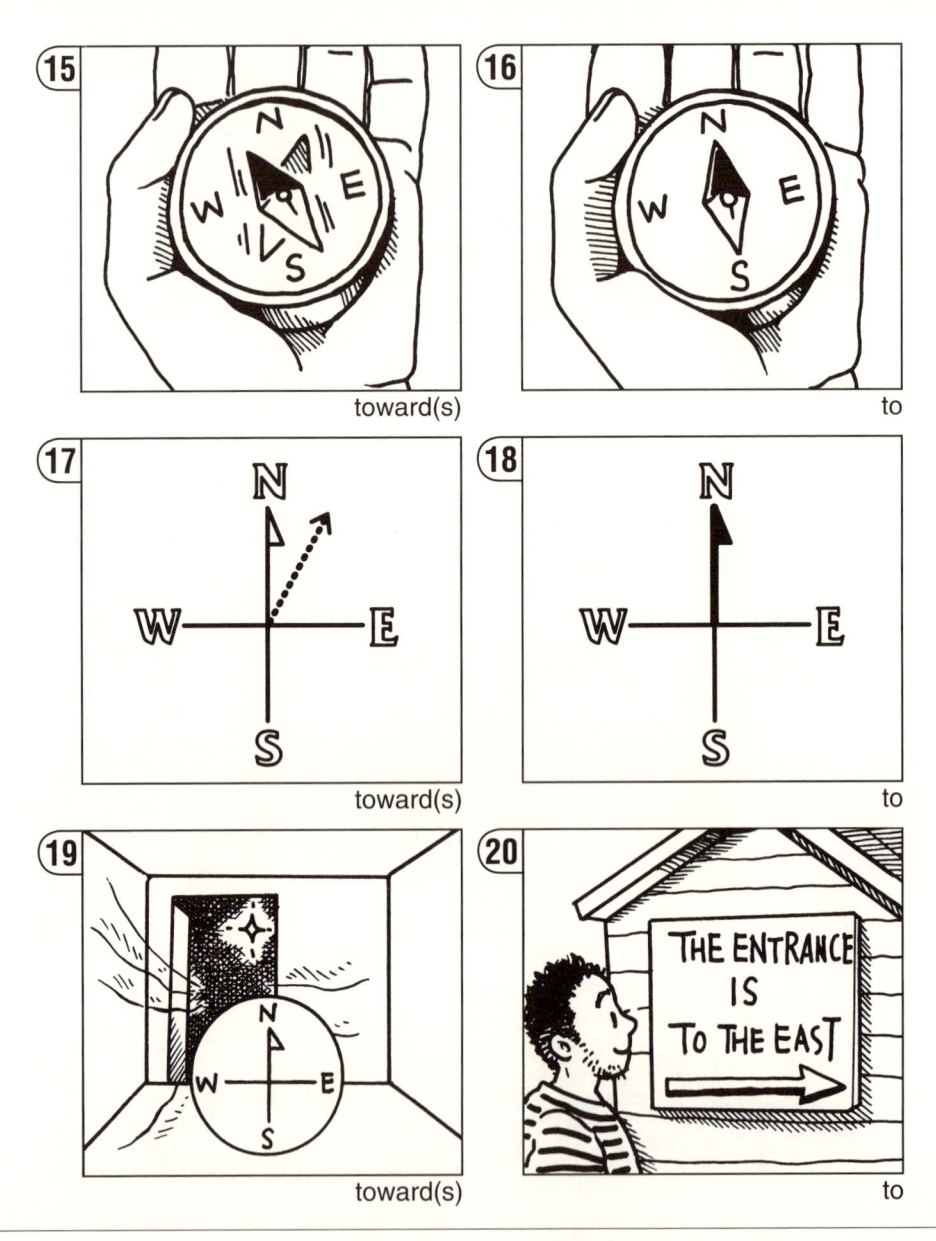

15 The compass needle is pointing toward(s) north.
16 The compass needle is pointing (to) north.
17 The arrow is pointing toward(s) north.
18 The arrow is pointing (to) north.
19 The entrance is toward(s) the north.
20 The entrance is to the east.

【Ⅱ】イメージを比べる 611

toward(s)

to

toward(s)

21　b, c. The car is turning toward(s) the right.
22　b. The car is turning right/to the right.
23　b. Leaf is talking toward(s) her father, Borizi.

612 ··· toward(s)：3Dと見る
② toward(s), to, at

toward(s)

to

at

24　c. Butch is waving toward(s)/to Sylvia.
25　c. Butch is waving to Sylvia.
26　Butch is waving at Sylvia.

【Ⅱ】イメージを比べる

27 Bakunsai is aiming the arrow toward(s) the target.
28 Bakunsai is pointing the arrow to/at the target.
29 The children are pointing at Tim.
30 Puppy is running toward(s) the intersection.
31 Puppy is running into the intersection. Now Puppy is at the corner.
32 Puppy turned at the intersection.

①前に向かう forward(s)

come **forward(s)**

1 Teria is coming forward(s).
2 Teria is going forward(s).
3 Teria is walking forward(s).

②先に行く ahead of

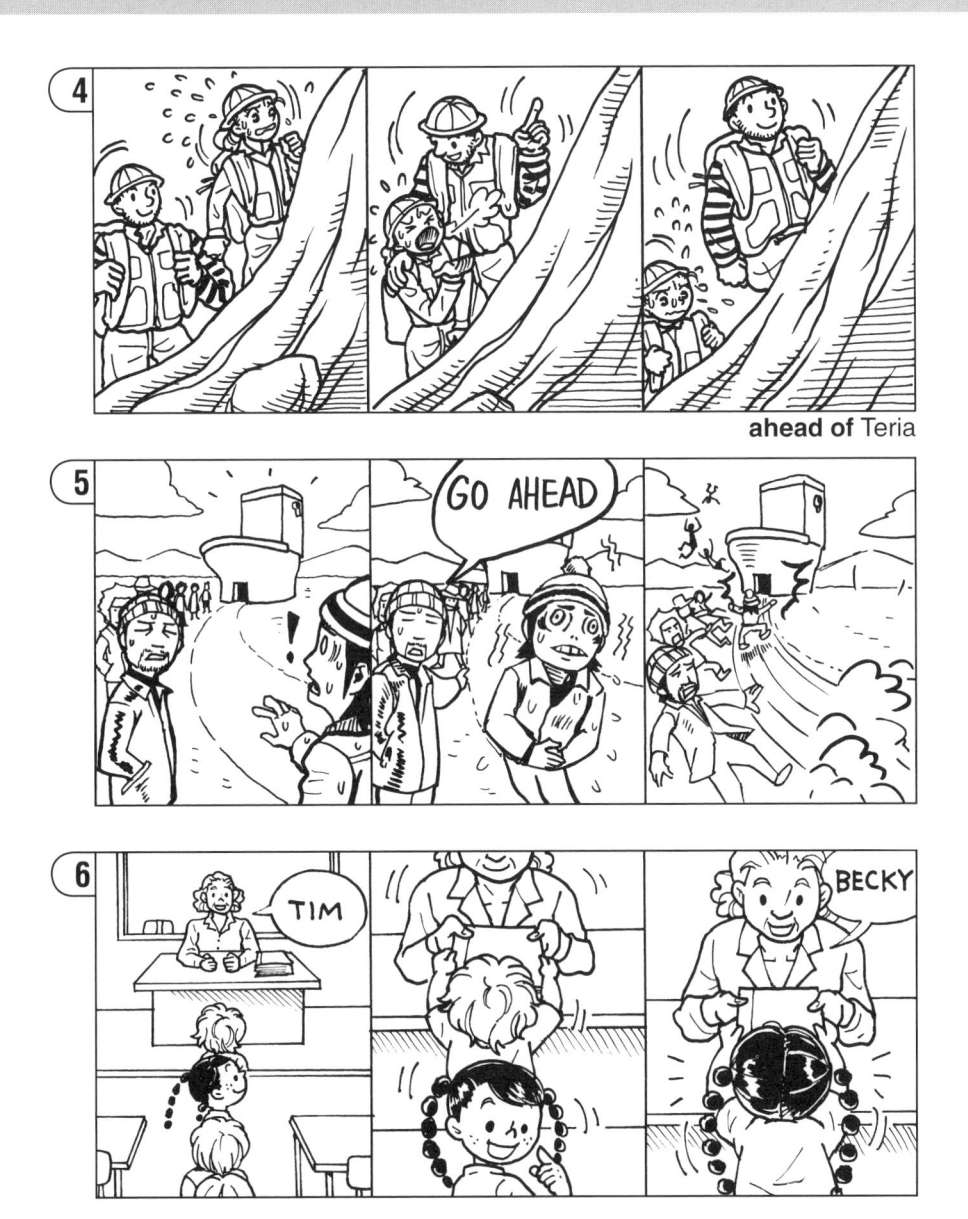

ahead of Teria

4　Butch went ahead of Teria.
5　Bowsheeman went ahead of everybody in the line.
6　Tim got his report card ahead of the girl with braids.

① forward(s) と ahead

come forward

forward

ahead

7　The teacher told Teria to come forward.
8　Butch signaled the dog to come forward.
9　Butch signaled the dog to come ahead/to him.
　　Butch told the dog, "Come on."

10　The lady is walking forward(s).
11　a. Bakunsai said, "Come on ahead." / "Come here."
　　c. Bowsheeman is walking backwards.
12　b. Vampire Tom told Ken, "Come here."　　c. Ken has come to Vampire Tom.

backward(s)

①後ろに下がる backwards

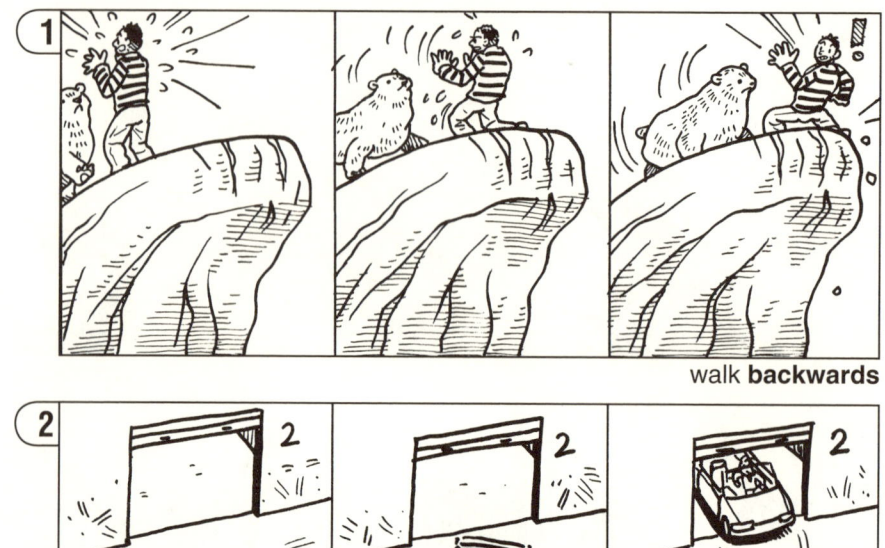

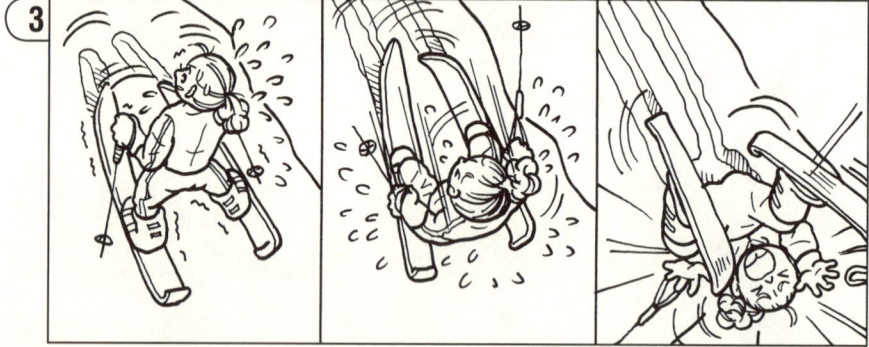

walk **backwards**

1. Butch is walking backwards.
   Butch is backing up.
2. Oton drove the car backwards (into the garage).
   Oton backed up the car/backed the car into the garage.
3. Teria fell over backwards.

② 逆向きの **backward(s)**

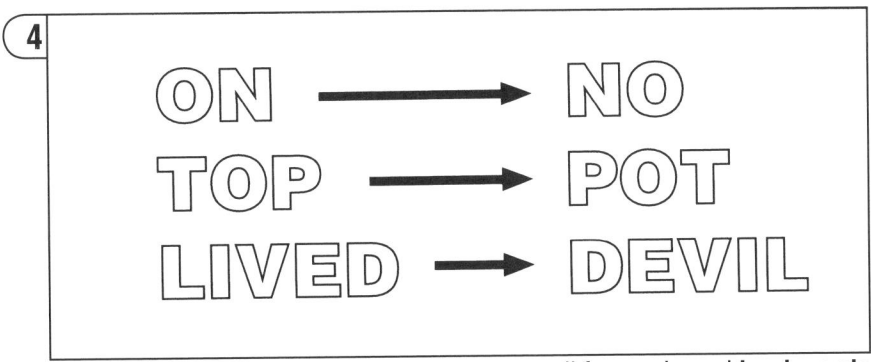

4

ON → NO
TOP → POT
LIVED → DEVIL

spell forwards and **backwards**

5

6

upside down

7

4　The words are spelled forwards and backwards.
5　Tim is bent over backward(s).　　6　The turtle is upside down.
7　Teria is facing backwards.

backward(s)

①もとにかえる back

put the book back

8 c. Albert put the book back.
9 c. Tim gave the piece of cake back to Olivia.
    Olivia took the piece of cake back from Tim.
10 c. Papa came back to the office.

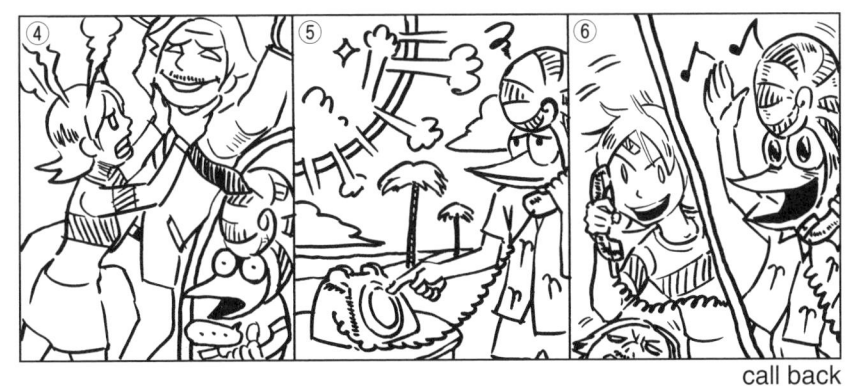

11 ① Nautilus is calling Ruby.
　⑤⑥ Nautilus is calling Ruby back.
12　Papa is massaging Mama's back/ Mama on her back.
13　Teria wears a ponytail in back.

beyond：3Dと見る

①はるか遠くを越えている **beyond**

beyond the mountains

1　③ The UFO went beyond the mountains.

【Ⅰ】基本のイメージ 623

beyond the top of the clock tower

2　② The balloon went beyond her reach.
　　　The balloon is above her reach.
　　③ The balloon went beyond the top of the clock tower.

624 … **beyond**：3Dと見る

②はるか遠くを過ぎている **beyond**

beyond / past the moon

3　③ The rocket flew beyond/past the moon.

beyond / past

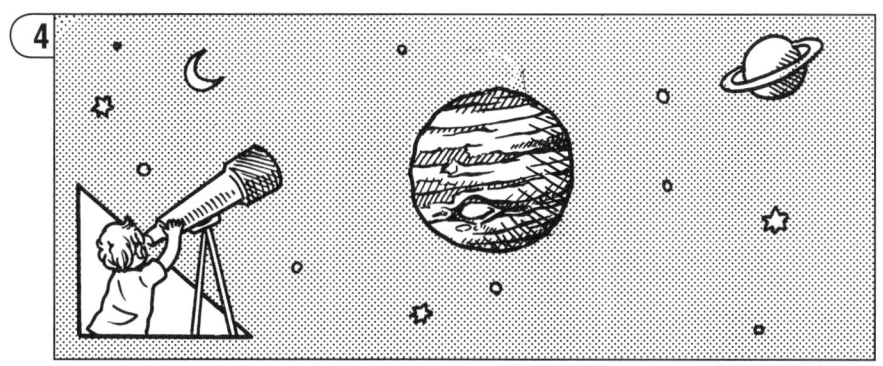

beyond / past

beyond / past

4　Saturn is beyond/past Jupiter.
5　The mountains are beyond/past the house.
6　The horse is beyond/past the village.

| 626 | **beyond**：3D と見る |

①はるか遠くを越えている／over と比べる

7　⑫ Leaf kicked her sandal beyond the line.

【Ⅱ】連想するイメージ

over the ocean　beyond the horizon

beyond / over

beyond / over

8　The birds flew beyond the horizon.
　　The bird flew over the ocean.
9　The caravan/The travellers walked beyond the horizon.
　　The caravan/The travellers walked over the desert.
10　The car drove beyond/over the horizon.

628 ... **beyond** : 3Dと見る

① **over, past, beyond**

over

past

beyond

11　The cat climbed over the roof (top).
12　The cat went past the house.
13　The cat went beyond the house.

【Ⅲ】イメージを比べる

over

past

beyond

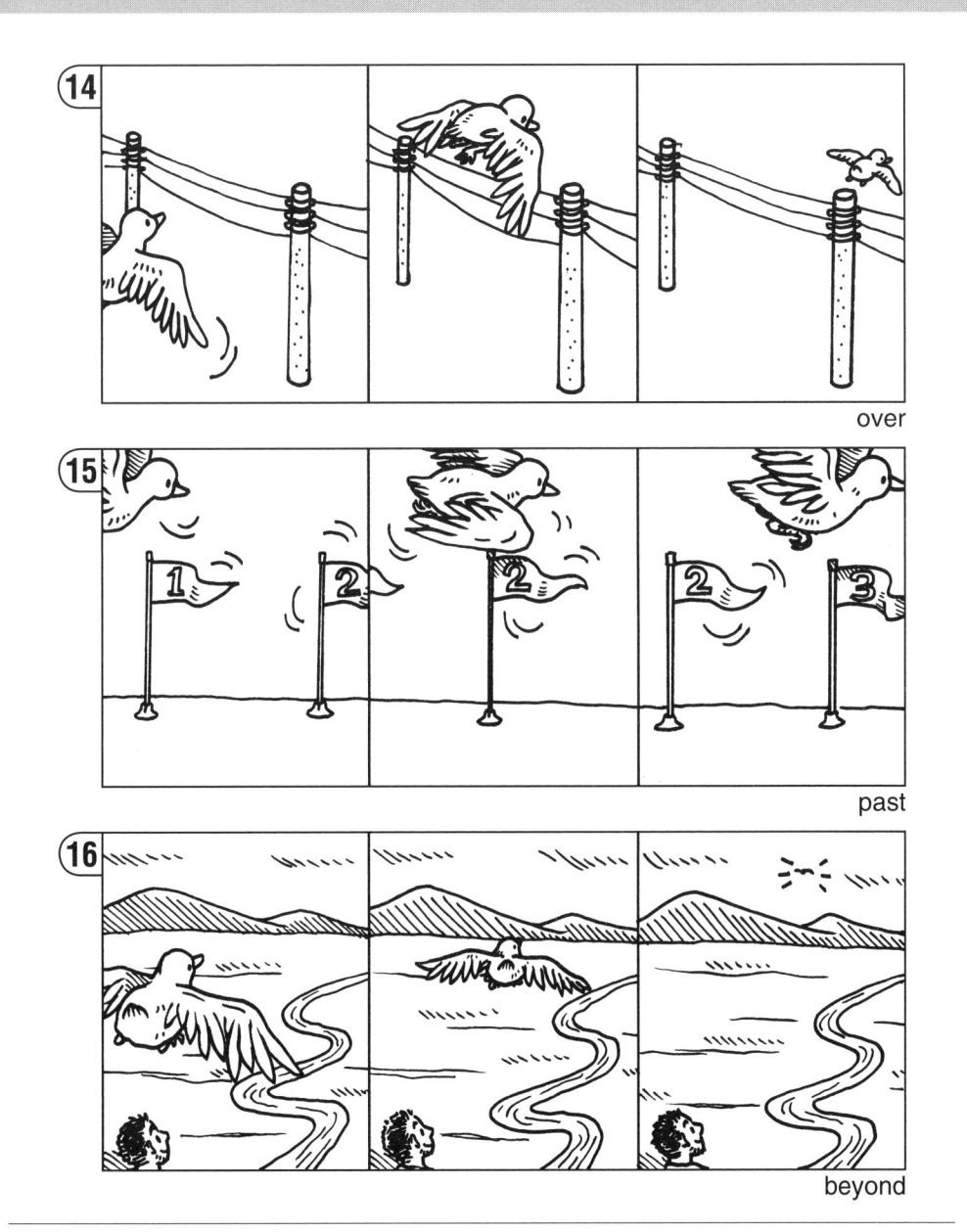

14　The bird flew over the power line.
15　The bird flew past flag #2.
16　The bird flew beyond/out of Butch's sight.

above：3Dと見る

①立体より高いところにいる / ある above

above the pyramid

above the cube

1 The moon is above the pyramid.
2 The pyramids are above the cube.
3 The bait is above the fish.
4 The pig is above the flames.
5 The dandelion seeds have risen above the Kobit's head.

【Ⅰ】基本のイメージ 631

above the white block

6 The teddy bear is above the books.
8 Olivia sleeps above Tim.
10 The shelf is above/over the sink.
7 The soccer ball is above the glove.
9 The black block is above the white one/block.
11 The dance school is above the bookstore.

above : 3Dと見る

②より高い above

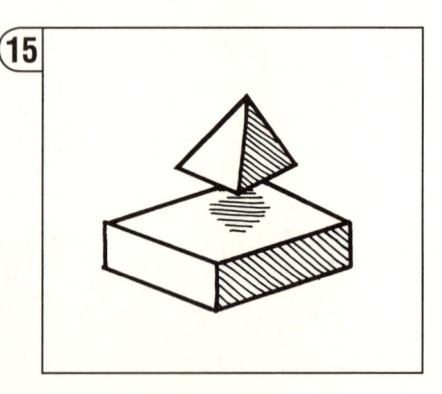

above / over the table

12 There is a lamp above/over the table.
14 The pig is above/over the flames.
16 The fairy is hovering above/over the flowers.

13 The moon is above/over the observatory.
15 The pyramid is above/over the block.
17 There is a cloud above/over the mountains.

【Ⅰ】基本のイメージ 633

above Tim's head

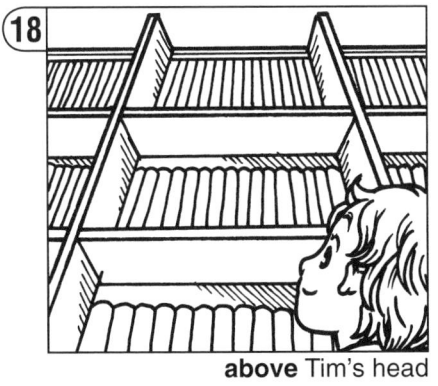

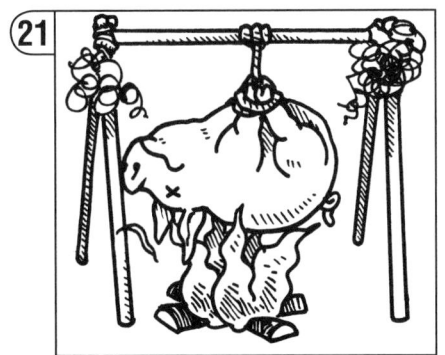

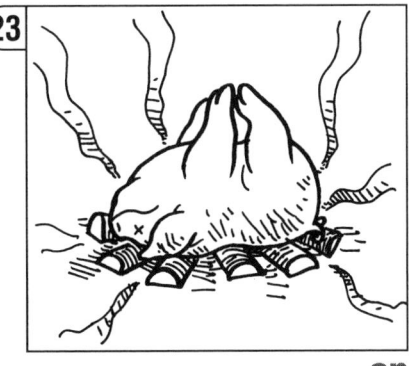

on

18　The bookshelves tower above Tim's head.
19　The skyscrapers tower above the rest of the buildings in the city.
20　Inond is towering above the Kobit.
21　The pig is over/on the fire.
　　The pig is directly above the fire.
22　The medium sized turtle is above/on the biggest one.
23　The pig is on the fire.

below：3Dと見る

①立体より低いところにいる／ある below

below the tree

below the cube

1　The treasure box is buried below/beneath the tree.
2　The pyramids are below the cube.
3　The house is below the tree.
4　Dora is below the man's feet/the man.
5　The bridge is below the cottage.
6　Butch is below the cat.
　　The cat is falling from above.

【 I 】基本のイメージ

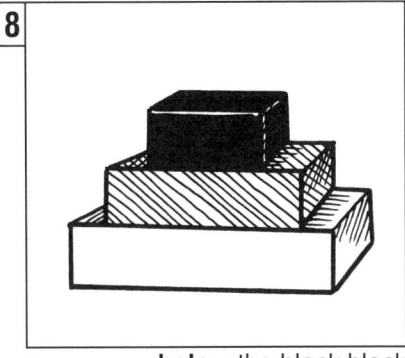

below the small turtle

below the black block

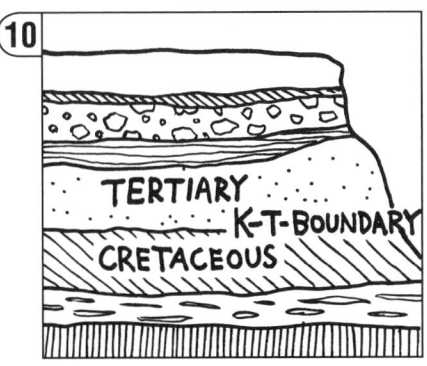

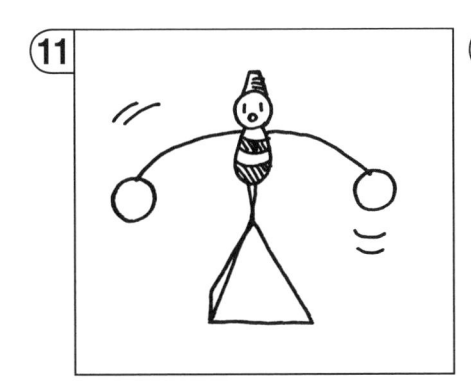

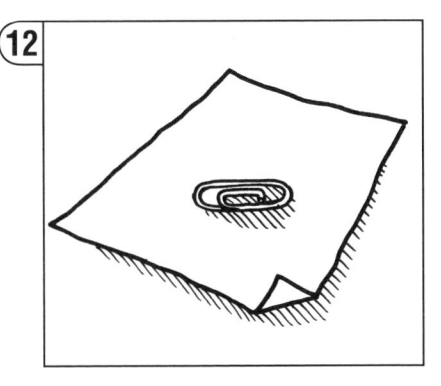

PLEASE SEE THE PICTURE BELOW.

TERTIARY
K-T-BOUNDARY
CRETACEOUS

7 The mother turtle is below the small/the little one.
8 The white block is below the black one.
9 This is a rare frog. See the picture below.
10 The Cretaceous layer is below the Tertiary layer. [beneath, underneath, under]
11 The pyramid is below/under the balancing toy.
12 The piece of paper is below the paperclip.

②より低い below

below the mountain

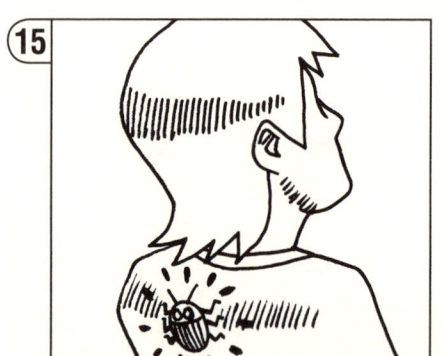

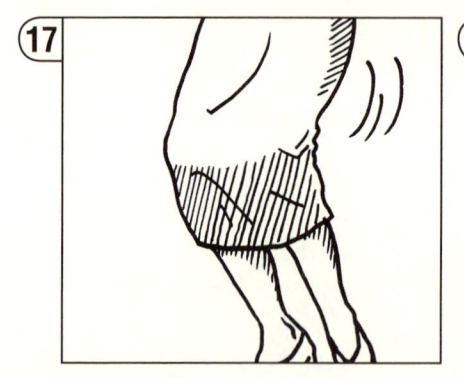

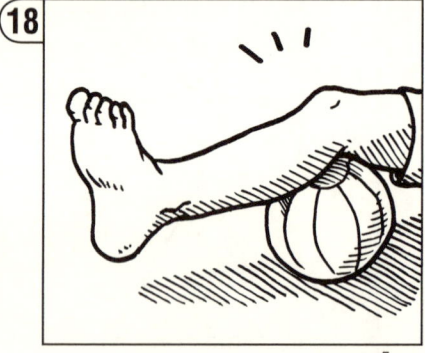

under

13　The town is below the mountain.
15　There is a bug below the man's hair.
17　The skirt comes (down) below her knees.
14　The town is below the cliffs.
16　The fire is below the pig.
18　The ball is under the girl's knee.

【Ⅰ】基本のイメージ 637

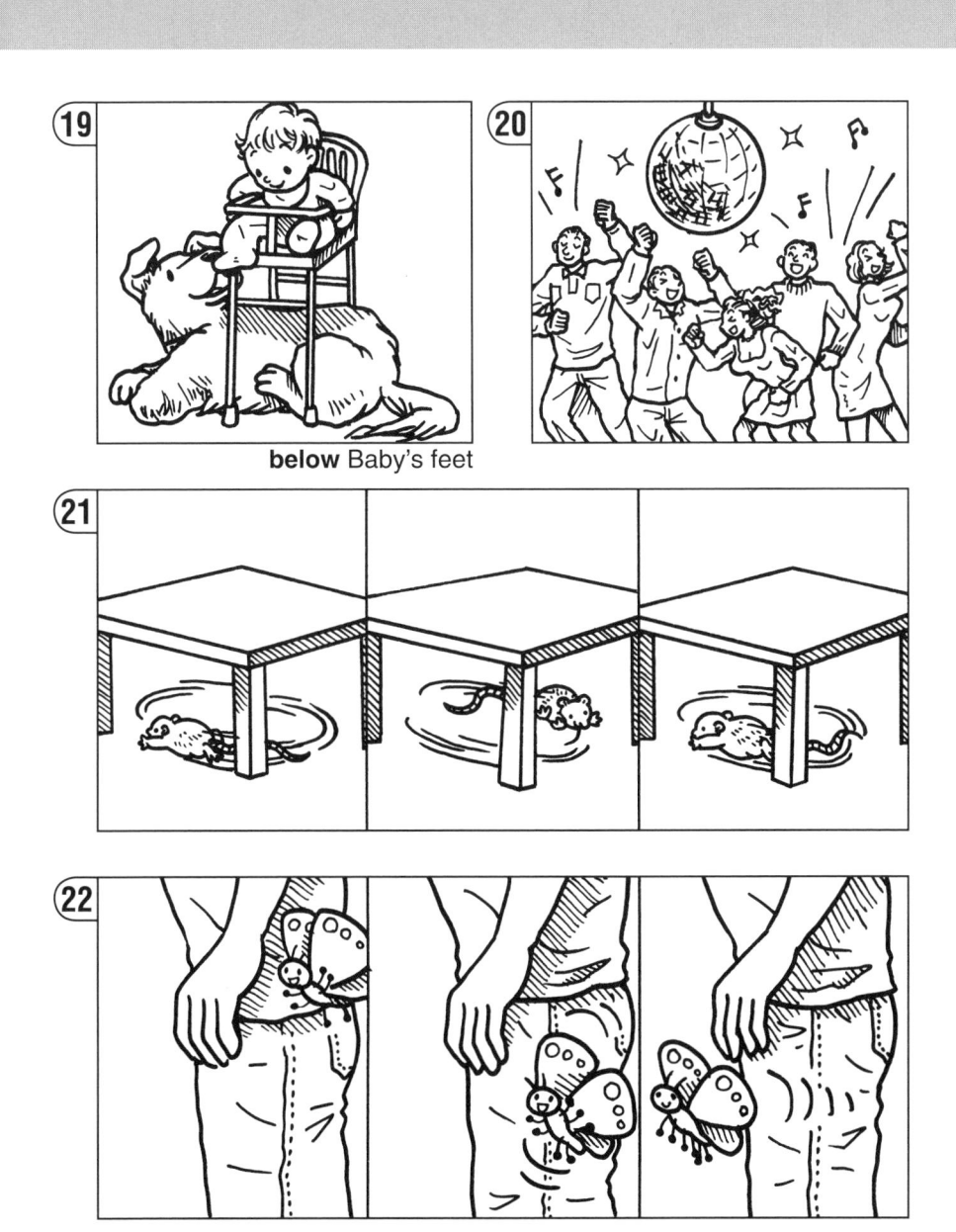

below Baby's feet

19 Pooch is below Baby's feet.
20 The people are dancing below the glitter ball. [under, beneath]
21 The mouse is running around below the table.
22 The butterfly is flying below the girl's arm.

① below と under

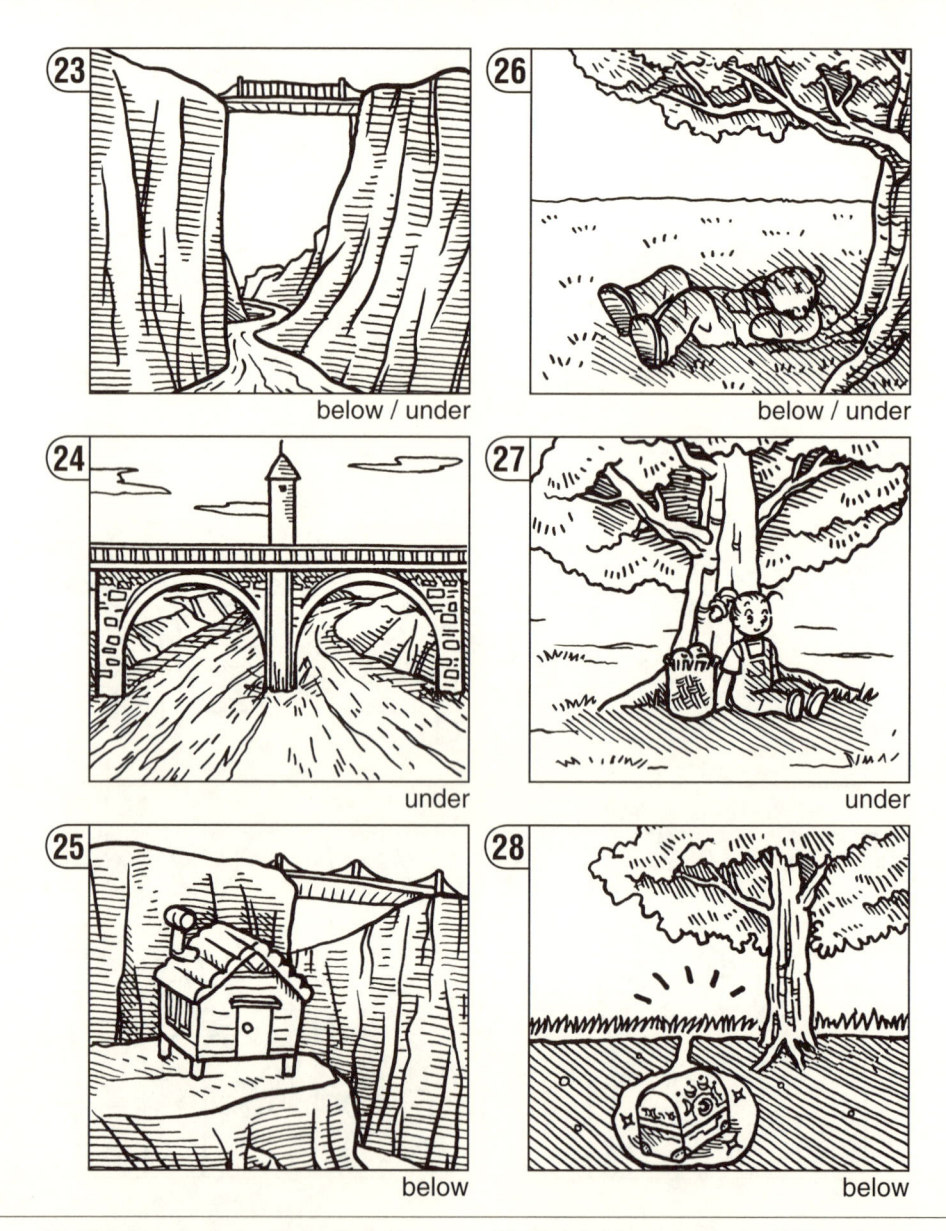

23　The river runs below/under the bridge.
24　The river runs under the bridge.
　　[beneath, underneath]
25　The cottage is below the bridge.
26　Teria is lying below/under the branches.
　　Teria is lying under the tree.
27　Teria is sitting under/beneath the tree.
28　The treasure box is buried below the tree.
　　[under, beneath]

【Ⅱ】イメージを比べる

29 below / under

30 under

31 below

32 under / below

33 under

34 in

29 The town is below/under the mountain. [beneath, underneath]
30 The monster lives under/inside the mountain.
31 The town is located below the mountain.
32 The triangle is under/below the line.
33 Olivia is under the arch of roses.
34 The monster lives in/inside the mountain.

① below と under

35 under / below

36 under

37 below

38 below / under

39 under

40 below

35 The girl's eyes are under/ below her hair. [beneath]
36 The girl's eyes are under her hair. [beneath, underneath]
37 The girl's eyes are below her hair.
38 Teria's name is written below/under her arm.
39 The bat is under/beneath the boy's arm.
40 Pooch is below the man's arm.

41 The pipe is below/under Teria's drawer.
42 The watch is stored under 'Teria.'
43 Baby and Olivia are below the file drawers in height.
44 The glove is below/under the soccer ball.
45 Albert is filed under 'A.'
46 The prince is below Rapunzel's hair.

642 … underneath：3Dと見る
①下にかくれている underneath

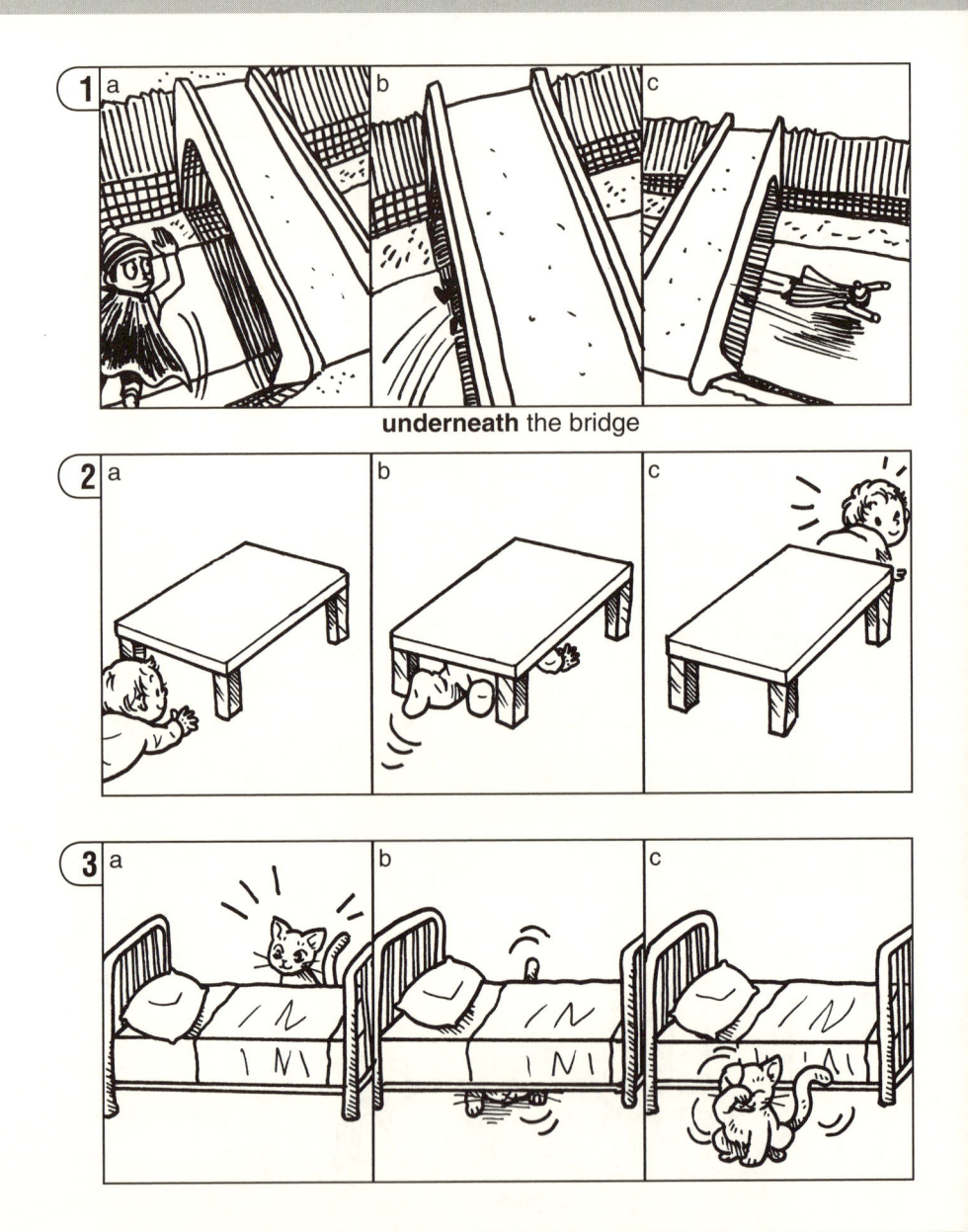

underneath the bridge

1. b. Bowsheeman is flying underneath/under the bridge.　c. He flew under the bridge.
2. b. Baby is crawling underneath/under the table.　c. He crawled under the table.
3. b. Kitten is walking underneath/under the bed.　c. She walked under the bed.

underneath his foot

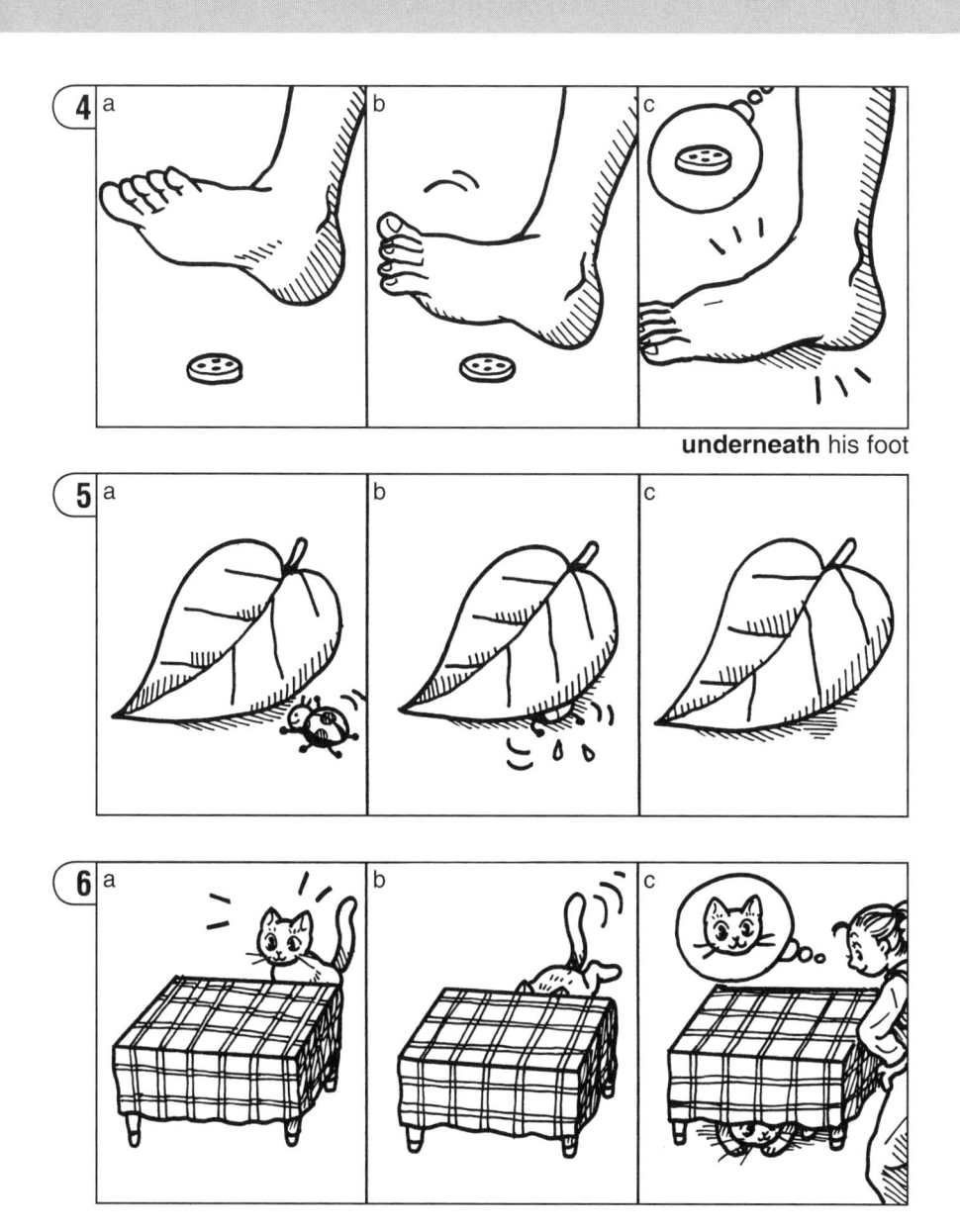

4　c. The button is underneath/under his/the foot. [beneath, below]
5　c. Now the bug is underneath/under the leaf. [beneath]
6　c. Kitten is hiding underneath/under the table. [beneath, below]

②かくれている **underneath**

underneath the covers

7　c. Olivia is shaking with fear underneath the covers. [under, beneath]
8　c. There is a sweet face underneath that scary mask. [under, beneath]
9　c. There is a chicken underneath the cover.

③下の方にいる / ある underneath

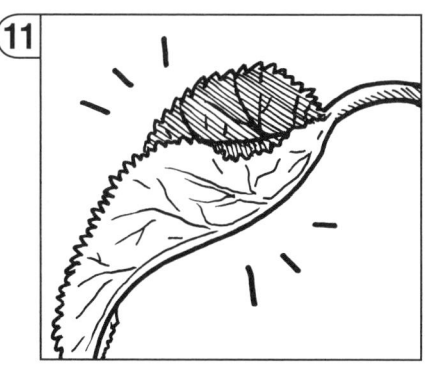

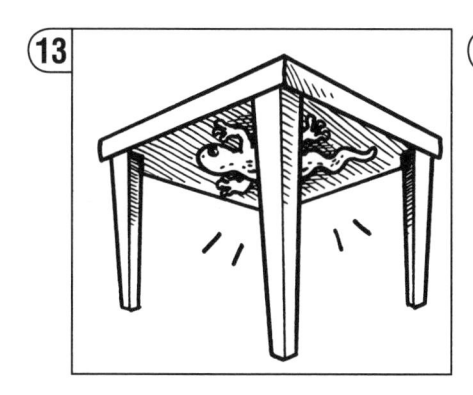

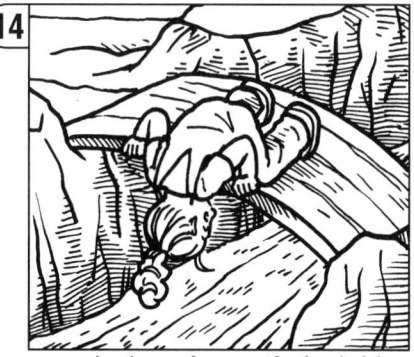

10 The fish is white underneath.
11 The leaf is white underneath.
12 Teria packed the eggs on top and the potatoes underneath.
13 The salamander is underneath/under the tabletop. [on the bottom of the table]
14 Teria is looking underneath the bridge.

underneath：3Dと見る
①かくれている underneath / under, below と比べる

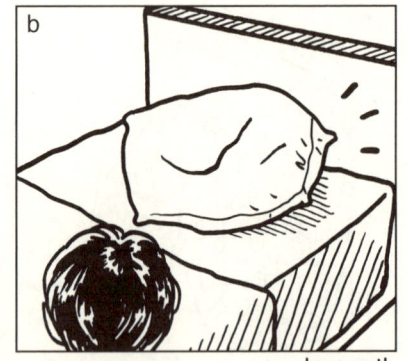

15 b, c. The chick is underneath Totto.
16 b. The man hid his gun underneath the pillow. [under, beneath]
17 Tim is looking underneath the table.　　18 Tim is looking under the table.

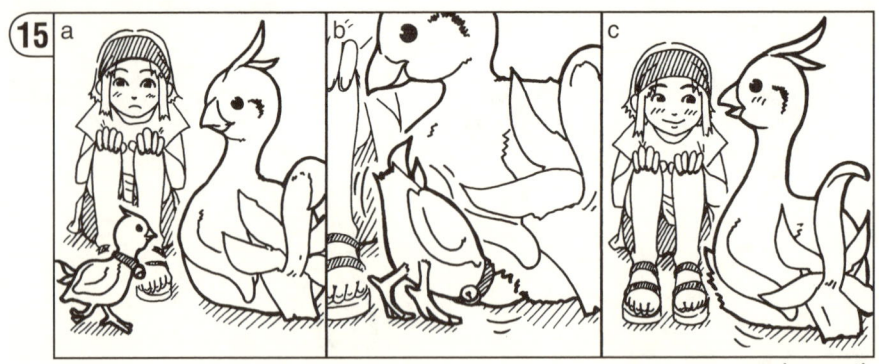

【Ⅱ】イメージを比べる

⑲ under	⑳ below
㉑ under	㉒ below
㉓ beneath	㉔ below

19　The chicks are under Totto.
20　The eggs are below/under Totto.
21　The picture is under the pillow.
22　The bed frame is below the mattress.
23　Teria is looking under/beneath the bridge.
24　Butch is looking below the cliff.
　　Butch is looking down.

①はるかに深い beneath

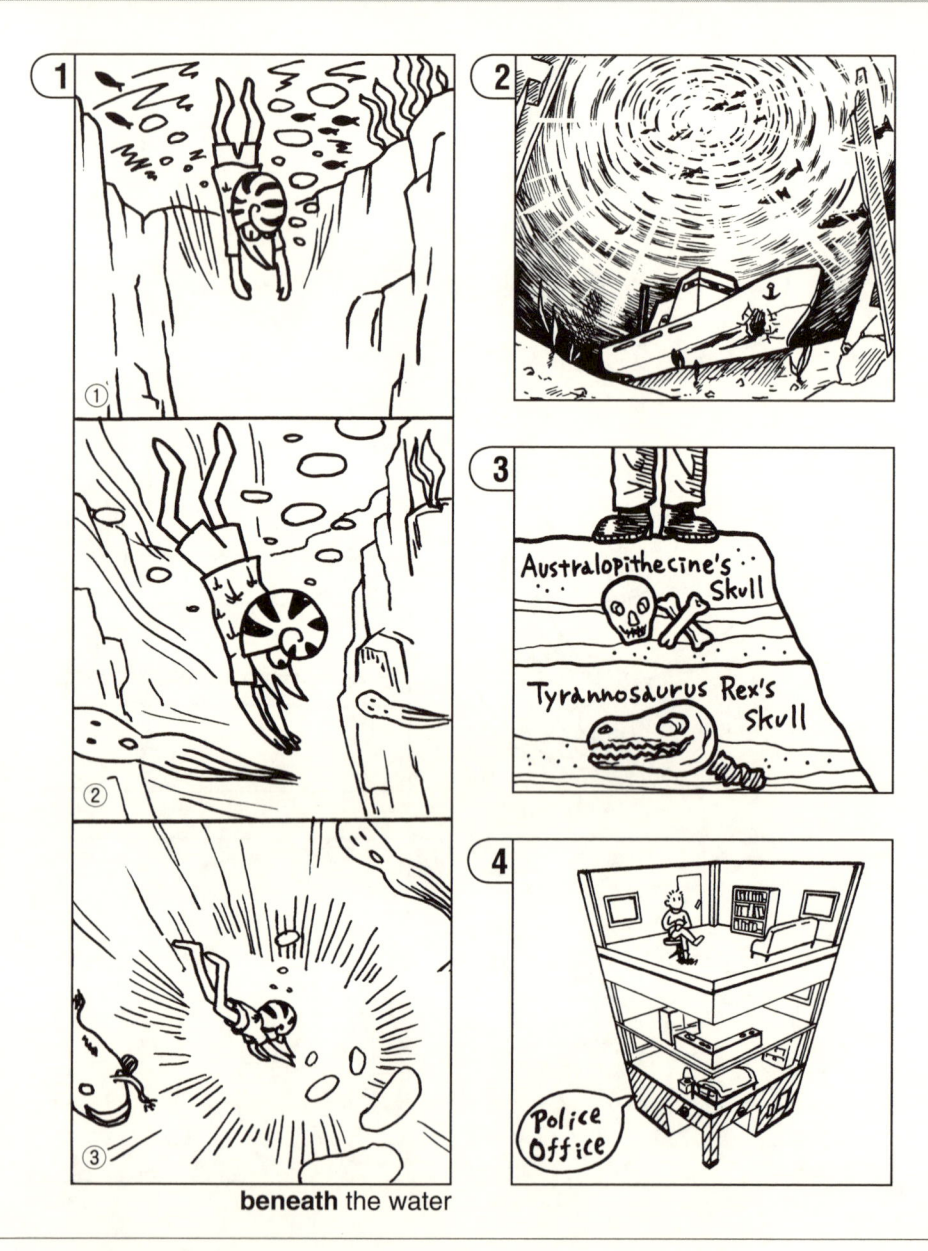

beneath the water

1. Nautilus swam beneath the water/the surface of water.
2. The boat is beneath the sea/the water.　The boat is under/underneath/ below the surface.
3. There is a Tyrannosaurus Rex's skull beneath the man's feet. [below, under]
   There is an Australopithecine's skull under the man's feet. [beneath, below]
4. The police office is beneath Sorel's floors. [below, under]

②重さのかかる beneath

beneath the laundry basket

5 c. There are dirty pants beneath/under the laundry basket.
6 The paper is beneath the dumbbell. [under, below]
7 The money is beneath the stack of books. [under, below]
8 The knife is beneath/under a pile of dishes.

beneath：3Dと見る

①影響をおよぼしている

9　The town is beneath the castle.
10　The village is beneath the volcano.
11　There is a house beneath the tree. (under, below)

②まったく気づかない

12　Borizi is beneath Leaf's notice.

①影響をおよぼす beneath / under と比べる

beneath

beneath

beneath / under

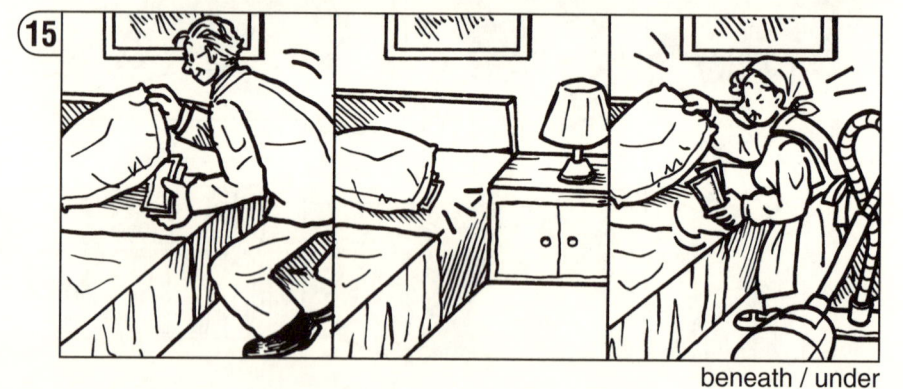

13　Candy put a hedgehog beneath/under Bowsheeman's head.
14　The prisoner's legs are beneath two heavy stones.
15　Papa left a tip beneath/under the pillow.

【Ⅲ】イメージを比べる 653

under

under

under

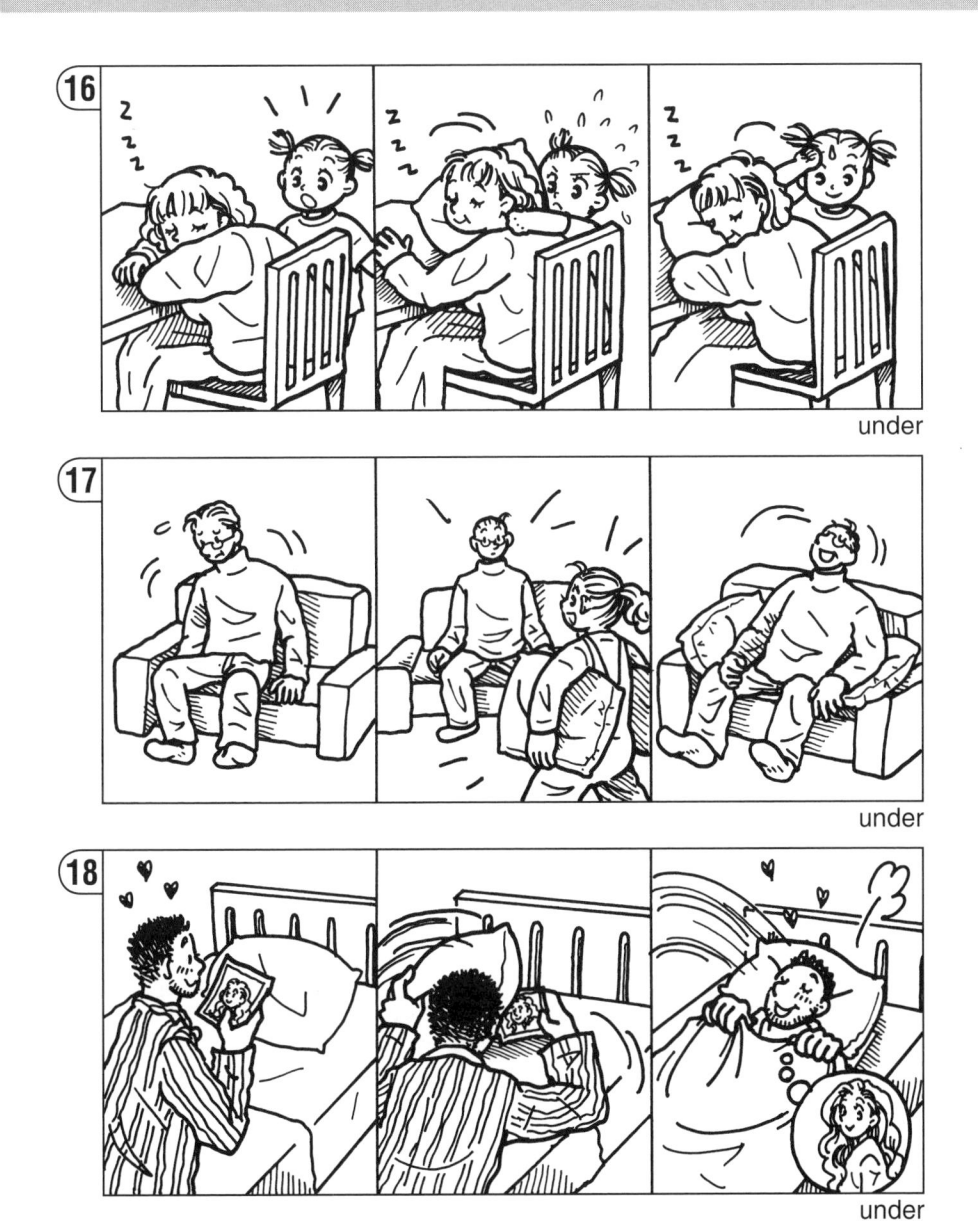

16　Olivia put a pillow under Mama's head.
17　Teria put pillows under Papa's arms.
18　Butch put a picture of Sylvia under his pillow. [underneath, beneath]

① **Time** を点として見る **at**

at 8:00 a.m.

at 12:00 p.m.

1. At 8:00 a.m., Mama and Papa eat breakfast.
2. Papa has lunch at 12.00 p.m.
3. Papa has lunch at 12:00 p.m.
4. Dinner is served at 9:00 p.m.
5. At midnight, Sylvia ran out of the castle.

at dawn

at sunset

at noon

at night

6 Butch and Sylvia woke up at dawn.
7 The farmers quit working at sunset.
8 The tree's shadow is shortest at noon.
9 Pooch takes a nap at midday.
10 Oton snuck/sneaked out of the house at night.

① Time を点として見る at

at the moment

at the same time

at the last minute

11 "What are you doing, Albert?" "At the moment I'm drawing."
12 Candy and Bowsheeman opened the door at the same time.
13 Teria finished her homework at the last minute.

14 At one time, the black monkey was king of the hill.
15 At one time, Bowsheeman was rich.
16 After Tim and Olivia broke the dishes, they swept them up at once.

① Time を点として見る at

17 Butch eats rice at breakfast, at lunch and at dinner.
   Butch eats rice for breakfast, lunch and dinner.

18 Albert has parties/a party at Thanksgiving, at Christmas and at New Year's.

19 Grandma began using glasses at seventy.

20 a. At first Teria was winning.   b. At last Olivia pulled ahead.   c. In the end, she won.
21 The convenience store is open at all hours.
22 The clock chimes on the hour.

②日にちの on

(23) on

(24) on

(25) in the Christmas season

23　On Albert's birthday, Sylvia gave him a pen.
24　Many friends were present on Mama and Papa's wedding day.
25　In/During the Christmas season, Bowsheeman works as Santa Claus.

③意識している「時」の for

26　Sylvia is buying a pen for Albert for his birthday.
27　Teria is calling the dentist for an appointment.
28　Grandma is going to visit her family for Christmas.

④ 一点の at, 線上の on, 境界内の in

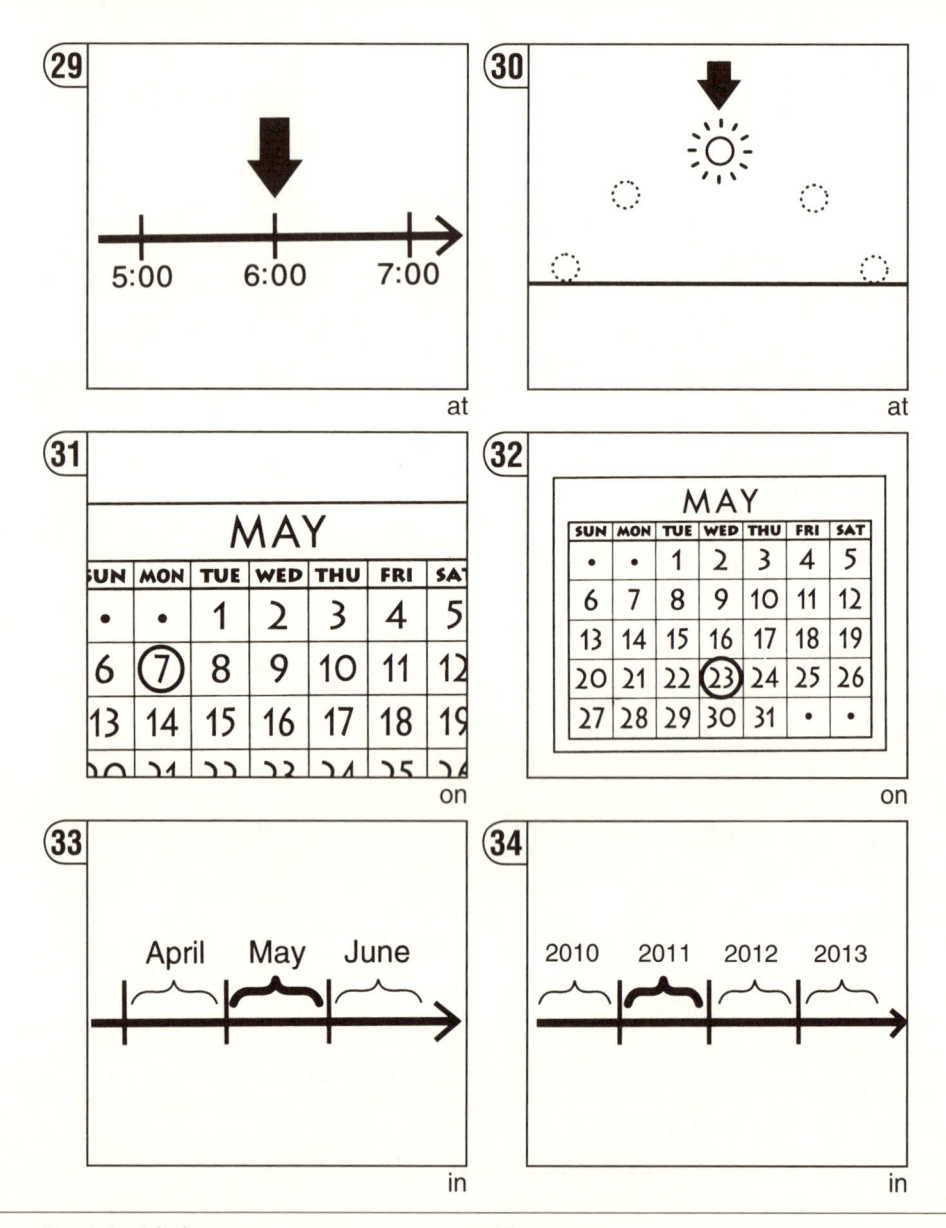

29 at six o'clock
30 at noon
31 on the seventh, on May seventh
32 on Wednesday
33 in May
34 in (the year) 2011

㉟

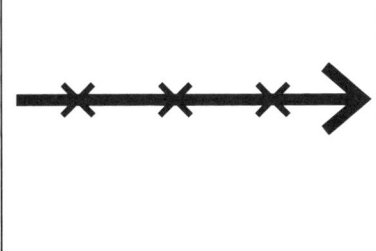

① at 6:00 p.m.

② at 6:43

③ at noon

④ at night

㊱

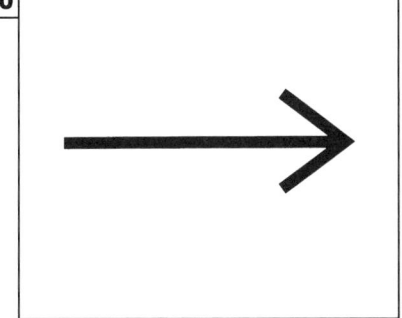

① on June 7th

② on Sunday

③ on my birthday

④ on Christmas Day

㊲

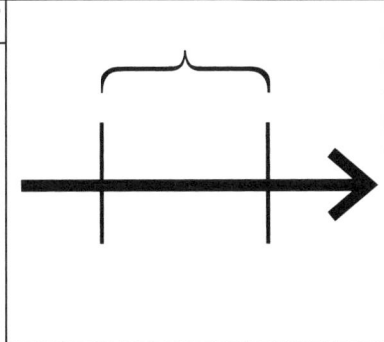

① in August

② in 2010

③ in the afternoon

④ in the evening

---

35 ① Dinner is at 6:00 p.m.
    ④ Teria plays with Olivia at night.
36 ④ Teria sees her grandparents on Christmas Day.
37 ① Teria's birthday is in August.
    ② Olivia became 5 (years old) in 2010.

⑤ at the / on / in time

at the time

in time   on time

in time

38 At the time when Candy met Bowsheeman, he was living (with his father) in the Gold Building.

39 b. Butch arrived at the coffee shop in time to drink a cup of coffee before Sylvia showed up.
   c. Sylvia arrived at the coffee shop on time.

40 Bowsheeman escaped just in time.

⑥「〜から〜まで」の from 〜 to 〜

from 1:00 to 3:00

from 7:55 to 8:00

since the early morning

41 Teria swam from 1:00 to 3:00.
42 She walked from 7:55 to 8:00.
　It takes 5 minutes to get from Teria's house to her (high) school.
43 Butch has been playing baseball since the early morning.

⑦ 〜から今も続いている since

since last April

44 Sylvia has been working as a waitress since last April.
45 It has been raining since noon.
46 Albert has been writing his novel since five years ago.

⑧ ～から（～まで）の **from**

from April to August

47 Sylvia worked as a waitress from April to August.
48 It rained from noon until/to early (in the) afternoon.
49 From start to finish, it took Albert four years to write his book.

⑨ 時間の長さを表わす **for**

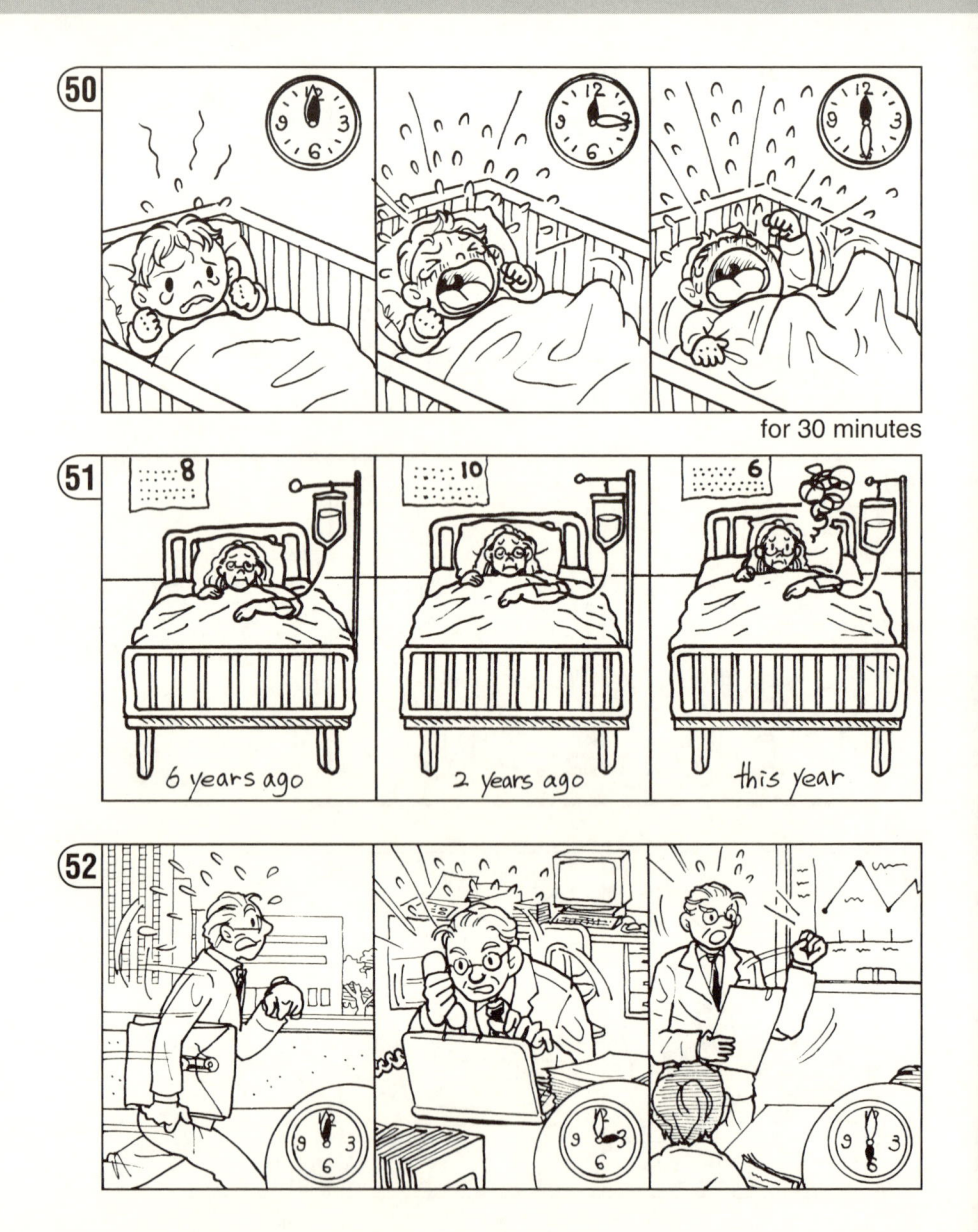

for 30 minutes

6 years ago   2 years ago   this year

50 Baby has been crying for thirty minutes.
51 The old woman has been in bed for more than six years.
52 Papa has been working for a long time/six hours.

⑩ 距離を表わす for

53 for 4km

54 for 100m

55

53 b. Teria has been hiking for 4 kilometers.　c. Teria hiked 5 kilometers.
　　　　　　　　　　　　　　　　　　　　　　Teria hiked for about 1 hour and 40 minutes.
54 b. Butch has been running for 100 meters.　c. Butch ran more than 200 meters.
　　　　　　　　　　　　　　　　　　　　　　Butch ran for less than 30 seconds.
55 Teria has to walk for 500m to get to her boyfriend's house.
　　It takes 10 minutes to get to her boyfriend's house.

⑪「(2日)後には」の in

56　a. Eluca will see Leaf in two days.
57　a. Inond will visit his girlfriend in two days.
58　c. Inond walked/got to his girlfriend's house in two days.　　He walked for two days.

⑫「(2日)間」の for

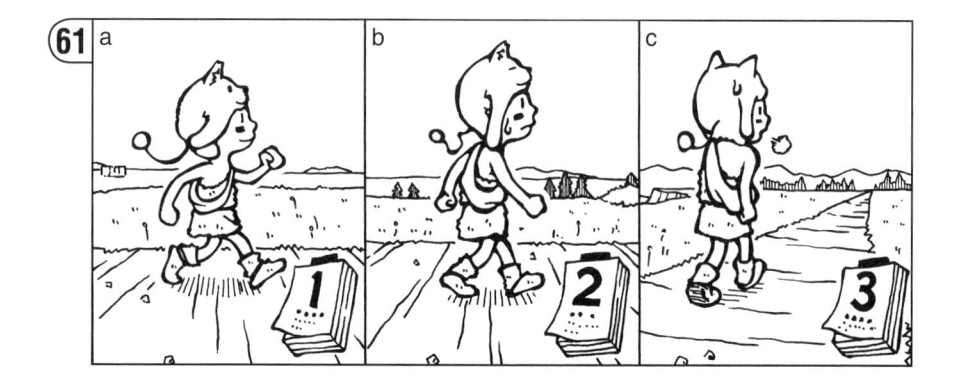

for 2 days

59 a. Eluca will visit Leaf for two days.
60 a. Inond and his girlfriend will be together for two days.
61 c. The kobit has been walking for two or three days.

⑬「〜の間に」の **during**

during the summer

62 Sunflowers bloom during (the) summer.
63 Baby woke up during the night.
64 Tim fell asleep during (his) class.

⑭「〜の間ずっと」の **throughout**

throughout the summer

during

65 Throughout the (whole) summer, the boy with glasses was in bad health.
66 Tim stayed in bed throughout August.
67 During January and February, the town is covered with snow.

⑮ in, during, throughout, for

in summer

during the summer

throughout the summer

68 a. In (the) winter Leaf skis.   c. In (the) summer she swims.
69 During (the) summer Chicori plays in the water.
70 Fennel swam throughout the summer/all summer long.

71 b. In May, Eluca visited Leaf.
72 Sometime during May, Eluca visited Leaf.
73 Eluca visited Leaf for three days in May.

⑯ before と after

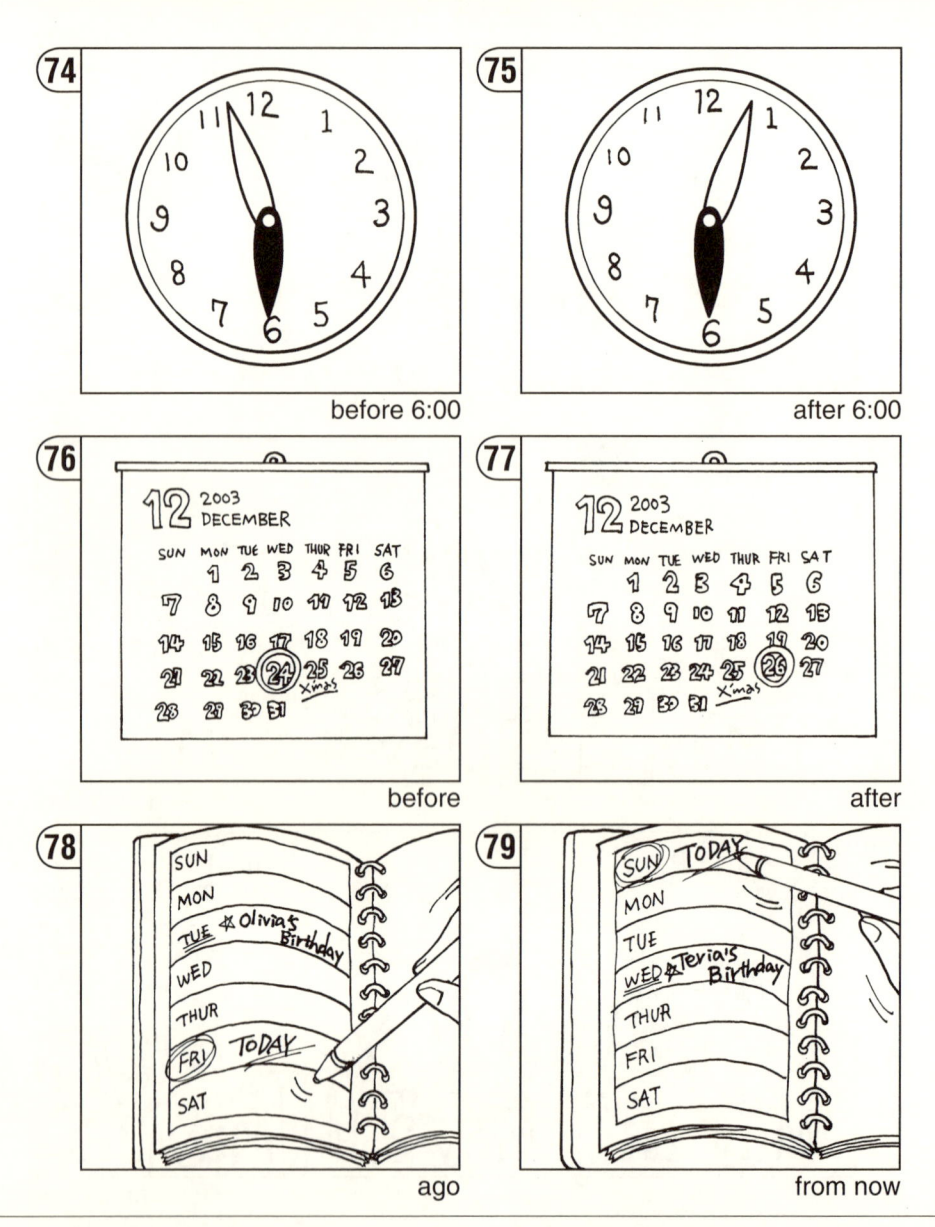

74 before 6:00

75 after 6:00

76 before

77 after

78 ago

79 from now

74　It's four minutes before six.
76　December 24th is the day before Christmas.
78　Today is Friday. Olivia's birthday was three days ago.
　　Today is 3 days after her birthday.
75　It's four minutes after six.
77　December 26th is the day after Christmas.
79　Today is Sunday. Teria's birthday will be three days from now.

⑰ in, before, after

in 3 hours

before 6:00

after 6:00

80 a. Teria is going to play tennis in three hours.
81 a. Teria is going to start playing tennis before six.
82 a. Teria is going to play tennis after six.

⑱ 通過する時間を表わす by

by night

by day

by 12:00

83 Sylvia works by day and studies by/at night.
84 Owls sleep by day.
85 Cinderella had to leave by twelve o'clock.

⑲ (6時)までずっとの until / till, (6時)前までの before, (6時)までにの by

until 6:00

before / by 6:00

by 6:00

86 a. Teria is going to play tennis until/till 6:00.
87 a. Teria is going to finish playing tennis before/by 6:00.
88 a. Teria is going to finish playing tennis by/before 6:00.

Time を表わすおもな前置詞

from　to

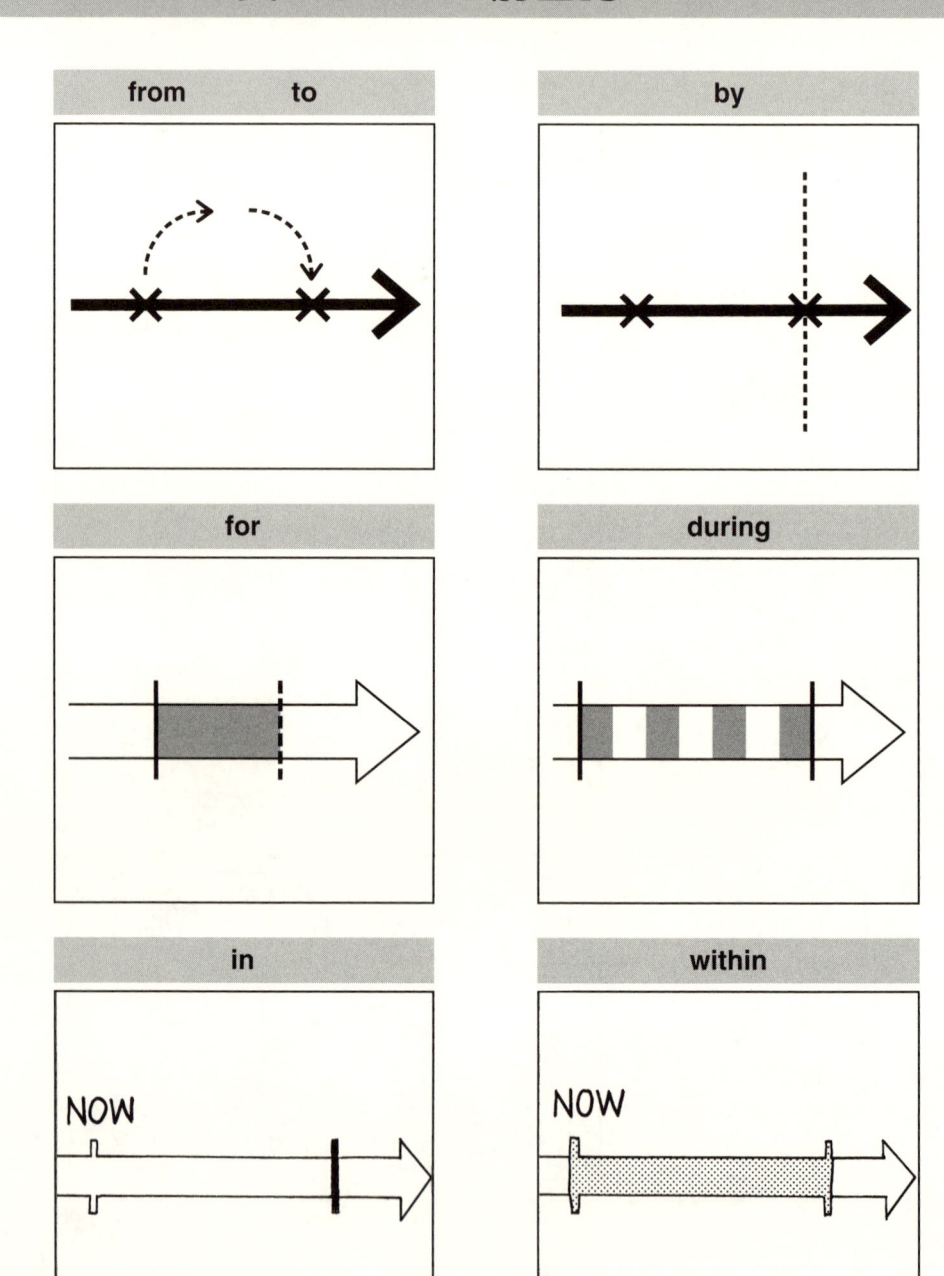

by

for

during

in

within

since	until / till

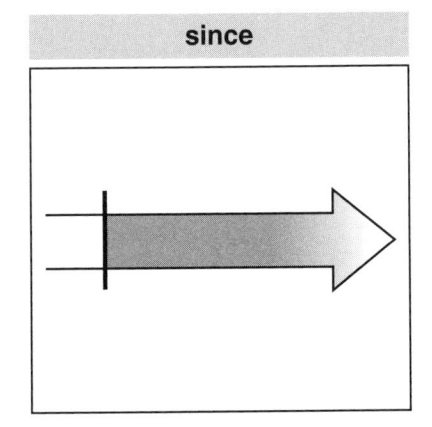

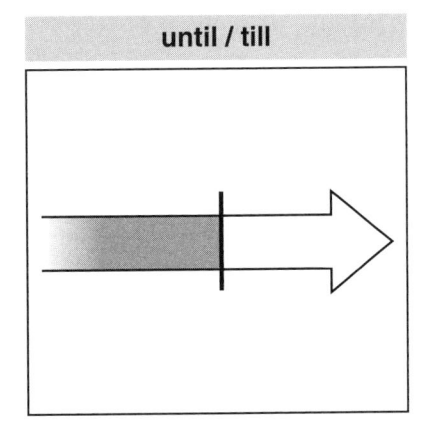

before	after

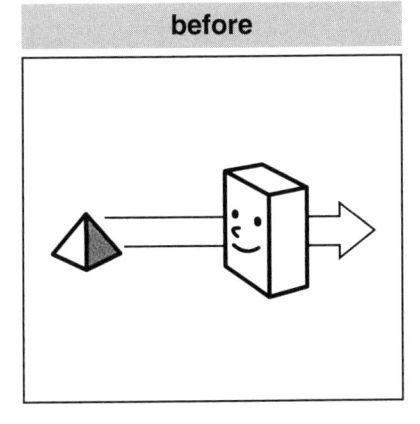

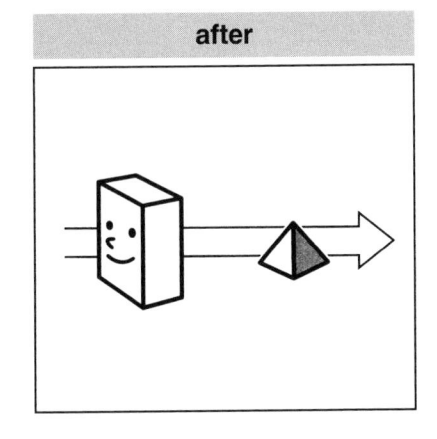

ago	from now
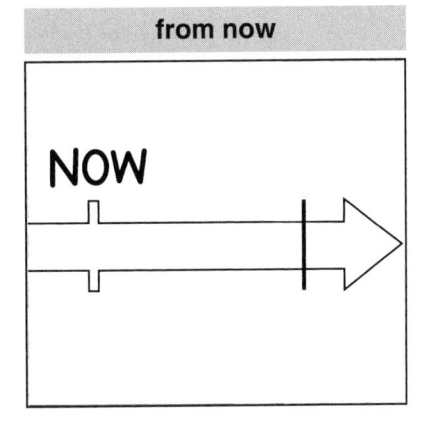 NOW	NOW

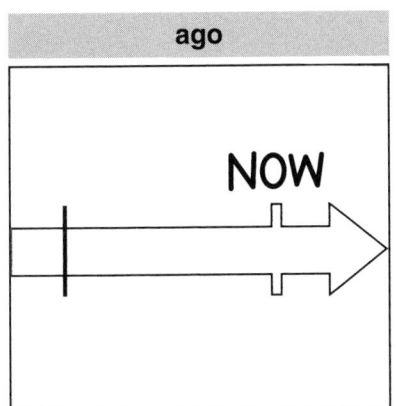

Spaceを表わすおもな前置詞

①場を1次元(線)と見るように指示している

on

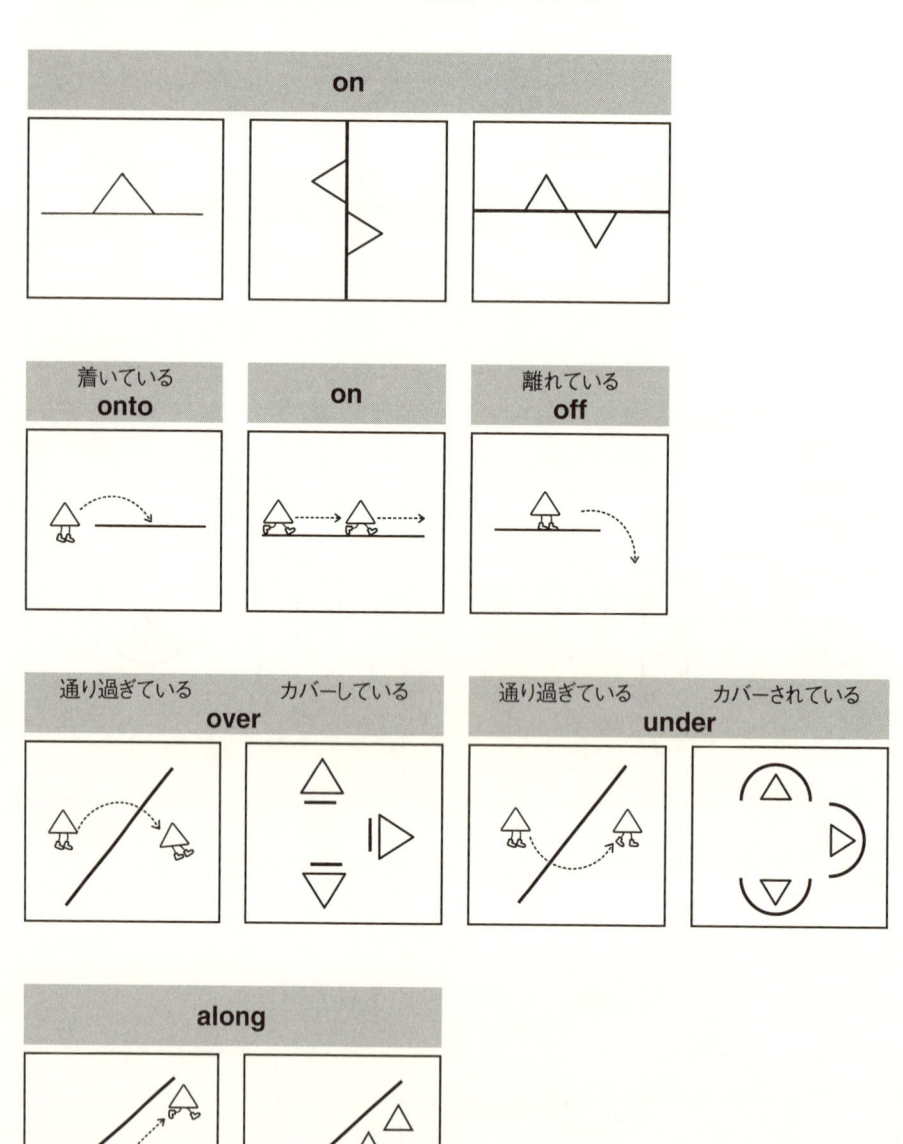

| 着いている **onto** | **on** | 離れている **off** |

| 通り過ぎている **over** | カバーしている | 通り過ぎている **under** | カバーされている |

along

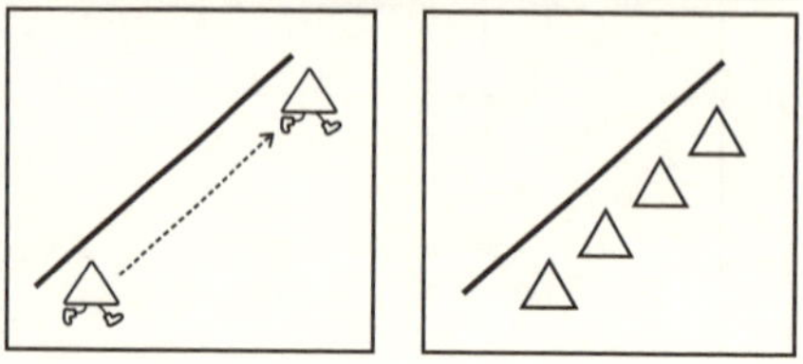

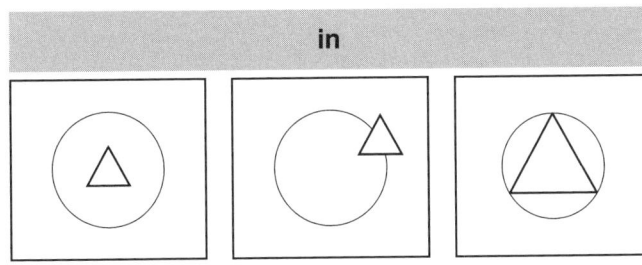

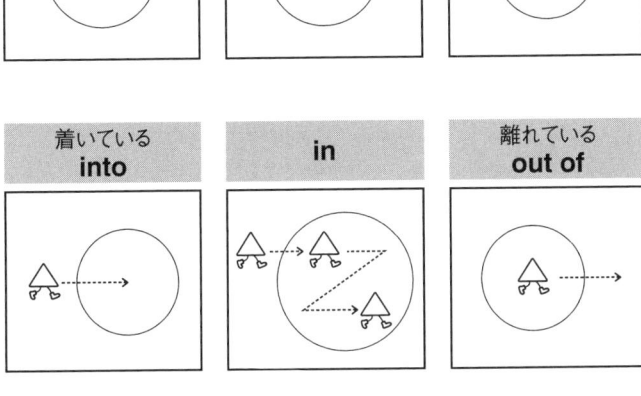

② 場を 2 次元(面)と見るように指示している

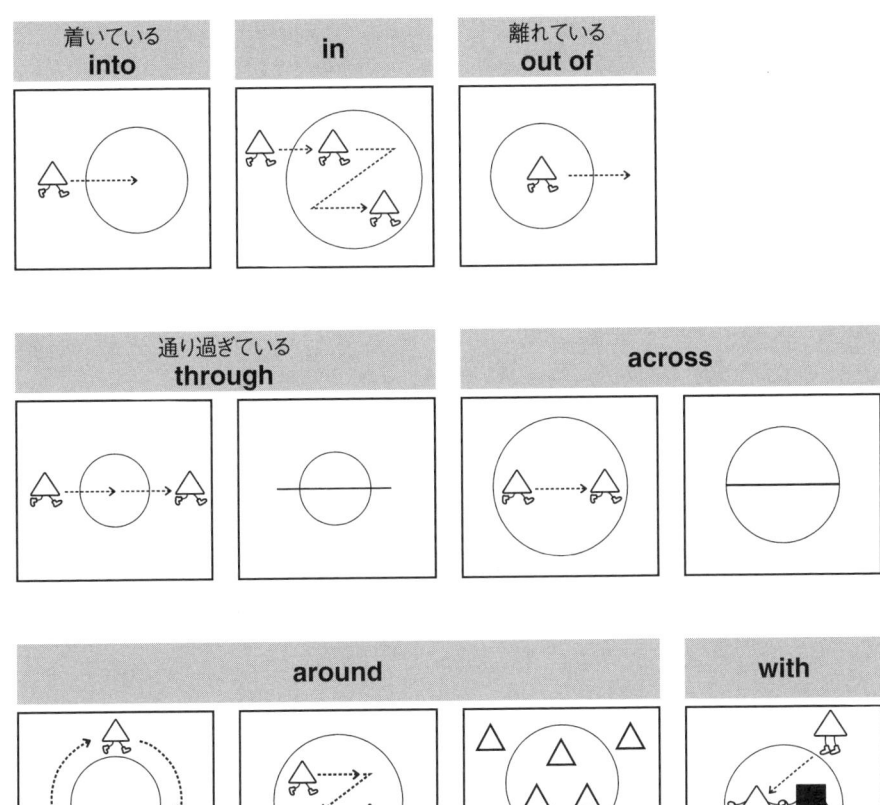

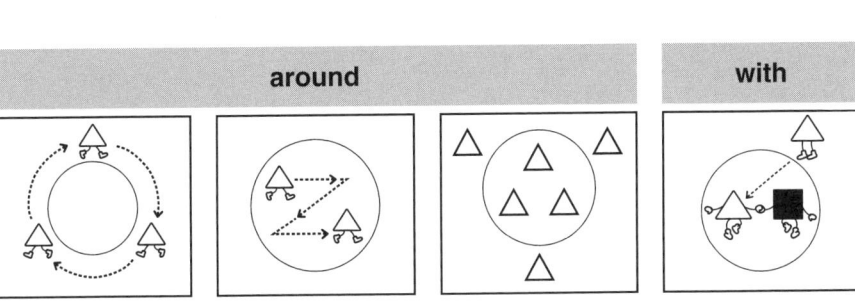

in

into 着いている **in** **out of** 離れている

through 通り過ぎている **across**

around **with**

③場を 0 次元（点）と見るように指示している

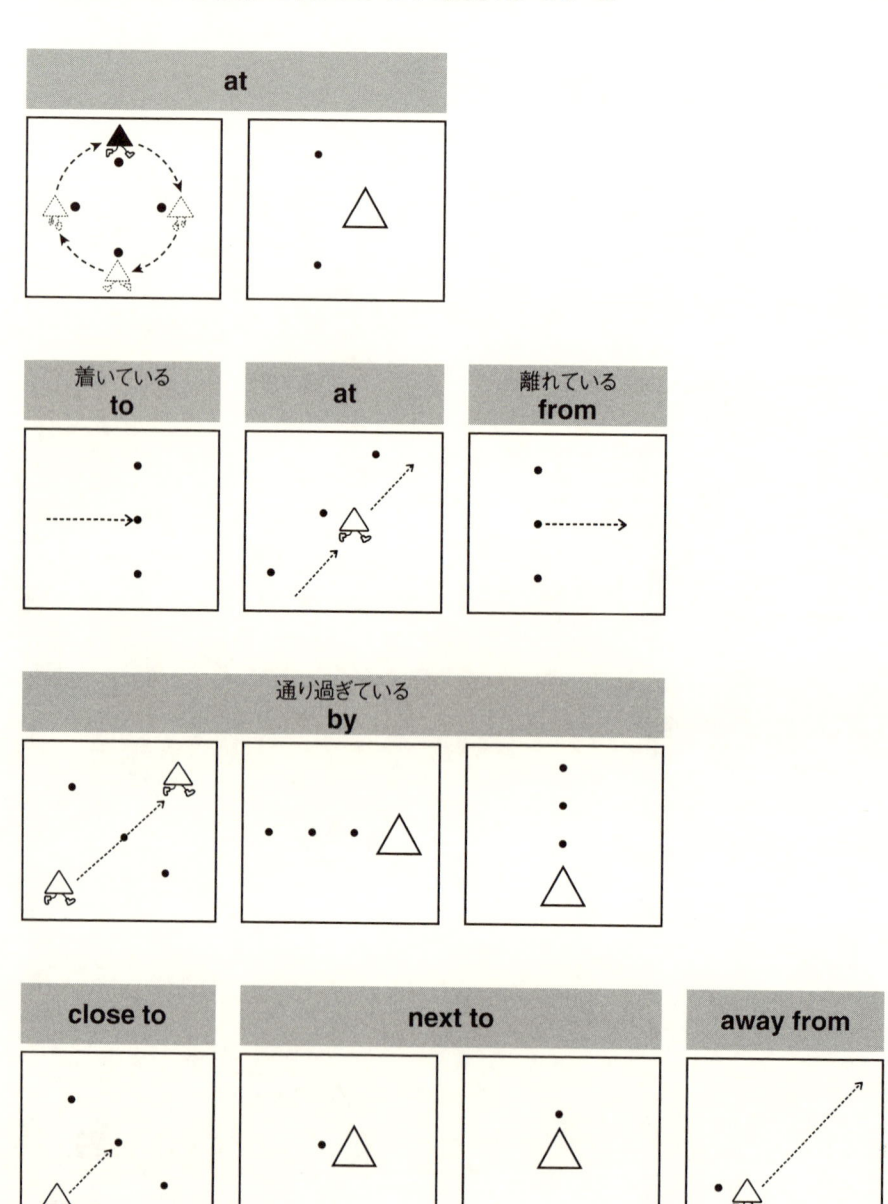

at

着いている to	at	離れている from

通り過ぎている by

close to	next to	away from

④場を 3D(立体)と見るように指示している

beside	alongside

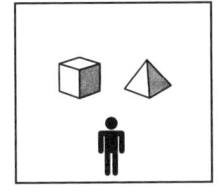

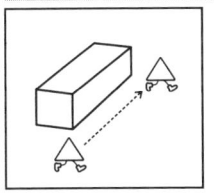

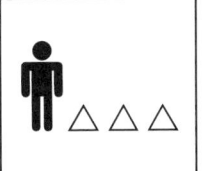

向かっている toward(s)	near	inside : outside	behind

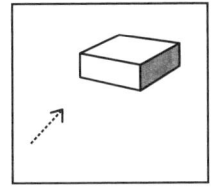

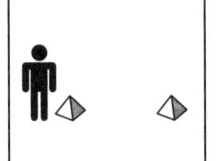

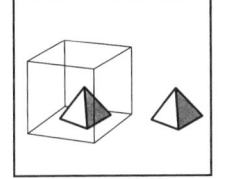

通り過ぎる beyond		beneath	underneath

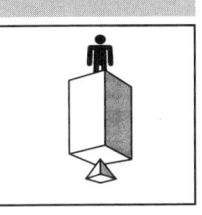

above	below	(2D) in front of	in back of

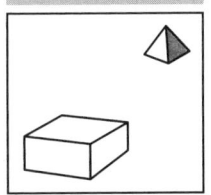

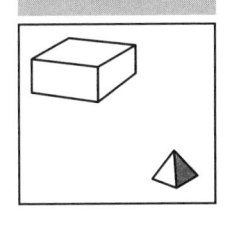

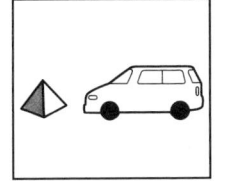

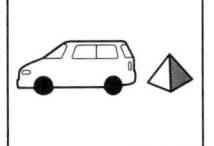

キャラクター紹介

Olivia
Tim
Mama & Baby
Papa
Grandma
Teria
Pooch
Sylvia
Albert
Butch
Kitten Puppy

Nautilus

Ruby Dad

sea munchkin

Mr. Gold

Dr. Bizarro

Candy

Bowsheeman

Katarina

Okan

Oton

Bakunsai Indy

Malow Borizi Fennel Chicori

Eluca Leaf

Earl Sorel Kobit Inond

あとがき

　1999 年、本書の元となった『ネイティブの感覚で前置詞が使える』が発行されました。そして 2000 年には続編の『ネイティブの感覚でもっと前置詞が使える』が、2005 年には『ネイティブの感覚でもっともっと前置詞が使える』が発行され、これら 3 冊をもってよく使われるほぼすべての前置詞 {副詞} を取り上げ、それぞれの前置詞がどのようなイメージをもっているのかを探ってきました。

　前作 3 冊に対しては幅広い年齢層の方々、英語初心者の方、英語の先生、英語を学ぶ多くの方々からご支持のお声をたくさんいただき心から感謝しています。
　「今までなかった！こういう本がもっと早くあったらよかったのに…」
　「自分でいろいろ気づくとおもしろく、はまりこんでいます」
　「実際の場面で自分の言いたい英語が思わず出てきました。パラパラ見ていただけなのにスゴイ！」など、ここでは全部ご紹介できないほどたくさんのご感想をいただきありがとうございました。この場を借りて御礼申し上げます。

　そして 2010 年。本書では前作 3 冊の絵を使い、新しい視点から 1 冊にまとめました。
　前作よりもさらにわかりやすく、そして読者の皆さんが好奇心をもって自分自身で前置詞のクライテリアを発見することができるような構成にしたい！という新たな思いで制作に取り組みました。

　そもそも私の研究のきっかけは数学者 Dr. Caleb Gattegno との出会いを通してのことであり、英語の文法には代数のようにプラスしたりマイナスしたり、置換したりするルールと、幾何のようにイメージとなるクライテリアがあるということに気がつきました。

数多くの前置詞を子どもが習得していくようにシンプルに理解するためにイメージを強調したイラストをさまざまな角度から観察し洞察し、共通したイメージをもつ絵を集めてグループにまとめてみました。そして最も基礎となるイメージは0次元（点）、1次元（線）、2次元（面）、3次元（立体）のイメージであり、それぞれのグループごとに共通のイメージがあることを発見しました。例えば点をクライテリアとするグループの前置詞にはいつでも場に点々と「もの」があることや、線をクライテリアとする場合には線の上下左右どこにでも位置することができることや、「3Dと見る」場合にはその場を見ている人がいることを暗黙の了解としていることなどです。

　今回の制作中にも本書の絵からいろいろな新しい発見をしています。例えばinは「面」とイメージするよりも「境界」とイメージしたほうがより多くの場面や状況を連想しやすくなり、納得できるなどです。クライテリアはだんだん研ぎすまされていきます。読者の皆様にもこれらの絵からいろいろ発見してほしく、あえて多数の絵をそのまま残しました。

　このような作業を経てたくさんの絵から私の仮説が証明され、日本語でもやはり1次元、2次元、3次元のイメージがクライテリアとなっていることを確信し、学術論文にまとめる準備を始めました。既存の論文を調べてみるとCelce Murcia著『現代アメリカ英語文法書』（1983年ニューベリハウス出版）の中でもat, from, to／on, off／in, out ofを点、線、面で分類していました。

　このクライテリアに確信がもてると、前置詞は名詞の前に位置しているので「名詞（場や時など）を0次元（点）と見なさい」「1次元（線）と見なさい」「2次元（面）と見なさい」「3次元（立体）と見なさい」と命令しているのだ！ということに気がついたことは「はじめに」でもお伝えしたとおりです。

　私自身が名詞を「点と見なさい」「線と見なさい」「面と見なさい」「立体と見なさい」ということを意識して前置詞を見始めると、英語を聞いたり読んだりす

るときにその英語の表わすイメージがより鮮明になり、話したり書いたりするときには自分がどう伝えたいか、そのためのことばの選択が楽になりました。特に間違いを指摘されたときには、なぜ間違いなのかがよくわかるようになりました。

　さらに多くのさまざまな状況や状態、場面を表わすのに、なじみのある動詞と前置詞｛副詞｝で簡単に表現できるようになり、本書の制作を手がけてから日常の英会話がとても楽になっています。前作を教科書として使い始めてからは私の学生も簡単な英語でさまざまなことが表現できることを納得したようで、学生の作る英作文がとてもわかりやすくなり、彼らの書く英文の量も増えてきました。また本書の制作にたずさわった仲間の一人が英語の書物を読んだときに英語がそのまますっと入ってきて、その情景が生き生きと浮かんできたのは嬉しい驚きだった！と話してくれました。

　本書を通して皆様が英語を学ぶ喜びに、英語で表現する喜びに、英語で理解し合う喜びに、より強くつながることを願っています。

　本書はベレ出版の脇山和美編集長のお力添えがあったからこそ本となる機会を賜ることができました。ありがとうございました。

　そして編集の新谷友佳子さんには前作を含めて大変長い間お世話になり、感謝しています。ありがとうございました。

　この場を借りて厚く御礼申し上げます。

企画・著者：ロス典子（**Noriko Ross**）
法政大学文学部英文学科卒、ワシントン州立大学 English BA 取得。ウィスコンシン州立大学 English MA 取得。現在、法政大学英語講師、国立音楽大学英語講師。

アドバイザー：モーリス・タック（**Dr. Maurice Tuck**）
コロラド州立大学言語学 MA、法学博士 JD 取得。タック法律事務所弁護士。東京電機大学英語准教授を経て現在は作家としてコロラドにて活動中。

監修：ピーター・ロス（**Peter Ross**）
ウィスコンシン州立大学応用言語学 MA 取得。コロンビア大学 MEd 取得。現在、東京経済大学英語准教授。

イラスト：
有賀真理
イラストレーター。桑沢デザイン研究所リビングデザイン科卒。
主な仕事として広告、書籍からキャラクター制作までと幅広く活動中。
飛永真一郎
クリエイター。様々な方面で活動中。東京造形大学デザイン科卒。
細沼　徹
イラストレーター、デザイナーとして活動中。東京造形大学デザイン科卒。

編集：武田　綾
英語学習書籍、CD、DVD 教材などの企画、制作にたずさわる。
1996 年よりクライテリア研究所に参加。

制作協力：有賀章子、安藤芙美子（クライテリア研究所）、ロス研太

クライテリア研究所のホームページ

http://www.criteria.jp/

本書の iPad 用、iPhone 用などの電子書籍化を準備中です。ホームページにてお知らせします。

【索引】

a

about…235, 317, 356, 357, 366 〜 375, 435
above…112, 120, 121, 134, 135, 148 〜 153, 325, 623, 630 〜 633
across…113, 130, 133,135,149, 330, 343, 344 〜 353, 533, 683
after…101, 184, 597, 676 〜 677, 681
against…53, 117, 198, 204 〜 208, 386, 397, 405
ago…676, 681
ahead (of)…247, 615 〜 617
all over…136, 343, 365
along…42, 43, 180 〜 189, 363, 404, 436, 532, 533, 542, 543, 597, 682
alongside…181, 186 〜 189, 532 〜 533, 539, 542, 685
among…377, 380 〜 389
apart (from)…384, 513, 527
around…354 〜 364, 367, 369 〜 371, 374, 435, 542, 637, 683
as…197, 210, 254, 257, 660, 666, 667
aside…100, 591
at [1章]…58, 67, 71, 161, 198, 211
at [2章]…225, 237, 252, 262 〜 265, 322, 370
at [3章]…416 〜 469, 542, 543, 557
at [4章]…612 〜 613, 654 〜 659, 662 〜 664, 678, 684
at the bottom of…444 〜 445, 465, 466
at the corner…262 〜 263, 419
at the edge of…264
at the end (of)…265, 442 〜 443
at the side (of)…237, 444, 468, 469
at the top (of)…340, 444 〜 445, 462 〜 465
away (from)…97, 103, 184, 226, 304 〜 309, 514 〜 526, 684

b

back…191, 521, 620〜621

backward(s)…617〜619

because of…237, 507

before…600〜603, 676〜677, 679, 681, 684

behind…171, 184, 297, 440, 469, 589, 594〜597, 685

below…158〜163, 170〜173, 634〜641, 643, 647〜650, 685

beneath…156〜160, 162〜166, 170〜174, 635, 637〜640, 643, 644, 646〜653, 685

beside…42, 188〜189, 264, 435, 442〜445, 457, 511, 513, 532〜533, 539, 542〜543, 588〜590, 685

besides…412〜413

between…242, 335, 376〜379, 383〜385

beyond…150, 153, 622〜629, 685

by [1章]…42, 140, 141

by [2章]…226, 258, 264, 339, 394, 401, 405〜408, 412

by [3章]…435, 442〜444, 457, 463, 464, 482, 506〜507, 511, 528〜545

by [4章]…678, 679, 681, 684

by means of…529, 535

by way of …528

c

close to…264, 435, 442〜444, 457, 458, 463, 469, 510〜513, 532〜533, 539, 542〜543, 684

d

down…140〜146, 189, 563, 567, 572〜585, 590, 591, 647

during…672〜675, 680

e

except (for)…411

f

face to face…351, 482
far away (from)…512 〜 513
for [1 章]…121, 126, 127, 167, 190 〜 203
for [2 章]…236, 299, 314, 324, 325, 332, 335, 366, 367
for [3 章]…452 〜 453, 549
for [4 章]…593, 658, 661, 668 〜 671, 675, 680, 682
forward(s)…614 〜 617, 619
from [1 章]…39, 60, 84 〜 85, 95, 97, 103, 184
from [2 章]…290, 293, 297, 300, 304 〜 308, 318, 338 〜 340, 349 〜 353
from [3 章]…483 〜 509, 512 〜 521, 526, 527, 578
from [4 章]…665, 667, 680, 684
from now…676, 681

i

in [1 章]…73 〜 81, 91, 98 〜 99, 151, 166 〜 168, 170, 172 〜 175
in [2 章]…214 〜 266, 268 〜 281, 298 〜 302, 313, 315, 327, 332, 338 〜 340, 343, 351, 378, 388 〜 389, 394, 409, 411
in [3 章]…451 〜 455, 473, 489, 537, 546, 561, 569, 570
in [4 章]…592 〜 593, 633, 641, 659, 660, 662 〜 664, 674 〜 675, 677, 680, 683
in addition to…412
in back (of)…246, 469, 589, 595, 598, 621, 685
in front of…246 〜 247, 457, 458, 511, 533, 589, 600 〜 604, 685
in his/her mind…266
in his/her side…468, 469
in the back of…246, 599

in the bottom of…467

in the center (of)…245

in the edge of…264

in the end of…265

in the front of…246, 604, 605

in the middle (of)…245

in the/his way (of)…247

in the/a corner (of)…262〜263

inside…217, 268〜275, 592, 593, 685

in spite of…65

into…45, 73, 97, 174, 175, 204, 205, 276〜284, 446, 449, 536, 613, 618, 683

l

like…97, 210〜211, 316

n

near…264, 435, 441〜444, 457, 458, 463〜465, 469, 510〜513, 532〜533, 539, 542〜543, 685

next to…42, 264, 351, 435, 440〜443, 457, 458, 469, 511, 513, 532〜533, 539, 542〜543, 588〜590, 684

o

of [1章]…81, 88〜91, 102, 155, 165

of [2章]…230, 240, 254〜255, 257〜258, 271, 281, 286〜295, 298, 300, 301〜309, 310〜325, 336, 361, 374〜375, 380, 393, 400, 406

of [3章]…492, 493, 495, 497, 499, 502〜509, 517, 520, 523, 569

of [4章]…602, 603, 620, 633, 649, 657

off…60, 62, 64, 87, 94〜108, 139, 142〜143, 190, 194, 303〜309, 317, 387, 493, 495, 508, 515, 516, 521, 522, 524〜525, 682

off of…493, 495, 508

off to⋯309

on [1章]⋯36 〜 91, 93, 94 〜 99, 101, 105, 108, 115, 119, 136, 139, 148 〜 149, 162, 163, 208

on [2章]⋯214, 215, 221 〜 223, 224, 237, 239, 241 〜 243, 249, 262 〜 263, 264 〜 265, 266 〜 267, 279, 303, 324 〜 325, 338 〜 340, 351, 353, 373, 374 〜 375, 399

on [3章]⋯420, 435 〜 437, 440 〜 443, 450, 459, 463 〜 469, 543, 563

on [4章]⋯593, 616, 617, 633, 659 〜 660, 662 〜 664, 682

on (the) top (of)⋯46, 47, 163, 463 〜 465, 467, 645

on and on⋯45, 70, 71

on hand⋯447

on his/her mind⋯266 〜 267, 374 〜 375

on the border (between)⋯43

on the bottom of⋯41, 83, 465, 467, 645

on the corner⋯262 〜 263

on the edge (of)⋯43, 90, 91, 264

on the end of⋯265

on the other side of⋯110, 594

on the outside of⋯39, 593

on the side (of)⋯39, 88 〜 91, 468

on the/his /her back (of)⋯48, 49, 52, 621

on the/his/her way (to)⋯44, 101

onto⋯85, 92 〜 93, 95, 260 〜 261, 682

opposite⋯209, 350 〜 351

out from⋯297

out (of) [1章]⋯98 〜 99, 100, 102, 107, 109, 145, 150, 176, 178, 192, 208

out (of) [2章]⋯270, 286 〜 309, 333, 406, 409

out (of) [3章]⋯480, 484, 491, 495, 501 〜 503, 548, 563

out (of) [4章]⋯592, 602, 629, 683

outside⋯274, 592 〜 593, 685

over [1章]⋯110 〜 153, 177

over [2章]…335, 337, 345～348, 352, 353, 358, 359, 363, 365, 373, 379
over [4章]…618, 619, 627～629, 631～633, 682
over and over…125

p

past…530～531, 624～625, 628～629

s

side by side…351, 539
since…318, 319, 665, 666, 681

t

through…127, 137, 155, 326～340, 343, 347, 349, 353, 394, 528～529, 683
throughout…342～343, 673, 674
to [1章]…41, 44, 66, 67, 88～90, 100, 101, 130, 182～183, 191, 201～203
to [2章]…244, 256, 264, 284～285, 324, 351, 403
to [3章]…427, 435, 440～444, 450, 457, 458, 461, 463, 469, 470～483, 485, 510～513, 523, 532～533, 539, 542～543, 582～584
to [4章]…588～590, 607, 609～613, 616～617, 620, 665, 667, 669, 670, 680, 684
to the edge of…471
together…384～387, 391, 671
toward(s)…132, 448, 606～613, 685

u

under…40～41, 82～83, 154～176, 418, 584, 589, 635～650, 652～653, 682
underneath…156～162, 170～173, 635, 638, 639, 642～648, 653, 685
until/till…667, 679, 681

up…69, 127, 180, 195, 375, 492, 493, 522, 546〜571, 582〜585, 618, 655, 657

up and down…585

up and up…552

up from…546

up on…549, 550, 553

up to…474, 476, 478, 551, 555, 559, 584

upside down…619

W

with…145, 182, 185, 191, 227, 323, 335, 351, 374, 390〜409, 541, 568, 683

within…217, 268〜275, 508, 680

without…410, 544

> "〜"は、同じテーマや比較するイメージが異なるページでつながっている場合に使っています。同時に見て参考にしてください。
> ","はそれぞれが独立したページです。

著者紹介

ロス典子

法政大学文学部英文学科卒、ワシントン州立大学 English BA 取得。ウィスコンシン州立大学 English MA 取得。元、法政大学英語講師、国立音楽大学英語講師。

[アドバイザー] モーリス・タック

コロラド州立大学言語学 MA、法学博士 JD 取得。タック法律事務所弁護士。東京電機大学英語准教授を経て現在は作家としてコロラドにて活動中。

[監修] ピーター・ロス

ウィスコンシン州立大学応用言語学 MA 取得。コロンビア大学 MEd 取得。現在、東京経済大学英語准教授。

改訂合本　ネイティブの感覚で前置詞が使える

2010年11月25日	初版発行
2024年 5月14日	第9刷発行
著者	ロス典子（のりこ）
カバーデザイン	竹内 雄二
DTP	WAVE 清水 康広

©Noriko Ross 2010. Printed in Japan

発行者	内田　真介
発行・発売	ベレ出版 〒162-0832　東京都新宿区岩戸町12 レベッカビル TEL.03-5225-4790 FAX.03-5225-4795 ホームページ　https://www.beret.co.jp/
印刷	株式会社 三光デジプロ
製本	根本製本株式会社

落丁本・乱丁本は小社編集部あてにお送りください。送料小社負担にてお取り替えします。

ISBN 978-4-86064-275-4 C2082　　　　　編集担当　新谷友佳子